AN ILLUSTRATED ENCYCLOPEDIA
of
AQUARIUM FISH

AN ILLUSTRATED ENCYCLOPEDIA

of

AQUARIUM FISH

**A COMPREHENSIVE DIRECTORY OF
EXOTIC FRESHWATER AND MARINE SPECIES**

Gina Sandford

GREENWICH EDITIONS

A QUANTUM BOOK

This edition published by
Greenwich Editions
10 Blenheim Court
Brewery Road
London N7 9NT

A member of the Chrysalis Group plc

ISBN 0-86288-323-7

QUMEQF

This book was produced by
Quantum Publishing
6 Blundell Street
London N7 9BH

Printed in Singapore by Star Standard Industries (Pte) Ltd

PHOTOGRAPHIC ACKNOWLEDGEMENTS

*Page numbers are listed with the letters a, b, c, or d
to distinguish the order on the page.*

The Publishers wish to thank all those contributing photographs to this volume. **M. W. Sandford** placed his transparency collection at our disposal and all the photographs in this book are contributed by him, *except* those gratefully acknowledged from: **G. R. Allen** pages 163b, 234b; **D. A. Allison,** 37b, 44a, 48b, 59b, 67a, 100c, 125c, 128a, 134a, c, 148a, 153c, 181a, 210a, b, 211a, 245c, 247b, 250a; **G. Axelrod** 118a; **H. A. Axelrod** 28b, 40c, 46b, c, 54b, 64a, 72a, 74b, 75a, 78b, 83b, 85b, 86a, 90c, 92a, c, 94a, 96b, 102a, b, 104a, 105c, 109a, c, 110c, 111b, 117b, 119c, 120b, 123b, 124a, 127a, b, 142a, b, 144c, 146c, 152b, 158c, 159a, c, 163c, 186b, 189b, 197a, 199c, 200c, 204b, 207a, 208a, c, 214a, 221b, 222b, 229a, 230c, 233a, 234a, 237a, c, 240a, 243a, 246a, b, c, 248c, 251c; **W. B. Burgess** 36a, 193b; **K. H. Choo** 230b, 234c, 235b, 236c, 243c; **W. Conkel** 116c; **V. Elek** 161c; **U. Erich Friese** 213b; **Exotarium Frankfurt** 90a; **S. Frank** 141b; **A Frisby** 196c, 198a; **N. Gray** 199b; **H. Hansen** 101c; **W. Hoppe** 230a; **R. Jonklaas** 197c; **E. Kennedy** 242c, 247a; **K. Knaack** 25c, 40a, 83c, 121c, 125b, 159b, 192b, 202b, 238a, c, 239c, 244a; **D. Lambert** 166c, 167c, 169b, 170a, 170c, 171a, 172c, 173b, 174a, 175b, c, 176a, b, c, 177b, 178b, c, 179b, 187b; **K. Lucas** 5, 102c, 107a, 189c, 194a, 203a, 209c, 236b, 244b, 245a; **G. Marcuse** 242a; **G. Meola** 121a; **M. Meyer** 167a, 169c; **A. Van den Nieuwenhuizen** 27c, 30b, 71b, 83a, 90b, 94c, 136c, 140b, 160a, 161a, 164a, 203c, 210c, 253a; **J. H. O'Neill** 235c; **K. Paysan** 160b, 205b, 223c, 228c, 229b, 239a, 249a, b, c, 253c; **Photomax Aquarium Picture Library** 5, 53c, 54a, 54c, 61a, 65a, 97c, 98a, 130b, 133a, 135d, 149b, 186a, 215b, 220b, 223b, 232c, 239b; **H. J. Richter** 22, 28a, c, 31a, b, 38b, 46a, d, 55b, 70b, 72c, 77b, 78a, 81a, b, c, 85a, 86b, c, 88a, 91a, b, 96d, 97a, 98b, c, 99b, 105b, 108c, 10b, 111a, 118b, 125d, 130a, 138c, 141a, 144b, 149a, 153a, 162a, 163d, 166b, 167b, 171c, 173a, 173c, 175a, 182b, 183c, 187c, 190c, 200a, 202a, 212a, c, 213a, 214d, 222a, 224c, 225c; **M. Roberts** 96a; **E. Roloff** 69b; **A. Roth** 29c, 66b, 71d, 77a, 77c, 103a, 105a, 117a, 132c, 137a, 140c, 147a, 170b, 174c, 179a, 177c, 178a, 206b, 208b, 223a; **D. D. Sands** 43b; **J. Scheel** 160d, 162c, 160c; **H. Scultz** 64c, 73c, 88c, 89d, 92b, 162b; **W. M. Stephens** 164b; **W. Tanaka** 163a; **E. Taylor** 41b; **W. A. Tomey** 2, 136b, 183b, 184a, 195b, 212b, 225b; **R. Zukal** 53b, 146d, 151c, 172b, 177a.

Contents

Introduction

The Directory

Introduction

The purpose of writing this book is to introduce enquiring aquarists to some species which they may not have considered keeping before. Although this initial section has some notes on setting up an aquarium, filtration systems, plants, etc, it is assumed that readers already have a basic knowledge of these things and have been keeping fish for some time but now wish to try their hand at something else: to find the next challenge, if you like.

If you are just beginning in the hobby, then by all means treat this work as a reference point for all the wonderful creatures you may like to keep in the future. But before you try to keep them, go out and get yourself a good beginners' guide, which will explain fully the principles of filtration and water chemistry. Just because water is clear does not mean it is ideal for fishes – a container of sulphuric acid is also clear, but I wouldn't care to try and keep fish in it! There are also many books which deal with specific subjects: aquarium plants, marine fish, brackish water fish, and so on. Read as many as you can, and then gradually start out on your new hobby. Progress may seem slow, but when you are dealing with living creatures there are no short cuts, and the two things you cannot buy are time and patience.

Fishkeeping is a challenge from the outset. You are dealing with creatures that live in an environment that is alien to us. It is necessary to learn a little physics and chemistry, as well as some biology, and to accomplish all this without killing the creatures in your charge. But provide the creatures with the environment they need, and you are part way there. Give them food that is as close to their natural foods as possible, and you have cleared another hurdle. The fish section aims to give you as much basic information as possible to enable you to keep each species and – where the information is available – breed that species too.

As things stand today, many habitats are under threat. Vast areas of forest are being cut down, and this affects the water courses within them. Marshes are being drained for redevelopment, reefs being dredged up to provide coral for building. Land is at a premium, and fish are low on the list of priorities. Some species are clinging to the edge of extinction in the confines of aquarists' tanks, their natural habitats destroyed forever. Some of these creatures are included in this book. It is a sad thought that, in ten years' time, some of the creatures listed here may be known only from photographs. It is up to us to help maintain breeding stocks and encourage others to do the same.

LEFT: The well-balanced, healthy, mature marine aquarium will grace any home. To achieve such a set-up requires an investment, not only in monetary terms, but also in time and patience.

ABOVE: Good retail outlets are clean, have good quality plants, well cared for fish and experienced staff who can usually help solve any problems you may have.

UNDERSTANDING FISH

Fish species are vast in number and almost infinite in variety. But, of course, they all have one simple thing in common. They are all creatures adapted to living in an aquatic environment, a world apart from our terrestrial existence.

Water is much denser than air, so their bodies have to be more streamlined to pass through it. Pelagic fishes have torpedo-shaped bodies to cleave their way with ease; but if we look at fishes from fast-flowing waters, we find that they have depressed (flattened) bodies and expanded fins, so that when the water flows across them it pushes them onto the substrate.

A fish's body is usually covered to a greater or lesser extent by scales which provide protection. Those that do not have scales may have thick skin, while others may have bony plates to afford them protection.

The various fins perform different functions. The single (i.e. unpaired) fins are the dorsal, adipose (if present), anal and caudal. Of these the dorsal, adipose and anal help keep the fish upright when swimming, while the caudal is used to initiate forward movement. The paired fins help with steering the fish.

In order to maintain a certain position in the water column – neither rising to the surface nor sinking to the bed below – a fish uses its swimbladder. This is a gas-filled bladder which extends from behind the head for about a third of the body length. Combined with the fish's fatty tissues it gives the fish lift which helps compensate for the negative buoyancy of other, heavier parts of the body such as the skeleton and some visceral organs.

The great majority of fish breathe by extracting the dissolved oxygen from water passing over their gills. In these organs the blood vessels are close to the surface,

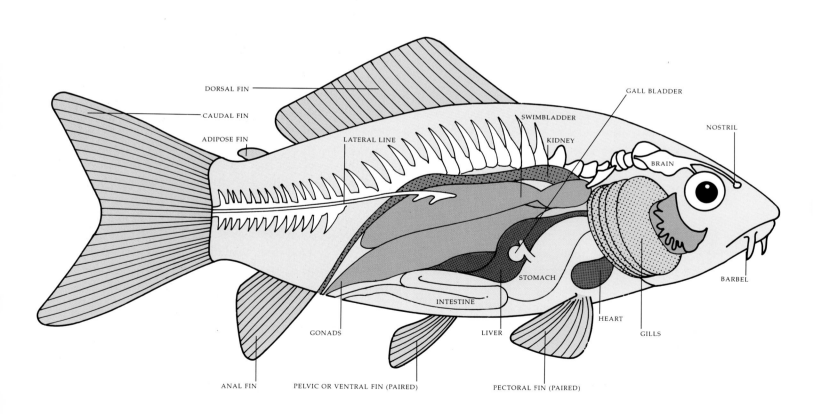

ABOVE: The internal anatomy of a fish.

ABOVE: To fish such as this cichlid, their eyes are very important. Poor water conditions can lead to cloudy eyes and thus diminished vision so the fish is unable to hunt or avoid predators efficiently.

allowing oxygen to be absorbed and waste gases exchanged. Although fish have nostrils, these are not used for breathing but purely for smell: as water is passed through them, lung-like rosettes test for anything edible in the vicinity.

Using their nostrils, fish can sense food from a distance; but to taste it, they must touch it. There is no single organ of taste. Instead, taste receptors are scattered across the head and body surface. For those fish with barbels, the barbels are also covered in taste receptors, which allow the fish to feel through the silty substrate until it touches food.

Most fish have eyes – although they do not have eyelids because their eyes are cleaned by the water. The position of the eyes on the head is indicative of life style. Bottom dwellers usually have their eyes on the top of their heads; and if the environment is silty the eyes are greatly reduced in size, as the fish relies more on its senses of taste and smell rather than on sight. Midwater fish have their eyes on the sides of the head, to give them almost all-round vision. There are some predators, noteably the pike, which have binocular vision. In some species such as *Caecobarbus*, the eyes have regressed and the fish are now blind. This is an adaptation to living in a cave environment.

Water transmits sound far better than air, and some fish have evolved a system whereby they can produce sound either by vibrating their swim bladder or by stridating their fin spines.

Electricity passes freely through water and some fish have managed to utilise this. The mormyrids use echo location to find their way around in the murky waters they inhabit. Electric catfish and electric eels use electricity to stun their prey.

AQUATIC ENVIRONMENTS

Fish have managed to colonise most bodies of water, from the deepest oceans to the highest mountain pools. Because of this ubiquity, they have been widely exploited by man for food.

So, when we think of freshwater fish, we envisage the minnows in our local streams, or the trout and salmon on the fishmonger's slab, both of which come from habitats that we are readily familiar with. But, all you have to do is think about a place where you find water, and it's 99.9% certain that you'll find a fish that lives in it.

For example, much of our fresh water is stored in natural underground aquifers; yet even in these seemingly inhospitable conditions, we find fish which inhabit caves and live their whole lives in total darkness. Even where these underground water sources emerge as sulphurous hot springs, there are fish to be found.

In the tropics, seasonal pools are home to some of the Killifish. At the onset of the dry season, the adult fish lay eggs which lie dormant in the mud until the next rains, the adults perishing as pools dry out. With the first of the rains only a small proportion of the eggs hatch, a precaution to ensure the survival of the species if the rains then fail.

Different types of fish inhabit various stretches of a river from its source to the sea. Fishes from fast-flowing waters have their fins adapted and expanded, to allow

ABOVE: Even in the most inhospitable regions, fish can be found. Some fish migrate upstream to breed in the shallower, warmer waters.

ABOVE: Nutrient rich, slow-flowing lowland rivers have a wide variety of plant, invertebrate and fish life.

them to hold station in the swift waters. Others have flattened body shapes designed for a life on the substrate, the flat fish and sting rays are prime examples of this.

For the aquarist it is a challenge to try to re-create some of these environments in the home aquarium. A forest creek, for example, with leaf litter on the substrate, plants which grow out of the water, and dappled lighting. Such a world would be home to some of the Banjo Catfish, which mimic leaf litter, or to the Splash Tetras which lay their eggs on the undersides of broad leaves above the water.

Consider the brackish water regions. Here we find such interesting little fish as the Mudskippers. An aquarium set up for these would utilise wood in the form of roots coming down into the water, and a sloping silty, wave-washed area for the fish to slither out on to, where they can display to each other. Alternatively you may wish to keep the Archer Fish, that will spit at insects from his watery lair.

Then there is the undoubted beauty of the coral reef, with its invertebrate life as well as its fishes. Unfortunately, we do not have the space here to consider invertebrates, as these are a separate specialised topic, but due consideration is given to many tropical marine species.

Creatures from the more inhospitable regions probably provide the greatest challenge to the aquarist. How do you maintain torrent-dwelling species in the relative calm of an aquarium? How do you breed some of the marine fish and successfully raise the fry? No book can give all the answers; but here we at least hope to whet your appetite, and encourage you to find some of those answers for yourself.

CHOICE OF TANK AND SET-UP

Just a wander round your local aquatic retailer will give you an idea of the number of different aquaria that are on offer. The question is, which one is the right one for you? Basically, an aquarium is simply an open-topped glass box that holds water. What matters is what you do with it, to ensure that it enhances your home and provides the right environment for your fish.

Probably the first thing to consider is size: the larger the aquarium, the easier it is to manage. However, the maximum size will be determined by the site you have chosen. If possible position the aquarium away from a heat source such as a radiator, and where sunlight will not fall on it. Alcoves are a popular choice but, with larger, modern homes, aquaria are sometimes used as room dividers. If a ready-made tank is not quite the right size or shape, custom-built aquaria may be ordered, although the cost is usually higher.

When full of water, rocks, gravel, etc, your glass box will be heavy. Water alone weighs approximately 1kg per litre (10lb per gallon). Add to this the weight of the glass, plus the internal decorations, and the total can be frightening. Modern aquarium stands are designed to take the weight, but do check the floor can also stand the strain. If building your own stand, double check your calculations to make sure it will take the strain. It is essential to use a sheet of polystyrene between the tank and stand, to even out any minor imperfections and so avoid cracking the tank.

Having organised your stand and got your tank home, the fun now starts. First of all check the tank for leaks by filling it with water before you put anything else into it. It is far easier to dry out a tank and seal a leak, than have to scrape out gravel and clean up the leaking area before sealing it. Once you have checked everything is all right, empty the tank again.

RIGHT: High intensity lighting is required to keep the deep red colour of the water lily leaves. A thoughtful design allows for this, provides plenty of open water for shoaling fishes and still allows shady areas for other plants that need a less intense light.

LIGHTING

The type of lighting you employ will depend on the effect you wish to create. If you wish to create a river bank environment with tree roots and the like, then dappled lighting is essential to emulate the sun on the ripples. However, if you heart's desire is to reproduce a tropical underwater paradise, with living tropical plants, then light of the right intensity and day length will be essential, if they are to flourish.

The most popular form of lighting is fluorescent tubes. These come in a range of lengths, wattages and colour ranges, to enable you to provide the right conditions for growing plants or marine algae, or even to let you observe nocturnal fish. Fitting these lights is a relatively simple operation. The lights are positioned in the hood of the tank, and held in place by clips. The inside of the hood is usually silvered or white to act as a reflector. The leads from the control units are pro-

BELOW: A carefully planned, planted and well illuminated aquarium makes a good focal point for any room.

vided with waterproof end caps so that, in the high humidity levels of the hood, water and electricity will not mix in a lethal combination. Control units themselves give out a lot of heat, and are best sited outside the hood to lessen the temperature build-up in the minimal space between the cover glass and the hood. However, sometimes the only place to position these units is in the hood – in which case, ensure that there is plenty of ventilation to disperse the heat.

For a furnished aquarium – that is, one with growing plants – a time switch is essential to control the lighting. In this type of tank you will have four or even five tubes running, and these should be timed to go on and off in sequence. In this way you can build the light source to imitate the tropical 12-hour day, with a period of high intensity over the six or seven hours when the sun would be highest in the sky. But of course, if you have plastic plants all you need is sufficient light to observe your fishes.

In the same way, you will want to select the type of tubes to be used. Specialized tubes are now available which cover the ideal spectral range for growing plants, while others are designed to promote the healthy growth of marine corals and invertebrates.

For open-topped aquaria, metal halide units or spotlights are very effective, as they can create dappled effects and shady areas especially in deep tanks. For marine use, metal halide lamps are often combined with actinic blue fluorescents to promote healthy coral and invertebrate life. Spotlights are also useful for highlighting the focal point of an aquarium, which may be a specimen plant or an attractive piece of wood.

Most aquaria come complete with matching hoods and the lighting units are installed in these – indeed, with some you just need to plug into the mains and the lights come on.

FILTRATION SYSTEMS

The filtration system is the life support for your fish. If the water quality deteriorates, the fish suffer and may even die; so it is essential that the filtration system is suitable for the creatures you are keeping.

The purpose of filtration is to break down waste products from the fish and convert them into harmless products. In nature this is known as the nitrogen cycle – the process whereby ammonia-loving bacteria convert ammonia into nitrites, and *nitrosomas* bacteria in turn convert nitrites into harmless nitrates which are then absorbed by plant life. In the confines of an aquarium it is necessary to employ a filtration system to improve the efficiency of this cycle.

The four main types of filtration employed by aquarists are undergravel filters, external power filters, trickle filters and biological systems.

BELOW: The nitrogen cycle

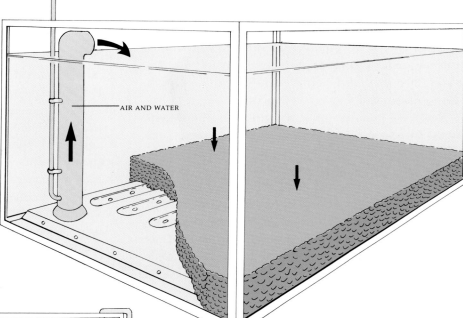

Fish excrete ammonia (NH_3) produced by breaking down proteins, mostly through the gills

Plants absorb the nitrate

Nitrosomas bacteria convert ammonia to nitrite (NO_2)

Nitrobacter bacteria convert nitrite to nitrate (NO_3)

RIGHT: An **undergravel filter** is the simplest system. Gravel or sand substrate covers the base of the tank, acting as a filter bed. Supported by oxygen from the downward flow of water, bacteria builds up within it and acts to break down waste products.

AIR

AIR AND WATER

BELOW: In a reverse flow undergravel filter the water is taken up by pump and returned by forcing it up through the gravel

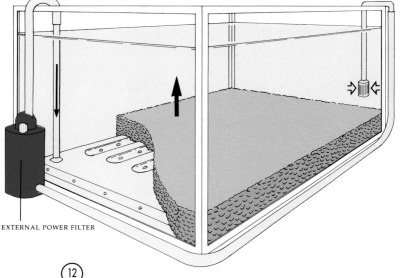

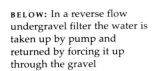

EXTERNAL POWER FILTER

Undergravel filtration This is the cheapest and easiest system to install. A perforated base plate is placed on the bare base of the aquarium and covered with the substrate. Water is either drawn down through the substrate and returned via an uplift tube to the top of the aquarium, or else the water is forced down the tube and so pushed up through the substrate. This latter method is referred to as reverse-flow undergravel filtration. Either method is effective, in that water passes through the filter bed (i.e. the substrate) allowing the aerobic bacteria to function and break down the ammonia and nitrites.

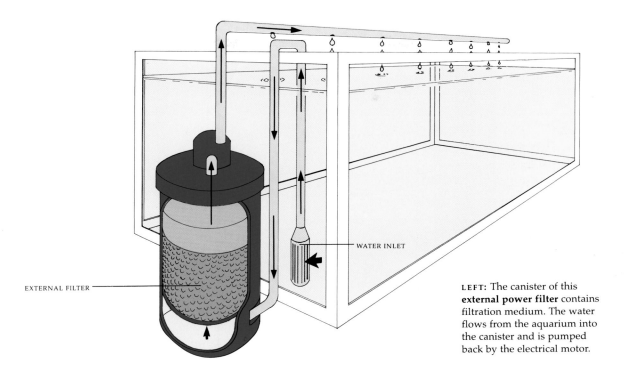

WATER INLET

EXTERNAL FILTER

LEFT: The canister of this **external power filter** contains filtration medium. The water flows from the aquarium into the canister and is pumped back by the electrical motor.

External power filters These are more expensive but very efficient. Water is drawn out of the aquarium and passes through a cannister containing a filter medium – which may be ceramic tubes, carbon, filter wool, or a combination of these. The filter medium provides the bed for the bacteria to live in, while the pump keeps the water constantly flowing through the filter bed to keep the bacteria alive.

Trickle filters A series of trays, one above the other, provide filter beds for the bacteria. Each tray has perforations in the base, and water is pumped to the top of the system and allowed to trickle through until it finally passes back into the aquarium. The filter medium can be a fine layer of filter matting, ceramic beads or similar, half-exposed to the air. Thus an oxygen-rich environment is created for the bacteria.

FILTER WOOL HALF SUBMERGED IN TRAY

AQUARIUM WATER VIA SPRAY BAR

RIGHT: Trickle filters are often coupled with other systems to supplement filtration. The exposed filter beds allow greater oxygen exchange to support a large number of bacteria.

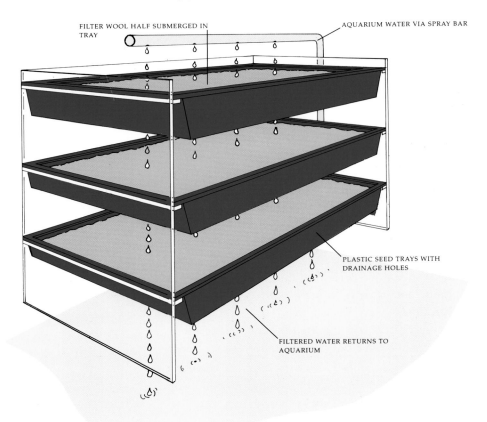

PLASTIC SEED TRAYS WITH DRAINAGE HOLES

FILTERED WATER RETURNS TO AQUARIUM

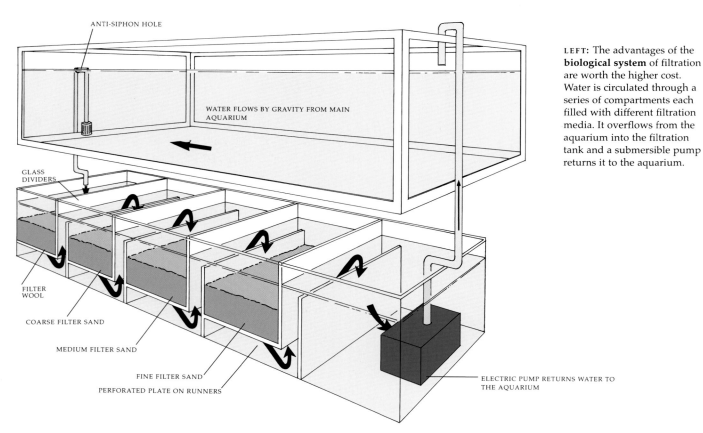

ANTI-SIPHON HOLE

WATER FLOWS BY GRAVITY FROM MAIN
AQUARIUM

GLASS
DIVIDERS

FILTER
WOOL

COARSE FILTER SAND

MEDIUM FILTER SAND

FINE FILTER SAND

PERFORATED PLATE ON RUNNERS

ELECTRIC PUMP RETURNS WATER TO
THE AQUARIUM

LEFT: The advantages of the
biological system of filtration
are worth the higher cost.
Water is circulated through a
series of compartments each
filled with different filtration
media. It overflows from the
aquarium into the filtration
tank and a submersible pump
returns it to the aquarium.

Biological systems A separate, specially constructed
tank is required for this type of filtration. However, they
are worth the extra cost involved. The principle is the
same as the other systems, only this time the water
passes through a series of compartments with a different filter medium in each, and then is pumped back
to the main aquarium. This system is often used in
combination with a trickle filter.

Maturing the system It is well known that it takes
time for a marine system to mature, but the same is true
for a freshwater system if you want to avoid problems.
The numbers of bacteria have to build up, to be able to
cope with waste products. In a new tank, there will be
an ammonia peak first, then when the ammonia-loving
bacteria have multiplied sufficiently to cope with this
there will be a nitrite peak. This in turn will encourage
nitrosomas bacteria to increase, to feed on the nitrites,
and as the maturation of the system continues, the
nitrite levels will drop off. At this point a few fish may
be added, and so the cycle continues with increases in
the number of bacteria to cope with the increase in
waste produced.

Even with a fully functioning filtration system, there
is still a need to carry out regular water changes once
every 10 days or so. This is also a good time to carry out
general tank maintenance, and to remove any build-up
of fish faeces, dead leaves, etc.

THE WATER

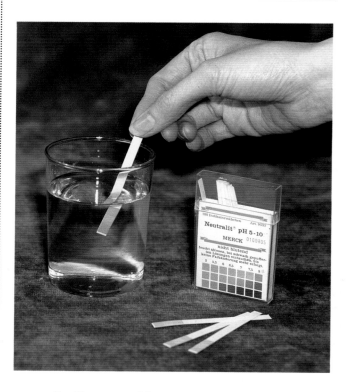

ABOVE: Test kits are essential
to check that the water
conditions are right for your
fish, but bear in mind that
these have a limited shelf life.

There is a wide selection of fishes given in the Directory of this book, some requiring soft acid conditions, some hard alkaline, others brackish water, and yet others marine conditions.

The hardness of water is a measure of the amount of dissolved salts. In fishkeeping terms, soft water would be about 3°dH (0–50mg/1 $CaCO_3$) and very hard 25°dH (more than 450mg/1 $CaCO_3$).

pH is a measure of the acidity or alkalinity of the water. pH7 is regarded as neutral. At the bottom of the scale, 0 would be very acid and at the top, 14 very alkaline. It is a logarithimic scale so, for example, pH 6 is ten times more acidic than pH 7, and pH 5 is 100 times more acidic than pH 7.

Most freshwater aquarium fish live within the range pH 6.5 to 8.5, and will tolerate a hardness of say 9–14°dH. However there are some that have specific requirements and these are detailed in the species section.

For marine aquaria, use a good quality marine salt and mix to a salinity of 1.023 to 1.027 at a temperature of 24–26°C (75–79°F). The alkalinity of marine water is also fairly constant at about pH 8.4.

RIGHT: The pH scale is logarithmic, that is to say, for each step from pH7–8 the water becomes ten times more alkaline with pH7 being termed neutral. Likewise pH6 is ten times more acidic than pH7 and pH5 would be 100 times more acidic.

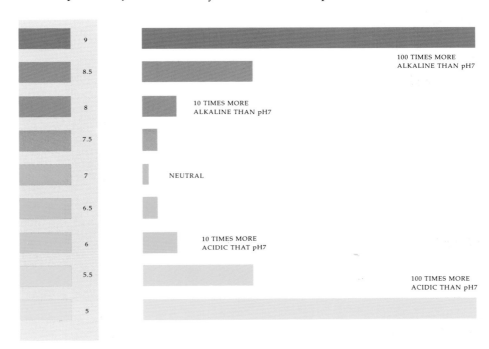

9

8.5

8

7.5

7

6.5

6

5.5

5

100 TIMES MORE ALKALINE THAN pH7

10 TIMES MORE ALKALINE THAN pH7

NEUTRAL

10 TIMES MORE ACIDIC THAT pH7

100 TIMES MORE ACIDIC THAN pH7

HEATING

There are various methods of heating a tropical aquarium, the most popular being the combined heater/thermostat. This is pre-set at the factory to about 23°C (74°F) and, should you need to alter the temperature, there is a dial or knob at the top which is turned left or right to increase or decrease the temperature – do check the instructions that come with the unit to determine which direction to turn the knob. The unit often has a light to indicate whether or not the thermostat is functioning.

Some people prefer to use separate heaters and outside thermostats. The advantage of these is that the temperature can easily be controlled by turning the dial on the external thermostat. A disadvantage is that small children have been known to play with these dials, with disastrous results for the fish. So, if you are opting for this method, make sure that any tiny hands cannot tamper with it.

Other alternatives are undertank heating mats, and heating cables which can be buried in the gravel.

The size of heater/thermostat will depend on the size of the aquarium but, as a rough guide, allow 10 watts per 4.5 litres (1 gallon). Thus a 68 litre (15 gallon) tank will require a 150 watt heater/thermostat. For larger aquaria you may need to use two or three heater/thermostats. These units are available in several sizes, of 50, 75, 100, 125, 150, 200 and 300 watts, so if you require 600 watts you can use either 2 x 300 watts or 3 x 200 watts. It is always best to fit two units running at half-power, to avoid overheating.

Check the temperature every day. As you become more experienced, a hand against the tank and a glance at the inmates will tell you whether all is well. But, for safety, use a thermometer and get used to checking it whenever you pass the aquarium.

After installing the heating system **do not** switch it on until there is water in the tank. **Never** switch on the heaters unless they are submerged in water.

DECORATING AND FILLING THE TANK

What you use to decorate your aquarium is a purely personal choice. It will also depend on the type of environment you wish to create – freshwater, marine, brackish, rift lake, etc. So let's start at the bottom.

SUBSTRATES

Gravel is the most obvious choice for freshwater set-ups. Three sizes are available, the smallest a fine grit which is often quite sharp when you run your fingers through it. Although fine for growing plants, this is not suitable if you have bottom-dwelling fishes which like to dig or bury themselves, as it scratches their bodies and can damage their barbels. The next size, medium pea gravel, is the most commonly used. As the name suggests, this has rounded stones and is well suited to aquarium use. But for larger aquaria with big fish, the size of gravel they use for road surfacing can look very effective.

Sand is a good alternative. For freshwater aquaria, non-compacting filtration sand makes a welcome alternative to gravel. The rounded grains allow free passage of water and do not damage delicate barbels.

Coral sand is used in marine aquaria, and also in some specialised freshwater aquaria where the fishes require hard alkaline water, such as Rift Lake tanks.

Always wash your substrate well to remove all dust and debris before putting it into the aquarium.

ROCKS

There are a number of different types of rock available from stores for you to choose from, including slate, granite, Westmoreland stone, etc. These are inert – that is, they will not dissolve and change the composition of your water. It is not advisable to go out and collect your own unless you know what you are collecting. The addition of a piece of limestone to a soft water aquarium could prove disastrous, with the calcium slowly leaching out of the rock and hardening the water. Scrub the rocks to remove dust and loose fragments before using them.

One very effective way to decorate an aquarium is to use large rounded pebbles to create a stream bed.

Tufa rock is the mainstay for marine aquaria. This is rather crumbly rock which is high in calcium, and thus helps to stabilise the pH at around 8.0. Dead corals and barnacle shells may also be employed to create a reef-like environment for your fish.

ABOVE: Dramatic effects can be achieved using lots of rockwork in the aquarium but be sure that the structure is stable.

WOOD

For versatility, wood is hard to beat in the aquarium. Not only is it decorative, it also provides an anchorage point for such plants as *Microsorium pteropus* (Java Fern). In addition, for some fish such as the various Bristlenose Catfish (*Ancistrus* sp.), it forms part of their diet and they happily rasp away at it.

Bog wood should be soaked for a few days to remove excess dust and dirt, and to allow some of the tannins to leach out. Vine roots also provide another alternative.

For those who do not wish to use the real thing, several companies offer realistic looking pieces of ceramic wood.

PLANTS

You have two options if you are going to have plants in your aquarium: live or artificial. Many of the artificial plants available today are so realistic that you would certainly be forgiven for confusing them with the real thing. But they are purely decorative, and do nothing to enhance the quality of the water in the aquarium nor to help combat any algal problems that may occur. Nevertheless, some very attractive effects can be achieved using artificial plants and, provided your filtration system is well-established and efficient, there should be no problems.

Live plants, in comparison, can be a bit more of a problem, because unless you plant them properly, and give them sufficient light and good water conditions, they die. Some fish also have a habit of eating them, but this is easily overcome by feeding more vegetable matter in the diet.

Choose your plants with care, ensuring that you have true aquatic plants. Here your local dealer will be happy to advise you. In nature, there are some species of plant that spend the whole year submerged, such as the various *Cabomba* species, and others which spend the dry season growing out of water in damp soil, only to be submerged when the rains swell the water course. Some of the *Cryptocoryne* and *Echinodorus* species (Amazon Sword plants) are examples of these. Ideally, you should have some plants which grow fairly tall and will be used towards the back of the aquarium, and others which are short for foreground use. The trouble is that, when you buy them, some may look like short plants, but within a few months you find they have grown to be too big for the position you put them in. So

ABOVE: This type of aquarium can be quite spectacular, especially if plants are allowed to grow down into the water. An ideal habitat aquarium for Archer fish.

LEFT: For the best effects, be sure to choose your plants so that their leaf shapes and colours compliment each other.

LEFT: If you have made the right choices of equipment, decor and animals, and been patient, you will be rewarded with a well-balanced aquarium in which fish, invertebrates and algae flourish.

take a little time to do some research and plan the aqua-scaping before going to the shop.

Another thing to consider is the shape, size and colour of the leaves. Plants should compliment each other, so position a broad-leaved species next to a fine-leaved, a dark red one next to a mid green, or a tall thin-leaved plant next to a bushy variety. It is easier to achieve the effect you want if you first plan it out on paper; and when you do get to the shop, try the plants next to each other just to see what you think.

When it comes to planting them, consider what you would do for garden plants – they would be planted in-dividually and well spaced out. Apply the same prin-ciple to your aquarium plants and you will have a much better chance of success. Plant the cuttings in rows and stagger the rows. Using this technique, you will see a wall of plants when viewed from the front, but when seen from the top each plant will have its own space. Allow space around large plants such as Amazon Swords. They have a great spread and provide a won-derful focal point but, if you plant too close to them, the shade their broad leaves creates can be detrimental to other plants. There are, however, some shade-loving plants that will thrive; for example, some of the smaller *Cryptocoryne* species.

When the plants are established, it will be necessary to cut them back every now and again and to remove some of the old dead leaves. You can carry this out dur-ing normal maintenance, just dealing with one group of plants each time.

One thing to bear in mind is that some of the cuttings you purchase may be marginal plants which are only submerged for part of the year. If these have been col-lected during the dry season and you plunge them into your tank, be prepared for the leaves to fall off! Leave the stems in position and, with a little bit of luck, shoots will appear from the old leaf joints. When these are long enough, they can be nipped off and planted, just as you would any other cutting.

FILLING THE AQUARIUM

Now you can fill the aquarium. Place an upturned saucer, plate or a sheet of clean paper over the substrate, and pour the water gently onto this. In this way you can prevent the gravel from being washed into mounds or the plants being washed-up, leaving the aquarium looking a little like a battle-zone. It is better to use warm water if you have tropical plants, for these do not benefit from being chilled with very cold water.

Finally, tidy up all the trailing wires and pipe-work. To make things easier, cable tidies are available, and these allow you to wire all the electrical items into one unit and have a single cable going to the mains.

FEEDING

The variety of foods available today is astounding, of every type from flake to frozen to live. Fish require a balanced diet in order to thrive and, while the commercially prepared flake and tablet foods provide this, the addition of frozen and live foods to the diet is also beneficial. There is always a heated debate over whether or not live foods should be fed to your fish. Some say it introduces disease, while others claim that the fish cannot live without it. The choice is yours, but a variety of foods is greatly recommended.

OMNIVORES

Of all the fishes, these are probably the easiest to feed. As their name suggests, they eat anything and everything they can fit in their mouths. Flake foods, tablet and pelletted foods, frozen and live foods, are all consumed with relish. Omnivores seem to do well being fed small amounts of nutrient a couple of times a day.

INSECTIVORES

These feed not only on aquatic invertebrates but also on terrestial insects that fall onto the water. Indeed, in the case of the Archer Fish, the creature actively "shoots down" insects that are resting on overhanging branches. Most of these fish will also accept flake foods, but be sure to include plenty of frozen *Daphnia*, bloodworm, *Mysis* shrimp and the like in their diet. Insectivores benefit from a variety of foods twice a day.

HERBIVORES

Now to the vegetarians of the fish world, the fish which have the reputation of devouring all the plants in your aquarium and being a very good reason for using plastic greenery. In fact, given plenty of other foods to browse on, herbivores should leave your plants alone. Offer them lettuce leaves, but "plant" them in the gravel so that the fish think they are growing. Frozen peas, squashed to removed the seed coat, are also readily taken, as are slices of courgette and potato. In addition, food manufacturers also produce vegetable flake and algae tablets which can be used regularly. Herbivores are almost constantly grazing, so keep a good supply of food available.

CARNIVORES

The bad guys of the fish world – the predators. As you may guess, these feed on fish and other animals. If you are keeping a predator, nine times out of ten it can be weaned onto dead food such as pieces of fish, shrimp, bits of meat, etc; but there is always one awkward creature that will not take anything unless it moves. If you are considering keeping a large predatory fish, think carefully. Can you feed it live fish if you really have to? If not, are you prepared to watch it starve? It's a hard choice but one that has to be taken. Nobody relishes feeding one live animal to another but sometimes it has to be done, if only for a short time to settle the predator in. It is very rare indeed that a captive fish has to be fed other live fish for the whole of its life. Predatory fish are used to gorging themselves and then to fasting for a while, so it is normal to feed them only two or three times in a week.

RIGHT: Plenty of live foods, such as *Daphnia*, are often the key to successful fish keeping and breeding.

BREEDING

Sometimes we set out to breed our fishes, at other times this event occurs by chance and the first we know about it is a few small fry appear in the aquarium. Where known, the breeding strategies, e.g. substrate spawner, egg scatterer, are given in the text for a particular species but the main methods are more fully explained here. There are two basic methods by which fish reproduce: egg laying and livebearing. Within the egg layers there are several different methods.

EGG SCATTERERS

Fishes which breed in this way may either spawn as pairs or as a shoal. Males and females release milt and eggs into the water almost simultaneously. These mix together and the eggs are fertilised. The fertilised eggs may either float away in the current or fall to the substrate to lie among the stones and/or plants until they hatch. There is no parental care and large numbers of eggs are produced to allow for predation.

The parents should be well conditioned before spawning. The aquarium may be set up with marbles across the bottom so that the eggs can fall between them and not be eaten. Alternatively a mesh screen can be placed across the tank, allowing the eggs to fall through to safety. Remove the parents after spawning.

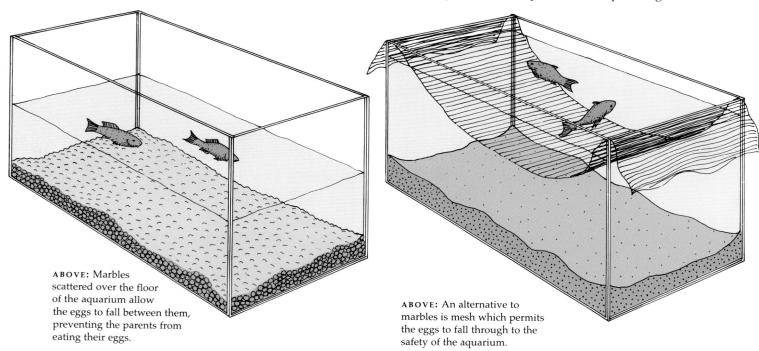

ABOVE: Marbles scattered over the floor of the aquarium allow the eggs to fall between them, preventing the parents from eating their eggs.

ABOVE: An alternative to marbles is mesh which permits the eggs to fall through to the safety of the aquarium.

NEST BUILDERS

Many species build nests of one form or another, some excavate large depressions in the substrate and guard them while others dig into the banks of rivers, laying their eggs in a tunnel. Probably the best known in the aquarium is the bubble nest constructed by many of the Gouramis and some Catfish.

No special breeding set-up is required. When ready to spawn, the fish construct the nest by blowing bubbles and will often incorporate bits of vegetation to help hold the nest together. After spawning, remove the female or provide her with plenty of plant-cover so that she can recover.

Care is needed to raise the fry. Take the precaution of fitting a tight cover glass to keep the area between the water surface and the cover glass warm and humid. Without this protection the nest and, more importantly, the fry can be chilled and may perish.

EGG DEPOSITORS

In this case, the eggs may either be laid on a flat surface such as a rock or plant leaf or they may be placed individually amongst fine leaved plants such as Java Moss. Egg depositors which utilise a flat surface usually form pairs and will guard the eggs and fry. Cichlids and some Catfish are probably the best known for this. Those fish using fine-leaved plants, for example some of the Rainbows, can be spawned in pairs or trios.

Spawning mops make ideal substitutes for fine leaved plants, and the breeding aquarium can be set up with these. This method is used for some of the Killifish and also for the Rainbows. In both cases spawn is laid over several days and individual eggs can easily be seen on the mops. They can be removed for hatching and rearing in another aquarium.

The set-up for Cichlids and Catfish will depend on the species, but generally, provide a flat stone, broad-leaved plant, cave, upturned flower pot or pipe, and allow the fish plenty of space to create a territory in which they can rear their brood. It is also possible to remove the eggs, still attached to the leaf, stone or whatever and raise them separately.

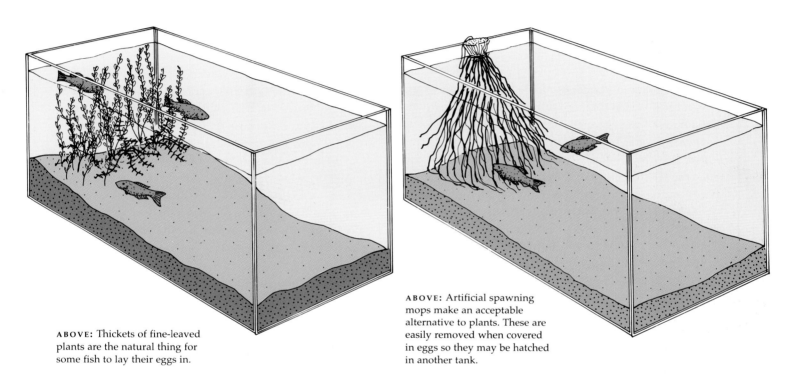

ABOVE: Thickets of fine-leaved plants are the natural thing for some fish to lay their eggs in.

ABOVE: Artificial spawning mops make an acceptable alternative to plants. These are easily removed when covered in eggs so they may be hatched in another tank.

EGG BURIERS

The annual Killifish are the best known for this method of reproduction. As their pools dry out, the fish spawn, pressing their eggs down into the substrate. The adults perish when the waters evaporate but the eggs remain dormant in the dried out mud. At the onset of the rains, some eggs hatch but, to allow for the failure of these rains, some of the eggs still remain dormant until they receive a second soaking.

To breed them in the aquarium, provide a layer of peat on the bottom. Condition the parents well and, if possible, use one male and two females as the males can drive the females very hard when breeding. After spawning, the substrate and eggs are dried out and stored for several weeks before they will hatch.

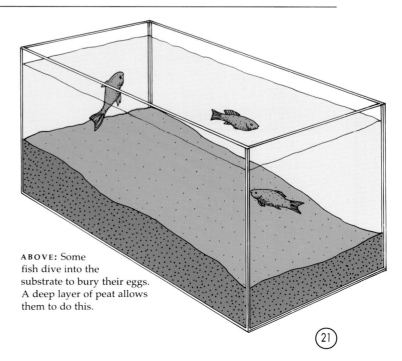

ABOVE: Some fish dive into the substrate to bury their eggs. A deep layer of peat allows them to do this.

MOUTH BROODERS

ABOVE: *Pseudotropheus socolofi* is a typical mouthbrooding cichlid.

The best known of the mouth brooders are some of the African Lake Cichlids and a few species of Catfish. The female lays the eggs on a flat surface where they are fertilised by the male before being taken up into the females mouth. They are held here until they hatch and even the fry still return to the parents' mouth for shelter. Brood numbers are usually low as, by the time of their release, the fry are fairly well grown so losses are minimal.

Fish which mouth brood require no special tank set up other than a flat surface or an area of open substrate on which to lay the eggs in the first instant.

LIVEBEARERS

Possibly the best known and also one of the first fish that everyone keeps is the Guppy. This Livebearer will produce several broods of fry every 4 to 5 weeks from a single mating, the female being able to store the male's sperm in her body. Other Livebearers need to be fertilised before producing every brood.

In order to raise the fry it is best to use a specially set up tank in which the female can give birth. This should have a false, slatted bottom that allows the fry to sink to the lower levels while, at the same time, preventing the female from eating them. Provided it is large enough to accommodate the female, a commercial breeding trap may also be used.

PROBLEMS

It is far better to try and prevent a problem occurring than to cope with it once it has happened. For straight-forward emergencies such as heater or pump failure, always ensure that you have spares. If there is a power cut, the fish will survive quite happily for a short time, as the temperature drop and the subsequent rise on restoration of the power supply will both be gradual. Should the disruption in service be of any length, then a blanket wrapped around the aquarium will help prevent heat loss. Also bottles full of hot water can be floated in the tank to help maintain the temperature – this is supposing you have an alternative source to heat the water in the first place!

It is always advisable to quarantine new stock, even if you know precisely where it has come from. But at some time in our career as aquarists, our fish are going to get some sort of disease. Good aquarium practices, such as using different nets for each aquarium, or dis-infecting nets before using them in another aquarium, help to prevent the spread of infection. Most of the common diseases such as White Spot and fungus can be treated using the proprietary medicaments available from your aquarium stores. Read the instructions carefully before use and be careful not to overdose. It is only in exceptional circumstances that veterinary advice has to be sought.

Develop the habit of touching the tanks as you pass and glancing at the fish, because they are the best guide to what if anything may be going wrong. They're looking sluggish and the tank feels cool – check the heater. In cool conditions tropical fish tend to slow down and become lethargic, so there is a chance the heater may have failed. They are near the filter inlet pipe but not swimming as usual and the tank feels warm – again, check the heater. In warmer conditions, oxygen levels drop and the fish move nearer the surface, in this case near the input pipe from the filter where the water will be carrying the most oxygen. If the behaviour of your fish changes, it will be for a reason – whether good (perhaps they have spawned) or possibly bad. While we all try to have thermometers in or on our tanks, there is no substitute for learning to live with your fish and constantly observe their behaviour.

LEFT: Livebearers are probably the first fish that an aquarist breeds. Here a *Heterandria formosa* gives birth.

The Directory

Anabantids

Anabantidae
Belontiidae
Helostomatidae
Osphronemidae

ANABAS TESTUDINEUS

(BLOCH, 1795)

Family: ANABANTIDAE	
Common name: CLIMBING PERCH, CLIMBING BASS	
Distribution: Malaysia, Indonesia, southern China, India	
Size: 23 cm (9 in)	
Food: OMNIVOROUS. Flake, live or frozen aquatic invertebrates, vegetable matter	
Temperature range: 22–28°C / 72–82°F	
pH: 7.0–8.0 dH: to 25°	

One of the earliest fishes imported for the hobby. Being very hardy, they were able to withstand long sea journeys to England, and specimens were displayed at the London Zoo Aquarium in 1870. In the wild, when their habitats dry up, these fish can travel across land on their pectoral fins. They have even been found up trees; whether they climbed to these heights or were taken there by predatory birds is questionable, but this has given rise to their common name – Climbing Perch. They can survive out of water for up to 48 hours in damp and humid conditions – or, if things get really dire, they may dig into the mud to survive. The male's anal fin is longer than the female's.

Breeding
The eggs float, and hatch in 24 hours at 26–28°C / 79–82°F. Feed the fry infusoria and newly hatched brine shrimp.

Tank Set-up
Can be aggressive so only keep with larger community fish. Provide plenty of plant cover, and some floating plants to discourage jumping. Use a tight-fitting cover glass.

22–28°C 72–82°F		23 cm (9 in)

CTENOPOMA ACUTIROSTRE

PELLEGRIN, 1899

23–28°C 73–82°F		15 cm (6 in)

Family: ANABANTIDAE	
Common name: SPOTTED CLIMBING PERCH	
Distribution: Zaire	
Size: 15 cm (6 in)	
Food: CARNIVOROUS. Live and frozen mosquito larvae, bloodworm, etc, and flake	
Temperature range: 23–28°C / 73–82°F	
pH: 6.5–7.5 dH: to 10°	

Can be a timid fish if kept with more robust companions. But given plenty of hiding places, so that it feels secure, it will swim about quite happily. Males have patches of spines on the body; there may be fewer spots on the fins of females.

Breeding
This bubble-nest builder requires very soft (2–4°), slightly acidic (pH 6.5–7.0) water and a high temperature (26–28°C / 79–82°F). Keep the tank well covered, to maintain high humidity in the space between water surface and cover glass. Feed fry on newly hatched brine shrimp.

Tank Set-up
Roots and plant for cover. Good filtration but not too fast a water flow. Subdued lighting.

CTENOPOMA ANSORGII

(BOULENGER, 1912)

Family: ANABANTIDAE	
Common name: ORNATE CTENOPOMA	
Distribution: Tropical west Africa	
Size: 8 cm (3 in)	
Food: CARNIVOROUS. Live foods of all kinds, will take flake and frozen food	
Temperature range: 26–28°C / 79–82°F	
pH: 6.5–7.5 dH: to 20°	

Rarely imported, this fish does not travel well and can be difficult to acclimatise to aquarium conditions. May take smaller tank mates, so keep with peaceful fish it cannot eat.

Breeding
Not very much known. They construct a bubble nest in shallow water, at a depth of 12 cm (4½ in). The fry require very small foods such as infusoria.

Tank Set-up
Well-planted aquarium with soft water. Good, mature filtration system to maintain the water quality.

26–28°C 79–82°F		8 cm (3 in)

CTENOPOMA KINGSLEYAE
GUENTHER, 1896

24–28°C
75–82°F

19 cm (7½ in)

Family: ANABANTIDAE	
Common name: KINGSLEY'S CTENOPOMA	
Distribution: Zaire to Gambia	
Size: 19 cm (7½ in)	
Food: OMNIVOROUS. Eats anything from live fish to flake and pellets	
Temperature range: 24–28°C / 75–82°F	
pH: 6.5–7.5 dH: to 15°	

Should be kept with quiet companions. Males have a prominent spiney patch behind the eye and at the base of the caudal fin.

Breeding
A large aquarium is needed. Up to 20,000 eggs are produced and these float to the surface. They hatch in about 24 hours if the water temperature is high (29°C / 84°F). When free-swimming (some two days after hatching) they may be fed newly hatched brine shrimp.

Tank Set-up
A roomy aquarium with roots and plants for decoration. Efficient filtration is essential as is a good turnover of water.

CTENOPOMA OXYRHYNCHUS
(BOULENGER, 1902)

24–28°C
75–82°F

10 cm (4 in)

Family: ANABANTIDAE	
Common name: MOTTLED CTENOPOMA	
Distribution: Stanley Pool (Zaire)	
Size: 10 cm (4 in)	
Food: CARNIVOROUS. Small live foods, will accept frozen and flake	
Temperature range: 24–28°C / 75–82°F	
pH: 6.2–7.0 dH: to 15°	

Not for the standard community aquarium, this fish will take smaller fish and should only be kept with larger companions. On males the dorsal and anal fins are pointed.

Breeding
The floating eggs hatch in about three to four days. Feed fry on newly hatched brine shrimp.

Tank Set-up
Open waters for swimming, but provide plenty of plant cover and roots or caves for hiding places. Gentle water flow is beneficial. Good filtration.

BELONTIA HASSELTI
(CUVIER & VALENCIENNES, 1831)

Family: BELONTIIDAE	
Common name: NONE	
Distribution: Singapore, Sumatra, Java, Borneo	
Size: 19 cm (7½ in)	
Food: OMNIVOROUS. Predominantly meaty foods, but include some vegetable matter	
Temperature range: 25–28°C / 77–82°F	
pH: 6.5–8.0 dH: to 35°	

Generally a peaceful fish unless it is spawning. Then males become very pugnacious, and even the female should be removed after spawning has taken place. When spawning, males lose the lace-like pattern on the fins.

Breeding
Use a breeding tank with shallow water, no more than 15 cm (6 in) deep, and a high temperature at about 28°C / 82°F. Males may or may not build a bubble nest. Up to 700 eggs may be produced and these hatch in about 36 hours. First foods are infusoria and brine shrimp nauplii.

Tank Set-up
Brightly lit, densely planted aquarium. Water should be hard and alkaline. Good filtration.

25–28°C
77–82°F

19 cm (7½ in)

Family: BELONTIDAE

Common name: COMBTAIL

Distribution: Sri Lanka

Size: 13 cm (5 in)

Food: OMNIVOROUS. Live foods, flake, vegetable matter

Temperature range: 24–28°C / 75–82°F

pH: 6.5–7.5 dH: to 25°

A very hardy fish, it can be aggressive, and should only be kept with other creatures who can stand up for themselves. Males have an extended dorsal fin.

Breeding

Eggs are laid beneath plant leaves. Clumps of eggs are surrounded by a single bubble, rather than the frothy bubble nest of some other anabantids. Fry are free-swimming after six days and will feed on newly hatched brine shrimp and powdered foods.

BELONTIA SIGNATA
(GUENTHER, 1861)

Tank Set-up

Plenty of hiding places such as roots, clumps of plants and caves. Water conditions are fairly unimportant so long as extremes are avoided. Gentle filtration.

| 24–28°C 75–82°F | | 13 cm (5 in) |

BETTA BREDERI
MYERS, 1935

Family: BELONTIIDAE

Common name: NONE

Distribution: Indonesia

Size: 11 cm (4½ in)

Food: OMNIVOROUS. Insect larvae, flake, frozen food

Temperature range: 23–28°C / 73–82°F

pH: 6.5–7.5 dH: to 15°

Can be aggressive, so keep with fish of a similar size. Males are larger than females and more colourful.

| 23–28°C 73–82°F | | 11 cm (4½ in) |

Breeding

These are mouth brooders, incubating the eggs for about 40 hours until the fry hatch. Once the young are released they may be fed on brine shrimp nauplii.

Tank Set-up

Planted tank with a good cover as these fish jump. Good filtration and a slight water flow.

Family: BELONTIIDAE

Common name: NONE

Distribution: Malay Peninsula

Size: 4.5 cm (2 in)

Food: CARNIVOROUS. Small aquatic invertebrates, flake

Temperature range: 23–27°C / 73–81°F

pH: 6.0–7.5 dH: to 15°

A timid fish, probably best kept in a species aquarium. It does not appear to be aggressive towards its own kind.

Breeding

Up to 60 eggs may be produced. Young may be fed on brine shrimp nauplii.

Tank Set-up

Thickets of tall plants. Very gentle filtration. Does best in soft acidic water.

| 23–27°C 73–81°F | | 4.5 cm (2 in) |

BETTA COCCINA
VIERKE, 1979

BETTA IMBELLIS
LADIGES, 1975

Family: BELONTIIDAE	
Common name: NONE	
Distribution: Indonesia	
Size: 4.5 cm (2 in)	
Food: OMNIVOROUS. Live foods for preference but will take flake and frozen food	
Temperature range: 24–25°C / 75–77°F	
pH: 7.0 dH: to 10°	

Males may be kept together and will engage in mock fights and displays, but little or no damage is done to either participant. Best kept in groups that include both males and females.

Breeding
Breeding and rearing as for *Betta splendens*, but far fewer eggs are produced.

Tank Set-up
Community aquarium with other peaceful species. Soft, well-filtered water. Plants, roots and caves for cover.

24–25°C 75–77°F		4.5 cm (2 in)

BETTA MACROSTOMA
REGAN, 1910

24–26°C 75–79°F		11 cm (4½ in)

Family: BELONTIIDAE	
Common name: BRUNEI BEAUTY	
Distribution: Sarawak, Brunei	
Size: 11 cm (4½ in)	
Food: OMNIVOROUS. Insect larvae, etc, but will take flake and tablet foods	
Temperature range: 24–26°C / 75–79°F	
pH: 6.5–7.5 dH: to 10°	

Rarely imported, and then it is usually only males that are available. Keep males singly in a species tank. Males are highly coloured, red and black, females, in contrast, are plain.

Breeding
Mouth brooders. The eggs are brooded for about two weeks and the young may be fed on newly hatched brine shrimp.

Tank Set-up
Well-planted tank with good filtration system giving a fast flow of water. Ensure plenty of hiding places. Keep the tank well covered. This fish is sensitive to any build-up of nitrates.

BETTA PUGNAX
(CANTOR, 1850)

Family: BELONTIIDAE	
Common name: PENANG MOUTHBROODING FIGHTER	
Distribution: Cambodia, Malaysia, Indonesia	
Size: 10 cm (4 in)	
Food: CARNIVOROUS. Live foods, but may take flake and frozen food	
Temperature range: 22–28°C / 72–82°F	
pH: 6.0–7.0 dH: to 12°	

A softwater fish that can be kept in a community aquarium. Keep as pairs. Males have longer finnage and brighter coloration.

Breeding
Up to 100 eggs are mouthbrooded by the male. First foods for the fry include infusoria and newly hatched brine shrimp.

Tank Set-up
Clean, clear water with a good rate of flow, such as that produced by an external power filter. Some plants for cover.

22–28°C 72–82°F		10 cm (4 in)

BETTA SPLENDENS
REGAN, 1910

24–29°C
75–84°F
7 cm (3 in)

Family: BELONTIIDAE
Common name: SIAMESE FIGHTER
Distribution: Cambodia, Thailand
Size: 7 cm (3 in)
Food: CARNIVOROUS. All small live foods, frozen foods and flake
Temperature range: 24–29°C / 75–84°F
pH: 6.0–8.0 dH: to 25°

A popular aquarium fish, it has been bred over the years to enhance not only the finnage and colour of males but also their pugnacity. Males should be kept as individuals otherwise they fight and tear their finnage to shreds, and these duals may even end in the death of one of the protagonists. The smaller, shorter-finned and more drab females may be kept together in a community aquarium.

Breeding
Males construct a bubble nest. They entice the female beneath the nest and the spawning embrace ensues. Males guard the nest and the eggs hatch in 24 hours. First foods need to be very fine: powdered flake, newly hatched brine shrimp, etc.

Tank Set-up
Community tank with very slight water movement.

COLISA FASCIATA
(BLOCH & SCHNEIDER, 1801)

22–28°C
72–82°F
10 cm (4 in)

Family: BELONTIIDAE
Common name: BANDED GOURAMI, INDIAN GOURAMI
Distribution: India through to Burma
Size: 10 cm (4 in)
Food: OMNIVOROUS. Flake, frozen and live foods
Temperature range: 22–28°C / 72–82°F
pH: 6.0–7.5 dH: to 15°

A beautiful fish for the community aquarium. Buy and keep as pairs. The male has a more elongated body and is more colourful, and his dorsal fin ends in a point. In India it is regarded as a food fish, being dried before it is eaten.

Breeding
Classic bubble nest builder. After the spawning embrace, the eggs float up to the nest and are guarded by the male. Remove the female after spawning, taking care not to disturb the nest. Eggs hatch in 24 hours. Feed the fry newly hatched brine shrimp and other fine foods.

Tank Set-up
Well-planted community tank with some caves as hiding places. Gentle filtration.

COLISA LABIOSA
(DAY, 1878)

Family: BELONTIIDAE
Common name: THICK-LIPPED GOURAMI
Distribution: Northern India and Burma
Size: 9 cm (3½ in)
Food: OMNIVOROUS. Live, flake and frozen foods, and vegetable matter
Temperature range: 22–28°C / 72–82°F
pH: 6.0–7.5 dH: to 10°

A good fish for the community aquarium. Should be kept as pairs. Males are more colourful and have a pointed dorsal fin.

Breeding
Typical bubble-nest builder, constructing a large nest. Up to 600 eggs may be produced, and hatch in 24 hours. Feed fry on infusoria and brine shrimp nauplii.

Tank Set-up
Larger community aquarium decorated with plenty of plants. A gentle flow of water is beneficial.

22–28°C
72–82°F
9 cm (3½ in)

COLISA LALIA
(HAMILTON, 1822)

22–28°C	5 cm (2 in)
72–82°F	

Family: BELONTIIDAE	
Common name: DWARF GOURAMI	
Distribution: India	
Size: 5 cm (2 in)	
Food: OMNIVOROUS. Plenty of vegetable matter, plus live foods, flake, etc	
Temperature range: 22–28°C / 72–82°F	
pH: 6.5–7.5 dH: to 15°	

A delightful fish for the mature community aquarium, it should be kept with peaceful fishes. Males are more colourful, having red and blue stripes down the body. Females in contrast are plain with a silvery body with just a hint of red-brown stripes. Keep in pairs.

Breeding
Constructs a bubble nest which includes pieces of plant material. Male guards the eggs and resultant fry. Remove the female after spawning and the male after the fry are free-swimming. Very fine first foods.

Tank Set-up
Mature, well-planted community aquarium. Very efficient filtration system as these fish are prone to disease and any decline in water quality will render them open to infection.

MACROPODUS OCELLATUS
(CANTOR, 1842)

Family: BELONTIIDAE	
Common name: NONE	
Distribution: Eastern China, Korea, Vietnam	
Size: 8 cm (3 in)	
Food: OMNIVOROUS. Flake, frozen and live foods	
Temperature range: 15–22°C / 59–72°F	
pH: 6.0–7.5 dH: to 25°	

Seldom imported, this attractive fish is ideal for the home aquarium, being much less aggressive than *Macropodus opercularis*. The finnage on males is spectacular, both dorsal and anal fins are extended and the caudal is bright red-orange.

Breeding
They breed in the same way as *M. opercularis*, but far fewer eggs are produced.

Tank Set-up
Well-planted tank with some floating plants. Good filtration.

15–22°C	8 cm (3 in)
59–72°F	

MACROPODUS OPERCULARIS
(LINNAEUS, 1758)

16–26°C	10 cm (4 in)
61–79°F	

Family: BELONTIIDAE	
Common name: PARADISE FISH	
Distribution: Widespread in eastern Asia	
Size: 10 cm (4 in)	
Food: OMNIVOROUS. Flake, frozen and live food	
Temperature range: 16–26°C / 61–79°F	
pH: 6.0–8.0 dH: to 30°	

A very hardy and adaptable fish, it was able to withstand the rigours of transportation by sea and was first imported to France in 1869. Males are more brightly coloured and have much longer fins than females. Adult males may fight.

Breeding
Easy to breed, they construct a bubble nest beneath a large leaf or other floating object, and produce up to 500 eggs. Feed fry on powdered flake, infusoria and newly hatched brine shrimp.

Tank Set-up
A large aquarium as they are boisterous fish. Males chase females, so provide hiding places in the form of clumps of plants, caves, etc. Gentle filtration.

MALPULUTTA KRETSERI
DERANIYAGALA, 1937

Family: BELONTIIDAE

Common name: NONE

Distribution: Sri Lanka

Size: Males 9 cm (3½ in), females 4 cm (1½ in)

Food: CARNIVOROUS. Prefers live foods but will take flake and frozen food

Temperature range: 24–28°C / 75–82°F

pH: 6.0–7.5 dH: to 20°

Very quiet, timid fish which needs equally quiet companions. Males are larger and have extended finnage. These fish will jump. They can be difficult to acclimatise to the aquarium and provide the aquarist with a challenge.

Breeding
They spawn in caves. Fry may be raised on brine shrimp. The young are rarely eaten by the parents.

Tank Set-up
Well-planted aquarium with some floating plants. Provide caves and other hiding places.

24–28°C
75–82°F

9 cm (3½ in)

PAROSPHROMENUS DEISSNERI
(BLEEKER, 1859)

24–28°C
75–82°F

7.5 cm (3 in)

Family: BELONTIIDAE

Common name: NONE

Distribution: Sumatra, Malaysia, Singapore

Size: 7.5 cm (3 in)

Food: CARNIVOROUS. Thrives on small live foods, but will accept prepared food

Temperature range: 24–28°C / 75–82°F

pH: 5.6–7.2 dH: to 10°

A fish for the specialist, it requires very precise conditions to thrive in captivity. It is best kept in a species aquarium. Males are more brightly coloured than females.

Breeding
It spawns in caves and, after spawning, the male guards the nest. The eggs hatch in about 72 hours, but are not free-swimming for another six days. Fry will be lost if the water conditions deteriorate – they must have very clean, clear, well-filtered water. Growth is slow. First foods: infusoria and brine shrimp nauplii.

Tank Set-up
Soft, slightly acidic, well-filtered, mature water. Planted aquarium with some caves.

PSEUDOSPHROMENUS CUPANUS
(CUVIER & VALENCIENNES, 1813)

24–26°C
75–79°F

6 cm (2½ in)

Family: BELONTIIDAE

Common name: SPIKE-TAILED PARADISE FISH

Distribution: Southern India and Sri Lanka

Size: 6 cm (2½ in)

Food: OMNIVOROUS. Live, flake and frozen food

Temperature range: 24–26°C / 75–79°F

pH: 6.5–7.5 dH: to 15°

A fish which is overlooked because, unless kept in good conditions, it does not show its true colours. It is difficult to tell the sexes apart unless they are about to breed, when males show a great deal of red and females are almost black.

Breeding
A bubble nest is built with plant material added. The male guards the nest until the eggs hatch and the fry are free-swimming. Feed young on newly hatched brine shrimp.

Tank Set-up
Well-planted tank with caves and roots to provide hiding places. Gentle filtration.

PSEUDOSPHROMENUS DAYI
(KOEHLER, 1909)

24–28°C	7.5 cm (3 in)
75–82°F	

Family: BELONTIIDAE

Common name: BROWN SPIKE-TAILED PARADISE FISH

Distribution: Western India

Size: 7.5 cm (3 in)

Food: OMNIVOROUS. Live, flake and frozen foods

Temperature range: 24–28°C / 75–82°F

pH: 6.5–7.5 dH: to 15°

A very peaceful fish that requires equally peaceful companions. Provided there is sufficient cover and an area of still water, it will breed in the community aquarium but few fry will be saved. Males can easily be distinguished by the pronounced spike on the tail (the central rays are extended).

Breeding

Builds a bubble nest into which plant material is added. Both parents guard the nest and tend the fry. The eggs hatch in 30 hours and the fry may be fed on fine foods.

Tank Set-up

Plenty of plants to give cover. Good quality water is essential, especially if you are to see the fish in their best colours.

SPHAERICHTHYS OSPHROMENOIDES
CANSTRINI, 1860

25–30°C	5 cm (2 in)
77–86°F	

Family: BELONTIIDAE

Common name: CHOCOLATE GOURAMI

Distribution: Malay Peninsula, Sumatra, Borneo

Size: 5 cm (2 in)

Food: OMNIVOROUS. Predominantly small live foods, but will take flake and frozen food

Temperature range: 25–30°C / 77–86°F

pH: 6.0–7.0 dH: to 2–4°

One for the specialist, this fish can be prone to bacterial infections and skin parasites, so water conditions are all important. It may be kept in pairs but seems to do better in shoals, where fish are allowed to pair themselves. It is difficult to tell the sexes unless the fish are in good health, when males have gold edges to their anal and caudal fins.

Breeding

A mouthbrooder or nest builder. Eggs are placed on the substrate and the female takes them into her mouth. Broods average 30 and incubation is 14 days. Young require very small foods.

Tank Set-up

The most important thing is water quality. Unless you can maintain soft, slightly acidic, well-filtered water you are doomed to failure. Regular water changes are essential. Plenty of plants to provide cover.

Family: BELONTIIDAE

Common name: PEARL GOURAMI, LEERI

Distribution: Malaysia, Sumatra, Borneo

Size: 12 cm (4½ in)

Food: OMNIVOROUS. Flake, frozen, live and vegetable foods

Temperature range: 24–28°C / 75–82°F

pH: 6.5–8.0 dH: to 30°

A wonderful fish for the larger community aquarium. Keep as pairs and they will display to each other, showing their true colours. Males have a pointed dorsal fin, the anal fin rays are extended and they show more red on the body.

Breeding

A large bubble nest is constructed among plants or below floating plants. The male guards the nest and fry. Feed young on newly hatched brine shrimp.

Tank Set-up

Planted community aquarium with some floating plants. Good filtration but not so strong a water flow as would destroy the nest.

24–28°C	12 cm (4½ in)
75–82°F	

TRICHOGASTER LEERI
(BLEEKER, 1852)

TRICHOGASTER MICROLEPIS
GUENTHER, 1861

25–30°C
77–86°F

15 cm (6 in)

Family: BELONTIIDAE
Common name: MOONLIGHT GOURAMI
Distribution: Thailand, Cambodia
Size: 15 cm (6 in)
Food: OMNIVOROUS. All live food, vegetable matter
Temperature range: 25–30°C / 77–86°F
pH: 6.0–7.0 dH: to 25°

A good sized, peaceful and somewhat timid fish. In mature fish the ventral fins are red and in females, yellow. They may damage fine-leaved plants when nest building. Moonlight Gouramis are considered excellent food fishes in their native countries.

Breeding
A bubble nest is constructed, incorporating some plant material to help bind it together. As many as 1,000 eggs may be produced. The fry are tiny and should be raised first on infusoria and then newly hatched brine shrimp.

Tank Set-up
A large aquarium with dense thickets of robust plants to provide cover. Gentle filtration.

TRICHOGASTER PECTORALIS
(REGAN, 1910)

23–27°C
73–81°F

20 cm (8 in)

Family: BELONTIIDAE
Common name: SNAKESKIN GOURAMI
Distribution: Cambodia, Thailand, Malay Peninsula
Size: 20 cm (8 in)
Food: OMNIVOROUS. Flake, frozen and live foods
Temperature range: 23–27°C / 73–81°F
pH: 6.0–8.0 dH: to 30°

A very accommodating and peaceful species, it is not kept as often as it should be. Males have a pointed dorsal fin.

Breeding
Builds a bubble nest and cares for it and the fry. First foods, infusoria and brine shrimp nauplii. The female need not be removed after spawning.

Tank Set-up
Community aquarium with other peaceful fish. Plants are beneficial. Good filtration but a gentle flow of water.

TRICHOGASTER TRICHOPTERUS
(PALLAS, 1777)

22–28°C
72–82°F

10 cm (4 in)

Family: BELONTIIDAE
Common name: BLUE GOURAMI, THREE-SPOT GOURAMI
Distribution: Widespread from southeast Asia through to the islands of the Indo-Australian Archipelago
Size: 10 cm (4 in)
Food: OMNIVOROUS. Flake, pelletted, frozen and vegetable food
Temperature range: 22–28°C / 72–82°F
pH: 6.0–8.5 dH: to 35°

A very hardy fish, it has been produced commercially in various colour forms: gold, opaline, etc. Keep with other

peaceful fishes, since if its companions are aggressive it will retire and hide away. Males have a pointed dorsal fin.

Breeding
Easy to breed and prolific. Males construct a bubble nest and guard it and the fry. Remove females after spawning. Raise fry on newly hatched brine shrimp and crumbled flake.

Tank Set-up
Planted community aquarium. Good filtration.

TRICHOPSIS PUMILIS
(ARNOLD, 1936)

25–28°C
77–82°F

3.5 cm (1½ in)

Family: BELONTIIDAE
Common name: DWARF CROAKING GOURAMI
Distribution: Vietnam, Thailand, Sumatra
Size: 3.5 cm (1½ in)
Food: OMNIVOROUS. Live, flake and frozen food
Temperature range: 25–28°C / 77–82°F
pH: 5.5–7.0 dH: to 10°

A delicate creature which does best in a species aquarium. When it is excited or courting, croaking sounds are produced. Males have a pointed dorsal fin. In females that are ready to spawn, the eggs can be seen through the body wall.

Breeding
Tiny bubble nests are constructed. About 150 eggs may be produced and these hatch in 48 hours. The fry are small, and are free-swimming after another two days.

Tank Set-up
Thickets of fine-leaved plants and clumps of *Cryptocorynes*. Soft, acidic water and gentle filtration.

TRICHOPSIS VITTATUS
(CUVIER & VALENCIENNES, 1831)

22–28°C
72–82°F
6.5 cm (2½ in)

Family: BELONTIIDAE

Common name: CROAKING GOURAMI

Distribution: Widespread from eastern India through to Malaysia and Indonesia

Size: 6.5 cm (2½ in)

Food: OMNIVOROUS. Small aquatic invertebrates, flake, frozen foods

Temperature range: 22–28°C/72–82°F

pH: 6.5–7.5 dH: to 15°

A very peaceful fish that will coexist quite happily with other quiet fish such as small Characins, Barbs and other small Anabantids. Males have more colour than females and their anal fin is extended. Both males and females are capable of producing a croaking sound.

Breeding
Can be difficult to breed – lowering the water level and raising the temperature to 30°C/86°F may induce them to spawn. Builds a bubble nest. Not many eggs are produced. The young are tiny and should be fed infusoria.

Tank Set-up
Well-planted community tank, with some floating plants. Gentle filtration.

HELOSTOMA TEMMINCKII
CUVIER & VALENCIENNES, 1831

22–28°C
72–82°F
15–30 cm (6–12 in)

Family: HELOSTOMATIDAE

Common name: KISSING GOURAMI

Distribution: Thailand (green form), Java (pink form)

Size: 15–30 cm (6–12 in)

Food: OMNIVOROUS. All live foods, vegetable matter

Temperature range: 22–28°C/72–82°F

pH: 6.5–8.5 dH: to 30°

An interesting fish most often bought because of its habit of "kissing". These are trials of strength between males, and do not usually result in any damage to either fish.

Breeding
Sexes are virtually impossible to distinguish. The eggs float, and lettuce leaves should be floated in the tank to provide infusoria and bacteria for the fry to feed on.

Tank Set-up
A large aquarium with plenty of open space. Use only tough plants such as Java Fern and Java Moss, as most fine-leaved plants are regarded as food. Otherwise use plastic plants. They like to browse on algae, so large, flat stones on which the algae can grow are both useful and decorative.

OSPHRONEMUS GORAMI
(LACEPEDE, 1802)

Family: OSPHRONEMIDAE

Common name: GIANT GOURAMI

Distribution: Malaysia, Java, China, eastern India

Size: 65 cm (26 in), possibly larger

Food: OMNIVOROUS. All live food, vegetable matter

Temperature range: 20–30°C/68–86°F

pH: 6.5–78.0 dH: to 25°

Young specimens may be quarrelsome between themselves, but may be kept with other species of similar size. Growth is rapid so be prepared to provide larger accommodation as required. Mature males have pointed dorsal and anal fins.

Breeding
Unlikely in an aquarium. A floating, ball-shaped nest of plant material is constructed and the eggs placed therein. Nest and fry are guarded for 2–3 weeks.

Tank Set-up
A large aquarium with plenty of robust plants including some floating plants. Good filtration is essential.

20–30°C
68–86°F
65 cm (26 in)

Catfish

Amphiliidae
Ariidae
Aspredinidae
Auchenipteridae
Bagridae
Callichthyidae
Chacidae
Doradidae
Heteropneustidae
Ictaluridae
Loricariidae
Malapteruridae
Mochokidae
Pimelodidae
Siluridae

AMPHILIUS PLATYCHIR
(GÜNTHER, 1864)

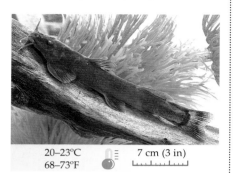

20–23°C 68–73°F	7 cm (3 in)

Family: AMPHILIIDAE

Common name: NONE

Distribution: Sierra Leone (W. Africa)

Size: 7 cm (3 in)

Food: OMNIVOROUS. Will accept prepared aquarium flakes, prefers live food invertebrates (Bloodworm, Mosquito larvae, *Tubifex*, etc.)

Temperature range: 20–23°C/68–73°F

pH: 6.5–7.3 dH: 8–20°

This naked loach-like Catfish that lives among stones and boulders of fast-flowing hill streams is occasionally imported for the aquarium trade. It is best kept in small groups rather than individually.

Breeding
Information is limited. The eggs are most probably laid on the underside of stones on the substrate.

Tank Set-up
A fast turnover of water from a power filter or similar and a coarse substrate of pebbles is recommended.

PHRACTURA ANSORGII
(BOULENGER, 1901)

Family: AMPHILIIDAE

Common name: AFRICAN WHIPTAIL CATFISH

Distribution: Nigeria, Zaire

Size: 9 cm (3½ in)

Food: INSECTIVOROUS. Bloodworm, *Daphnia*, etc.

Temperature range: 20–23°C/68–73°F

pH: 6.5–7.5 dH: 7–20°

Unlike the similar looking but unrelated South American Whiptailed Loricriid Catfish, the armouring of *Phractura* is not an external layer of dermal bone, but extensions of the internal skeleton. This possibly serves a similar function of protecting the fish in the fast-flowing water at the river margin it inhabits. It is generally to be found in the mid strata of the water column, resting amongst the plants in which it finds its food. It is a rather delicate and sedentary aquarium species.

Breeding
Males are more slender than females, especially when the females are full of roe. During spawning the fish are very active and the courtship may be violent. The eggs are approximately 1 mm in diameter and blue-green in colour. Between 100 and 400 may be produced at each spawning. The fry are quite

20–23°C 68–73°F	9 cm (3½ in)

slow growing, only reaching 15 mm (½ in) at two months old.

Tank Set-up
Use a fairly densely planted aquarium, yet with a high turnover of water. The fish is intolerant to high temperatures.

ARIUS SEEMANI
GÜNTHER, 1864

Family: ARIIDAE

Common name: SHARK CATFISH

Distribution: Estuaries of rivers draining into the Pacific Ocean, from southern California to Columbia in South America.

Size: 30 cm (12 in)

Food: OMNIVOROUS

Temperature range: 22–26°C/72–79°F

pH: 6.8–8.0 dH: 8–25°

This shoaling mid-water swimming Catfish is best kept in small groups. Its colours fade with age.

Breeding
There has been no reported breeding success with captive specimens so far. Females are more robust than males, especially specimens larger than 12 cm (4½ in). Observations have been made of a supplementary appendage at the base of, and similar in form to, the ventral fin. It is possibly a mouthbrooder.

22–26°C 72–79°F	30 cm (12 in)

Tank Set-up
Provide a large tank with open swimming spaces and fast flowing water. Most specimens fare better in slightly brackish water, retaining their colour longer and growing faster, than when kept in freshwater.

BUNOCEPHALICHTHYS VERRUCOSUS SCABRICEPS

(EIGENMANN AND EIGENMANN, 1889)

Family: ASPREDINIDAE	
Common name: CRAGGY-HEADED BANJO CATFISH	
Distribution: Northeastern South America	
Size: 8 cm (3 in)	
Food: OMNIVOROUS	
Temperature range: 21–24°C / 70–75°F	
pH: 6.6–7.0 dH: 7–12°	

The fish is a poor swimmer whose best line of defence is its ability to conceal itself amongst the forest litter, which its craggy appearance, similar to bark in both colour and form, does much to assist.

 21–24°C 70–75°F 8 cm (3 in)

Breeding
Not known.

Tank Set-up
A reasonably dense planted tank is preferred, where *B. v. scabriceps* will spend much of its time amongst the mid layers of plants. Without the plants, it has a tendency to bury itself. It is fairly inactive and only seems to come to life in the presence of live foods such as *Tubifex, Daphnia*, etc.

Family: ASPREDINIDAE	
Common name: NONE	
Distribution: Branco River (Brazil)	
Size: 10 cm (4 in)	
Food: OMNIVOROUS	
Temperature range: 21–24°C / 70–75°F	
pH: 6.7–7.0 dH: 7–12°	

This species always has the appearance of being emaciated, no matter how well fed it is. It has a curious ridge along the back, which may help it to conceal itself amongst other forest debris.

Breeding
Not known.

Tank Set-up
This species is rarely imported, and then as an additional species amongst the more common Banjo Catfish. It tends to bury, therefore a sandy or fine gravel bottom should be provided.

 21–24°C 70–75°F 10 cm (4 in)

BUNOCEPHALUS HYPSIURUS
KNER, 1855

PLATYSTACUS COTYLEPHORUS
BLOCH, 1794

Family: ASPREDINIDAE	
Common name: WHIPTAILED BANJO CATFISH	
Distribution: Northern South America	
Size: 25 cm (10 in)	
Food: OMNIVOROUS. Accepts flake or tablet food, prefers live aquatic invertebrates	
Temperature range: 22–25°C / 72–77°F	
pH: 6.8–8.0 dH: 8–20°	

A peaceful species except with very small fry-sized fish, it has a tolerance for brackish conditions due to its estuarine habitat.

Breeding
Males are more intensely mottled, and have a short extension to the dorsal spine. Females are more drab and have expanded ventral fins. Once the eggs are hatched and fertilised, the female attaches the eggs to her underside, carrying them about until they hatch.

 22–25°C 72–77°F 25 cm (10 in)

Tank Set-up
Unless tidal change in salinity can be replicated in the aquarium, this species is best kept in freshwater, with a fine or sandy substrate.

AUCHENIPTERICHTHYS THORACATUS
(KNER, 1858)

21–25°C
70–77°F
11 cm (4½ in)

Family: AUCHENIPTERIDAE	
Common name: ZAMORA CATFISH, MIDNIGHT CATFISH	
Distribution: Upper Amazonian tributaries (South America)	
Size: 11 cm (4½ in)	
Food: INSECTIVOROUS. Accepts aquarium flake and tablet food	
Temperature range: 21–25°C / 70–77°F	
pH: 6.5–7.2 dH: 7–14°	

The natural habitat of this Catfish is near the river bank.

Breeding

The sex is determined by body form (females are more robust) and shape of anal fin (slightly convex in females, straight in males). Males also exhibit a thickened appendage at the front of the anal fin. Eggs are fertilised prior to laying.

Tank Set-up

Provide secluded hollows, preferably in wood, in which the Midnight Catfish can hide during the diurnal hours. Whilst not aggressive or actively predatory, it is best kept with fish of similar size.

ENTOMOCORUS GAMEROI
MAGO-LÉCCIAF, 1983

22–25°C
72–77°F
11 cm (4½ in)

Family: AUCHENIPTERIDAE	
Common name: NONE	
Distribution: Apuré River (Venezuela)	
Size: 11 cm (4½ in)	
Food: INSECTIVOROUS. Accepts aquarium flakes	
Temperature range: 22–25°C / 72–77°F	
pH: 6.5–7.3 dH: 8–16°	

A rarely imported, but worthwhile addition for the Catfish enthusiast.

Breeding

Males differ from females in the shape of the dorsal fin which is longer and curved along the front edge, the pelvic fin which is longer and broader, and the presence of an intromittent organ just anterior to the anal fin, used to fertilise the eggs prior to laying.

Tank Set-up

A quiet tank with not too many 'dither' fish, yet with plenty of seclusion in the form of wood and rockwork in which to hide is best. The naked body (no armouring or similar protection) of this species can easily become damaged from sharp objects. Water should be moderately fast flowing.

LIOSOMADORAS ONCINUS
(SCHOMBURGK, 1841)

21–25°C
70–77°F
20 cm (8 in)

Family: AUCHENIPTERIDAE	
Common name: JAGUAR CATFISH	
Distribution: Ucayali and Negro Rivers (South America)	
Size: 20 cm (8 in)	
Food: CARNIVOROUS. Beef-heart, Whitebait, etc., when acclimatised will accept pelleted food	
Temperature range: 21–25°C / 70–77°F	
pH: 5.5–6.8 dH: 3–12°	

Colour patterning and intensity can vary considerably depending on the location of the fish. Some of the intensity can be enhanced with correct feeding of meaty rather than pelleted foods.

Breeding

It is similar to other Auchenipterids in that eggs are fertilised internally by the male prior to hatching. Males exhibit an intromittent organ at the anterior of the anal fin and are less robust than females. Males can also be more intensely coloured.

Tank Set-up

Wood with plenty of hollows is essential as this species is rarely out foraging for food until after dark. Water should not be alkaline, but acidic and fast flowing. It is advisable to keep them in pairs (both sexes) rather than as individuals, one pair to a tank.

TATIA CREUTZBERGI
(BOESEMAN, 1953)

20–24°C
68–75°F
4 cm (1½ in)

Family: AUCHENIPTERIDAE	
Common name: DWARF DRIFTWOOD CATFISH	
Distribution: Surinam	
Size: 4 cm (1½ in)	
Food: OMNIVOROUS. Prefers aquatic invertebrates (Daphnia, Tubifex, Bloodworm, etc.)	
Temperature range: 20–24°C / 68–75°F	
pH: 6.5–7.2 dH: 8–16°	

This species is sedentary during much of the day, only venturing out for food as the opportunity arises. Whilst at rest, the maxiliary barbel is housed in a groove in the head under the eye. In contrast, these barbels are held outstretched at 90° to the body axis when it searches for food over the substrate.

Breeding

As with other members of this family of Catfish, the eggs are fertilised internally before laying.

Tank Set-up

A well planted aquarium with plenty of seclusion is preferable. Clean well-oxygenated water is essential for the fish's well-being. It does not like being kept in the company of far larger species of fish.

Family: BAGRIDAE
Common name: GIRAFFE CATFISH
Distribution: Widespread throughout tropical Africa, including the Nile, Niger and Congo Rivers, and Lakes Chad and Tanganyika
Size: To 60 cm (24 in)
Food: OMNIVOROUS
Temperature range: 22–25°C / 72–77°F
pH: 6.5–7.8 dH: 10–28°

Despite its potential size *A. occidentalis* is a very peaceful species that will co-exist with much smaller species. In its natural environment its size makes it of commercial importance as a food item, whereas in captivity it can become a long-lived family pet.

Breeding
Not known.

Tank Set-up
The fish requires a large aquarium with sound water filtration as it can be a little filthy in its eating habits! Often it is best kept in isolation or with only a few other fish as space permits.

22–25°C 72–77°F		60 cm (24 in)

AUCHENOGLANIS OCCIDENTALIS
(VALENCIENNES, 1840)

CHRYSICHTHYS ORNATUS
BOULENGER, 1902

20–25°C 68–77°F		18 cm (7 in)

Family: BAGRIDAE
Common name: AFRICAN WOOD CATFISH
Distribution: Tropical West Africa
Size: 18 cm (7 in)
Food: CARNIVOROUS. Grudgingly accepts aquarium tablet food
Temperature range: 20–25°C / 68–77°F
pH: 6.8–7.5 dH: 8–16°

This species can be a voracious feeder. Its coloration helps conceal it amongst the debris in which it is found naturally. The dorsal and pectoral spines are sharp, therefore handle with care; whilst these spines are not themselves poisonous, the copious covering of body slime can lead to blood poisoning if the spines puncture your skin.

Breeding
Not known.

Tank Set-up
Use rock and wood to provide the seclusion in which this species will lurk, waiting for any suitable food to swim by. Furnish sparsely with plants as they are liable to become uprooted. Power water filtration is recommended as undergravel filters will quickly become disturbed and their efficiency lost. Keep only with fish too big to swallow.

HETEROBAGRUS BOCOURTI
BLEEKER, 1864

Family: BAGRIDAE
Common name: KING BAGRID
Distribution: Southeast Asia
Size: 20 cm (8 in)
Food: CARNIVOROUS. Opportunist feeder rather than active predator
Temperature range: 21–25°C / 70–77°F
pH: 6.5–7.2 dH: 10–20°

This species can be a delicate fish in captivity, which takes some time to acclimatise.

21–25°C 70–77°F		20 cm (8 in)

Breeding
Not known.

Tank Set-up
The tank should be large with a lot of free swimming space, and wide enough to prevent the long maxilliary barbels touching both front and back panes of glass simultaneously. Hiding places should be provided, as should open swimming areas. Fast turnover of well-filtered and oxygenated water is virtually essential.

LEIOCASSIS SIAMENSIS
REGAN, 1913

Family: BAGRIDAE
Common name: ASIAN BUMBLEBEE CATFISH
Distribution: Thailand
Size: 18 cm (7 in)
Food: INSECTIVOROUS
Temperature range: 22–25°C / 72–77°F
pH: 6.2–7.5 dH: 10–20°

In juvenile form this species prefers to be kept in small shoals, however as they reach adulthood they can become quarrelsome.

22–25°C 72–77°F	18 cm (7 in)

Breeding
Not known. Sex can be determined by the presence of a small fleshy appendage just anterior to the male's anal fin.

Tank Set-up
Provide plants and rockwork to help conceal the Asian Bumblebee Catfish during the daytime. Subdued lighting is recommended, as is a moderately fast water flow.

Family: BAGRIDAE
Common name: NONE
Distribution: Java
Size: 12 cm (4½ in)
Food: INSECTIVOROUS
Temperature range: 22–26°C / 72–79°F
pH: 6.5–7.2 dH: 10–18°

A less colourful species than *L. siamensis*, this species is also less aggressive when adult than *L. siamensis* and is better suited to the community aquarium with fish larger than 5 cm (2 in).

Breeding
Sexing and breeding as for *L. siamensis*.

Tank Set-up
Provide secluded areas and moderate water flow.

22–26°C 72–79°F	12 cm (4½ in)

LEIOCASSIS STENOMUS
(VALENCIENNES, 1839)

LOPHIOBAGRUS CYCLURUS
(WORTHINGTON AND RICARDO, 1937)

Family: BAGRIDAE
Common name: TANGANYIKAN CATFISH, AFRICAN BULLHEAD
Distribution: Lake Tanganyika (Africa)
Size: 10 cm (4 in)
Food: CARNIVOROUS. Insect larvae and small fish
Temperature range: 23–26°C / 73–79°F
pH: 7.3–8.0 dH: 15–25°

It is possible that *L. cyclurus* emits a poisonous substance into the water if disturbed, which effects other fish in the vicinity.

Breeding
The fish has been bred in captivity. Sexual differences are not known. Adhesive milk-coloured eggs are laid to the walls of rocky hollows and there is parental care of eggs.

23–26°C 73–79°F	10 cm (4 in)

Tank Set-up
Decorate heavily with rocks to form caves in which the fish will spend much of its time.

MYSTUS MICRACANTHUS
(BLEEKER, 1846)

Family: BAGRIDAE	
Common name: TWO-SPOT PINK BAGRID	
Distribution: Thailand, Borneo, Java and Sumatra	
Size: 12 cm (4½ in)	
Food: OMNIVOROUS. Will eat small fish	
Temperature range: 20–25°C / 68–77°F	
pH: 6.5–7.2 dH: 8–20°	

The fish is best kept in small shoals rather than individually. It will forage constantly in search of food.

20–25°C 68–77°F	12 cm (4½ in)

Breeding
Not known, but like some other Asian Bagrids (*Leiocassis* for example) males develop a small fleshy appendage near the vent.

Tank Set-up
Provide a large aquarium with open swimming areas. Clean, well oxygenated water is advisable, with a reasonable water flow.

Family: BAGRIDAE	
Common name: ASIAN RED-TAILED BAGRID	
Distribution: Southeast Asia	
Size: 60 cm (24 in)	
Food: CARNIVOROUS	
Temperature range: 22–25°C / 72–77°F	
pH: 7.0–8.2 dH: 13–24°	

This species is best kept in isolation. Its size and carnivorous nature do not lend themselves to sharing space with other tank inmates. Ensure all tank decoration is well secured from demolition from this powerful Catfish, and that sharp edges, on which the Catfish could easily scratch its naked body, are absent.

Breeding
Not known.

Tank Set-up
Provide a large tank with abundant swimming areas. A securely fitted hood or cover is required as this Catfish is a strong jumper. Ensure that all heaters, thermostats, filtration pipes and similar equipment is secure.

22–25°C 72–77°F	60 cm (24 in)

MYSTUS NEMURUS
(VALENCIENNES, 1839)

MYSTUS WYCKII
(BLEEKER, 1858)

22–26°C 72–79°F	70 cm (27½ in)

Family: BAGRIDAE	
Common name: NONE	
Distribution: Thailand, Sumatra, Borneo, Burma and Java	
Size: 70 cm (27½ in)	
Food: OMNIVOROUS. Adults inclined towards piscivorous diet	
Temperature range: 22–26°C / 72–79°F	
pH: 6.6–7.3 dH: 8–22°	

The very flat broad head and distinctive creamy white flashes on the upper and lower caudal fin lobes make for easy identification of this species. The maxilliary barbels are long, extending beyond the anal fin base, while the mandibular barbels can extend to the tips of the pectoral fin. This is an extremely powerful fish, and can be aggressive.

Breeding
Not known.

Tank Set-up
The fish is best kept in isolation, in a tank large enough to house it in its potential adult size. Good filtration and protection of heaters, thermostats and indeed anything else which could become damaged from this boisterous fish is advisable! Adult specimens will often feed only on live fish.

PELTEOBAGRUS FULVIDRACO
(RICHARDSON, 1846)

Family:	BAGRIDAE
Common name:	AMUR CATFISH
Distribution:	Amur River basin (Russia), China and Siberia
Size:	35 cm (14 in)
Food:	INSECTIVOROUS. Will accept flake and tablet food
Temperature range:	16–24°C / 60–75°F
pH: 6.5–7.2 dH: 7–20°	

Their distribution range does not make them readily available. *P. fulvidraco* can be kept outdoors in ponds for much of the year, but is not advisable to keep it with other spawning fish as their fry will probably be taken as nutrient. Whilst the body is naked and unprotected, there are pungent dorsal and pectoral fin spines that can inflict painful wounds to the unwary handler.

16–24°C
60–75°F 35 cm (14 in)

Breeding
Eggs are layed in a depression in the substrate. These and the subsequent fry are tended by the male.

Tank Set-up
Water conditions are not critical so long as extremes are avoided, even heaters can be dispensed with. The tank should have open swimming spaces as well as areas of seclusion such as that offered by plants, rockwork and wood.

22–25°C
72–77°F 4 cm (1½ in)

PELTEOBAGRUS ORNATUS
(DUNCKER, 1904)

Family:	BAGRIDAE
Common name:	DWARF ORNATE BAGRID
Distribution:	Malaysia and Indonesia
Size:	4 cm (1½ in)
Food:	INSECTIVOROUS. Partial to *Daphnia* and *Tubifex*, will accept flake
Temperature range:	22–25°C / 72–77°F
pH: 6.5–7.2 dH: 8–18°	

P. ornatus is one of the few diurnally active Catfish. Its body is transparent to such a degree that not only are the internal organs visible, but so too are the body markings on the opposite side.

Breeding
Around 12–20 light green eggs about 2 mm in diameter can be seen from time to time in the body cavity of females. These are laid among the fronds of fine-leaved plants.

Tank Set-up
The fish is ideally suited to the community aquarium with other similar-sized fish, and is best kept in small shoals. An abundance of plants, particularly Java Moss is recommended. Water should be reasonably well oxygenated and slow flowing. Feed abundantly with *Daphnia* to bring to breeding condition.

ASPIDORAS PAUCIRADIATUS
(WEITZMAN AND NIJSSEN, 1970)

Family:	CALLICHTHYIDAE
Common name:	FALSE CORYDORAS
Distribution:	Araguaia River (Brazil)
Size:	2.5 cm (1 in)
Food:	OMNIVOROUS. Accepts small invertebrates – (*Daphnia*, etc.) and flake
Temperature range:	22–25°C / 72–77°F
pH: 6.2–7.0 dH: 6–12°	

Superficially similar to *Corydoras*, *Aspidoras* are differentiated by anatomical features of the skull: a dual fontanel, openings in the top of the skull, as opposed to only one in *Corydoras*. *Aspidoras* species are generally smaller and can be more retiring than their close relatives, *Corydoras*, and hence care should be taken in the selection of fellow tank inmates.

22–25°C
72–77°F 2.5 cm (1 in)

Breeding
Not known.

Tank Set-up
Provide a quiet well-planted aquarium with few other species. Water should be well filtered and oxygenated. A soft sandy substrate is recommended.

BROCHIS BRITSKII

NIJSSEN AND ISRÜCKER, 1983

22–25°C
72–77°F

8 cm (3 in)

Family: CALLICHTHYDAE	
Common name: NONE	
Distribution: Mato Grosso River (Brazil)	
Size: 8 cm (3 in)	
Food: OMNIVOROUS	
Temperature range: 22–25°C / 72–77°F	
pH: 6.7–7.2 dH: 8–20°	

This species has only recently been discovered, and is fairly similarly coloured to the other two species of *Brochis*. Unique among the Callichthyidae, *B. britskii* has a bony shield that completely covers the underside of the head.

Breeding

So far unrecorded. Sexes can be distinguished by the profile of the snout, which is more rounded in females, and in males slightly concave.

Tank Set-up

It is ideally suited to the community tank containing similar-sized fish. Provide good water filtration and subdued lighting. Open areas for feeding, and quiet areas for hiding should also be provided.

Family: CALLICHTHYIDAE	
Common name: HOG-NOSED BROCHIS	
Distribution: Upper Napo River (Ecuador)	
Size: 9 cm (3½ in)	
Food: OMNIVOROUS	
Temperature range: 22–24°C / 72–75°F	
pH: 6.5–7.2 dH: 8–20°	

The very distinctive snout helps differentiate this species from other *Brochis* species.

Breeding

Sexing is not known and there is no documented spawning record.

Tank Set-up

Soft substrate is essential as this species is fond of digging in search of food, and can easily damage the sensory barbels if the medium is too coarse. Good filtration is required as *B. multiradiatus* is not tolerant of poor quality water.

22–24°C
72–75°F

9 cm (3½ in)

BROCHIS MULTIRADIATUS

(ORCÉS-VILLAGOMEZ, 1960)

BROCHIS SPLENDENS

(CASTELNAU, 1855)

Family: CALLICHTHYIDAE	
Common name: SAILFIN CORYDORAS	
Distribution: Brazil, Peru and Ecuador	
Size: 7 cm (2¾ in)	
Food: OMNIVOROUS. Easy to satisfy, likes small aquatic invertebrates, will take flake food	
Temperature range: 21–27°C / 70–80°F	
pH: 6.0–7.5 dH: 6–25°	

The common name, Sailfin Corydoras, alludes to the appearance of juvenile specimens having a large sail-like dorsal fin. It is often confused with *Corydoras aeneus*, the Bronze Corydoras, which is similarly pigmented. However the longer dorsal fin of *Brochis*, with 10–12 spines, against the six to seven spines of the *Corydoras*, and its larger size, help in distinguishing the two.

21–27°C
70–80°F

7 cm (2¾ in)

Breeding

Adhesive eggs are laid individually on the underside of plant leaves. There is no parental care.

Tank Set-up

Well suited to the community aquarium, *B. splendens* is active for much of the day. Keep as a small group, not individually. Provide broad-leaved plants for spawning, and fine sandy substrate.

CALLICHTHYS CALLICHTHYS
(LINNAEUS, 1758)

Family: CALLICHTHYIDAE
Common name: ARMOURED CATFISH
Distribution: Widespread through much of tropical South America
Size: 20 cm (8 in)
Food: OMNIVOROUS
Temperature range: 20–26°C / 68–79°F
pH: 6.0–7.8 dH: 6–30°

In order to survive in low oxygenated waters, *C. callichthys* can take in atmospheric air for absorption into the bloodstream via the highly vascular covered hind gut. As a result, it makes regular excursions to the water surface, irrespective of the saturated oxygen levels. Sometimes the air can be seen emitted from the vent.

20–26°C
68–79°F
20 cm (8 in)

Breeding
Males have stouter pectoral fin spines, which often turn upward distally with age. Females have a more robust body form. Males build a bubble nest at the water's surface from an aggregate of floating plant or debris and sticky bubbles of air. The female clasps the eggs as they leave her vent, presenting the eggs for fertilisation by the male, after which the eggs are deposited in the bubble nest, and guarded aggressively by the male.

Tank Set-up
The fish is tolerant of a wide range of water conditions. As it is fairly inactive during the daytime it requires secluded areas of the tank in the form of wood or rockwork. For spawning, either floating plant or other material (polystyrene for instance) is needed to provide the anchorage for the bubble nest, otherwise rooted plants will be removed for the purpose. It can be boisterous, even aggressive during spawning.

GENERAL TIPS FOR KEEPING *CORYDORAS*
With the majority of *Corydoras* species, keeping, sexing and breeding are somewhat similar. Most species are undemanding of water conditions and will tolerate wide variations of temperature, pH and hardness. As a general indication these should ideally be in the following range: temperature: 22–26°C/72–79°F; pH: 6.2–7.8; dH 4–25°

Soft sandy substrate is essential to prevent damage to Barbels. For breeding purposes, stock two males to a single female.
Sexing can usually be determined by body form, with males more slender than females. Also, females invariably have larger fan-like ventral fins, often used to clasp the eggs during spawning. Adhesive eggs are laid on broad-leaved plants or the aquarium glass.
In order to create a degree of categorisation of the *Corydoras*, ichthyologists have grouped the various varieties principally on pattern. These group types are shown with each species of *Corydoras* described here.

CORYDORAS ARCUATUS
(ARCUATUS GROUP)
ELWIN, 1939

Family: CALLICHTHYIDAE
Common name: ARCHED CORYDORAS
Distribution: Ecuador, Peru and Brazil
Size: 4 cm (1½ in)
Food: OMNIVOROUS
Temperature range: 22–26°C / 72–79°F
pH: 6.2–7.8 dH: 4–25°

Similar to *C. narcissus* which has a more pronounced snout, *C. arcuatus* has a rounded snout. Refer to 'General tips for keeping *Corydoras*' above.

Breeding
There are no recorded instances of captive breeding.

Tank Set-up
Refer above.

22–26°C
72–79°F
4 cm (1½ in)

CORYDORAS AXELRODI
(AENEUS GROUP)
RÖSSEL, 1962

Family: CALLICHTHYIDAE
Common name: AXELROD'S CORYDORAS
Distribution: Meta River (Columbia)
Size: 4 cm (1½ in)
Food: OMNIVOROUS
Temperature range: 22–26°C / 72–79°F
pH: 6.2–7.8 dH: 4–25°

C. axelrodi is sometimes confused with *C. loxozonas* which lacks the dark stripe along the back. Refer to 'General tips for keeping *Corydoras*' above regarding keeping and breeding.

Breeding
Refer above.

Tank Set-up
Refer above.

22–26°C
72–79°F
4 cm (1½ in)

CORYDORAS BARBATUS (BARBATUS GROUP)

QUOY AND GAIMARD, 1824

Family: CALLICHTHYIDAE
Common name: BARBATUS CATFISH
Distribution: Rio de Janeiro to São Paulo (Brazil)
Size: 6 cm (2½ in)
Food: OMNIVOROUS
Temperature range: 22–26°C / 72–79°F
pH: 6.2–7.8 dH: 4–25°

This is the largest species of the *Corydoras*. Two distinct colour forms exist that seem related to their locality. Those from the Rio de Janeiro area are

22–26°C / 72–79°F   6 cm (2½ in)

more colourful, particularly the males which exhibit bright gold-yellow reticulations on the head. While breeding is more or less common to other *Corydoras* species, the ratio of males to females should be 1:1. Refer to the general *Corydoras* description on page 44 for details regarding keeping.

Breeding
There are a number of recorded instances of captive breeding of this species.

Tank Set-up
Refer to page 44.

CORYDORAS CAUDIMACULATUS (PUNCTATUS GROUP)

RÖSSEL, 1961

Family: CALLICHTHYIDAE
Common name: TAIL-SPOT CORYDORAS
Distribution: Guaporé River (Brazil)
Size: 5 cm (2 in)
Food: OMNIVOROUS
Temperature range: 22–26°C / 72–79°F
pH: 6.2–7.8 dH: 4–25°

This species is a little more delicate than many other species of *Corydoras*, particularly in its requirements of good water quality and is also more retiring.

22–26°C / 72–79°F   5 cm (2 in)

It is similar to *C. guapore*, but stouter and with more defined spots on the body.

Breeding
Refer to page 44.

Tank Set-up
It likes a quiet aquarium with plenty of secluded areas. Refer also to page 44.

CORYDORAS GARBEI (BARBATUS GROUP)

R. VON IHERING, 1911

Family: CALLICHTHYIDAE
Common name: NONE
Distribution: São Francisco River (Brazil)
Size: 3.5 cm (1½ in)
Food: OMNIVOROUS
Temperature range: 22–26°C / 72–79°F
pH: 6.2–7.8 dH: 4–25°

A rather drab coloured *Corydoras*. Refer to the general *Corydoras* description on page 44 for details regarding keeping.

Breeding
There are no recorded instances of captive breeding.

Tank Set-up
Refer to page 44.

22–26°C / 72–79°F   3.5 cm (1½ in)

CORYDORAS HASTATUS (ELEGANS GROUP)

EIGENMANN AND EIGENMANN, 1888

Family: CALLICHTHYIDAE
Common name: DWARF CORYDORAS
Distribution: Amazon River (Brazil)
Size: 3 cm (1 in)
Food: OMNIVOROUS. Accepts aquarium flake food, does best on small aquatic invertebrates such as *Daphnia*.
Temperature range: 23–26°C / 73–79°F
pH: 6.5–7.2 dH: 4–18°

One of the smallest *Corydoras* species that is best kept in small groups of no fewer than six. This species spends most of the time shoaling in mid-water.

23–26°C / 73–79°F   3 cm (1 in)

Breeding
Refer to page 44.

Tank Set-up
Refer to page 44.

CORYDORAS PANDA (AENEUS GROUP)

NIJSSEN AND ISBRÜCKER, 1971

Family: CALLICHTHYIDAE	
Common name: PANDA CORYDORAS	
Distribution: Ucayali river system (Peru)	
Size: 3.5 cm (1½ in)	
Food: OMNIVOROUS	
Temperature range: 22–26°C / 72–79°F	
pH: 6.5–7.5 dH: 6–20°	

Juvenile specimens are more markedly coloured than adults. *C. panda* is not so robust in captivity as other *Corydoras* species, requiring particular attention paid to water quality. Refer to the general *Corydoras* description on page 44 for details regarding keeping and breeding.

Breeding
It has been bred in captivity, but not often.

 22–26°C 72–79°F   3.5 cm (1½ in)

Tank Set-up
Refer to page 44.

CORYDORAS POLYSTICTUS (PUNCTATUS GROUP)

REGAN, 1912

Family: CALLICHTHYIDAE	
Common name: NONE	
Distribution: Mato Grosso River (Brazil)	
Size: 4 cm (1½ in)	
Food: OMNIVOROUS	
Temperature range: 22–26°C / 72–79°F	
pH: 6.2–7.8 dH: 4–25°	

Refer to the general *Corydoras* description on page 44 for details regarding keeping.

Breeding
Refer to page 44.

Tank Set-up
Refer to page 44.

 22–26°C 72–79°F   4 cm (1½ in)

CORYDORAS ROBINEAE (PUNCTATUS GROUP)

BURGESS, 1983

Family: CALLICHTHYIDAE	
Common name: FLAG-TAILED CORYDORAS	
Distribution: Negro River (Brazil)	
Size: 4 cm (1½ in)	
Food: OMNIVOROUS	
Temperature range: 22–26°C / 72–79°F	
pH: 6.2–7.8 dH: 4–25°	

The striped tail, similar to that of its close relative, *Dianema urostriata*, makes this species easy to identify. Refer to the general *Corydoras* description on page 44 for details regarding keeping.

Breeding
Refer to page 44.

Tank Set-up
Refer to page 44.

22–26°C 72–79°F   4 cm (1½ in)

CORYDORAS SEPTENTRIONALIS (ARCUATUS GROUP)

GOSLINE, 1940

Family: CALLICHTHYIDAE	
Common name: DUSKY CORYDORAS	
Distribution: Venezuela	
Size: 4.5 cm (2 in)	
Food: OMNIVOROUS	
Temperature range: 22–26°C / 72–79°F	
pH: 6.2–7.8 dH: 4–25°	

Refer top general *Corydoras* description on page 44 for details regarding keeping.

Breeding
There are no recorded instances of captive breeding.

Tank Set-up
Refer to page 44.

 22–26°C 72–79°F   4.5 cm (2 in)

CORYDORAS STERBAI (PUNCTATUS GROUP)

KNAACK, 1962

Family: CALLICHTHYIDAE	
Common name: STERBA'S CORYDORAS	
Distribution: Guaporé River (Brazil)	
Size: 3.5 cm (1½ in)	
Food: OMNIVOROUS	
Temperature range: 22–26°C / 72–79°F	
pH: 6.2–7.8 dH: 4–25°	

This species is often confused with *C. haraldshultzi* which has a lighter ground colour and dark spots. Refer to the general *Corydoras* description on page 44 for details regarding keeping and breeding.

Breeding
Refer to page 44.

Tank Set-up
Refer to page 44.

 22–26°C 72–79°F   3.5 cm (1½ in)

DIANEMA LONGIBARBIS

COPE, 1870

Family: CALLICHTHYIDAE	
Common name: PORTHOLE CATFISH	
Distribution: Peru	
Size: 15 cm (6 in)	
Food: OMNIVOROUS / INSECTIVOROUS	
Temperature range: 22–26°C / 72–79°F	
pH: 6.5–7.2 dH: 7–20°	

Dianema are fairly peaceful, and not as boisterous as their *Hoplosternum* and *Callichthys* relatives. They are best kept in small groups of six or more, and tend to mope if isolated from others.

Breeding
Males have slightly thicker pectoral fin spines and are not so stocky as females. These fish are bubble nest spawners,

but there are few successful captive breeding attempts recorded.

Tank Set-up
A quiet tank is preferred. This mid- to lower-water strata swimmer, needs

 22–26°C 72–79°F   15 cm (6 in)

open space and will often rest on an elevated vantage place, such as a rocky ledge.

DIANEMA UROSTRIATA

(MIRANDA-RIBEIRO, 1912)

Family: CALLICHTHYIDAE	
Common name: FLAG-TAILED CATFISH	
Distribution: Brazil	
Size: 16 cm (6¼ in)	
Food: OMNIVOROUS / INSECTIVOROUS	
Temperature range: 22–26°C / 72–79°F	
pH: 6.5–7.2 dH: 7–20°	

Clearly identifiable from *D. longibarbis*, by the distinctive striped caudal fin. *D. urostriata* can also grow slightly larger than it. Both species are able to take in atmospheric air to supplement their oxygen supply when water contains low amounts of dissolved oxygen.

Breeding
Males have slightly thicker pectoral fin spines and are not so stout as females. The fish are bubble nest spawners.

Tank Set-up
Requirements are identical to those for *D. longibarbis*.

 22–26°C 72–79°F   16 cm (6¼ in)

HOPLOSTERNUM LITTORALE
(HANCOCK, 1828)

Family: CALLICHTHYIDAE	
Common name: NONE	
Distribution: Widespread through northern South America	
Size: 20 cm (8 in)	
Food: OMNIVOROUS	
Temperature range: 21–27°C / 70–80°F	
pH: 6.2–7.5 dH: 6–20°	

This is the largest member of the Callichthyidae family of Catfish. The slightly forked caudal fin helps distinguish this from other species of *Hoplosternum*. It is often found in poorly oxygenated rivers and streams near the bank.

Breeding
Females are more robust than males, but the pectoral spines of males are thicker and bend upwards at their extremities with age. It is a bubble nest spawner, in a similar fashion to its close relative, *Callichthys callichthys*.

Tank Set-up
It is not suited to the community aquarium, as while not aggressive except during breeding, it is a little boisterous. It is pretty undemanding of water conditions. Provide shelter,

21–27°C 70–80°F — 20 cm (8 in)

subdued lighting, and a tight cover to prevent the fish jumping out as it surfaces to take in oxygen from above the water surface.

HOPLOSTERNUM PECTORALE
(BOULENGER, 1895)

Family: CALLICHTHYIDAE	
Common name: NONE	
Distribution: Paraguay	
Size: 15 cm (6 in)	
Food: OMNIVOROUS	
Temperature range: 22–27°C / 72–80°F	
pH: 6.2–7.5 dH: 6–20°	

An identifying feature of this species is the rounded caudal, similar to that of *Callichthys callichthys*. Less boisterous

22–27°C 72–80°F — 15 cm (6 in)

than other *Hoplosternum*, it is found in muddy or silted rivers and streams.

Breeding
Its sex is determined by its body form, the male being less robust than the female. It is a bubble nest spawner.

Tank Set-up
It is not entirely suitable for a community tank of small fish, though it is generally undemanding and not aggressive outside spawning. It has a fairly wide tolerance of water quality and condition.

HOPLOSTERNUM THORACATUM
(VALENCIENNES, 1840)

Family: CALLICHTHYIDAE	
Common name: NONE	
Distribution: Fairly widespread throughout northern South America	
Size: 18 cm (7 in)	
Food: OMNIVOROUS	
Temperature range: 21–27°C / 70–80°F	
pH: 6.5–7.5 dH: 6–22°	

Found in muddy stretches of rivers and streams, *H. thoracutum*'s auxiliary intestinal breathing allows it to survive in poorly oxygenated water. Coloration varies considerably with this fish, dependant on its locality. The truncated shape of the caudal fin is the identifying feature of this species of *Hoplosternum*.

Breeding
This species is fairly easy to spawn. Males are more colourful and less robust, with thicker pectoral fin spines. It is a bubble nest spawner similar to *Callichthys callichthys*. Males aggressively guard eggs.

21–27°C 70–80°F — 18 cm (7 in)

Tank Set-up
Any plants will need to be hardy and require good roots as *H. thoracatum* can be boisterous. This very hardy fish will accept most aquarium conditions. Do not keep it with smaller fish.

CHACA BANKANENSIS
BLEEKER, 1852

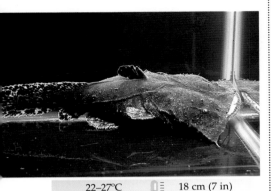

Family: CHACIDAE	
Common name: FROG-MOUTHED CATFISH	
Distribution: India, Burma, Malaya, Sumatra, and Borneo	
Size: 18 cm (7 in)	
Food: CARNIVOROUS. Will not accept dried fish flake or pellet	
Temperature range: 22–27°C / 72–80°F	
pH: 6.5–7.2 dH: 6–18°	

Despite its modest size, this fish has an enormous mouth. It lays motionless in wait at the bottom of muddy streams, well concealed amongst other stream debris, for its prey to come close. Sometimes it will flutter the fringe of barbels around the mouth to lure the prey closer. Once the prey is within reach, the gape is so large that when the mouth is opened the displaced water rushes into the cavity, drawing prey with it from some considerable distance. The fish hardly moves throughout this process.

Breeding
Not known.

Tank Set-up
It is totally unsuited to the community aquarium as *Chaca* will eat fishes up to the size of itself. The aquarium should have places for concealment, with low lighting levels. It is a voracious fish with a demanding appetite and not recommended for the novice fishkeeper.

22–27°C
72–80°F   18 cm (7 in)

ACANTHODORAS CATAPHRACTUS
(LINNAEUS, 1758)

Family: DORADIDAE	
Common name: NONE	
Distribution: Amazon River (Brazil)	
Size: 15 cm (6 in)	
Food: OMNIVOROUS. Readily accepts pelleted fish food	
Temperature range: 22–27°C / 72–80°F	
pH: 6.2–7.5 dH: 6–25°	

A. cataphractus spends much of the daylight hours hidden in hollows in wood or rocks, venturing out only at night to feed. It is quite gregarious, and will gorge itself to such an extent that the body becomes markedly bloated. The body has a series of deep plates down each side, each plate with numerous spines or thorns like the dorsal and pectoral fin spines and those of the humeral process. The fin spines are equipped with powerful muscles, and one line of defence is for *Acanthodoras* to clamp the aggressor between the pectoral spine and the humeral process, a strategy that has been painfully demonstrated to the author on a number of occasions!

Breeding
Sexual differences are not known. Eggs are laid in a depression in the substrate. Both sexes guard the eggs.

Tank Set-up
A. cataphractus is not to be trusted with smaller fish. While not an active predator, the presence of other sleeping fish may be too much of a temptation!

22–27°C
72–80°F   15 cm (6 in)

Provide many hollows in which it can hide, and feed it after the lighting is turned off. It will tolerate wide variations in water chemistry, and is extremely hardy and long lived.

AGAMYXIS PECTINIFRONS
(COPE, 1870)

Family: DORADIDAE	
Common name: SPOTTED DORAS	
Distribution: Rio Maranon, Peru	
Size: 14 cm (5½ in)	
Food: OMNIVOROUS. Flake, tablet, frozen and live food	
Temperature range: 21–26°C / 70–79°F	
pH: 5.5–7.5 dH: to 12°	

A sedentary catfish that fits in well in a community aquarium of medium to large peaceful fishes. It spends much of its time hiding away in caves or crevices in wood. Wood is better for it to hide in as it can rub the skin off its pectoral and dorsal fin spines if they are constantly scraping against a rough surface. Most active at dusk and into the night. If the water is too hard, a cloudy film can develop across the eyes.

21–26°C
70–79°F   14 cm (5½ in)

Breeding
Not known.

Tank Set-up
A well-established community aquarium with a sand or gravel substrate, rocks, wood and some plants for decor. Efficient filtration.

AMBLYDORAS HANCOCKI
(VALENCIENNES, 1840)

Family: DORADIDAE

Common name: TALKING CATFISH

Distribution: Northern South America and the freshwaters of the Amazon and Marañón Rivers

Size: 12 cm (4½ in)

Food: OMNIVOROUS. Especially aquatic invertebrates (*Daphnia, Tubifex, Chaoborus* larvae, etc.); will readily accept commercial fish food and flake

Temperature range: 21–25°C / 70–77°F

pH: 6.5–7.2 dH: 8–16°

A. hancocki is fairly placid, and can be kept in a community tank of similar-sized fish. They are more diurnally active if kept in small groups rather than singularly. The common name, Talking Catfish, alludes to the noises it produces, either by voluntary vibrating its swim bladder using the so-called elastic spring mechanism which connects this organ to the back of the skull, or by stridation of the pectoral fin joint. The sound created is used for communication, which transmits itself very easily in water.

22–27°C
72–80°F

12 cm (4½ in)

Breeding
Not known. Sexes can be determined by the shape of the coracoidal process on the underside of the fish: parallel processes for males, horse-shoe shaped in females.

Tank Set-up
Provision of secluded areas created with wood, rockwork and plants is recommended. The addition of waterlogged beech and oak tree leaves as a substrate acts as a playground for the Talking Catfish.

ANADORAS GRYPUS
(COPE, 1871)

22–27°C
72–80°F

17 cm (7 in)

Family: DORADIDAE

Common name: DUSKY DORADID

Distribution: Amazon basin (Brazil)

Size: 17 cm (7 in)

Food: OMNIVOROUS

Temperature range: 22–27°C / 72–80°F

pH: 6.5–7.2 dH: 8–15°

Not a diurnally active species, *A. grypus* is often confused with *Amblydoras hancockii*, the better known Talking Catfish. Both share the mottled coloration, but the lateral plates of *A. grypus* are deeper, and the caudal peduncle is covered by fulcra on the ventral and dorsal surfaces, looking somewhat like a series of overlapping plates or tiles. *A. grypus* also grows larger.

Breeding
Not known.

Tank Set-up
It is advisable to keep either single individuals or very small groups in a large tank. They are not communal fish, preferring solitude for much of the time. Do not keep them with fish smaller than 5 cm (2 in). Provide areas for hiding such as hollows in wood or rocky caves. Some water movement is preferred, though not too strong.

ASTRODORAS ASTERIFRONS
(HECKEL, 1855)

Family: DORADIDAE

Common name: STAR GAZING DORADID

Distribution: Brazilian Amazon and Bolivia

Size: To 9 cm (3½ in)

Food: OMNIVOROUS / INSECTIVOROUS. Readily accepts commercial fish food and flake

Temperature range: 21–25°C / 70–77°F

pH: 6.5–7.5 dH: 8–20°

21–25°C
70–77°F

9 cm (3½ in)

It is placid and sedentary, usually resting among submerged tree roots in wood and plants. Its diurnal activity is confined to short foraging excursions. Colour can vary slightly according to locality. It is not regularly imported.

Breeding
Not known.

Tank Set-up
This fish requires a quiet tank with moderately secluded areas in which to hide during the day. A moderately slow water flow is preferred.

HASSAR NOTOSPILUS
(EIGENMANN, 1912)

22–25°C	7 cm (3 in)
72–77°F	

Family: DORADIDAE

Common name: BLACK-FINNED DORADID

Distribution: Northeastern South America

Size: To 7 cm (3 in)

Food: OMNIVOROUS. Accepts flake food, but should be augmented by small live aquatic invertebrates

Temperature range: 22–25°C / 72–77°F

pH: 6.5–7.0 dH: 5–20°

A shy but inquisitive Doradid that is active diurnally. The barbels are branched to increase the area over which are spread the taste receptors. Much of the body is naked with only a narrow band of thorned plates down the lateral surface. Take care with handling, the sharp dorsal and pectoral fin spines can easily become entangled in nets.

Breeding

Males have a slight fleshy extension to the dorsal fin spine. Females are more stoutly built. Their breeding strategy is not known.

Tank Set-up

This fish fits in well in a community tank with fish of similar size. It prefers fairly dense planting through which it will forage during the day. The plant also affords *Hassar* with a sense of security as a hiding place if frightened. Soft sand or fine gravel base is essential otherwise the delicate fringed barbels can become easily damaged as it sifts through the substrate.

MEGALODORAS IRWINI
EIGENMANN, 1925

Family: DORADIDAE

Common name: SNAIL-EATING DORADID

Distribution: Brazilian Amazon and northeastern South America

Size: 60 cm (24 in)

Food: CARNIVOROUS. Juvenile fish have fed on snails, in captivity readily adapts to pelleted food, chopped earthworms, beef-heart

Temperature range: 22–26°C / 72–79°F

pH: 6.5–7.4 dH: 7–20°

The attractive marbled coloration of juveniles fades slightly with age. Growth in the aquarium can be slow, but the fish is long-lived. As it grows, so too do the lateral plates and the thorn on each. The dorsal and pectoral fins are also liberally equipped with serrations along their anterior and posterior edges. Despite its size, it has little local economic value as a food fish. Its flesh is reputed to be fairly tough and unpalatable.

22–26°C	60 cm (24 in)
72–79°F	

Breeding

Not known.

Tank Set-up

Provide a large tank with suitable hiding hollows, in which *Megalodoras* will spend much of the daylight hours. Open feeding areas should also be provided. Handle with care!

OPSODORAS STUBELII
(STEINDACHNER, 1882)

22–26°C	11 cm (4½ in)
72–79°F	

Family: DORADIDAE

Common name: NONE

Distribution: Brazil and Peru

Size: 11 cm (4½ in)

Food: OMNIVOROUS. Prefers insect larvae and other invertebrates, will accept flake food

Temperature range: 22–26°C / 72–79°F

pH: 6.5–7.2 dH: to 20°

A very peaceful species with delicate branched barbels, used to sift through sandy substrate in search of food, it is not always easy to acclimatise to a new aquarium. Once established it is fairly hardy. It is active to a degree during the daytime.

Breeding

Not known.

Tank Set-up

Suitable for a community tank with fish larger than 2 cm (1 in), it requires good water quality and moderate water flow. A soft sandy or fine gravel bottom is essential. While not a shoaling fish, it seems happier kept in small groups rather than as an individual specimen.

ORINOCODORAS EIGENMANNI
MYERS, 1927

21–26°C	18 cm (7 in)
70–79°F	

Family: DORADIDAE
Common name: NONE
Distribution: Orinoco River system
Size: 18 cm (7 in)
Food: OMNIVOROUS. Flake, tablet, frozen and live food
Temperature range: 21–26°C/70–79°F
pH: 5.5–7.5 dH: to 12°

A catfish well-suited to the companionship of other medium to large-sized peaceful fishes. *O. eigenmanni* is crepuscular, that is to say it is most active at dawn and dusk, sifting through the substrate for food. It is often confused with *Platydoras*

costatus. However, they can be differentiated by the size of the lateral plates along the body and the head shape: in *P. costatus* the plates cover most of the body and the head is short but in *O. eigenmanni* the plates are small and the head longer with a more pointed snout.

Breeding
Not known.

Tank Set-up
A well-established community aquarium with a sand or gravel substrate, rocks, wood and some plants for decor. Efficient filtration.

PSEUDODORAS NIGER
(VALENCIENNES, 1817)

21–24°C	80 cm (31 in)
70–75°F	

Family: DORADIDAE
Common name: BLACK DORADID
Distribution: Amazon
Size: To 80 cm (31 in)
Food: OMNIVOROUS/INSECTIVOROUS. Readily accepts pelleted food
Temperature range: 21–24°C/70–75°F
pH: 6.2–7.5 dH: to 7–20°

Despite its size, it is remarkably placid, even with fish much smaller than itself. Its sense of taste is refined by the presence of taste receptors within the mouth cavity hanging from appendages similar to stalagtites and stalagmites.

Breeding
Not known.

Tank Set-up
A large tank with good filtration and flow is essential. The fish does not thrive in isolation, so is best kept in pairs or small groups, depending on tank size.

PTERODORAS GRANULOSUS
(VALENCIENNES, 1811)

21–25°C	90 cm (35 in)
70–77°F	

Family: DORADIDAE
Common name: NONE
Distribution: Widespread in most large rivers in South America
Size: 90 cm (35 in)
Food: OMNIVOROUS. Flake, tablet, frozen and live food
Temperature range: 21–25°C/70–77°F
pH: 5.5–7.0 dH: to 12°

A large catfish that requires an equally large aquarium. Although peaceful it may "inadvertently" swallow smaller companions especially if hungry. It may be kept in the company of larger

Characins, Cichlids and Cyprinids. Seasonal migrations of these creatures occurs in the wild.

Breeding
Not known.

Tank Set-up
A well-established aquarium with a sand or gravel substrate, rocks, wood and some plants for decor. Ensure that the water remains on the acidic side of neutral as alkaline water can cause excess body mucus to be produced and the eyes to cloud over. Efficient filtration.

RHINODORAS DORBIGNYI
(KRÖYER, 1855)

21–25°C	17 cm (7 in)
70–77°F	

Family: DORADIDAE
Common name: CLOUDY DORADID
Distribution: South Brazil and Paraguay
Size: 17 cm (7 in)
Food: OMNIVOROUS. Accepts flake food, prefers live invertebrates such as *Tubifex*, beef-heart, finely chopped earthworms
Temperature range: 21–25°C/70–77°F
pH: 6.5–7.2 dH: to 10°

Not often imported, this fish has a fairly rapid growth rate.

Breeding
Not known.

Tank Set-up
Attention must be paid to the water chemistry, as hard water (above about 10°dH) is not well tolerated. Clean, well filtered water with moderate water flow is also a requirement. Supply areas of seclusion, hollows and caves, in which the fish can spend much of the daylight hours, and use subdued lighting.

HETEROPNEUSTES FOSSILIS
(BLOCH, 1797)

22–27°C 72–80°F	50 cm (20 in)

Family: HETEROPNEUSTIDAE

Common name: LIVER CATFISH, ASIAN STINGING CATFISH

Distribution: India, Thailand and Borneo

Size: 50 cm (20 in)

Food: OMNIVOROUS. Prefers earthworms, beefheart, etc., will accept tablet food

Temperature range: 22–27°C / 72–80°F

pH: 6.2–7.6 dH: to 25°

Handle with care, the pectoral spines are poisonous, and although not fatal the sensation is not one to be recommended. *H. fossilis* has a supplementary respiratory organ in the form of a vascular cavity close to the backbone and extending the full length of the fish, from the back of the head to the tail. This helps it live in poorly oxygenated waters caused by evaporation during the long dry summer months.

Breeding
Eggs are laid in a depression in the substrate, and guarded by the adults until past fry stage.

Tank Set-up
While water conditions are not critical, a tight cover on the aquarium is needed to prevent *H. fossilis* jumping out. A planted tank is preferred, though the plants will need to be well rooted, with hiding places provided by rockwork. It is not a community-tank fish, even when juvenile.

ICTALURUS MELAS
(RAFINESQUE, 1820)

10–30°C 50–86°F	20 cm (8 in)

Family: ICTALURIDAE

Common name: BLACK BULLHEAD CATFISH

Distribution: North America, from Ontario (Canada) down to the Gulf of Mexico

Size: 20 cm (8 in)

Food: OMNIVOROUS. Has a penchant for aquatic insect larvae and small fish or fry

Temperature range: 10–30°C / 50–86°F

pH: 6.5–7.8 dH: 5–20°

Considered both an ornamental and food fish, it is widespread in lakes and rivers and normally associated with soft sand or muddy bottoms.

Breeding
A circular depression is created in the substrate in which the eggs are laid. The eggs are guarded by the adults. On hatching, this care continues with the fry.

Tank Set-up
As can be seen from the water conditions given it can just about live in anything! This fish is more at home in the outdoor pond where it has ready access to its preferred foods, than in the confines of an aquarium. It is not to be trusted with your fancy carp breeding stock as it will eat the fry. Growth is rapid.

ACANTHICUS ADONIS
ISBRÜCKER AND NIJSSEN, 1988

Family: LORICARIIDAE

Common name: ADONIS CATFISH

Distribution: Tocantins River (Brazil)

Size: 40 cm (16 in)

Food: HERBIVOROUS

Temperature range: 21–24°C / 70–75°F

pH: 6.5–7.0 dH: 5–18°

This species that lives in fairly fast flowing waters, is superficially similar to *A. hystrix*, the difference being the presence of spots on the body. The armoured scutes enclosing the body are heavily covered with denticles – small, sharp, thorn-like appendages – that can easily become entangled in nets.

Breeding
Not known. Mature males have more spiny (heavily dentated) pectoral spines than females.

Tank Set-up
A large tank, about 2 m (6 ft), is the best choice with only a few of the same species, as territorial fights can occur, especially in confined quarters. Plants will become dislodged if not well rooted. A good choice of plant would be Java Moss or Java Fern, both of which will anchor themselves firmly to

21–24°C 70–75°F	40 cm (16 in)

wood. Water flow from a powerful pump or filter is essential to the fish's well-being.

ACANTHICUS HYSTRIX
SPIX, 1829

Family: LORICARIIDAE	
Common name: BLACK ADONIS CATFISH	
Distribution: Amazon River, French Guiana	
Size: 45 cm (18 in)	
Food: HERBIVOROUS	
Temperature range: 21–24°C / 70–75°F	
pH: 6.5–7.2 dH: 5–18°	

A striking Catfish which, although known to science for more than a century and a half, has only recently been for sale as aquarium specimens. These striking fish are identifiable from *A. adonis* by the jet black body, lacking any spots or blotches.

Breeding
Not known. Mature males have longer interopercular spines than females, and more heavily dentated pectoral spines.

Tank Set-up
A large tank is required in which *A. hystrix* can set up territories. Provide similar planting arrangements as for *A. adonis*.

21–24°C 70–75°F — 45 cm (18 in)

ANCISTRUS HOPLOGENYS
(GÜNTHER, 1864)

21–25°C 70–77°F — 15 cm (6 in)

Family: LORICARIIDAE	
Common name: SPOTTED BRISTLE-NOSED CATFISH	
Distribution: Amazon basin (South America)	
Size: 15 cm (6 in)	
Food: HERBIVOROUS	
Temperature range: 21–25°C / 70–77°F	
pH: 6.4–7.2 dH: 4–16°	

Living among wood debris near the banks of rivers and streams, males, in particular, can be aggressively territorial with other *Ancistrus*, and will attack intruders with their interopercular spines erect. It has been known for two males to become entangled this way, separation being exceptionally difficult.

Breeding
Males are easily distinguished by the bushy array of fleshy tentacles around the snout and up the centre of the head. Females have short thin tentacles only around the margin of the snout. Eggs are laid in a hollow in wood and guarded, generally by the male. Parental care continues with the fry, until they gain enough camouflage colouring (up to 3 weeks from hatching).

Tank Set-up
Plenty of bog wood or vine roots is essential. Broad-leaved plants will survive provided other softer plant material is fed. Water should be slightly acidic if attempting to breed *A. hoplogenys*. A reasonable flow of clean, oxygenated water is recommended.

CHAETOSTOMA THOMASI
REGAN, 1904

Family: LORICARIIDAE	
Common name: NONE	
Distribution: Columbia (South America)	
Size: 10 cm (4 in)	
Food: HERBIVOROUS / INSECTIVOROUS. Partial to small aquatic invertebrates such as *Daphnia*, *Tubifex*, etc.	
Temperature range: 20–24°C / 68–75°F	
pH: 6.7–7.2 dH: 6–20°	

Chaetostoma is distinguished by the fleshy snout, possibly evolved as an absorption fender to protect itself in the fast flowing waters in which it is found. They can be territorial amongst their own species, with short squabbles occurring from time to time.

Breeding
Not known.

Tank Set-up
Plenty of hiding places are required, hence a well planted aquarium with wood or rocky caves or hollows in which to hide. Fast flowing water is essential. (Often this species will be found near to the outlet of a power filter.) It will live happily with other fish of similar size, but note the territorial tendencies mentioned above.

20–24°C 68–75°F — 10 cm (4 in)

COCHLIODON COCHLIODON
(KNER, 1854)

Family: LORICARIIDAE	
Common name: COCHLIODON CATFISH	
Distribution: Paraguay (South America)	
Size: 12 cm (4½ in)	
Food: HERBIVOROUS. Spinach, lettuce or garden peas are ideal substitute food	
Temperature range: 21–24°C / 70–75°F	
pH: 6.3–7.2 dH: 5–12°	

A peaceful species that unfortunately is not frequently seen in the aquarium hobby.

Breeding
Neither sexing nor breeding is known.

Tank Set-up
Acclimatisation of this species can be difficult if the correct conditions are not met. Water should be slightly acidic and moderately soft.

 21–24°C 70–75°F   12 cm (4½ in)

FARLOWELLA ACUS
(KNER, 1854)

Family: LORICARIIDAE	
Common name: STICK OR TWIG CATFISH	
Distribution: Venezuela	
Size: 17 cm (7 in)	
Food: HERBIVOROUS. Frequently and regularly offer captive specimens garden peas, spinach and lettuce	
Temperature range: 21–25°C / 70–77°F	
pH: 6.5–7.2 dH: 6–15°	

It is not surprising that this species from forest creeks and rivers uses its likeness to twigs as a form of protection. Being herbivorous, it spends considerable time eating, to extract the low nutrient levels from plant material, and its camouflage permits this activity to be conducted with the minimum of concern.

Breeding
Females are slightly more robust than males. Adhesive eggs are laid, often in the presence of a moderate water current and in the aquarium these eggs are often attached to the tank glass near the outlet from a power filter. Eggs are cleaned and guarded by the parents.

Tank Set-up
Clean, oxygenated water with a reasonable flow is essential. Often *F. acus* will be found among the mid- to upper strata of the water column, on broad-leaved plants, wood or aquarium glass. Although an ideal community fish, this Catfish is not happy with skittish fish.

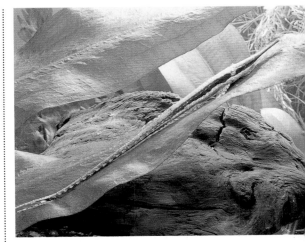

 21–25°C 70–77°F   17 cm (7 in)

GLYPTOPERICHTHYS GIBBICEPS
(KNER, 1854)

Family: LORICARIIDAE	
Common name: NONE	
Distribution: Peru	
Size: 50 cm (20 in)	
Food: HERBIVOROUS. Algae, green food	
Temperature range: 22–27°C / 72–80°F	
pH: 6.5–7.5 dH: to 20°	

A large gentle catfish that does little damage to plants provided it is fed enough green food. If there is insufficient algae available, peas, lettuce, etc. will be accepted. Can be slow growing if the aquarium is too small for it. Spends much of the day hiding and comes out at dusk.

Breeding
Not known.

 22–27°C 72–80°F   50 cm (20 in)

Tank Set-up
A well-established, large, understocked community aquarium with a sand or gravel substrate, rocks and robust plants for decor. Provide a good flow of water and very efficient filtration.

Family: LORICARIIDAE
Common name: ZEBRA PLEC, L46
Distribution: Xingu River (Brazil)
Size: 7 cm (3 in)
Food: OMNIVOROUS. Favour meaty food such as beef-heart more than vegetable
Temperature range: 22–75°C / 72–80°F
pH: 6.4–7.0 dH: 5–12°

When photographs of this fish were first published there was a rush of Catfish enthusiasts in pursuit of this extremely attractive Catfish. At that time it had not been scientifically described, and for commercial considerations was given the code number L46. Since then it has become more readily available.

Breeding
There are no reported instances of captive breeding. Males have a more conspicuous covering of hair-like denticles on the pectoral fin spine, and longer interopercular spines than females.

HYPANCISTRUS ZEBRA
ISBRÜCKER AND NIJSSEN, 1991

Tank Set-up
A reasonably quiet community aquarium with plenty of secluded areas provided by plants and wood is recommended. Water flow should be moderate and lighting subdued.

22–27°C
72–80°F   7 cm (3 in)

HYPOPTOPOMA INEXSPECTATUM
(HOLMBERG, 1893)

22–27°C
72–80°F   6 cm (2½ in)

Family: LORICARIIDAE
Common name: NONE
Distribution: Paraguay River (South America)
Size: 6 cm (2½ in)
Food: HERBIVOROUS
Temperature range: 22–27°C / 72–80°F
pH: 6.5–7.2 dH: 6–18°

The bony plates encasing the body of this fish are covered with small fine hair-like denticles, which can become entangled in nets.

Breeding
Not known. Males are slightly more slender than females.

Tank Set-up
This peaceful species is at home in the community aquarium, where it hides among the plants, often resting on a broad-leaved plant stem in the mid-water regions. Fairly fast flowing and clean water is essential.

LIPOSARCUS ANISITSI
(EIGENMANN AND KENNEDY, 1903)

Family: LORICARIIDAE
Common name: SNOW KING PLEC
Distribution: Paraguay River, Paraguay and Brazil
Size: 40 cm (16 in)
Food: HERBIVOROUS
Temperature range: 21–24°C / 70–75°F
pH: 6.5–8.0 dH: 6–20°

The rivers in which these fish are found are subject to fluctuating water levels. Should the levels become too low, *L. anisitsi* burrow into the bank, undergoing a period of aestivation which can exceed 12 months. Until a recent scientific revision of this group of Loricariids, the generic name was *Pterygoplichthys*.

Breeding
There are no reports of aquarium specimens breeding, and perhaps their natural method of breeding explains why this has not been achieved. In their natural environment they burrow deeply into the muddy bank, near the water surface, to lay their eggs. The male guards the eggs.

21–24°C
70–75°F   40 cm (16 in)

Tank Set-up
A large aquarium is required for this species, with only well-rooted plants, rocks or wood to provide hiding places. Good filtration is essential as they can foul the tank fairly rapidly with faeces from partially digested food.

LIPOSARCUS MULTIRADIATUS
(HANCOCK, 1828)

22–26°C
72–79°F   50 cm (20 in)

Family: LORICARIIDAE
Common name: NONE
Distribution: Peru, Amazonia, Bolivia, Paraguay
Size: 50 cm (20 in)
Food: HERBIVOROUS. Algae, green food
Temperature range: 22–26°C / 72–79°F
pH: 6.5–7.5 dH: to 18°

A large, peaceful catfish, that does little damage to plants despite being a herbivore. It relishes peas and lettuce in its diet. Makes an excellent companion fish for large Cyprinids. Take care when handling as the fin spines can become entangled in nets.

Breeding
Not known.

Tank Set-up
A well-established large aquarium with a sand or gravel substrate, rocks, wood and some large, robust plants for decor. Very efficient filtration.

OTOCINCLUS PAULINUS
REGAN, 1908

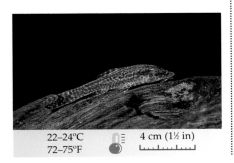

22–24°C
72–75°F   4 cm (1½ in)

Family: LORICARIIDAE
Common name: MARBLED OTOCINCLUS
Distribution: São Paulo region (Brazil)
Size: 4 cm (1½ in)
Food: HERBIVOROUS
Temperature range: 22–24°C / 72–75°F
pH: 6.5–7.4 dH: 5–20°

Active all day as they browse continuously on algae, mainly in the upper layers of the water column. It is here that the algae are likely to flourish, where the strong lighting will not be dissipated by the water depth.

Breeding
Not known, although often what appear to be females full of roe can be seen.

Tank Set-up
This is a very peaceful species. A community tank with an abundance of plant, particularly broad-leaved varieties is recommended. Clean, flowing water is essential.

OTOCINCLUS AFFINIS
STEINDACHNER, 1877

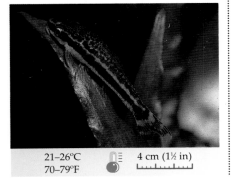

21–26°C
70–79°F   4 cm (1½ in)

Family: LORICARIIDAE
Common name: DWARF OTOCINCLUS
Distribution: Southeastern Brazil
Size: 4 cm (1½ in)
Food: HERBIVOROUS. Algae, green food
Temperature range: 21–26°C / 70–79°F
pH: 5.5–7.5 dH: to 12°

An ideal little catfish for the community aquarium. It can be difficult to acclimatise to aquarium conditions but, provided the water quality is right and plenty of green food is available it will usually settle. Keep as a group. Males are slimmer and slightly smaller than females.

Breeding
Eggs are laid on plant leaves. Raising the fry can be difficult, provide plenty of green food.

Tank Set-up
A well-established community aquarium with a sand or gravel substrate, rocks and plenty of plants for decor. Very efficient filtration.

PANAQUE NIGROLINEATUS
(PETERS, 1877)

22–26°C
72–79°F   25 cm (10 in)

Family: LORICARIIDAE
Common name: PIN-STRIPED PLEC
Distribution: Colombia (South America)
Size: 25 cm (10 in)
Food: HERBIVOROUS
Temperature range: 22–26°C / 72–79°F
pH: 6.5–7.5 dH: 5–18°

Adult males can fight, using their interopercular spines as weapons. There are a number of variations on the patterning which may be regional differences of the same species or a distinct new species in its own right.

Breeding
Unrecorded. Sexes can be distinguished by the length of the interopercular spines, which are longer on males.

Tank Set-up
A large tank with open spaces combined with secluded areas in which to hide should be provided. Flowing well-filtered water is essential.

PANAQUE SUTTONI
SCHULTZ, 1944

Family: LORICARIIDAE
Common name: BLUE-EYED PLEC
Distribution: Northern South America
Size: 18 cm (7 in)
Food: HERBIVOROUS
Temperature range: 21–24°C/70–75°F
pH: 6.0–7.2 dH: 4–18°

Once established, *P. suttoni* can be fairly hardy. However, acclimatisation can be difficult, particularly with juvenile specimens. Good specimens exhibit a slight copper sheen.

21–24°C
70–75°F

18 cm (7 in)

Breeding
Sex identification and breeding strategy is not known.

Tank Set-up
As with *P. nigrolineatus*, a tank with both open and secluded areas, and fast flowing clean water, should be provided. Before purchasing, look carefully for signs of emaciation and sunken eyes; this species does not acclimatise easily, and sick specimens will succumb.

PAROTOCINCLUS MACULICAUDA
(STEINDACHNER, 1877)

22–25°C
72–77°F

4.5 cm (2 in)

Family: LORICARIIDAE
Common name: NONE
Distribution: Southern Brazil
Size: 4.5 cm (2 in)
Food: HERBIVOROUS. Algae, etc., rarely accept pelleted or flake
Temperature range: 22–25°C/72–77°F
pH: 6.4–7.2 dH: 4–15°

This fish is often found in the upper layers of the water, browsing on algae growing on plants, wood and rock.

Breeding
Not known. Sexes may possibly be distinguished by the intensity of coloration and body form.

Tank Set-up
Ideally suited to the community aquarium with plenty of plants and woodwork that extends to the upper parts of the tank. This fish is very peaceful and should be kept in small groups of six or so. Moderately strong flowing water should be used.

PECKOLTIA ARENARIA
(EIGENMANN & ALLEN, 1942)

22–27°C
72–80°F

12 cm (4½ in)

Family: LORICARIIDAE
Common name: CLOWN PLEC
Distribution: Peru
Size: 12 cm (4½ in)
Food: HERBIVOROUS. Algae, green food
Temperature range: 22–27°C/72–80°F
pH: 6.0–7.0 dH: to 12°

One of the smaller suckermouthed Catfishes, it is suited to the community aquarium where it will not bother its companions. They may, however, be aggressive towards their own kind in as much as they are territorial, so only keep more than one specimen if you have a large enough aquarium to allow them to form their territories. Easy to feed, they will accept most substitute green food such as lettuce, peas and courgettes, and thus leave your plants alone.

Breeding
Not known.

Tank Set-up
A well-established community aquarium with plenty of plants and some caves to provide hiding places. Efficient filtration.

PECKOLTIA PULCHER
(STEINDACHNER, 1915)

Family: LORICARIIDAE
Common name: NONE
Distribution: Negro River (Brazil)
Size: 6 cm (2½ in)
Food: HERBIVOROUS. Will also eat small invertebrates such as *Daphnia*
Temperature range: 23–27°C/73–79°F
pH: 6.0–7.0 dH: 6–20°

P. pulcher is territorial among its own species, and will jealously guard what it considers to be its part of the tank. This

23–27°C
73–79°F

6 cm (2½ in)

is usually confined to a hollow in a piece of wood.

Breeding
Not known, neither is sexual dimorphism known.

Tank Set-up
It can be included in the community tank provided quiet areas and dim lighting are offered. Clean and well-oxygenated water essential, as it will not tolerate high nitrate levels. It can be a difficult species to initially acclimatise.

PSEUDACANTHICUS SPINOSUS
(DE CASTELNAU, 1855)

Family: LORICARIIDAE	
Common name: SPINY PLEC	
Distribution: Amazon basin	
Size: 25 cm (10 in)	
Food: OMNIVOROUS. Will eat vegetable matter, beef-heart, tablet food, etc.	
Temperature range: 22–26°C / 72–79°F	
pH: 6.4–7.3 dH: to 20°	

The body and head are covered with serrations and bristles which make for problems in handling. Their aggressive territorial behaviour, particularly by the males, should not be underestimated.

Breeding
Not known. Males are more colourful than females, with slightly thicker pectoral spines.

Tank Set-up
Unsuited to the community aquarium, these fish are extremely territorial and thus require a lot of space. Territorial

22–26°C 72–79°F		25 cm (10 in)

fights can lead to death. Water should be fast flowing and well-filtered. Do not overdo water changes, confined these to 10% water volume at any one time. Provide wood for cover and to help delineate territories.

RINELORICARIA LANCEOLATA
(GÜNTHER, 1868)

Family: LORICARIIDAE	
Common name: LANCEOLATE WHIPTAILED CATFISH	
Distribution: Paraguay River (South America)	
Size: 12.5 cm (4½ in)	
Food: OMNIVOROUS / HERBIVOROUS. Plants, algae, small aquatic invertebrates like *Daphnia*	
Temperature range: 21–25°C / 70–77°F	
pH: 6.4–7.0 dH: 6–20°	

The markings of this species, particularly the broad dark band in the anterior margin of the dorsal fin help in its recognition. Much of its nutrient is extracted from plant or algae material, but will also eat small aquatic invertebrates such as *Daphnia*.

21–25°C 70–77°F		12.5 cm (4½ in)

Breeding
Mature males have fine hair-like bristles around the 'cheeks' of the head and pectoral fin spines, features that are lacking on females. Adhesive eggs are laid in hollows. Eggs and fry are guarded by the parents. The aquarium plastic pipe used in plumbing (approx. 50 mm (2 in) diameter) can be used as spawning caves.

Tank Set-up
Although at home in the community aquarium, *R. lanceolata* is best kept isolated from other fish when attempting to spawn them. Slow flowing water is required, stagnant (still) water is not favoured. Provide caves or hollows from wood, rock and / or plastic pipe.

STURISOMA AUREUM
(STEINDACHNER, 1900)

Family: LORICARIIDAE	
Common name: GIANT WHIPTAIL	
Distribution: Columbia	
Size: 30 cm (12 in)	
Food: OMNIVOROUS. Vegetable and algae nutrient, also small invertebrates from among plants	
Temperature range: 22–27°C / 72–80°F	
pH: 6.4–7.5 dH: 6–20°	

Despite their potential size, this is a peaceful species. Breeding can be induced by attention to feeding, water quality and flow. It is more at home with slow moving fish than active species.

Breeding
Mature males have a prominent array of bristles on their 'cheeks', a feature lacking in females which are slightly more robust. Adhesive eggs are laid onto a smooth cleaned surface, often the aquarium glass in captivity, and are tended by the male. Hatching takes place some five days later. Fry require infusoria as the main nutrient in the early stages, and as their mouth and teeth develop, require an abundance of plant content on which to feed.

Tank Set-up
A reasonably large aquarium is needed to house adults. This should be planted, though not too densely, and furnished with bog wood or vine roots. Efficient and strong filtration is imperative.

22–27°C 72–80°F		30 cm (12 in)

STURISOMA PANAMENSE
EIGENMANN AND EIGENMANN, 1889

Family: LORICARIIDAE	
Common name: ROYAL WHIPTAIL, ROYAL FARLOWELLA	
Distribution: Panama (Central America)	
Size: 25 cm (10 in)	
Food: OMNIVOROUS. Vegetable and algae matter	
Temperature range: 22–27°C / 72–80°F	
pH: 6.5–7.2 dH: 6–20°	

S. panamense spends much of the time in the upper layers of the water, resting or grazing on wood or plant leaves. From aquarium observations there is some suggestion that the tail is used as a tactile sensing mechanism.

Breeding
Mature males have an array of bristles on their 'cheeks'. Smooth surfaced breeding site is first cleaned by the male, after which the adhesive eggs are laid by the female. The males fertilises

22–27°C 72–80°F		25 cm (10 in)

these eggs, guards and cleans them until the fry hatch. Infusoria is the main constituent part of their diet in the first few weeks of hatching.

Tank Set-up
Ideal exhibition fish in any furnished community aquarium, but pay heed to the potential size of adults. At this size plants need to be adequately rooted. Clean water and moderate flow is essential to their success.

MALAPTERURUS ELECTRICUS
(GMELIN, 1789)

22–28°C 72–82°F		40 cm (16 in)

Family: MALAPTERURIDAE
Common name: ELECTRIC CATFISH
Distribution: Widespread through tropical Africa, from the Nile to the Niger, Zaire and Zambesi river systems
Size: 40 cm (16 in)
Food: CARNIVOROUS
Temperature range: 22–28°C / 72–82°F
pH: 6.2–7.5 dH: 8–25°

M. electricus has an electrogenic organ surrounding the body, from just behind the head to the base of the caudal fin, capable of discharging up to 350 volts, according to size. The polarity is head negative, tail positive, and the discharge strong enough to stun other fish of similar size. This characteristic was known to the ancient Egyptians, who considered the electric discharges as a

healing remedy for a number of ailments, and depicted such in some of the heiroglyphics in their tombs.

Breeding
There are incomplete reports of *M. electricus* laying eggs in burrows in the river bank. Aquarium spawnings are unknown. Males are more slender than females.

Tank Set-up
This is a fish that is best kept in isolation – certainly not a community fish! They will fight one another if the aquarium is not large enough. Water conditions are not critical, but its messy feeding habits require good filtration. Slow or still water is preferred, with plenty of cover provided by plants and rocks.

HEMISYNODONTIS MEMBRANACEOUS
(GEOFFROY-ST. HILAIRE, 1809)

22–25°C 72–77°F		48 cm (19 in)

Family: MOCHOKIDAE
Common name: MOUSTACHE SYNODONTIS
Distribution: Widespread from tropical west Africa to the Nile basin
Size: 48 cm (19 in)
Food: INSECTIVOROUS. Will accept pelleted fish food
Temperature range: 22–25°C / 72–77°F
pH: 6.8–7.2 dH: to 25°

While the family Mochokidae are referred to as Upside-down Catfish, only an extremely small percentage of species swim inverted for more than 50% of the time. However, *H. membranaceous* is one that does spend the major part of its time inverted. The specific name alludes to the membrane

at the base of the short maxilliary barbels.

Breeding
Not known, neither are sexual differences.

Tank Set-up
Though peaceful, the fish is a little too large for the normal community aquarium. Water conditions for it are not critical. It prefers the company of others of the same species rather than living in isolation. Only well-established plants remain rooted, but are useful in providing some form of retreat.

MOCHOKIELLA PAYNEI
HOWES, 1980

Family: MOCHOKIDAE

Common name: PAYNE'S SYNODONTIS

Distribution: Sierra Leone

Size: 5 cm (2 in)

Food: INSECTIVOROUS. Will accept flake

Temperature range: 22–25°C / 72–77°F

pH: 6.5–7.2 dH: 6–12°

This small, peaceful species of Mochokid inhabits forest streams.

Breeding
Not known. It is not readily sexable except with ripe females.

Tank Set-up
It is one of the few Mochokids that can be accommodated in a community tank.

Provide both plant cover and open swimming areas. It is only active diurnally when food is offered.

22–25°C 72–77°F		5 cm (2 in)

SYNODONTIS ALBERTI
SCHILTHUIS, 1891

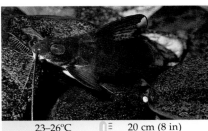

23–26°C 73–79°F		20 cm (8 in)

Family: MOCHOKIDAE

Common name: NONE

Distribution: Stanley Pool region (Zaire)

Size: 20 cm (8 in)

Food: INSECTIVOROUS

Temperature range: 23–26°C / 73–79°F

pH: 6.0–7.5 dH: 5–20°

This fish is easily recognisable by the long maxilliary barbels which can extend beyond the tips of the caudal fin, high lance-like dorsal fin and large eyes.

Breeding
Not known.

Tank Set-up
Though peaceful, this fish is not for the community tank. Provide a large aquarium with a mixture of open areas and hiding places. Thought should be given to the architecture of the tank, with special emphasis on avoiding sharp surfaces that can easily damage the naked body and long maxilliary barbels of *S. alberti*. Water flow should be slow, though well filtered.

Family: MOCHOKIDAE

Common name: ANGEL CATFISH

Distribution: Stanley Pool region (Zaire) and Cameroons

Size: 20 cm (8 in)

Food: INSECTIVOROUS. Will accept flake or tablet food

Temperature range: 22–27°C / 72–80°F

pH: 6.0–7.5 dH: 5–20°

Some specimens can be quarrelsome. The author has observed two specimens locked in mouth-to-mouth combat enduring for up to an hour, in which time the bodies became completely drained of colour. It is not known whether both participants were the same sex, or if this was a prelude to pair bonding.

Breeding
Sexing and breeding strategy is not known.

Tank Set-up
A moderately large aquarium, with wood and plants to provide privacy. Other species should be of similar size. Water conditions are not critical, though slow water flow is best.

SYNODONTIS ANGELICUS
SCHILTHUIS, 1891

22–27°C 72–80°F		20 cm (8 in)

SYNODONTIS BRICHARDI

POLL, 1959

22–25°C
72–77°F
18 cm (7 in)

Family: MOCHOKIDAE	
Common name: BRICHARD'S SYNODONTIS	
Distribution: Lower Zaire River	
Size: 18 cm (7 in)	
Food: OMNIVOROUS. Insect larvae preferred, but will accept aquarium flake and tablet food	
Temperature range: 22–25°C / 72–77°F	
pH: 6.5–7.5 dH: 6–18°	

The loach-like body is ideally suited to the fast-flowing environment of rapids and near waterfalls which they inhabit. Most of the time they are resting, with their head towards the flow of water. Juveniles are far more colourful than adults, which can look a little drab in comparison.

Breeding

Not known. Short papillae near the vent have been observed on some specimens, possibly males.

Tank Set-up

Extensive wood and rockwork combined with fast-flowing water is the ideal set-up. Other fish should be carefully chosen to match these criteria. It is a peaceful species, but should not be trusted with small fish or fry.

SYNODONTIS FLAVITAENIATUS

BOULENGER, 1919

Family: MOCHOKIDAE	
Common name: NONE	
Distribution: Stanley Pool region (Zaire)	
Size: 18 cm (7 in)	
Food: OMNIVOROUS. Will take aquarium food, but prefers insect larvae	
Temperature range: 23–26°C / 73–79°F	
pH: 6.0–7.5 dH: 5–20°	

The distinctive colour of this species remains in adults, though it is not quite as intense. Like *S. clarias*, this species has fimbriated maxilliary barbels, though these appear as small ramifications.

Breeding

Not known. Males have papillae adjacent to vent.

23–26°C
73–79°F
18 cm (7 in)

Tank Set-up

This is a peaceful species, though not to be trusted with very small fish or fry. Provide shelter and plants. Lighting should be subdued.

SYNODONTIS MULTIPUNCTATUS

(BOULENGER, 1898)

Family: MOCHOKIDAE	
Common name: CUCKOO SYNODONTIS	
Distribution: Lake Tanganyika (Africa)	
Size: 12 cm (4½ in)	
Food: INSECTIVOROUS. Will accept tablet food	
Temperature range: 21–25°C / 70–77°F	
pH: 6.8–7.8 dH: 15–30°	

The common name, Cuckoo Synodontis, is derived from a similar breeding strategy to that adopted by the bird.

Breeding

Males show a short papillae adjacent to the vent, a characteristic of many *Synodontis*. Breeding takes place amongst spawning Cichlids, the eggs laid in such a way that the Cichlids take on the parental care not just of their own species eggs and fry, but also those of this Catfish.

Tank Set-up

It is an ideal Catfish for a themed aquarium, complete with various Lake Tanganyika Cichlids. Plants are not essential, but extensive rockwork is a must, for both the Cichlids and this

21–25°C
70–77°F
12 cm (4½ in)

Catfish. Good well filtered and mature water is recommended. The fish is diurnally active.

SYNODONTIS NIGRIVENTRIS
DAVID, 1936

Family: MOCHOKIDAE	
Common name: COMMON UPSIDE-DOWN CATFISH	
Distribution: Zaire basin	
Size: 3 cm (1¼ in)	
Food: INSECTIVOROUS. Will take floating food, but is not their preferred choice	
Temperature range: 23–26°C / 73–79°F	
pH: 6.0–7.5 dH: 5–20°	

The fish lives near the banks of rivers and streams, usually inverted under overhanging logs. It is only active at twilight, when it swims inverted, searching for insects resting on the water surface. This species remains inverted for most of the time, and its coloration is modified such that its underside is darker than its back. This countershading is its means of concealment from birds and other aquatic predators. Predators find that the stout pectoral and dorsal spines makes *S. nigriventris* almost indigestible.

Breeding
Males are generally smaller and less sturdy than females. There have been isolated instances of aquarium spawnings. Eggs are attached to the underside of caves, hollows or wood. Parents do not seem to give undue care to their eggs.

Tank Set-up
Slow-flowing water, with numerous overhangs under which the fish will rest inverted during the day, is essential. Tall plants should also be included. Feed only after the tank lights are extinguished. The fish is perfectly at home in the furnished community tank.

23–26°C 73–79°F	3 cm (1¼ in)

Family: MOCHOKIDAE	
Common name: NONE	
Distribution: Upper Zaire River (Zaire)	
Size: 20 cm (8 in)	
Food: OMNIVOROUS. Prefers insect larvae	
Temperature range: 23–26°C / 73–79°F	
pH: 6.0–7.2 dH: 5–18°	

The attractive marbling of juveniles is diminished in adult specimens. The eye is, uncharacteristically for Catfish, rather large.

Breeding
Not known.

Tank Set-up
This is a timid species that requires suitable hiding retreats, provided by wood and rockwork. Mature, well-filtered water is needed, as is a subdued lighting level. Though very peaceful, the fish is not suitable for keeping with small fish.

23–26°C 73–79°F	20 cm (8 in)

SYNODONTIS PLEUROPS
(BOULENGER, 1897)

BRACHYPLATYSTOMA JURUENSE
(BOULENGER, 1898)

Family: PIMELODIDAE	
Common name: BANDED SHOVELNOSED CATFISH	
Distribution: Jurua River (Brazil)	
Size: 80 cm (31 in)	
Food: CARNIVOROUS. Live fish, earthworms, etc. Will not accept tablet food	
Temperature range: 22–27°C / 72–80°F	
pH: 6.5–7.4 dH: to 20°	

This is a migratory Catfish of deep swift-flowing rivers that will swim for considerable distances in the wild. Its size and attitude make it a fish best suited to the large public aquarium rather than the domestic set-up.

Breeding
Sexual dimorphism and breeding behaviour are not known.

Tank Set-up
A very large tank with efficient and strong flowing filtration is required. Only keep with similar-sized fish, or in isolation. An effective aquarium cover is required to combat any leaping. Furnish the tank with wood only, as only the strongest plants will remain rooted.

22–27°C 72–80°F	80 cm (31 in)

DUOPALATINUS MALARMO
(SCHULTZ, 1944)

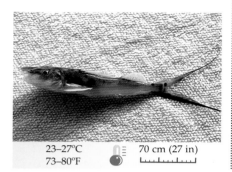

| 23–27°C 73–80°F | 70 cm (27 in) |

Family: PIMELODIDAE
Common name: MALARMO CATFISH
Distribution: Maracaibo basin and Negro River (South America)
Size: 70 cm (27 in)
Food: CARNIVOROUS. Live fish, earthworms, etc. Will not accept aquarium food
Temperature range: 23–27°C/73–80°F
pH: 6.2–7.0 dH: to 20°

This fish can be difficult to adjust to the aquarium, but once established is reasonably hardy. The demand for live foods must be considered before purchase.

Breeding
Not known.

Tank Set-up
A large tank should be furnished with wood or rockwork to provide suitable hiding places. Strong, established, well rooted plants such as Amazon Swords, should withstand inclusion in the aquarium. Lighting should be subdued, and water well filtered, with reasonable water current.

Family: PIMELODIDAE
Common name: SPOTTED SHOVELNOSED CATFISH
Distribution: Major river systems in northern South America (Suriname, Venezuela and Amazon)
Size: 50 cm (19½ in)
Food: CARNIVOROUS. Beef-heart, river shrimp, fish, etc. This diet can be supplemented with pelleted or flake
Temperature range: 22–27°C/72–80°F
pH: 6.5–7.2 dH: to 20°

This particular Shovelnosed Catfish lives in the deep sections or on the bottom of rivers and is readily identifiable by its protruding lower jaw and distinctive coloration. Indication of its condition is by the presence of a coppery sheen over the body of healthy specimens.

Breeding
Not known.

Tank Set-up
Provide a large aquarium with rocks (without sharp protrusions which could easily damage the fish's body, or more importantly its barbels) or wood, and soft sandy substrate. Subdued lighting

HEMISORUBIM PLATYRHYNCHOS
(VALENCIENNES, 1840)

and fast flowing water that has been efficiently filtered are essential. Initially growth is rapid, but from 25 cm (10 in) body length this slows dramatically. Keep it only with fish too large to eat!

| 22–27°C 72–80°F | 50 cm (19½ in) |

LEIARIUS PICTUS
(MÜLLER AND TROSCHEL, 1849)

Family: PIMELODIDAE
Common name: SAILFIN MARBLED CATFISH
Distribution: Amazon River regions
Size: 60 cm (24 in)
Food: CARNIVOROUS. Earthworms, beef-heart, other fish. Will not take aquarium food
Temperature range: 22–27°C/72–80°F
pH: 6.5–7.4 dH: 6–20°

This fish is not often imported, and then usually as a juvenile specimen. In the juvenile state the maxilliary barbels are exceptionally long, extending beyond the caudal fin, but in adults these barbels barely extend beyond the dorsal fin.

Breeding
Not known.

| 22–27°C 72–80°F | 60 cm (24 in) |

Tank Set-up
This species requires a large tank with few other inhabitants. It is aggressive to others of the same species and territorial. Fast-flowing well-filtered water, and low lighting levels are required.

MICROGLANIS IHERINGI
GOMES, 1946

21–26°C
70–79°F

5 cm (2 in)

Family: PIMELODIDAE

Common name: BUMBLE-BEE PIM

Distribution: Northern South America (Venezuela, Peru and Colombia)

Size: 5 cm (2 in)

Food: INSECTIVOROUS. Will readily take aquarium flake and tablet food

Temperature range: 21–26°C / 70–79°F

pH: 6.5–7.4 dH: to 18°

This is a very sedentary creature that is rarely seen during daylight hours. For this reason feeding must be conducted after the tank lights are extinguished.

Breeding

Not known. Females may appear slightly more robust than males.

Tank Set-up

It can be included in the community aquarium provided the other fish are too large to eat. Plenty of hiding places are required, suiting the use of a planted tank with wood or rock decor. The fish is long-lived.

PERRUNICHTHYS PERRUNO
SCHULTZ, 1944

21–25°C
70–77°F

65 cm (25½ in)

Family: PIMELODIDAE

Common name: RETICULATED PIM PERRUNO CATFISH

Distribution: Maracaibo basin (Venezuela)

Size: 65 cm (25½ in)

Food: CARNIVOROUS. Live fish, can be conditioned to accept dead meaty food (beef-heart, etc.). Will not accept commercial aquarium food

Temperature range: 21–25°C / 70–77°F

pH: 6.0–7.2 dH: to 18°

The barbels of *P. perruno* are particularly long and, like the barbels of other Catfish, are used in the search for food. The maxillary barbels can be a good indication of water quality, as instead of being fairly straight, they start to curl at the ends and then degenerate when the nitrate values of the water get too high.

Breeding

Not known.

Tank Set-up

A very large tank is required with plenty of swimming space, with few other inmates other than very large Cichlids and similar fish. Efficient filtration and reasonable flow are recommended.

PHRACTOCEPHALUS
HEMIOLIOPTERUS
(SCHNEIDER, 1801)

21–27°C
70–80°F

120 cm (47 in)

Family: PIMELODIDAE

Common name: RED-TAILED CATFISH

Distribution: Widespread in the Amazonian basin

Size: To 120 cm (47 in)

Food: CARNIVOROUS

Temperature range: 21–27°C / 70–80°F

pH: 7.2–7.6 dH: 8–20°

A very large Catfish that is best suited to the public aquarium. Small specimens approximately 5 cm (2 in) long have been available, but anyone considering buying this fish should think long and hard as to the implications and responsibilities it imposes.

Breeding

Not known, and probably impractical in the aquarium. Sexual dimorphism is also not known.

Tank Set-up

This Catfish is better suited to an indoor heated pool than a glass aquarium. Despite its size it can be trained to take food from its owners hand. It is usually kept in isolation and little decor is required, but very efficient filtration is essential.

PIMELODUS ALBOFASCIATUS
MEES, 1974

22–25°C
72–77°F

25 cm (10 in)

Family: PIMELODIDAE

Common name: WHITE-STRIPED PIM

Distribution: Northern South America

Size: 25 cm (10 in)

Food: CARNIVOROUS. Juveniles can be trained to take tablet food

Temperature range: 22–25°C / 72–77°F

pH: 6.2–7.4 dH: 6–15°

The streamlined shape of this fish makes it ideally suited to life in moderately fast flowing waters. It is diurnally active, though the majority of foraging will be done from twilight to dawn. Beware: sharp pectoral and dorsal fin spines can inflict painful wounds and become severely enmeshed in nets.

Breeding

Not known.

Tank Set-up

The fish is not too demanding of water chemistry, but water quality should be attended to. Mature filtration with low nitrate levels is essential. Provide open swimming areas as well as caves or hollows in which the fish can hide. It will prey on smaller fish.

PIMELODUS ORNATUS

KNER, 1857

22–25°C / 72–77°F   25 cm (10 in)

Family: PIMELODIDAE
Common name: ORNATE PIM
Distribution: French Guiana, Surinam and Paraguay
Size: 25 cm (10 in)
Food: CARNIVOROUS. Juvenile specimens will take pelleted food
Temperature range: 22–25°C / 72–77°F
pH: 6.3–7.2 dH: to 20°

The distinctive coloration of this fish can only be maintained and enhanced through correct feeding of meaty foods such as beef-heart and river shrimp. Beware when handling the fish as the dorsal and pectoral fin spines are especially sharp and stout, and can inflict painful wounds.

Breeding
Sexual differences and breeding strategy are not known.

Tank Set-up
Well matured and efficient filtration is essential. Provide hiding places in which this Catfish will spend most of the daylight hours. Soft sandy substrate with open areas for night-time foraging are recommended. Do not keep with small fish.

PIMELODUS PICTUS

STEINDACHNER, 1876

Family: PIMELODIDAE
Common name: ANGELICUS PIM
Distribution: Colombia (South America)
Size: 12 cm (4½ in)
Food: INSECTIVOROUS. Will take aquarium flake and tablet food
Temperature range: 22–25°C / 72–77°F
pH: 6.0–6.8 dH: to 12°

As with all species of *Pimelodus*, the sharp pectoral and dorsal spines make it difficult to handle. Never use a net as these spines are sure to become entangled and removal is both tricky and dangerous; harm can come to both fish (dislocated or broken fin spines) and to handler (painful stabs). The use of plastic bags in place of the net is probably the better method of transfer, even then watch for punctured bag.

Breeding
Not known.

Tank Set-up
One of the most peaceful species of *Pimelodus* which prefers being kept as a small group rather than individually.

Kept in this manner they are more likely to be seen during the day. The water must be well-matured and filtered, with a moderate water flow. Soft, slightly acid water is preferred, and with plenty of hiding places provided.

22–25°C / 72–77°F   12 cm (4½ in)

PLATYSTOMATICHTHYS STURIO

(KNER, 1857)

22–26°C / 72–79°F   40 cm (16 in)

Family: PIMELODIDAE
Common name: STURGEON CATFISH
Distribution: Amazon basin
Size: 40 cm (16 in)
Food: CARNIVOROUS. Earthworms, fish, beef-heart, etc. Will not take aquarium flake or tablet food
Temperature range: 22–26°C / 72–79°F
pH: 6.2–7.5 dH: to 20°

The maxillary barbels of these river fish are extremely long, often with a curious red patch at half distance, the function of which has yet to be explained. Many specimens exhibit an upturned snout that is not commensurate with damage. Difficult to initially acclimatise.

Breeding
Not known.

Tank Set-up
A large tank, the width of of which is enough to encompass the long barbels of *Platystomatichthys* is required. Only fish large enough not to be eaten should be selected for tank-mates. Plenty of seclusion and dim lighting are the order of the day, as are good filtration and a modest water flow.

PSEUDOPIMELODUS RANINUS RANINUS

(VALENCIENNES, 1840)

22–25°C
72–77°F

10 cm (4 in)

Family: PIMELODIDAE

Common name: BUMBLE-BEE PIM

Distribution: Amazon basin, French Guiana and Surinam

Size: 10 cm (4 in)

Food: CARNIVOROUS. Insect larvae, small fish, will accept tablet food

Temperature range: 22–25°C / 72–77°F

pH: 6.5–7.3 dH: to 20°

P. r. raninus is one of the smallest of the Pimelodids, one of the few that can be kept in a community tank (with reservations, see below). The main problem for the aquarist is that it is rarely seen during the day, venturing out only at night, though the presence of food can sometimes tempt it out in subdued light.

Breeding
Not known. Possibly females become distended when in spawning condition.

Tank Set-up
This species can be placed in the community tank provided all other inhabitants are about 4 cm (1½ in), too large to eat and no spawning activity is taking place. *P. r. raninus* hides during the daytime, therefore provision of hiding places is necessary.

KRYPTOPTERUS BICIRRHIS

(VALENCIENNES, 1839)

Family: SILURIDAE

Common name: ASIAN GLASS CATFISH, GHOST CATFISH

Distribution: Widespread through eastern India, and southeast Asia

Size: 10 cm (4 in)

Food: INSECTIVOROUS. Prefers small aquatic invertebrates such as *Daphnia*, will take flake food as a supplement

Temperature range: 22–26°C / 72–79°F

pH: 6.2–7.0 dH: 5–16°

Found in clear streams, the transparency of this fish allows its internal organs to be seen. The degree of transparency varies, possibly due to its geographical location, but also due to diet, which must include small live foods. At rest, *K. bicirrhis* lays at an angle of approximately 30°, but in motion it swims horizontally.

Breeding
No information on sexing and only scant breeding reports are available.

Tank Set-up
This is a shoaling mid-water Catfish that can be difficult to initially acclimatise, but once established is reasonably hardy. Keep only as a group, not individually. It is an ideal community Catfish that requires open swimming space with a moderate flow of water from an efficient filter. It will eat small fry, but otherwise it is harmless.

22–26°C
72–79°F

10 cm (4 in)

Family: SILURIDAE

Common name: EUROPEAN WELS

Distribution: Europe. Has been introduced into the UK

Size: 300 cm (118 in)

Food: ANYTHING!

Temperature range: 4–20°C / 39–68°F

pH: 6.0–7.6 dH: to 20°

The common name 'Wels' derives from the German for 'Catfish'. Its introduction into English waters has been mainly to satisfy the demands of anglers. *S. glanis* has a voracious appetite that includes other fish, water fowl and vegetable matter; indeed seemingly anything it can get into its large mouth. Although usually just over 3 m (9 ft) in length, one recorded specimen measured 5 m (16½ ft).

Breeding
Around 100,000 adhesive eggs are laid on plants and guarded by the male. Hatching takes place within 16–19 days according to temperature.

SILURUS GLANIS

LINNAEUS, 1758

4–20°C
39–68°F

300 cm (118 in)

Tank Set-up
It is unsuitable for tanks, except as juvenile, and more suited to private lakes.

Characacins

Family: ALESTIDAE	
Common name: RED-EYED TETRA	
Distribution: Lagos to the Niger Delta (West Africa)	
Size: 8 cm (3 in)	
Food: INSECTIVOROUS. Flake, small frozen invertebrates, live *Daphnia* and other aquatic invertebrates	
Temperature range: 23–28°C / 73–82°F	
pH: 6.0–7.5 dH: to 20°	

A peaceful but active, shoaling fish. Live foods such as *Daphnia*, bloodworm and mosquito larvae are appreciated, but frozen foods and flake are also accepted. In males the anal fin is convex with red, yellow and black stripes, whereas in females it is almost straight with a black tip.

Breeding
Soft, slightly acidic water. A pair may produce in excess of 1,000 eggs. They hatch in about 36 hours and are free-swimming within a week. Feed newly hatched fry on brine shrimp nauplii. Growth is rapid.

Tank Set-up
Aquarium at least 100 cm (39 in) long, with thickets of plants and open areas for swimming.

ARNOLDICHTHYS SPILOPTERUS
(BOULENGER, 1909)

23–28°C 73–82°F		8 cm (3 in)	

LADIGESIA ROLOFFI
GERY, 1968

22–25°C 72–77°F		4 cm (1½ in)

Family: ALESTIDAE	
Common name: JELLY BEAN TETRA	
Distribution: Liberia, Sierra Leone, Ivory Coast, Ghana	
Size: 4 cm (1½ in)	
Food: OMNIVOROUS. Takes flake and frozen but prefers live food	
Temperature range: 22–25°C / 72–77°F	
pH: 5.5–6.5 dH: to 10°	

Keep small shoals of these fish in a quiet community aquarium. Males have an extended anal fin. These do not travel well and can be difficult to acclimatise.

Breeding
A few eggs are laid over peat substrate. The fry require very fine live foods such as infusoria.

Tank Set-up
Planted aquarium with very good filtration. Allow plenty of swimming space as they are very active. They seem to appreciate the spray bar return from a power filter. Keep the tank well covered, as they jump. A few floating plants are also beneficial.

LEPIDARCHUS ADONIS
ROBERTS, 1966

22–25°C 72–77°F		2 cm (1 in)

Family: ALESTIDAE	
Common name: JELLY BEAN TETRA, ADONIS CHARACIN	
Distribution: West Africa	
Size: 2 cm (1 in)	
Food: INSECTIVOROUS. Flake, small frozen invertebrates, live *Daphnia* and other small aquatic invertebrates	
Temperature range: 22–25°C / 72–77°F	
pH: 5.8–6.5 dH: to 6°	

A delicate little Characin, this fish should be kept in a shoal with equally small, peaceful tankmates. Males have dark spots on the rear of the body, the female's body is almost transparent.

Breeding
Very soft, acidic water is required for breeding these creatures, less than 4°dH is fine. On average about 25 eggs are laid on the plants and these hatch in 36 hours. The fry are free-swimming within a week. First foods: newly hatched brine shrimp. Keep the tank darkened as the fry like to hide but, when feeding, light one corner to keep the brine shrimp in one place and the fry will come and feed.

Tank Set-up
Heavily planted aquarium with fine-leaved plants and very gentle filtration.

MICRALESTES INTERRUPTUS
(BOULENGER, 1899)

Family: ALESTIDAE

Common name: CONGO TETRA

Distribution: Zaire

Size: Males 8.5 cm (3½ in), females 6 cm (2½ in)

Food: INSECTIVOROUS. Flake, frozen invertebrates, live *Daphnia*, mosquito larvae and other aquatic invertebrates

Temperature range: 22–26°C / 72–79°F

pH: 6.0–7.0 dH: to 18°

A somewhat skittish fish that is easily frightened, and more confident when kept in a small shoal. Males are the more attractive, with long, flowing finnage on the adults. Females are relatively drab by comparison. To maintain the irridescent body sheen, feed copious amounts of live and/or frozen foods. They will sometimes nibble more tender plants.

Breeding
About 300 eggs are scattered over fine plants. Spawning usually occurs in the morning as the first rays of sunlight hit the tank, or it may be initiated by a water change. The eggs hatch in about six days. First foods are infusoria and newly hatched brine shrimp.

Tank Set-up
Planted aquarium with some fine-leaved plants and open areas for swimming. Good filtration system to create a flow of water.

22–26°C 72–79°F		8.5 cm (3½ in)

ABRAMITES HYPSELONOTUS
(GUENTHER, 1868)

Family: ANOSTOMIDAE

Common name: HIGH-BACKED HEADSTANDER

Distribution: Orinoco and Amazon basins

Size: 13 cm (5 in)

Food: HERBIVOROUS. Will also take detritus and small micro-organisms from the substrate; offer lettuce, flake and small live or frozen food

Temperature range: 22–26°C / 72–79°F

pH: 6.0–7.5 dH: to 18°

Young fish adapt well to the community aquarium, but as they mature the fish become intolerant of their own kind. Their preference for vegetable matter can cause problems with tank decor.

However, if plenty of green foods are offered, the fish will leave the aquatic plants alone.

Breeding
Nothing known.

Tank Set-up
Tank decor should consist of wood and large pebbles, with few hardy plants such as Amazon Swords (*Echinodorus*) and Java Fern (*Microsorium pteropus*) – the latter may be attached to the wood. Good filtration system to create a flow of water.

22–26°C 72–79°F		13 cm (5 in)

ANOSTOMUS ANOSTOMUS
(LINNAEUS, 1758)

Family: ANOSTOMIDAE

Common name: STRIPED ANOSTOMUS

Distribution: Upper Amazon above Manaus, Orinoco, Venezuela, Guyana, Colombia

Size: 18 cm (7 in)

Food: HERBIVOROUS. Offer lettuce, peas and the like; will also take live *Daphnia*, etc

Temperature range: 22–27°C / 72–81°F

pH: 5.8–7.5 dH: to 20°

A very attractive fish. Small groups of, say, four individuals will quarrel. But kept singly or in larger groups of, say, eight, they are peaceful, not bothering other fishes in the community aquarium. Individuals will, however, take up territories.

Breeding
Has been bred but no details available.

Tank Set-up
Planted aquarium with rockwork that provides vertical crevices. Good, powerful filtration system to create a fast flow of water. Strong lighting if you wish to provide good algal growth.

22–27°C 72–81°F		18 cm (7 in)

ANOSTOMUS TERNETZI
FERNANDEZ-YEPEZ, 1949

24–27°C
75–81°F
16 cm (6 in)

Family: ANOSTOMIDAE

Common name: NONE

Distribution: Orinoco, Xingu, Araguaia Rivers (Brazil)

Size: 16 cm (6 in)

Food: HERBIVOROUS. Offer the usual green foods plus some live or frozen food

Temperature range: 24–27°C / 75–81°F

pH: 6.0–7.5 dH: to 20°

Similar in appearance to *A. anostomus* but lacking the colourful finnage, this species is very peaceful and makes a welcome addition when combined with medium-sized community fishes. Is partial to eating plants, but this can be avoided by providing suitable alternatives in the form of lettuce and peas.

Breeding
Not known.

Tank Set-up
Planted aquarium with some wood or rocks to provide crevices. Appreciates a good flow of water such as that provided by a power filter.

LEPORINUS FASCIATUS
(BLOCH, 1794)

22–27°C
72–81°F
25 cm (10 in)

Family: ANOSTOMIDAE

Common name: BLACK-BANDED LEPORINUS

Distribution: Tributaries of the Amazon, Venezuela

Size: 25 cm (10 in)

Food: HERBIVOROUS. Offer the usual green food plus some live or frozen food

Temperature range: 22–27°C / 72–81°F

pH: 6.0–7.5 dH: to 20°

Although a little quarrelsome with their own kind (they may nip each other's fins), these fish are usually peaceful as far as other companions are concerned.

Breeding
Not known.

Tank Set-up
Decorate the aquarium predominantly with roots and rocks, as all but the toughest plants will be eaten. Good filtration with a fast flow of water through the aquarium.

APHYOCHARAX ANISITSI
EIGENMANN & KENNEDY, 1903

18–27°C
64–81°F
5 cm (2 in)

Family: CHARACIDAE

Common name: BLOODFIN

Distribution: Parana River, Argentina

Size: 5 cm (2 in)

Food: OMNIVOROUS. Small live or frozen food, flake

Temperature range: 18–27°C / 64–81°F

pH: 6.0–8.0 dH: to 28°

A undemanding, peaceful shoal fish that may be kept in an unheated aquarium. However, if kept at the cooler end of its range the colours fade. Males have a hook on the anal fin. A long-lived species: eight to 10 years is not uncommon if the fish are kept correctly. A good fish for the beginner.

Breeding
Scatter eggs over and through thickets of fine-leaved plants. Remove the adults or they will eat the eggs. Feed fry on fine flake and brine shrimp.

Tank Set-up
Planted aquarium with some open water.

ASTYANAX FASCIATUS MEXICANUS
(CUVIER, 1819)

22–25°C
72–77°F
9 cm (3½ in)

Family: CHARACIDAE

Common name: BLIND CAVEFISH

Distribution: Texas (USA), Mexico through to Panama

Size: 9 cm (3½ in)

Food: OMNIVOROUS. Flake, live and frozen food

Temperature range: 22–25°C / 72–77°F

pH: 6.0–8.0 dH: to 30°

This fish is widely available in the hobby, far more so than its sighted counterpart. It is undemanding, should be kept in shoals and makes an excellent community fish. Males are thinner than females.

Breeding
Breeds readily in cooler waters. The fry hatch in about 48 hours.and are free-swimming a few days later. Feed very small fine foods. The young fish have eyes but these regress as the fish grows.

Tank Set-up
Any standard community aquarium with reasonable filtration and a gentle flow of water.

Family: CHARACIDAE
Common name: PEPPER TETRA, WHITE-STAR TETRA
Distribution: Amazon basin
Size: 3 cm (1 in)
Food: CARNIVOROUS. Fine live food, but will accept flake and frozen
Temperature range: 22–26°C / 72–79°F
pH: 5.5–6.5 dH: to 8°

A delicate, small, shoaling fish which may be kept with others but only if they are equally peaceful. The white markings are more intense on males. When ready to breed, females are fuller in the body.

Breeding
Not known.

Tank Set-up
Planted aquarium with some floating plants. Wood for decoration. Good filtration, over peat, and a gentle flow of water.

AXELRODIA STIGMATIAS
(FOWLER, 1913)

 22–26°C / 72–79°F   3 cm (1 in)

BOEHLKEA FREDCOCHUI
GERY 1966

22–26°C / 72–79°F   5 cm (2 in)

Family: CHARACIDAE
Common name: NONE
Distribution: Maranon river (Peru)
Size: 5 cm (2 in)
Food: OMNIVOROUS. Live, flake and frozen food
Temperature range: 22–26°C / 72–79°F
pH: 5.5–7.5 dH: to 12°

Often overlooked in dealers' tanks as it does not show its true colours when under stress. Kept in acidic waters with low lighting, the delicate blues and irridescent sheens will become apparent on the body of the fish.

Breeding
Has been bred but no details could be found.

Tank Set-up
Soft, slightly acidic water. Good filtration. Low light levels. Wood and plant for decoration, but choose plants that are suited to these conditions.

BRYCONOPS MELANURUS
(BLOCH, 1795)

Family: CHARACIDAE
Common name: TAIL-LIGHT TETRA
Distribution: Eastern Brazil
Size: 10 cm (4 in)
Food: OMNIVOROUS. Predominantly live food but accepts flake and frozen food
Temperature range: 23–26°C / 73–79°F
pH: 5.5–6.5 dH: to 10°

A shoal of young fish is suited to the community aquarium. However, as these fish mature their nature changes and they may become quarrelsome. Males are slimmer than females.

Breeding
No reports of aquarium breeding, but details given suggest very soft water of about 4° and a temperature in the region of 28°C / 82°F. They are egg scatterers.

Tank Set-up
Large aquarium with very good water conditions. The water should be high in oxygen and fast flowing; this can be achieved with a large external power filter with the water returned via a

 23–26°C / 73–79°F   10 cm (4 in)

spray bar. Clumps of plants and some rock or wood, but leave open water for the fish to swim in.

CHALCEUS MACROLEPIDOTUS

CUVIER, 1817

Family: CHARACIDAE	
Common name: PINK-TAILED CHALCEUS	
Distribution: Amazon and the Guianas	
Size: 25 cm (10 in)	
Food: CARNIVOROUS. Takes meat, pieces of fish and tablet food	
Temperature range: 23–27°C / 73–81°F	
pH: 6.5–7.5 dH: to 18°	

A large, predatory Characin for the specialist. Easy to keep in a large tank, but fit a tight cover as the fish are prone to jumping. In the process they may dislodge scales, which leaves them open to secondary infections. Can be kept with fish of a similar size. Although a

23–27°C
73–81°F

25 cm (10 in)

predator, young fish will take flakes and tablet food.

Breeding
Not known.

Tank Set-up
Large aquarium at least 150 cm (59 in) in length. Sparsely planted, although the fish do not attack plants. Good filtration to create a current.

CHEIRODON KRIEGI

SCHINDLER, 1937

23–26°C
73–79°F

5 cm (2 in)

Family: CHARACIDAE	
Common name: THREE-SPOT TETRA	
Distribution: Basin of Paraguay River and upper reaches of Guaporé River (Central South America)	
Size: 5 cm (2 in)	
Food: OMNIVOROUS. Flake, small frozen and live food	
Temperature range: 23–26°C / 73–79°F	
pH: 6.0–7.0 dH: to 15°	

A peaceful, if not very colourful, fish for the community aquarium. The black spot above the vent is much like the gravid patch in female livebearers, but it is not indicative of sex or readiness to spawn. Females are fuller in the body when ripe.

Breeding
An egg scatterer, trios of two males to one female chase through fine-leaved plants or clumps of Java Moss. The eggs hatch after five days and the fry are free-swimming four days later. First foods: newly hatched brine shrimp nauplii and the like. Remove parents after spawning.

Tank Set-up
Planted aquarium with a gentle flow of water. Efficient filtration system as the fish dislike any deterioration in water quality.

COELURICHTHYS TENUIS

NICHOLS, 1913

Family: CHARACIDAE	
Common name: TENUIS TETRA	
Distribution: Northern Argentina across Paraguay and into southern Brazil	
Size: 5 cm (2 in)	
Food: OMNIVOROUS. Prefers live food but takes flake or frozen	
Temperature range: 19–22°C / 66–72°F	
pH: 5.5–6.5 dH: to 4°	

A peaceful fish, but definitely one for the specialist. Water conditions must be exact: cool, soft, slightly acid, high in oxygen and with a strong current.

Breeding
These fish practise internal fertilisation. After frantic courtship, the sperm packet is transferred to the female. She may then deposit her eggs at any time, even up to several weeks later. Eggs are placed on the undersides of plants or, if these are unavailable, on grass roots. Fry are minute and difficult to feed.

Tank Set-up
Partially planted aquarium with dim lighting. Very efficient filtration system which will also provide a strong flow of ultra-clean water.

19–22°C
66–72°F

5 cm (2 in)

Family: CHARACIDAE	
Common name: SWORDTAIL CHARACIN	
Distribution: Meta River (Colombia)	
Size: 6.5 cm (2½ in)	
Food: OMNIVOROUS. Live, flake and frozen food	
Temperature range: 22–27°C / 72–81°F	
pH: 6.0–7.5 dH: to 25°	

A gentle, shoaling fish for the community aquarium. Can be difficult to acclimatise, but once used to aquarium conditions it is very robust. Males have longer pectoral fins.

Breeding
Milt is placed in the oviduct of the female. This means that the male does not have to be present when the eggs are laid, as they are fertilised as they pass out of the female's body. Eggs hatch in about 30 hours and the fry should be fed on newly hatched brine shrimp.

Tank Set-up
Planted community aquarium with some floating plants. Gentle filtration.

CORYNOPOMA RIISEI
GILL, 1858

22–27°C 72–81°F 6.5 cm (2½ in)

CREAGRUTUS BENI
EIGENMANN, 1911

Family: CHARACIDAE	
Common name: BENNY TETRA	
Distribution: Lake Valencia (Venezuela), Peru Amazon, Bolivia, Tocantins River (Brazil)	
Size: 8 cm (3 in), but Venezuelan population only to 4.5 cm (2 in)	
Food: OMNIVOROUS. Flake, frozen and live food	
Temperature range: 22–26°C / 72–79°F	
pH: 6.0–7.0 dH: to 20°	

22–26°C 72–79°F 8 cm (3 in)

A community fish which will live happily with other smaller Tetras. Keep as a shoal. Females are more colourful and robust than males.

Breeding
Females can, if necessary, store sperm. About 60 eggs are laid and they hatch in approximately 24 hours. The fry are free-swimming after three days. Feed the fry on small foods, such as newly hatched brine shrimp, which they usually take from the bottom.

Tank Set-up
Partially planted aquarium with plenty of swimming space and bright lighting.

EXODON PARADOXUS
(MUELLER & TROSCHEL, 1845)

22–26°C 72–79°F 15 cm (6 in)

Family: CHARACIDAE	
Common name: BUCKTOOTHED TETRA	
Distribution: The Guyanas and northern Brazil	
Size: 15 cm (6 in)	
Food: CARNIVOROUS. Pieces of fish or meat, earthworms	
Temperature range: 22–26°C / 72–79°F	
pH: 5.5–7.5 dH: to 20°	

This fish is a predator and, as such, should not be kept with other fishes. Keep a dozen or so together and they will live reasonably peacefully, but if only three or four are kept they will sometimes attack each other, taking out the eyes or tearing out chunks of flesh if they cannot eat the prey fish whole.

Breeding
Eggs are scattered over plants and hatch in about 36 hours. Fry are cannibalistic and therefore difficult to raise in any number.

Tank Set-up
Planted aquarium with wood for decoration. Very efficient filtration system which will also provide a strong flow of clean water. Cover the tank as these fish jump.

GYMNOCORYMBUS SOCOLFI

GÉRY, 1964

Family: CHARACIDAE	
Common name: SOCOLF'S TETRA	
Distribution: Meta River (Colombia)	
Size: 5.5 cm (2 in)	
Food: OMNIVOROUS. Flake, insect larvae, vegetable matter	
Temperature range: 22–26°C/72–79°F	
pH: 5.5–7.5 dH: to 20°	

Juveniles, up to 3 cm (1¼ in) long, are very attractive and active, their unpaired fins being red-orange in colour. However, this fades with maturity and the fish become more sedate.

Breeding
Has been bred commercially.

Tank Set-up
Partially planted aquarium with shaded areas to afford the fish security.

22–26°C
72–79°F   5.5 cm (2 in)

HASEMANNIA NANA

(REINHARDT I. LUETKEN, 1874)

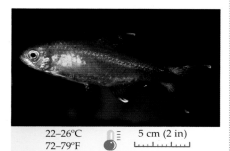

22–26°C
72–79°F   5 cm (2 in)

Family: CHARACIDAE	
Common name: SILVER TIP TETRA	
Distribution: Brazil	
Size: 5 cm (2 in)	
Food: OMNIVOROUS. Flake, insect larvae	
Temperature range: 22–26°C/72–79°F	
pH: 6.5–7.5 dH: to 15°	

An ideal fish for the community aquarium because of its longevity and peaceful temperament. Males are more slender and have more colour than the females. They also have a white tip to the anal fin, in females it is yellow.

Breeding
Relatively easy to breed provided the parents are well conditioned. Up to about 200 eggs may be scattered over fine-leaved plants or a synthetic medium. Remove the parents. Fry are easy to raise provided they are well fed.

Tank Set-up
Partially planted aquarium with open areas. Good filtration system to provide well-oxygenated, clean water with a good flow.

Family: CHARACIDAE	
Common name: RUMMY-NOSE TETRA	
Distribution: Vaupes River (Colombia), Negro River (Brazil)	
Size: 4.5 cm (2 in)	
Food: OMNIVOROUS. Flake, insect larvae	
Temperature range: 22–26°C/72–79°F	
pH: 6.0–7.0 dH: to 10°	

Can be difficult to keep unless the water conditions are correct. Regular water changes are necessary, as this fish is sensitive to any build-up of nitrates. When ready to breed, males are slimmer than females.

Breeding
Not easy to breed. Use soft (less than 4°dH), acidic (pH 6.0–6.5) water. Eggs may be laid on the substrate or on plants, and hatch in 36 hours. Fry are free-swimming after four days. Feed on newly hatched brine shrimp.

HEMIGRAMMUS BLEHERI

GÉRY, 1986

Tank Set-up
Planted aquarium with wood for decoration. Good filtration system to maintain clean water with a good flow.

22–26°C
72–79°F   4.5 cm (2 in)

HEMIGRAMMUS ERYTHROZONUS
DURBIN, 1909

Family: CHARACIDAE
Common name: GLOWLIGHT TETRA
Distribution: Essequito River (Guyana)
Size: 4 cm (1½ in)
Food: OMNIVOROUS. Flake, insect larvae
Temperature range: 22–26°C/72–79°F
pH: 6.0–7.5 dH: to 15°

Peaceful, shoaling fish for the planted community aquarium. Males are slimmer than females. This fish is bred commercially in large numbers.

Breeding
With soft, acid water and high temperatures (26°C/79°F), these Tetras spawn over and between fine-leaved plants.

Tank Set-up
Planted aquarium to provide some cover for the fish. Decorate with wood.

22–26°C 72–79°F		4 cm (1½ in)

HEMIGRAMMUS PULCHER
LADIGES, 1938

22–27°C 72–81°F		4.5 cm (2 in)

Family: CHARACIDAE
Common name: PRETTY TETRA
Distribution: Vicinity of Iquitos (Peru), Brazil
Size: 4.5 cm (2 in)
Food: OMNIVOROUS. Flake, insect larvae
Temperature range: 22–27°C/72–81°F
pH: 6.0–7.5 dH: to 15°

A good shoaling fish for the community aquarium. Males are slimmer than females and have a pointed swim bladder, whereas in females it is rounded. There are two subspecies: *H. pulcher pulcher* Ladiges, 1938 and *H. pulcher haraldi* Géry, 1961.

Breeding
They breed in similar fashion to other *Hemigrammus* spp., laying eggs over and through plants. Feed fry on newly hatched brine shrimp.

Tank Set-up
Planted aquarium with wood for decoration, and a reasonable flow of clean, soft water.

HEMIGRAMMUS ULREYI
(BOULENGER, 1895)

Family: CHARACIDAE
Common name: ULREY'S TETRA
Distribution: Upper Rio (Paraguay)
Size: 5 cm (2 in)
Food: OMNIVOROUS. Flake, insect larvae, and small aquatic invertebrates either live or frozen
Temperature range: 23–27°C/73–81°F
pH: 6.0–7.0 dH: to 10°

A timid fish when first introduced into the aquarium. Needs plenty of space and the company of other peaceful species. Males are slimmer than females. They display their best colours when seen in sunlight.

Breeding
No records found of this species having been bred.

Tank Set-up
Planted aquarium with wood for decoration and a fast flow of clean, soft water.

23–27°C 73–81°F		5 cm (2 in)

HYPHESSOBRYCON FLAMMEUS
MYERS, 1924

Family: CHARACIDAE
Common name: FLAME TETRA
Distribution: Vicinity of Rio de Janeiro (Brazil)
Size: 4 cm (1½ in)
Food: OMNIVOROUS. Flake, insect larvae
Temperature range: 22–27°C / 72–81°F
pH: 6.5–7.0 dH: to 22°

A community fish that is underrated because it fails to show its true colours under the harsh lighting conditions of dealers' tanks. The subtle red hues are best observed in subdued lighting. Males exhibit a dark, blood-red anal fin, and their pectoral fins have a black tip. In females there is no black tip to the pectorals, and the anal fin is a much lighter red and may even fade to yellow.

Breeding
Typical of the Tetras: eggs laid through plants; feed young on newly hatched brine shrimp. Frequent smaller feeds, say five to six times a day, promote better growth than one or two feeds a day.

Tank Set-up
Typical community tank of other small, peaceful species. Subdued lighting, which may be provided by the addition of some floating plants.

22–27°C
72–81°F
4 cm (1½ in)

HYPHESSOBRYCON LORETOENSIS
LADIGES, 1938

22–27°C
72–81°F
4 cm (1½ in)

Family: CHARACIDAE
Common name: LORETO TETRA
Distribution: Amazon, Peru
Size: 4 cm (1½ in)
Food: OMNIVOROUS. Flake, *Daphnia*, brine shrimp – small live or frozen foods
Temperature range: 22–27°C / 72–81°F
pH: 6.0–7.5 dH: to 15°

A more challenging fish for the community aquarium. Not often seen, newly imported specimens are sometimes thin and frequently difficult to feed. Offer fine live foods in the first instance, and later move on to frozen

and flake foods. Males are generally slimmer than females.

Breeding
No details available.

Tank Set-up
Community of other, small, peaceful fishes with plants and wood.

Family: CHARACIDAE
Common name: LEMON TETRA
Distribution: Brazil
Size: 4.5 cm (2 in)
Food: OMNIVOROUS. Live, frozen and flake
Temperature range: 23–27°C / 73–81°F
pH: 6.0–7.5 dH: to 20°

A pretty shoaling fish for the community aquarium, always swimming about. Males have a black edge to the anal fin.

Breeding
Can be difficult to spawn. The eggs are pale yellow in colour. Fry are easily raised on tiny live foods.

Tank Set-up
Well-maintained community aquarium. The key to success seems to be in maintaining good-quality water conditions.

23–27°C
73–81°F
4.5 cm (2 in)

HYPHESSOBRYCON PULCHRIPINNIS
AHL, 1937

HYPHESSOBRYCON SOCOLOFI
WEITZMAN, 1977

22–27°C
72–81°F

4.5 cm (2 in)

Family: CHARACIDAE

Common name: LESSER BLEEDING HEART TETRA

Distribution: Negro River (Brazil)

Size: 4.5 cm (2 in)

Food: OMNIVOROUS. Flake, *Daphnia*, brine shrimp, etc., either live or frozen

Temperature range: 22–27°C / 72–81°F

pH: 6.0–7.0 dH: to 10°

Best kept in shoals of six or more individuals. Peaceful fish, they make ideal companions for *Corydoras* and other bottom-dwelling species. In adults, the males are larger with a more intense blue dorsal and a blue anal fin. Females are more robust and have a red posterior edge to the anal and a red tip to the dorsal.

Breeding
Relatively easy to breed. Well-conditioned pairs may be placed in a 45 cm (18 in) breeding tank. Water temperature should be raised to the upper end of the range, 26–27°C / 79–81°F, the pH lowered to around 6.0 and the hardness to 4°. Provide plants in which the spawning fish may scatter the eggs.

Tank Set-up
Planted tank with open areas for swimming. Subdued lighting. Sensitive to poor water conditions: carry out regular weekly partial water change.

IGUANODECTES SPILURUS
(GUENTHER, 1864)

Family: CHARACIDAE

Common name: NONE

Distribution: Guyana, into central Brazil and south to the Madeira River

Size: 5–6 cm (2–2½ in)

Food: OMNIVOROUS. Flake, insect larvae and small aquatic invertebrates either live or frozen

Temperature range: 23–27°C / 73–81°F

pH: 5.5–7.5 dH: to 18°

Found over a large area of South America, these fish adapt well to aquarium conditions. The coloration of the various populations differs, but is generally somewhat nondescript. As a result, they are often overlooked; but they are breedable, and make a welcome addition to the enthusiasts' aquarium. Males have extensions to the first rays of the anal fin.

Breeding
The water conditions should be at the lower end of each scale, about 2°dH and a pH of 6.0. Pairs spawn over breeding mesh. Eggs hatch in about 12 days. First foods: newly hatched brine shrimp.

23–27°C
73–81°F

5–6 cm (2–2½ in)

Tank Set-up
Planted aquarium with wood for decoration and a fast flow of clean, well-oxygenated water.

INPAICHTHYS KERRI
GERY & JUNK, 1977

23–27°C
73–81°F

4 cm (1½ in)

Family: CHARACIDAE

Common name: NONE

Distribution: Aripuana River (Amazonia)

Size: Males 4 cm (1½ in), females 3 cm (1 in)

Food: OMNIVOROUS. Flake, insect larvae and small aquatic invertebrates either live or frozen

Temperature range: 23–27°C / 73–81°F

pH: 6.5–7.5 dH: to 10°

Very attractive fish for the community aquarium. Only the males exhibit the blue sheen on the body; but to ensure that they display at their best, they should be kept in shoals which include both males and females. These are active fish which require a reasonable amount of swimming space.

Breeding
Eggs are laid singly on fine-leaved plants such as Java Moss. Remove the parents after spawning or they will eat the eggs. First foods: infusoria and newly hatched brine shrimp. Water temperature should be around 27°C / 81°F.

Tank Set-up
Heavily planted aquarium but with some open areas and subdued lighting. Ensure that good water quality is maintained, as the fish will not display their best colours if they are under stress of any sort.

MEGALAMPHODUS SWEGLESI
GERY, 1961

20–23°C	4 cm (1½ in)
68–73°F	

Family: CHARACIDAE	
Common name: RED PHANTOM TETRA	
Distribution: Met and Muco Rivers (Colombia), and the upper Orinoco basin	
Size: 4 cm (1½ in)	
Food: OMNIVOROUS. Flake, insect larvae and small aquatic invertebrates either live or frozen	
Temperature range: 20–23°C / 68–73°F	
pH: 5.5–7.5 dH: to 18°	

A very beautiful, peaceful and somewhat delicate fish for a community aquarium. Pay careful attention to conditions and especially water temperature, as the most common cause of their demise is having the water temperature too high. Feed small amounts frequently rather than a single, large daily feed. In males the dorsal is red and extended, in females it is red, black and white.

Breeding
Very soft water and low temperatures are required: 1–2° of hardness, pH 5.5–6.0 and a temperature of 20–22°C / 68–72°F. Use Java Moss or a synthetic substitute over the bottom of the tank and reduce the lighting. The eggs are a rusty brown colour. Feed the fry when free-swimming on newly hatched brine shrimp.

Tank Set-up
Planted aquarium stocked with equally peaceful species. Ensure good water quality is maintained. Carry out frequent partial water changes.

MOENKHAUSIA PITTERI
EIGENMANN, 1920

Family: CHARACIDAE	
Common name: DIAMOND TETRA	
Distribution: Lake Valencia (Venezuela)	
Size: 6 cm (2½ in)	
Food: OMNIVOROUS. Flake, small frozen invertebrates, live *Daphnia* and other aquatic invertebrates	
Temperature range: 24–28°C / 75–82°F	
pH: 5.5–7.0 dH: 4–10°	

A shoaling fish for the well-planted community aquarium. To achieve good growth and finnage, feed well on live foods such as *Daphnia*, bloodworm and mosquito larvae. If live foods are unavailable, frozen substitutes may be used. Adult males can be distinguished from females by their extended finnage and more intense coloration.

Breeding
Use soft acidic water. Eggs are scattered on fine-leaved plants, and hatch after

24–28°C	6 cm (2½ in)
75–82°F	

two days. Once the yolk sac is absorbed, feed the fry on brine shrimp nauplii. Remove parents after spawning or they may eat the eggs.

Tank Set-up
Plants to provide shelter. A gentle current from power heads or from an external power filter is appreciated.

MOENKHAUSIA SANCTAEFILOMENAE
(STEINDACHNER, 1907)

Family: CHARACIDAE	
Common name: YELLOW-BANDED MOENKHAUSIA	
Distribution: Paraguay, Bolivia, Peru, Brazil	
Size: 7 cm (3 in)	
Food: OMNIVOROUS. Flake, frozen and live food	
Temperature range: 22–26°C / 72–79°F	
pH: 6.0–8.0 dH: to 25°	

Widely available within the trade, this fish is bred in large numbers by fish farmers. It is hardy and makes an excellent community fish. In mature fish, males are slimmer than females.

22–26°C	7 cm (3 in)
72–79°F	

Breeding
The fish will spawn in the roots of floating plants or on spawning mats. Eggs hatch in about 36 hours and require very fine foods.

Tank Set-up
General community aquarium with some plants.

NEMATOBRYCON PALMERI
EIGENMANN, 1911

23–27°C
73–81°F
5 cm (2 in)

Family: CHARACIDAE

Common name: EMPEROR TETRA

Distribution: West coast of Colombia

Size: 5 cm (2 in)

Food: OMNIVOROUS. Flake, insect larvae, and small aquatic invertebrates either live or frozen

Temperature range: 23–27°C/73–81°F

pH: 5.0–7.5 dH: to 22°

An excellent fish for a community of other peaceful fishes. In males the dorsal fin and the outer and central rays of the caudal fin are extended and the colour is intense. In females the finnage is not extended and the coloration is more drab.

Breeding
Soft water, with a temperature of about 27°C/81°F, and subdued lighting are required to induce these fish to spawn. Use Java Moss or a synthetic substitute over the bottom of the tank to prevent the parents eating the eggs. Remove the parents after spawning. Eggs hatch in about 36 hours and require very fine foods such as infusoria followed by newly hatched brine shrimp.

Tank Set-up
Heavily planted aquarium with other peaceful species. Regular water changes and an efficient filtration system to create a gentle flow of water.

PARACHEIRODON AXELRODI
(SCHULTZ, 1956)

22–26°C
72–79°F
5 cm (2 in)

Family: CHARACIDAE

Common name: CARDINAL TETRA

Distribution: Venezuela, through Brazil into eastern Colombia

Size: 5 cm (2 in)

Food: OMNIVOROUS. Flake, insect larvae, and small aquatic invertebrates either live or frozen

Temperature range: 22–26°C/72–79°F

pH: 4.5–6.0 dH: to 4°

A very desirable fish for the community aquarium. The majority of Cardinals imported for the trade are wild caught. Males are generally slimmer than females.

Breeding
As for the Neon Tetra, but use a larger aquarium. They usually spawn in the evening, releasing about 500 eggs.

Tank Set-up
Planted aquarium, with some floating plants to cut down the light, and stocked with equally peaceful species. Keep a careful check on the water conditions and carry out water changes regularly.

PARACHEIRODON INNESI
(MYERS, 1936)

Family: CHARACIDAE

Common name: NEON TETRA

Distribution: Putumayo River (Peru)

Size: 4 cm (1½ in)

Food: OMNIVOROUS. Flake, insect larvae, and small aquatic invertebrates either live or frozen

Temperature range: 20–26°C/68–79°F

pH: 7.0 dH: to 20°

Probably the most popular of all aquarium fish, Neons are now bred in vast numbers for the aquatic trade and are able to tolerate a wide range of aquarium conditions. Males are slimmer than females and have a straight blue line. In females the line is bent and they are deeper in the body. Keep in a small shoal of six or more.

Breeding
Soft water, 1–2° of hardness, pH 5.0–6.0, and a temperature of about 24°C/75°F. Use Java Moss or a synthetic substitute over the bottom of the tank and reduce the lighting. The male embraces the female when spawning. Remove the parents. Eggs hatch in about 24 hours

20–26°C
68–79°F
4 cm (1½ in)

and the fry are free-swimming after five days. Feed the fry on infusoria and later on newly hatched brine shrimp.

Tank Set-up
Planted aquarium stocked with equally peaceful species. Check water conditions and carry out water changes regularly.

PARACHEIRODON SIMULANS
(GERY, 1963)

23–26°C	3 cm (1 in)
73–79°F	

Family: CHARACIDAE
Common name: NONE
Distribution: Brazil
Size: 3 cm (1 in)
Food: OMNIVOROUS. Flake, insect larvae, and small aquatic invertebrates either live or frozen
Temperature range: 23–26°C / 73–79°F
pH: 5.5–6.0 dH: to 15°

Although an ideal community fish, it can be difficult to keep and is seldom imported. Pay attention to water conditions as they are delicate creatures and very sensitive to a build up of nitrates. They are also prone to infection by *Oodinium* and prompt treatment is recommended. Keep as a shoal. Males are slimmer than females.

Breeding
As for *P. innesi*, but more difficult to induce to spawn.

Tank Set-up
The correct water conditions and their maintenance are crucial to the successful keeping of this species. Carry out water changes regularly. Planted community aquarium with other peaceful species.

PETITELLA GEORGIAE
(GERY & BOUTIERE, 1964)

Family: CHARACIDAE
Common name: FALSE RUMMY-NOSE TETRA
Distribution: Peru
Size: 5 cm (2 in)
Food: OMNIVOROUS. Flake, insect larvae, and small aquatic invertebrates either live or frozen
Temperature range: 23–26°C / 73–79°F
pH: 5.5–7.0 dH: to 10°

These are suitable companions for *Corydoras*, the dwarf South American Cichlids and the like, but can be difficult to keep. However, they are more colourful than *Hemigrammus rhodostomus*, the true Rummy-nose Tetra, and therefore worth persevering with. Males and females are difficult to distinguish, but in healthy specimens males have more contrast between the stripes in the caudal fin.

Breeding
Not known.

Tank Set-up
Heavily planted aquarium with secluded areas. Soft, acidic water is preferred and a gentle flow of water.

23–26°C	5 cm (2 in)
73–79°F	

Regular partial water changes with aged or well-conditioned water will help to maintain this fish in good health.

PHENAGONIATES MACROLEPIS
(MEEK & HILDEBRAND, 1913)

Family: CHARACIDAE
Common name: BARRED GLASS TETRA
Distribution: Southern Panama
Size: 6 cm (2½ in)
Food: CARNIVOROUS. Small live food of all kinds
Temperature range: 22–24°C / 72–75°F
pH: 6.5–7.0 dH: to 8°

These fish like soft, slightly acidic water. They can be very aggressive towards each other, but other inhabitants of the aquarium are not usually attacked. In the wild they are found as lone specimens or in small groups.

Breeding
Not known.

Tank Set-up
Provide very good filtration and a high turnover of water. Partial water changes every 10–14 days. Thickets of plants and not too intense lighting. Cover the aquarium, as these fish jump.

22–24°C	6 cm (2½ in)
72–75°F	

THAYERIA BOEHLKEI
WEITZMAN, 1957

22–28°C
72–82°F

6 cm (2½ in)

Family: CHARACIDAE

Common name: NONE

Distribution: Peru and western Brazil

Size: 6 cm (2½ in)

Food: OMNIVOROUS. Flake, frozen and live food

Temperature range: 22–28°C/72–82°F

pH: 5.5–7.5 dH: to 20°

An undemanding fish for the community aquarium as long as nitrites and nitrates are not allowed to build up. The fish swim at an angle in the water. Females, when ready to spawn, have a distended belly.

Breeding
Prolific, producing around 1,000 eggs.

Tank Set-up
Well-planted aquarium. Carry out regular partial water changes, say 25% every 10–14 days. These fish can also tolerate saline conditions.

THAYERIA OBLIQUA
EIGENMANN, 1908

22–28°C
72–82°F

8 cm (3 in)

Family: CHARACIDAE

Common name: PENGUIN FISH

Distribution: Brazil

Size: 8 cm (3 in)

Food: OMNIVOROUS. Flake, frozen and live food

Temperature range: 22–28°C/72–82°F

pH: 5.5–7.5 dH: to 18°

Excellent fish for the community aquarium. Make sure the water is well-oxygenated and clean. When ready to breed, females are plumper than males.

Breeding
Not known.

Tank Set-up
Densely planted aquarium. Ensure a good, well-maintained filtration system that will supply the well-oxygenated water these fish require.

TRIPORTHEUS ANGULATUS
(SPIX, 1829)

22–28°C
72–82°F

10 cm (4 in)

Family: CHARACIDAE

Common name: NONE

Distribution: Amazon basin and Orinoco

Size: Over 10 cm (4 in)

Food: CARNIVOROUS. Flake, frozen food and live insect larvae

Temperature range: 22–28°C/72–82°F

pH: 6.0–7.5 dH: to 15°

Though peaceful with fish of similar size, this may harrass smaller species. A surface-dwelling fish, it often jumps. Allow plenty of space for this creature, as it can be very active. The water should be well-oxygenated. Sensitive to atmospheric pressure.

Breeding
Not known.

Tank Set-up
Aquarium at least 1.25 m (4 ft) long, with plenty of open water. Ensure a tight-fitting cover glass to prevent the fish jumping out of the tank. Power filter with spray bar return is beneficial.

CHARACIDIUM FASCIATUM
REINHARDT, 1866

19–24°C
66–75°F

10 cm (4 in)

Family: CHARACIDAE

Common name: BANDED CHARACIDIUM

Distribution: Widespread in South America

Size: 10 cm (4 in)

Food: CARNIVOROUS. Tablet food, and live or frozen insect larvae, etc.

Temperature range: 19–24°C/66–75°F

pH: 5.5–7.5 dH: to 24°

Peaceful with other fishes, but can be territorial with its own kind. Loach-like in its habits and movements. Males have spots along the edge of the dorsal fin, females have a clear dorsal fin.

Breeding
Egg-scatterers, the eggs falling between stones and gravel. They hatch in about 36 hours. Provide the fry with hiding places in the form of plants. Feed infusoria followed by newly hatched brine shrimp.

Tank Set-up
Planted aquarium with a good flow of well-oxygenated water. Soft, slightly acidic water is preferred, although these fish will adapt to harder water.

CHARACIDIUM RACHOVII
(REGAN, 1913)

Family: CHARACIDAE

Common name: NONE

Distribution: Southern Brazil

Size: 7 cm (3 in)

Food: CARNIVOROUS. Tablet food, and live or frozen insect larvae, etc.

Temperature range: 20–24°C / 68–75°F

pH: 5.5–7.5 dH: to 24°

Peaceful with other fishes. Loach-like in its habits and movements. Males have a spotted dorsal fin; females have a transparent dorsal fin.

Breeding
Not known.

Tank Set-up
Planted aquarium with a good flow of soft, slightly acidic, well-oxygenated water.

 20–24°C
68–75°F   7 cm (3 in)

ELACHOCHARAX GEORGIAE
GERY, 1965

Family: CHARACIDAE

Common name: DWARF DARTER CHARACIN

Distribution: Brazil

Size: 3 cm (1 in)

Food: CARNIVOROUS. Very small live foods, will also take flake and nibble at tablet foods

Temperature range: 23–29°C / 73–84°F

pH: 5.5–6.5 dH: to 8°

A fish for the enthusiast, it is best kept in a well-planted species aquarium or with other small very peaceful fish. Gregarious, so keep in large groups of 10 or more individuals. Rarely imported.

 23–29°C
73–84°F   3 cm (1 in)

Breeding
Not known.

Tank Set-up
Densely planted aquarium with soft, slightly acidic, well-oxygenated water. Provide flat stones or wood for the fish to rest on.

CITHARINUS CITHARUS
(GEOFFROY, 1809)

Family: CITHARINIDAE

Common name: NONE

Distribution: Senegal to the Nile basin

Size: 50 cm (20 in)

Food: OMNIVOROUS. Tablet, flake, live and frozen food

Temperature range: 22–28°C / 72–82°F

pH: 7.0–8.5 dH: to 15°

A large, deep-bodied fish which needs a very large aquarium. In the wild they feed by sifting through the mud on the substrate.

Breeding
Not known.

Tank Set-up
Large aquarium with plenty of open water. Good filtration and a reasonable flow of water. Soft substrate.

 22–28°C
72–82°F   50 cm (20 in)

DISTICHODUS LUSOSSO
SCHILTHUIS, 1891

22–26°C
72–79°F

40 cm (16 in)

Family: CITHARINIDAE	
Common name: NONE	
Distribution: Angola, Zaire basin, Cameroon	
Size: 40 cm (16 in)	
Food: HERBIVOROUS. Lettuce, peas, etc	
Temperature range: 22–26°C / 72–79°F	
pH: 6.0–7.5 dH: to 18°	

A peaceful fish, it makes a suitable companion for other large peaceful species. Feed copious amounts of green food. Can be distinguished from *D. sexfasciatus* by its longer snout.

Breeding
Not known.

Tank Set-up
A large aquarium with plenty of swimming space. Use either hardy plants, such as Java Moss or Java Fern, or artificial plants. A steady flow of water from a power filter is beneficial.

DISTICHODUS SEXFASCIATUS
BOULENGER, 1897

22–26°C
72–79°F

25 cm (10 in)

Family: CITHARINIDAE	
Common name: NONE	
Distribution: Angola, Zaire basin	
Size: 25 cm (10 in)	
Food: HERBIVOROUS. Lettuce, peas, etc	
Temperature range: 22–26°C / 72–79°F	
pH: 6.0–7.5 dH: to 18°	

A peaceful, community fish, provided its companions are of similar size. Juveniles are far more colourful than adults, whose red coloration fades to grey. Provide plenty of vegetable matter in the diet.

Breeding
Not known.

Tank Set-up
A large aquarium with well-filtered, soft, slightly acidic water for preference. Such plants as Java Fern may be grown, but any soft-leaved species will be eaten. Provide cover by using wood as decoration.

NANNAETHIOPS UNITAENIATUS
GUENTHER, 1871

22–26°C
72–79°F

6.5 cm (2½ in)

Family: CITHARINIDAE	
Common name: ONE-STRIPED AFRICAN CHARACIN	
Distribution: Niger to Zaire and east to the White Nile	
Size: 6.5 cm (2½ in)	
Food: CARNIVOROUS. Small live foods such as *Daphnia* and bloodworm, plus flake and frozen food	
Temperature range: 22–26°C / 72–79°F	
pH: 6.5–7.5 dH: to 10°	

A delicately coloured shoaling fish. Males have more intense coloration and are slimmer than females. When breeding, areas of the dorsal fin and the upper half of the caudal fin may show some colour on males.

Breeding
Soft slightly acidic water. Spawning is stimulated by sunlight. Eggs are scattered over plants and stones, and hatch in about 30 hours. The fry are free-swimming after five days. First foods: infusoria and newly hatched brine shrimp.

Tank Set-up
A planted aquarium with clear, well-filtered water.

NANNOCHARAX FASCIATUS
GUENTHER, 1867

22–26°C
72–79°F

7 cm (3 in)

Family: CITHARINIDAE	
Common name: NONE	
Distribution: Western Africa from Volta through to Gabon	
Size: 7 cm (3 in)	
Food: CARNIVOROUS. Small live food, also flake and frozen food	
Temperature range: 22–26°C / 72–79°F	
pH: 6.5–7.5 dH: to 12°	

A fish for the specialist. Can be kept in a community tank provided the water is well-oxygenated and has a good flow. Its companions should be other small, peaceful species. Spends much of its time resting on its pectoral, anal and caudal fins among the plants. Can be difficult to feed: start with small live foods and, as the fish settles in, introduce flake foods into the outflow from the filter.

Breeding
Not known.

Tank Set-up
A planted aquarium with some broad-leaved plants for the fish to rest on. Good filtration is essential, as is a steady flow of well-oxygenated water.

NEOLEBIAS ANSORGEI
BOULENGER, 1912

23–28°C	3.5 cm (1½ in)
73–82°F	

Family: CITHARINIDAE
Common name: ANSORGE'S NEOLEBIAS
Distribution: Central Africa
Size: 3.5 cm (1½ in)
Food: CARNIVOROUS. Small live food such as *Daphnia* and bloodworm, plus flake and frozen food
Temperature range: 23–28°C / 73–82°F
pH: 6.0–7.0 dH: to 10°

If you are looking for a challenge, this is a magnificent fish for a well-matured species tank. In community aquaria it suffers from bullying. Males are far more intensely coloured than females. Susceptible to too much freshwater.

Always use well-conditioned aged water for water changes.

Breeding
Eggs are scattered over moss or peat fibre and hatch in 24 hours. The tiny fry hang at the surface for several days and should be fed on infusoria followed by newly hatched brine shrimp.

Tank Set-up
A small aquarium, say 50 cm (20 in) long. Very gentle filtration if any. A water depth of about 20 cm (8 in) and a few fine-leaved plants.

PARAPHAGO ROSTRATUS
BOULENGER, 1899

Family: CITHARINIDAE
Common name: STRIPED FIN-EATER
Distribution: Congo Basin, Zaire
Size: 18 cm (7 in)
Food: CARNIVOROUS. Small fish, pieces of fish fins, etc
Temperature range: 24–26°C / 75–79°F
pH: 6.0–7.0 dH: to 12°

Highly predatory, this fish should be kept alone or only with bottom-dwelling species such as larger Catfish. It feeds by severing parts of the fins from other fish. Its upper jaw is moveable, so it is able to use its jaws like a pair of scissors to slice through the fins.

24–26°C	18 cm (7 in)
75–79°F	

Breeding
Not known.

Tank Set-up
Thickets of plants with open areas for hunting. Good filtration.

Family: CITHARINIDAE
Common name: AFRICAN PIKE CHARACIN
Distribution: Niger delta (West Africa)
Size: 14 cm (5½ in)
Food: CARNIVOROUS. Juveniles take small live foods, older specimens eat fish
Temperature range: 23–28°C / 73–82°F
pH: 6.5–7.5 dH: to 20°

Typical of a hunter, it spends much time lurking among plants and roots. Should be kept alone or with larger fishes that it cannot swallow. It does have a nasty habit of biting the tails of other fish. Be prepared to feed live fish if all else fails.

Breeding
Not known.

Tank Set-up
Use plenty of roots and plants to provide places of concealment. Undemanding as far as water conditions are concerned.

23–28°C	14 cm (5½ in)
73–82°F	

PHAGO MACULATUS
AHL, 1922

PHAGOBORUS ORNATUS
(BOULENGER, 1899)

Family:	CITHARINIDAE
Common name:	NONE
Distribution:	Zaire basin
Size:	20 cm (8 in)
Food:	CARNIVOROUS. Small fish, larger insect larvae and fish fins
Temperature range:	22–26°C / 72–79°F
pH:	5.5–7.0 dH: to 12°

A hunter best kept alone or with bottom-dwelling Catfish such as some of the larger Loricariids. Young fish take insect larvae, but adults prefer to hunt fish.

Breeding
Not known.

Tank Set-up
Large aquarium with open areas and thickets of dense plants. Good filtration and regular water changes to maintain water quality.

22–26°C
72–79°F 20 cm (8 in)

CRENUCHUS SPILURUS
GUNTHER, 1863

24–27°C
75–81°F 6 cm (2½ in)

Family:	CRENUCHIDAE
Common name:	SAILFIN CHARACIN
Distribution:	Guyana
Size:	6 cm (2½ in)
Food:	CARNIVOROUS. Insect larvae, small fish, etc; will also take flake and frozen food
Temperature range:	24–27°C / 75–81°F
pH:	5.5–6.5 dH: to 8°

A fish for the species aquarium, since it is very timid if kept with boisterous fishes. Usually peaceful but older males can be a little territorial. Males have a longer dorsal fin which ends in a point, females are smaller and paler.

Breeding
It is believed to lay its eggs on stones and fan the eggs. In nature the spawning season is from October to February.

Tank Set-up
A small aquarium, heavily planted with some pebbles and roots to give shelter. Efficient filtration.

POECILOCHARAX WEITZMANI
GÉRY, 1965

Family:	CRENUCHIDAE
Common name:	NONE
Distribution:	Upper Solimoes region, upper Rio Negro / Orinoco regions
Size:	3.5 cm (1½ in)
Food:	CARNIVOROUS. Small live aquatic invertebrates, Daphnia, etc
Temperature range:	24–27°C / 75–81°F
pH:	5.0–6.5 dH: to 6°

Best kept in a species aquarium. These fish do not travel well and can be difficult to acclimatise, requiring very precise water conditions and lots of live foods. Newly imported fish require a mature system. Males have longer fins than females and are slimmer fish.

Breeding
Not yet accomplished in aquaria.

24–27°C
75–81°F 3.5 cm (1½ in)

Tank Set-up
Very soft, acidic water with very efficient filtration. Well-planted thickets of Java Moss are useful for this. Fine gravel and wood or pebbles for decoration.

BOULENGERELLA LATERISTRIGA
(BOULENGER, 1895)

Family: CTENOLUCIIDAE
Common name: STRIPED PIKE CHARACIN
Distribution: Negro and Urubu Rivers (Brazil)
Size: 40 cm (16 in)
Food: CARNIVOROUS. Insects and small fish
Temperature range: 22–27°C / 72–81°F
pH: 5.5–6.5 dH: to 10°

Solitary or group hunters, these fish should only be kept with other quiet species that are too large for them to swallow. Because they are nervous fish, newly imported specimens are often damaged in transit. Check that the fish are feeding before purchase.

Breeding
Not known.

Tank Set-up
A spacious aquarium with good cover and plenty of swimming space at the surface. A few floating plants are beneficial to give the fish security. This species requires a high oxygen content in the water and is susceptible to poor

 22–27°C
72–81°F   40 cm (16 in)

water conditions, so ensure that your filtration system is working at peak efficiency. Water changes of up to one third should be carried out on a fortnightly basis. Use well-conditioned water to replenish the aquarium.

BOULENGERELLA MACULATA
(VALENCIENNES, 1849)

Family: CTENOLUCIIDAE
Common name: NONE
Distribution: Amazon
Size: 35 cm (14 in)
Food: CARNIVOROUS. Juveniles take flake, adults eat insects and small fish
Temperature range: 22–27°C / 72–81°F
pH: 6.0–7.5 dH: to 18°

A surface-dwelling fish that likes the company of its own kind. Can be kept with other, larger fish. Easily frightened, it may dash about and injure itself or jump and hit itself against the cover glass. The long snout is especially susceptible to damage. Requires plenty of space and clean, well-oxygenated water.

22–27°C
72–81°F   35 cm (14 in)

Breeding
Not known.

Tank Set-up
A large aquarium with plenty of swimming space at the surface. A gentle current, provided by the spray bar return from a power filter, is beneficial. Decorate the aquarium with broad-leaved plants and wood.

CTENOLUCIUS HUJETA
(VALENCIENNES, 1849)

Family: CTENOLUCIIDAE
Common name: HUJET PIKE CHARACIN, SLANT-NOSED GAR
Distribution: Central and South America
Size: 70 cm (28 in), but usually only to 20 cm (8 in)
Food: CARNIVOROUS. Insects, insect larvae and, primarily, fish
Temperature range: 22–25°C / 72–77°F
pH: 6.5–7.5 dH: to 20°

A pack hunter, small shoals swim actively in a gentle current, searching for prey near the surface. Easily frightened, so care should be taken when cleaning the aquarium as they may dash about causing themselves injury. In captivity males are, in general, smaller than females. The male's ventral fin has a ragged edge, with the central fin rays longer than the outer. The female has a straight edge to the ventral fin.

Breeding
Can be accomplished with pairs or with trios – two males to one female. Over 1,000 eggs may be produced, hatch in 20 hours in water of 27°C / 81°F. First foods: newly hatched brine shrimp. Young can be cannibalistic.

22–25°C
72–77°F   70 cm (28 in)

Tank Set-up
A large aquarium planted at the rear and sides to provide cover. Low light levels or floating plants to reduce the light. Use an external power filter to help create good water movement. Susceptible to poor water conditions: change up to half the water once a week.

CURIMATA SPILURA

GUNTHER, 1864

Family: CURIMATIDAE

Common name: DIAMOND-SPOT CURIMATA

Distribution: Widespread throughout South America

Size: 9 cm (3½ in)

Food: HERBIVOROUS. Predominantly vegetable foods, but will take flake

Temperature range: 21–27°C / 70–81°F

pH: 6.0–7.5 dH: to 25°

Very peaceful shoaling fish for the larger community aquarium, provided the plants are hardy enough to withstand the onslaught! However, if copious amounts of green foods are offered they will leave the plants alone.

Breeding

Not yet accomplished in aquaria. In nature they spawn in flood plains at the start of the rainy season.

Tank Set-up

Large aquarium with a mix of real and plastic plants and decorated with wood. Good filtration. Bright lighting will encourage both strong plant growth and algae for the fish to browse on.

 21–27°C 70–81°F 9 cm (3½ in)

SEMAPROCHILODUS TAENIURUS

(VALENCIENNES, 1817)

Family: CURIMATIDAE

Common name: NONE

Distribution: Western Colombia and Brazil

Size: 30 cm (12 in)

Food: HERBIVOROUS. Algae, peas, etc

Temperature range: 22–25°C / 72–77°F

pH: 5.5–7.5 dH: to 20°

Kept with other peaceful fish in a large aquarium, this species will live for a long time. They prefer the water conditions to be at the lower end of the range: at about pH 6.0 and a hardness of about 10° the fish grow well and seem to show their best colours. Not

only will they feed on peas, lettuce and the like, which should form the bulk of their diet, they will also accept tablet foods.

Breeding

Not known.

Tank Set-up

A large aquarium decorated with wood onto which has been attached Java Fern – since this hard-leaved plant seems to withstand the fish's browsing habits. A soft sand substrate, as this species does like to dig. Good filtration required.

 22–25°C 72–77°F 30 cm (12 in)

ERYTHRINUS ERYTHRINUS

(SCHNEIDER, 1801)

Family: ERYTHRINIDAE

Common name: NONE

Distribution: Brazil

Size: 25 cm (10 in)

Food: CARNIVOROUS. Live fish, larger insect larvae, etc; some specimens can be weaned onto dead food

Temperature range: 22–26°C / 72–79°F

pH: 6.0–7.5 dH: to 20°

An out-and-out predator, it should be kept alone. As it requires live foods, you must be prepared to feed them; if you are not, do not keep this fish. The swimbladder has a secondary function, since it may be used as a respiratory organ thus enabling the fish to survive in waters poor in oxygen. It is one of the Characins that lacks an adipose fin.

22–26°C 72–79°F 25 cm (10 in)

Breeding

Not known.

Tank Set-up

Plants and wood for decoration and to give hiding places. Gentle filtration.

HOPLIAS MALABARICUS
(BLOCH 1794)

21–25°C
70–77°F

50 cm (20 in)

Family: ERYTHRINIDAE	
Common name: TIGER FISH	
Distribution: Central and northern South America	
Size: 50 cm (20 in)	
Food: CARNIVOROUS. Fish (alive or dead), pieces of meat, earthworms, etc	
Temperature range: 21–25°C / 70–77°F	
pH: 6.0–8.0 dH: to 24°	

A loner, which should only be kept with other fish much larger than itself, such as the Catfish *Pseudodoras niger*. Much of its time is spent lurking among plants. Highly predatory, it will attack anything it considers will fit in its mouth. Males are slimmer, their ventral profile being almost straight, while in females the ventral profile is more curved. Take care when cleaning the aquarium – frightened specimens may bite! Tiger fish have an accessory breathing organ which allows them to survive in very poor conditions.

Breeding
Possible in a very large aquarium.

Tank Set-up
Decorate the aquarium with wood and large plants. The filtration system needs to be able to cope with large amounts of high protein waste.

CARNEGIELLA STRIGATA
(GUENTHER, 1864)

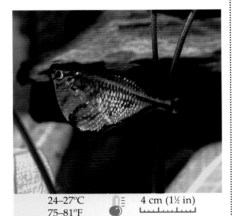

24–27°C
75–81°F

4 cm (1½ in)

Family: GASTEROPELECIDAE	
Common name: MARBLED HATCHET	
Distribution: Peru	
Size: 4 cm (1½ in)	
Food: CARNIVOROUS. Predominantly small live food, although they will take some flake	
Temperature range: 24–27°C / 75–81°F	
pH: 5.5–7.5 dH: to 18°	

True surface dwellers, these fish thrive on a diet of mosquito larvae and fruit flies. They need to be kept in shoals of at least six fish, otherwise they seem to pine away. They will sometimes dart around the aquarium, and at other times remain motionless in a strong current. Females are more rounded in the body, and when they are ready to spawn the eggs can usually be seen in the body cavity. All fishes of this genus lack an adipose fin.

Breeding
Soft water of about 5° with a pH around 6.0. If conditioned well on mosquito larvae and small flies, the fish will spawn, depositing their eggs on floating plants. The eggs hatch in 30 hours. First foods should be very fine: infusoria, powdered flake, brine shrimp nauplii, etc.

Tank Set-up
Mature community aquarium with a good filtration system that produces a strong current. Thickets of plants with some clear surface areas. These fish jump, so a tight-fitting cover glass is essential.

GASTEROPELECUS STERNICLA
(LINNAEUS, 1758)

23–26°C
73–79°F

6.5 cm (2½ in)

Family: GASTEROPELECIDAE	
Common name: COMMON HATCHET	
Distribution: Brazil, Guyana, Surinam	
Size: 6.5 cm (2½ in)	
Food: CARNIVOROUS. Small flies, mosquito larvae, will take flake	
Temperature range: 23–26°C / 73–79°F	
pH: 6.0–7.0 dH: to 12°	

Can be a very timid fish if there is insufficient cover in the aquarium. Provide some floating plants, but still leave enough clear surface area for the fish to feed. May be kept in a community aquarium. Males are slimmer than females, when viewed from above.

Breeding
Not accomplished in captivity but may be similar to *Carnegiella strigata*.

Tank Set-up
Community aquarium with plants and wood for decoration, plus some floating plants. Good filtration. Cover glass needed, as these fish will jump.

HEMIODOPSIS GRACILIS
(GUNTHER, 1864)

23–27°C
73–81°F

16 cm (6 in)

Family: HEMIODIDAE	
Common name: SLENDER HEMIODUS	
Distribution: Brazil, Guyana	
Size: 16 cm (6 in)	
Food: OMNIVOROUS. Plankton, aufwuchs, flake, small aquatic invertebrates	
Temperature range: 23–27°C / 73–81°F	
pH: 5.5–7.0 dH: to 15°	

An active shoaling fish that is ideal for the larger community aquarium of like-sized, peaceful fishes. It requires high oxygen levels so do not overstock the aquarium. Care needs to be taken when acclimatising the fish: pay careful attention to water conditions.

Breeding
Not known.

Tank Set-up
Large aquarium with plenty of open water. Very efficient filtration with a high turnover rate – twice an hour is ideal – and high oxygen levels.

HEPSETUS ODOE
(BLOCH, 1794)

26–28°C
79–82°F

70 cm (28 in)

Family:	HEPSETIDAE
Common name:	AFRICAN PIKE CHARACIN
Distribution:	Tropical Africa excluding Nile Basin
Size:	70 cm (28 in)
Food:	CARNIVOROUS. Live fish, pieces of fish or meat
Temperature range:	26–28°C / 79–82°F
pH:	6.0–7.5 dH: to 15°

An out-and-out predator, this fish should only be kept by dedicated aquarists who can cater for its needs. Small specimens acclimatise easily, but beware, they grow quickly and then need a very large aquarium if they are not to injure themselves. Can be skittish in temperament. In the wild this is a food fish and is often caught by rod and line.

Breeding
Not accomplished in captivity. In the wild they construct a free-floating bubble nest which is guarded by one or both parents.

Tank Set-up
Large aquarium with an equally large and very efficient filtration system. Good cover glass, as they will jump. Sparse planting and some wood for decoration. Avoid anything with sharp edges on which the fish may damage itself if it takes fright.

COPELLA NATTERERI
(STEINDACHNER, 1875)

23–26°C
73–79°F

5 cm (2 in)

Family:	LEBIASINIDAE
Common name:	BEAUTIFUL SCALED TETRA
Distribution:	Lower Amazon to the Negro River
Size:	5 cm (2 in)
Food:	OMNIVOROUS. Predominantly live food but will accept flake and frozen food
Temperature range:	23–26°C / 73–79°F
pH:	5.5–7.0 dH: to 20°

A fish ideally suited to the heavily planted, peaceful community aquarium. Males of this species are more colourful and have a larger dorsal fin than females. Keep as a small group of both sexes to avoid fighting between males.

Breeding
The eggs are laid on broad leaves such as those of *Echinodus*. The male will guard the eggs until they hatch, which takes about 30 hours. First foods: infusoria and other micro foods.

Tank Set-up
Community aquarium with a few floating plants. Wood for decoration. Good filtration with a gentle water flow.

LEBIASINA MULTIMACULATA
BOULENGER, 1911

23–27°C
73–81°F

7 cm (3 in)

Family:	LEBIASINIDAE
Common name:	MULTI-SPOTTED LEBIASINA
Distribution:	Northwest Colombia
Size:	7 cm (3 in)
Food:	CARNIVOROUS. Mosquito larvae, and similar sized live foods; will also take small fry and frozen food
Temperature range:	23–27°C / 73–81°F
pH:	6.0–7.5 dH: to 22°

Because this fish is predatory, it should be kept with equal or only slightly smaller companions. It is not too particular about water conditions, as in the wild it can exist in water that is oxygen deficient. It accomplishes this by using its swim bladder as a secondary breathing apparatus. Males are more slender and more colourful than females.

Breeding
Not known.

Tank Set-up
Planted aquarium with plenty of hiding places. Gentle filtration.

NANNOBRYCON EQUES
(STEINDACHNER, 1876)

23–28°C
73–82°F

5 cm (2 in)

Family:	LEBIASINIDAE
Common name:	THREE-STRIPED PENCILFISH, HOCKEY STICK PENCILFISH
Distribution:	Western Colombia, Guyana, Negro River
Size:	5 cm (2 in)
Food:	CARNIVOROUS. Insect larvae, *Daphnia*, etc
Temperature range:	23–28°C / 73–82°F
pH:	5.5–7.0 dH: to 10°

Gentle fish, these may be kept with other equally peaceful fishes. They prefer the company of their own kind, so keep in a shoal. Most of the time they are found motionless near the surface, in between plant roots, twigs and the like. They have a different nocturnal colour patterning: the horizontal stripes all but disappear and vertical bars show on the body.

Breeding
Very soft acidic water. Pairs will spawn over Java Moss or a breeding mat. Remove parents or they will eat the eggs. First foods: infusoria and newly hatched brine shrimp.

Tank Set-up
Well-planted aquarium. Pay particular attention to the water conditions if you wish to succeed with these fish.

NANNOSTOMUS ESPEI
(MEINKEN, 1956)

Family: LEBIASINIDAE	
Common name: ESPE'S PENCILFISH	
Distribution: Southwestern Guyana	
Size: 3.5 cm (1½ in)	
Food: OMNIVOROUS. Small live food, flake and frozen food	
Temperature range: 22–25°C / 72–77°F	
pH: 5.5–7.0 dH: to 8°	

A delicate little Characin that needs to be kept in a shoal of at least a dozen individuals. Males have a more intense gold stripe along the body than females.

Breeding
Condition the fish well on live foods such as mosquito larvae. As they will eat their eggs, provide a spawning trap or large clump of Java Moss to protect them. Hatching time averages 48 hours. Feed fry fine foods such as rotifers followed by brine shrimp nauplii.

 22–25°C 72–77°F   3.5 cm (1½ in)

Tank Set-up
Well-planted community aquarium with other peaceful fish. Soft, acidic water. Good filtration and regular water changes.

PYRRHULINA VITTATA
REGAN, 1912

24–27°C 75–81°F   6 cm (2½ in)

Family: LEBIASINIDAE	
Common name: STRIPED PYRRHULINA	
Distribution: Amazon basin, Madeira River	
Size: 6 cm (2½ in)	
Food: CARNIVOROUS. Small live food, frozen food and flake	
Temperature range: 24–27°C / 75–81°F	
pH: 6.0–7.5 dH: to 15°	

Can be somewhat aggressive towards their own kind, with stronger males dominating weaker ones, but as far as other tankmates are concerned they are quite peaceable. Females are less aggressive. Keep several fish together, but make sure the tank is quite large so that they can each have their own space.

Breeding
The male cleans a broad leaf or a stone and defends the eggs until they hatch some two days later. Feed fry brine shrimp nauplii.

Tank Set-up
Large community aquarium with plenty of plants, including some broad-leaved species. Some areas of open water for swimming. Good filtration with a high turnover to create a good flow of water.

Family: SERRASALMIDAE	
Common name: WIMPLE PIRANHA	
Distribution: Guyana and the Mato Grosso region of the southern Amazon	
Size: 15 cm (6 in)	
Food: CARNIVOROUS. Fish scales and flesh, live food	
Temperature range: 23–26°C / 73–79°F	
pH: 5.5–6.5 dH: to 5°	

These are best kept as single fish, or with fish of a similar size in a very large, well-maintained aquarium. Young specimens are quite sociable, but as they mature they become more likely to take scales from other fish.

Breeding
Not known.

Tank Set-up
Large aquarium with large plants and decorated with roots and wood. High turnover filtration unit giving a strong current of water.

 23–26°C 73–79°F   15 cm (6 in)

CATOPRION MENTO
(CUVIER, 1819)

MYLEUS RUBRIPINNIS
(MUELLER & TROSCHEL, 1844)

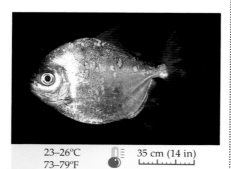

23–26°C 73–79°F	35 cm (14 in)

Family: SERRASALMIDAE
Common name: NONE
Distribution: Guyana, Amazon
Size: 35 cm (14 in), but only to about 12 cm (4½ in) in captivity
Food: OMNIVOROUS. Any small food such as *Daphnia*, flake, peas, etc
Temperature range: 23–26°C / 73–79°F
pH: 6.0–7.0 dH: to 20°

Only attempt keeping these fish if you can provide good quality, well-oxygenated water and plenty of swimming space. They retain a silvery body coloration into adulthood, and this combined with the red on their anal fin makes them very attractive. Specimens are sometimes seen with what look like tiny spots or blisters on their flanks; these blemishes are the result of an as yet unidentified disease.

Breeding
Not known.

Tank Set-up
A spacious aquarium with rounded stones, wood and plants. Pay particular attention to the water conditions if you wish to succeed with these fish.

Family: SERRASALMIDAE
Common name: BLACK-BARRED MYLEUS
Distribution: Brazil, Venezuela
Size: 12 cm (4½ in)
Food: OMNIVOROUS. All kinds of vegetable food (mango, peach, lettuce, peas, etc), and small live food
Temperature range: 24–27°C / 75–81°F
pH: 5.5–7.0 dH: to 10°

A very attractive fish, its one drawback for the community aquarium is its love of plants. Males have an elongated, pointed dorsal fin, and their anal fin is bi-lobed and elongated.

Breeding
Nothing known.

Tank Set-up
A large aquarium decorated with roots, some tough plants such as Java Moss, Java Fern and Amazon Sword plants, plus some artificial plants. Use a sand substrate as the fish like to sift through it for food. Good filtration.

24–27°C 75–81°F	12 cm (4½ in)

MYLEUS SCHOMBURGKII
(JARDINE, 1841)

SERRASALMUS RHOMBEUS
(LINNAEUS, 1766)

23–26°C 73–79°F	38 cm (15 in)

Family: SERRASALMIDAE
Common name: SPOTTED PIRANHA
Distribution: Amazon basin and Guyana
Size: 38 cm (15 in)
Food: CARNIVOROUS. Live fish, pieces of meat or fish, some flake
Temperature range: 23–26°C / 73–79°F
pH: 5.5–7.0 dH: to 10°

A predator, the Piranha has a great reputation for stripping flesh from bones. However, it does not usually attack humans unless it is frightened. Its teeth are razor sharp and can cause nasty wounds, so take care when carrying out regular tank maintenance. On males the front of the anal fin is extended. Feed two or three times a week.

Breeding
Has been bred in captivity but information is limited. The eggs hatch in about two days, but the fry are not free-swimming until about a week later. Feed fry on live foods. You will need a regularly supply of progressively larger and larger foods.

Tank Set-up
A large species aquarium is best, as they will not attack each other unless the prospective prey fish is weakened for some reason. Good filtration and water turnover to cope with the waste from these greedy carnivores. Remove uneaten food regularly. Roots to provide hiding places and thickets of large plants.

Cichlids

Cichlidae

ACARICHTHYS HECKELLI
(MÜLLER & TROSCHEL, 1848)

Family:	CICHLIDAE
Common name:	THREAD-FINNED CICHLID
Distribution:	Guyana, Surinam, Brazil, Peru
Size:	20 cm (8 in)
Food:	OMNIVOROUS. Live, frozen, flake food
Temperature range:	23–25°C / 73–77°F
pH:	6.5–7.5 dH: to 18°

A graceful, peaceful Cichlid which, although territorial, does not bother other fishes. It gets its common name from the extended rays at the rear of the dorsal fin. If you have wild-caught specimens they may not accept flake or frozen food so offer live food at first and gradually introduce flake and frozen food.

Breeding
The fish spawn in caves, laying groups of 5 or 6 eggs with gaps between each group until they have produced a few hundred eggs. The female tends the

23–25°C 73–77°F		20 cm (8 in)

eggs and fry, the male the territory. Newly hatched brine shrimp and other fine foods for the fry.

Tank Set-up
Use a good-sized aquarium with plenty of caves for the fish to hide in. Some plants are beneficial. Good filtration and regular water changes are necessary.

AEQUIDENS PULCHER
(GILL, 1858)

19–23°C 66–73°F		20 cm (8 in)

Family:	CICHLIDAE
Common name:	BLUE ACARA
Distribution:	Northern South America, Trinidad
Size:	20 cm (8 in)
Food:	OMNIVOROUS. Live, flake, frozen food
Temperature range:	19–23°C / 66–73°F
pH:	6.5–8.0 dH: to 25°

An easy fish to keep as long as you pay attention to regular aquarium maintenance. They suffer if there is any deterioration in water quality. The dorsal and anal fins on the males are extended.

Breeding
Easy to breed and raise, the eggs are laid on rocks and tended by the parents who continue to guard the fry. They get into a cycle and produce broods regularly.

Tank Set-up
In a larger community aquarium, provide plenty of rocks and plants so they have hiding places. Good filtration is essential, as are regular water changes in order to maintain water quality.

AEQUIDENS RIVULATUS
(GUNTHER, 1859)

Family:	CICHLIDAE
Common name:	GREEN TERROR
Distribution:	Ecuador, Peru
Size:	20 cm (8 in)
Food:	OMNIVOROUS. Live food if possible, will take flake and frozen food
Temperature range:	21–24°C / 70–75°F
pH:	6.5–7.5 dH: to 15°

Noted for its aggression, they should be kept only with fishes able to fend for themselves. They take up territories and will defend them especially when breeding. Males are generally larger, females are darker in colour.

21–24°C 70–75°F		20 cm (8 in)

Breeding
They form a family unit with both parents tending the eggs and fry. Initially the fry grow slowly, but on a diet of newly hatched brine shrimp they soon grow faster.

Tank Set-up
Have a large community aquarium with plenty of open water and areas to which the fish can stake a territorial claim. Good filtration and regular water changes are beneficial.

AEQUIDENS TETRAMERUS
(HECKEL, 1840)

24–26°C
75–79°F
20 cm (8 in)

Family: CICHLIDAE
Common name: SADDLE CICHLID
Distribution: Central and north-eastern South America
Size: 20 cm (8 in)
Food: CARNIVOROUS. Mostly live food, will accept frozen and flake
Temperature range: 24–26°C / 75–79°F
pH: 6.5–7.0 dH: to 12°

A beautiful fish of slow moving rivers and pools, not often offered for sale. Most of those for sale are commercially bred and never attain the size or colour of wild specimens. Adults can be very intolerant of other fishes, the fry are more tolerant. It is a food fish in its native lands.

Breeding
They spawn on a flat surface, with the parents sharing the care. Up to 1,000 eggs may be produced.

Tank Set-up
Use a good-sized aquarium with robust plants and rock and wood. Good filtration and regular water changes are necessary.

AMPHILOPHUS ALFARI
(MEEK, 1907)

Family: CICHLIDAE
Common name: PASTEL CICHLID
Distribution: Central America
Size: 22 cm (9 in)
Food: OMNIVOROUS. Live, flake, frozen food
Temperature range: 23–26°C / 73–79°F
pH: 6.5–7.0 dH: to 10°

Variations can be seen in the colour, body and finnage shape of this fish, even in fishes from the same river system. In the aquarium it is domineering and also likes to dig in the substrate. Males are much larger than females.

Breeding
Eggs are usually deposited on a hard, vertical surface. The female protects the eggs and fry.

Tank Set-up
Reasonable sized aquarium with rocks, wood and plant to give cover is best. Good filtration to cope with the debris the fish stir up when digging is required.

23–26°C
73–79°F
22 cm (9 in)

AMPHILOPHUS CITRINELLUS
(GÜNTHER, 1864)

Family: CICHLIDAE
Common name: MIDAS CICHLID
Distribution: Central America
Size: 30 cm (12 in)
Food: OMNIVOROUS. Live, flake, frozen food
Temperature range: 21–25°C / 70–77°F
pH: 6.5–7.5 dH: to 18°

This is a rather belligerent fish especially when breeding. They love to dig and move large quantities of gravel around the aquarium, so plants in the aquarium are a waste of space. Males have a conical genital papilla, longer finnage and a hump on their heads. Females have a wider, half-lobed genital papilla.

Breeding
They are prolific and spawn on rocks. The parents care for the fry. Feed fry brine shrimp and fine flake food and they grow rapidly.

Tank Set-up
Use a large aquarium with some rocks and wood which should be seated on the base glass of the aquarium so that the fish cannot undermine them when digging. Provide good filtration.

21–25°C
70–77°F
30 cm (12 in)

AMPHILOPHUS LABIATUS
(GUNTHER, 1864)

Family:	CICHLIDAE
Common name:	RED DEVIL
Distribution:	Central America
Size:	25 cm (10 in)
Food:	OMNIVOROUS. Live, frozen, flake, tablet food
Temperature range:	24–26°C / 75–79°F
pH:	6.5–7.5 dH: to 15°

A greedy fish, it will eat anything and everything. Growth is rapid. Aggressive and territorial, they should only be kept

24–26°C 75–79°F	25 cm (10 in)

with other fishes that are able to take care of themselves. Males are bigger than females and have a pointed genital papilla, whereas females have a blunt one.

Breeding
After laying her eggs, it is the female's responsibility to care for the brood. When free-swimming the fry can be offered newly hatched brine shrimp.

Tank Set-up
As for *A. citrinellus*.

ANOMALOCHROMIS THOMASI
(BOULENGER, 1915)

Family:	CICHLIDAE
Common name:	AFRICAN BUTTERFLY CICHLID
Distribution:	Liberia, Guinea, Sierra Leone
Size:	Males 10 cm (4 in); females 7 cm (3 in)
Food:	OMNIVOROUS. Live, frozen, flake, green food
Temperature range:	23–27°C / 73–80°F
pH:	6.5–7.0 dH: to 10°

This very peaceful fish may be kept with others of a similar nature. Unless they are spawning, males and females are virtually indistinguishable, but when breeding the males have more black on them.

23–27°C 73–80°F	10 cm (4 in)

Breeding
Eggs are deposited on a pre-cleaned leaf or rock and both the eggs and fry are guarded by the parents. If you are using a tank that is too small, the parents may eat the eggs or fry.

Tank Set-up
Provide a planted, mature aquarium with some broad-leaved plants and flat stones. Also provide hiding places and good filtration.

APISTOGRAMMA AGASSIZII
(STEINDACHNER, 1875)

Family:	CICHLIDAE
Common name:	AGASSIZ' DWARF CICHLID
Distribution:	Southern tributaries of the Amazon
Size:	8 cm (3 in)
Food:	OMNIVOROUS. Live, flake, frozen food
Temperature range:	22–24°C / 72–75°F
pH:	6.0–6.5 dH: to 10°

They are a peaceful fish but will claim a territory. The male's territory may encompass the territories of several females who will defend their boundaries against each other but not against the male. It is likely that the male will spawn with each of the females within his territory. Males are

22–24°C 72–75°F	8 cm (3 in)

more colourful, have extended finnage and are usually larger than females.

Breeding
They spawn in caves – flowerpots make excellent caves – with the female protecting the eggs and the male defending the territory. On hatching the fry are still protected and moved around the aquarium.

Tank Set-up
A well-planted, mature community aquarium with caves and hiding places; good filtration and regular water changes is ideal.

APISTOGRAMMA BITAENIATA
PELLEGRIN, 1936

Family:	CICHLIDAE
Common name:	BANDED DWARF CICHLID
Distribution:	Peru, Brazil
Size:	Males 6 cm (2½ in); females 4 cm (1½ in)
Food:	CARNIVOROUS. Small live food
Temperature range:	23–25°C / 73–77°F
pH:	5.0–6.0 dH: to 7°

A delicate little fish not often seen. They should be kept as several females to one male, each female having a territory within the male's overall territory. Males are larger, more colourful and have larger finnage than females.

23–25°C 73–77°F	6 cm (2½ in)

Breeding
In soft acidic water at about 26°C / 79°F, they are typical cave spawners. After hatching, the fry are led by the female around the aquarium.

Tank Set-up
Provide a well-planted aquarium with caves. Check water quality, keep it soft (below 10°) and acidic. Good filtration and regular water changes are required.

APISTOGRAMMA BORELLII
(REGAN, 1906)

Family: CICHLIDAE

Common name: BORELLI'S DWARF CICHLID

Distribution: Mato and Paraguay Rivers and nearby water courses (South America)

Size: Males 8 cm (3 in); females 4.5 cm (2 in)

Food: CARNIVOROUS. Predominantly small live food

Temperature range: 24–25°C / 75–77°F

pH: 6.0–6.5 dH: to 12°

A beautiful fish that makes a lovely addition to a well-balanced, mature, under-stocked, community aquarium of very peaceful fishes. These creatures are territorial but problems only arise when they are breeding. Males are far more colourful than females but allow several females to one male. It has been recorded that barren females occur within a batch. Sometimes young males will take on the guise of a female to avoid conflict with other males.

Breeding
Some 60 or so eggs are laid in a cave. They are guarded by the female and, on hatching, she herds the fry around the aquarium. Meanwhile the male defends the territory.

24–25°C
75–77°F

8 cm (3 in)

Tank Set-up
A planted aquarium with caves and hollows and good filtration is ideal.

APISTOGRAMMA CACATUOIDES
HOEDEMAN, 1951

Family: CICHLIDAE

Common name: COCKATOO DWARF CICHLID, CRESTED DWARF CICHLID

Distribution: Amazon basin

Size: Males 9 cm (3½ in); females 5 cm (2 in)

Food: CARNIVOROUS. Small live food, will accept flake

Temperature range: 24–25°C / 75–77°F

pH: 7.0 dH: to 10°

This fish derives its common names from the extended rays at the beginning of the dorsal fin. Males are much larger than females and have longer fins. Keep several females with each male. He will remain in the mid levels of the aquarium while the females claim their breeding territories on the substrate.

While taking care of her brood, the female may become bright yellow.

Breeding
Females lay their eggs in caves and carry out the guarding of the eggs and fry while the male protects the whole territory. As he may breed with more than one female at the same time, the fry from different broods may become intermingled but are still protected by a female even if they are not her own. Do not use fungus treatments on the eggs as these fish are sensitive to chemicals.

Tank Set-up
Use plants, wood and rocks to provide caves and territories, and provide good filtration to maintain water conditions.

24–25°C
75–77°F

9 cm (3½ in)

APISTOGRAMMA MACMASTERI
KULLANDER, 1979

Family: CICHLIDAE

Common name: MACMASTERS DWARF CICHLID

Distribution: Orinoco basin

Size: 8 cm (3 in)

Food: CARNIVOROUS. Live food

Temperature range: 24–30°C / 75–86°F

pH: 6.0–6.5 dH: to 8°

A delightful little fish that has a wonderful territorial defensive display which can be seen quite often if the group is kept with a few other peaceful fishes. Males are larger and more colourful, the caudal is bright red on its upper and lower edges.

Breeding
They are polygamous and typical cave spawners. The female tends the eggs and fry, the male the territory.

Tank Set-up
In a well-planned, mature aquarium ensure there are caves and hollows and well-filtered water.

24–30°C
75–86°F

8 cm (3 in)

APISTOGRAMMA NIJSSENI
KULLANDER, 1979

24–30°C
75–86°F

6.5 cm (2½ in)

Family: CICHLIDAE

Common name: NIJSSEN'S DWARF CICHLID, PANDA DWARF CICHLID

Distribution: Peru

Size: Males 6.5 cm (2½ in); females 4 cm (1½ in)

Food: CARNIVOROUS. Live food, will eventually take frozen and flake

Temperature range: 24–30°C/75–86°F

pH: 5.5 dH: below 5°

A very beautiful fish that only shows its true potential if the correct water conditions can be maintained. Males are larger and incredibly colourful while the female has a strange black and yellow coloration. Peaceful and may be kept with other fishes.

Breeding
They have been bred in captivity but details are not available.

Tank Set-up
A well planted, mature aquarium with plenty of wood is best. Use half coconut shells to provide spawning sites and shelter. Efficient filtration to maintain the water quality is required and it should be remembered they are only really happy in very soft acidic water.

APISTOGRAMMA STEINDACHNERI
(REGAN, 1908)

Family: CICHLIDAE

Common name: STEINDACHNER'S DWARF CICHLID

Distribution: Guyana

Size: Males 10 cm (4 in); females 7 cm (3 in)

Food: CARNIVOROUS. Live food

Temperature range: 23–25°C/73–77°F

pH: 6.0–7.0 dH: to 10°

Only aggressive when spawning, these fish may be housed with other fishes, but be prepared for the other fish to be herded to one section of the aquarium if the Cichlids breed. Males are larger, more colourful.

Breeding
The male keeps a harem. They spawn in caves and the female tends the eggs. Both parents may guard the fry.

Tank Set-up
Provide a well planted community aquarium with caves and hiding places and good filtration.

23–25°C
73–77°F

10 cm (4 in)

APISTOGRAMMA TRIFASCIATA
(EIGENMANN & KENNEDY, 1903)

Family: CICHLIDAE

Common name: THREE-STRIPED DWARF CICHLID

Distribution: Paraguay and Guaporé Rivers (South America)

Size: Males 6 cm (2½ in); females 4.5 cm (2 in)

Food: CARNIVOROUS. Small live food

Temperature range: 26–29°C/79–84°F

pH: 6.0–6.5 dH: to 8°

A peaceful but territorial fish. Males are easily distinguishable, they are more colourful and the third to fifth rays of the dorsal are elongated. Keep several females with each male.

26–29°C
79–84°F

6 cm (2½ in)

Breeding
Use soft, slightly acidic water. They spawn in caves with the female tending the eggs and fry and the male the overall territory.

Tank Set-up
Use a planted aquarium with rocks and wood set out to allow the females to claim territories and, if possible have a cave (flowerpot) in each territory. Provide a sand substrate. Check the water quality and make only small water changes, ensuring the filtration system is efficient.

ARCHOCENTRUS NIGROFASCIATUS
(GUENTHER, 1866)

Family: CICHLIDAE	
Common name: CONVICT CICHLID, ZEBRA CICHLID	
Distribution: Central America	
Size: 15 cm (6 in)	
Food: OMNIVOROUS. Live, frozen, flake, green food	
Temperature range: 20–24°C / 68–75°F	
pH: 6.5–8.0 dH: to 20°	

An undemanding fish, this alone should make it appealing, however, its belligerent attitude towards other fish makes it most suitable for a species aquarium. They pair off and spawn readily. Males are larger and have longer fins; as they mature they develop a fatty lump on the forehead. Females have a scattering of orange scales on the lower part of the body. There is an albino variety of this fish.

Breeding
Straightforwardly, the pair select a suitable site, which may be in a cave or in the open, and deposit their eggs. Both parents care for the eggs and fry which are easy to raise on newly hatched brine shrimp.

20–24°C 68–75°F		15 cm (6 in)

Tank Set-up
A good-sized aquarium is needed if more than one pair are kept to allow them to have territories. Provide rocks, wood and robust plant cover. Regular water changes are required.

ARCHOCENTRUS SAJICA
(BUSSING, 1974)

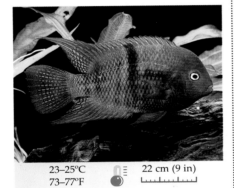

23–25°C 73–77°F		22 cm (9 in)

Family: CICHLIDAE	
Common name: T-BAR CICHLID	
Distribution: Costa Rica	
Size: Males 22 cm (9 in); females 17 cm (7 in)	
Food: OMNIVOROUS. Live, flake, frozen food	
Temperature range: 23–25°C / 73–77°F	
pH: 7.0–7.0 dH: to 15°	

A smaller Cichlid whose peaceable temperament allows it to be kept with other fishes, even in a community tank of medium-sized fishes. They form pairs and will breed in a community aquarium. Males are larger and their dorsal and anal fins are elongated. Do not keep with *A. nigrofasciatus* as the two species will interbreed.

Breeding
For preference they spawn in caves and the female carries out guard duties on the eggs and newly hatched fry while the male deals with territory defence. These roles are sometimes reversed. There can be a problem with rearing the fry as only part of the brood grows normally and the remainder are stunted.

Tank Set-up
The fish need a well-planted, mature aquarium with plenty of hiding places, including some caves, and efficient filtration.

Family: CICHLIDAE	
Common name: NONE	
Distribution: Guatemala	
Size: Males 12 cm (4½ in); females 8 cm (3 in)	
Food: OMNIVOROUS. Live, flake, frozen, green food	
Temperature range: 22–25°C / 72–77°F	
pH: 6.5–7.5 dH: to 12°	

Very peaceful, they will breed regularly if conditions are right. Males are larger and have pointed dorsal and ventral fins. Mature males also have a bump on their foreheads.

Breeding
They spawn in caves. Once hatched the fry are removed to pits and tended by both parents.

Tank Set-up
Provide a planted aquarium with several caves and good filtration.

ARCHOCENTRUS SPILURUS
(GUENTHER, 1862)

22–25°C 72–77°F		12 cm (4½ in)

ASTATOTILAPIA BURTONI
(GUNTHER, 1893)

Family: CICHLIDAE	
Common name: BURTON'S MOUTHBROODER	
Distribution: East and central Africa	
Size: Males 12 cm (4½ in); females 7 cm (3 in)	
Food: OMNIVOROUS. Live, flake, frozen, green food	
Temperature range: 20–24°C / 68–75°F	
pH: 8.0–9.0 dH: to 20°	

A territorial and quarrelsome fish with its own kind that usually lives quietly with other species. Males are larger, more colourful and have dummy egg spots on their anal fin. Keep several females with each male.

Breeding
These fish are mouthbrooders. They lay their eggs in pits and the female picks them up in her mouth. Some 30 plus

20–24°C
68–75°F

12 cm (4½ in)

eggs may be produced. After hatching the fry may still return to the female's mouth.

Tank Set-up
Thickets of plants and plenty of rocks to give hiding places are necessary, as is a gravel and/or sand substrate. Regular water changes are beneficial.

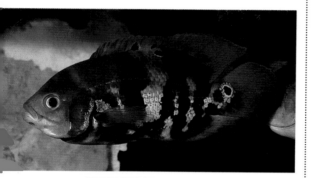

ASTRONOTUS OCELLATUS
(CUVIER, 1829)

22–25°C
72–77°F

33 cm (13 in)

Family: CICHLIDAE	
Common name: OSCAR	
Distribution: South America	
Size: 33 cm (13 in)	
Food: CARNIVOROUS. Meaty food both live and dead, tablet food	
Temperature range: 22–25°C / 72–77°F	
pH: 6.5–7.5 dH: to 20°	

These undemanding fish are often the aquarist's first encounter with Cichlids – the young fish are very attractive, but unfortunately grow rapidly to a large size. They are undemanding as far as water is concerned, tolerating soft or hard, acid or alkaline, just as long as extremes are avoided.

Breeding
A large aquarium is required as the pair can be quite boisterous when spawning. Some 1,000 to 2,000 eggs may be laid on cleaned rock. Both parents tend the eggs and young.

Tank Set-up
Provide a large aquarium with plenty of swimming space. Use rocks and wood for decor. Plants are best potted or they should be well-established large plants if planted in the substrate. Either way, place rocks around the crown of the plant to prevent the fish from digging it up. Alternatively use plastic plants. Good filtration is needed to cope with the waste from these greedy feeders.

AULONOCARA BAENSCHI
MEYER & RIEHL, 1985

Family: CICHLIDAE	
Common name: BAENSCH'S PEACOCK, YELLOW REGAL CICHLID	
Distribution: Lake Malawi	
Size: 10 cm (4 in)	
Food: OMNIVOROUS. Live, flake, frozen food	
Temperature range: 22–25°C / 72–77°F	
pH: 7.5–8.5 dH: to 25°	

The males of this striking fish are yellow and blue, the degree of one or other of the colours depends on the locality the fish are from. Females are a drab brown. Peaceable and suitable for most community Malawi aquaria.

Breeding
Typical mouthbrooder. The eggs are fertilised while in the female's mouth.

Tank Set-up
Use a standard Malawi aquarium with plenty of rocks and hiding places.

22–25°C
72–77°F

10 cm (4 in)

AULONOCARA JACOPFREIBERGI
(JOHNSON, 1974)

24–26°C
75–79°F
15 cm (6 in)

Family: CICHLIDAE
Common name: NONE
Distribution: Lake Malawi
Size: 15 cm (6 in)
Food: CARNIVOROUS. Live, frozen food
Temperature range: 24–26°C/75–79°F
pH: 7.5–8.0 dH: to 18°

The colour on dominant males is beautiful. In the wild they live in shoals, each group only having one fully coloured male. Males are larger, have longer ventral fins and more pointed dorsal and anal fins than females. Females have a red stripe on the dorsal fin. These fish have many sensory pits around their head, these form part of the lateral line.

Breeding
The female mouthbroods the eggs and they are fertilised while they are in her mouth.

Tank Set-up
Use a typical rocky set-up to allow the fish to claim territories. Provide good filtration.

AULONOCARA NYASSAE
REGAN, 1921

25–26°C
77–79°F
18 cm (7 in)

Family: CICHLIDAE
Common name: AFRICAN PEACOCK
Distribution: Lake Malawi
Size: 18 cm (7 in)
Food: CARNIVOROUS. Live food but accepts flake and frozen food
Temperature range: 25–26°C/77–79°F
pH: 8.0 dH: to 18°

A beautiful Malawi Cichlid, the males are dark blue with a lighter edge to the dorsal fin while females are plain. Although they are predominantly carnivores, in the aquarium they will take frozen and flake food without any trouble.

Breeding
The female mouthbroods the eggs. She lays them on the substrate and immediately picks them up in her mouth. The male displays the dummy eggs on his anal fin in front of the female whilst expelling his milt. She mouths for the dummy eggs and takes in the milt thus fertilising the eggs in her mouth.

Tank Set-up
Use a typical Malawi set up with hard alkaline water and plenty of rockwork to give the fish hiding places and territories. Good filtration is required.

CHALINOCHROMIS BRICHARDI
POLL, 1974

25–27°C
77–80°F
15 cm (6 in)

Family: CICHLIDAE
Common name: NONE
Distribution: Lake Tanganyika
Size: 15 cm (6in)
Food: CARNIVOROUS. Live food for preference, will take flake
Temperature range: 25–27°C/77–80°F
pH: 7.0–9.0 dH: to 15°

This fish lives off the rocky shores of Lake Tanganyika about 2–10 m (6–30 ft) down. A territorial but peaceful Cichlid, the males and females form strongly bonded pairs. Males have a well defined black spot in the dorsal fin but in females this spot is less clear.

Breeding
They spawn on the walls or ceiling of caves or in a crevice, the eggs hatching in about three days. Fry will take newly hatched brine shrimp. The fry remain in the parents' territory.

Tank Set-up
Provide plenty of caves and crevices in amongst rocks, robust plants and good filtration.

BIOTODOMA CUPIDO
(HECKEL, 1840)

23–25°C
73–77°F
13 cm (5 in)

Family: CICHLIDAE
Common name: NONE
Distribution: Western Guyana
Size: 12.5 cm (5 in)
Food: CARNIVOROUS. Small live food
Temperature range: 23–25°C/73–77°F
pH: 7.0 dH: to 10°

A pugnacious and territorial fish that may be kept with larger fish that are able to defend themselves. Telling the sexes can be difficult, however the dorsal and anal fins of males are usually pointed.

Breeding
They form pairs and spawn in a hollow dug by the male. The eggs stick to the ground, clumped together, the female guards the eggs. Both parents guard the fry. Feed fry on the very finest live foods.

Tank Set-up
Use rocks to build up hollows, caves and crevices with a few robust plants in front and to the sides. Good filtration is required.

CHROMIDOTILAPIA GUNTHERI
(SAUVAGE, 1882)

Family: CICHLIDAE
Common name: GUENTHER'S CICHLID
Distribution: West Africa
Size: 18 cm (7 in)
Food: OMNIVOROUS. Live, flake, frozen food
Temperature range: 23–25°C/73–77°F
pH: 7.0 dH: to 12°

A fish of coastal rivers and lagoons, it is aggressive towards its own kind. When several are kept together a hierarchy develops. Males are larger than the more colourful females. They form permanent pairs.

Breeding
Eggs are laid on the substrate and immediately taken into the male's mouth. When the fry are free-

23–25°C 73–77°F		18 cm (7 in)

swimming both parents share brood-care, and even the female will take fry into her mouth if danger threatens.

Tank Set-up
Provide a species aquarium with plenty of hiding places created out of rocks, wood, pots etc; sand substrate; and good filtration.

CICHLA OCELLARIS
BLOCH & SCHNEIDER, 1801

Family: CICHLIDAE
Common name: PEACOCK CICHLID, PEACOCK BASS
Distribution: Northern South America
Size: Males 60 cm (24 in)
Food: CARNIVOROUS. Live food of all kinds, especially fish, will take dead food
Temperature range: 24–28°C/75–82°F
pH: 6.5–7.5 dH: to 15°

A predator that is best kept in a species aquarium. Undemanding as far as water quality is concerned provided extremes are avoided. Older males develop a nuchal hump. In their native lands they are an important food fish and are raised on fish farms.

Breeding
It is unlikely in the aquarium. In the wild they breed in shallow water, laying their eggs on stones. Parental care is practised.

24–28°C 75–82°F		60 cm (24 in)

Tank Set-up
Use a large aquarium with plants, rocks and wood. Leave some open areas for swimming and provide good filtration.

CICHLASOMA BIMACULATUM
(LINNAEUS, 1758)

Family: CICHLIDAE
Common name: TWIN-SPOT CICHLID, TWO-SPOT CICHLID
Distribution: Northern South America
Size: 20 cm (8 in)
Food: OMNIVOROUS. Live, flake, frozen food
Temperature range: 22–26°C/72–79°F
pH: 6.5–7.5 dH: to 12°

This is an undemanding fish that is reasonably peaceful. Keep as pairs, males become slightly larger, in with other similarly-sized and mannered species. Easy to feed, they accept most commercially available foods.

Breeding
The pair spawn on a pre-cleaned flat rock and both parents take care of the eggs and fry. The youngsters grow rapidly.

Tank Set-up
The Cichlid may be kept in a planted aquarium provided the plants are robust. Use rocks and wood arranged to form hiding places. Provide good filtration.

22–26°C 72–79°F		20 cm (8 in)

CICHLASOMA PORTALEGRENSIS
(HENSEL, 1870)

Family: CICHLIDAE	
Common name: BROWN ACARA, PORT ACARA	
Distribution: Brazil, Bolivia, Paraguay	
Size: 15 cm (6 in)	
Food: OMNIVOROUS. Live, flake, frozen food	
Temperature range: 19–24°C / 66–75°F	
pH: 6.0–7.0 dH: to 10°	

A hardy fish well suited to beginners, they are easy to keep, feed and breed. It is not easy to tell the sexes unless the fish are ready to breed, males tend to be greenish in colour while the female is brownish.

Breeding
Slightly acid, soft to medium hard water in warmish water – 25–26°C / 77–79°F. The eggs are laid on a

19–24°C 66–75°F	15 cm (6 in)

flat surface and parental care is practised by both parents. Easy to rear fry on normal fry foods.

Tank Set-up
Use rocks and wood to provide hiding places and spawning sites; robust plants; and gravel substrate.

CLEITHRACARA MARONII
(STEINDACHNER, 1882)

Family: CICHLIDAE	
Common name: KEYHOLE CICHLID	
Distribution: Guyana	
Size: 15 cm (6 in)	
Food: OMNIVOROUS. Live, flake, frozen food	
Temperature range: 22–25°C / 72–77°F	
pH: 6.0–8.0 dH: to 20°	

Commercially bred, they are now becoming so inbred that their size has diminished. It is rare to see a specimen of 14–15 cm (5½–6 in) unless it is a wild fish. It is difficult to determine the sexes, as although males have a longer anal fin it is often hard to tell unless the fish are near spawning and you can see a difference in the genital papillae. A peaceful fish, it is ideal for a larger community aquarium.

Breeding
Eggs are laid on a flat surface and both parents tend the eggs and young.

Tank Set-up
A general community aquarium is adequate.

22–25°C 72–77°F	15 cm (6 in)

COPADICHROMIS BOADZULU
(ILES, 1960)

Family: CICHLIDAE	
Common name: NONE	
Distribution: Lake Malawi	
Size: 15 cm (6 in)	
Food: OMNIVOROUS. Live, frozen, flake	
Temperature range: 24–26°C / 75–79°F	
pH: 8.0–8.5 dH: to 15°	

These active fish require plenty of open water for swimming. They are quite peaceful and may be combined with other Malawi Cichlids. Males are far

more colourful and their dorsal and anal fins are elongated.

Breeding
These fish will breed in a community Malawi aquarium. Keep two females with the male. The female mouthbroods the eggs. When released the young are quite large and easy to raise.

Tank Set-up
Use a typical rocky Malawi set up.

24–26°C 75–79°F	15 cm (6 in)

COPADICHROMIS CHRYSONOTA
(BOULENGER, 1908)

Family:	CICHLIDAE
Common name:	NONE
Distribution:	Lake Malawi
Size:	15 cm (6 in)
Food:	OMNIVOROUS. Live, frozen, flake
Temperature range:	23–26°C / 73–79°F
pH: 8.0–8.5 dH: 10–15°	

A very peaceful fish, so much so that several males can be kept together with the females and each one stakes out a small territory. Their one bad habit is attacking plants but the fish can be kept just as well without plants. Males are larger and more brightly coloured than females and have egg spots on the anal fin.

23–26°C
73–79°F

15 cm (6 in)

Breeding
Much the same as all other *Copadichromis* species. The male digs pits in the substrate and invites females to spawn with him. Females mouthbrood the eggs.

Tank Set-up
A typical rocky, Malawi set-up with some open areas for the fish to breed in and good filtration is required.

COPORA NICARAGUENSIS
(GUNTHER, 1864)

Family:	CICHLIDAE
Common name:	NICARAGUA CICHLID
Distribution:	Nicaragua, Costa Rica
Size:	To 25 cm (10 in)
Food:	OMNIVOROUS. Live, flake, frozen food
Temperature range:	23–26°C / 73–79°F
pH: 7.0–8.0 dH: to 15°	

In the main peaceful, if territorial, *C. nicaraguensis* is a very beautiful fish that can be kept with other species. Males are generally larger than females and may have a slight cephalic hump. Their one drawback is that they eat some plants.

Breeding
These fish lay non-adhesive eggs which remain on the floor in a dark corner of a cave until they hatch. The female takes

23–26°C
73–79°F
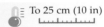
To 25 cm (10 in)

care of the eggs and newly hatched fry, the male defends the territory. Feed fry newly hatched brine shrimp.

Tank Set-up
Use an aquarium with plenty of caves and hiding places and some robust plants such as Java Fern. Give good filtration.

CRENICICHLA JOHANNA
HECKEL, 1840

Family:	CICHLIDAE
Common name:	GRAY PIKE CICHLID, RED-FINNED PIKE CICHLID
Distribution:	Brazil and northern South America
Size:	35 cm (14 in) plus
Food:	CARNIVOROUS. Live and dead food
Temperature range:	23–26°C / 73–79°F
pH: 6.5–7.5 dH: to 15°	

Although it is a predator, it may be kept with large fishes that have deep bodies, that is those that do not look like a possible meal. Newly imported specimens may need to be fed live food to settle them in but should then adapt to meaty food and even tablets and flakes.

23–26°C
73–79°F
35 cm (14 in)

Breeding
Little is known – they spawn in caves.

Tank Set-up
A large aquarium with rocky overhangs and caves is best. Plants may be added.

Water conditions are not important so long as extremes of hardness and alkalinity / acidity are avoided but they do need reasonable filtration.

CRENICICHLA LEPIDOTA
HECKEL, 1840

23–27°C
73–80°F

 To 45 cm (18 in)

Family: CICHLIDAE

Common name: TWO-SPOT PIKE CICHLID, COMB PIKE CICHLID

Distribution: Brazil, Bolivia

Size: To 45 cm (18 in)

Food: CARNIVOROUS. Live and dead food

Temperature range: 23–27°C / 73–80°F

pH: 6.5–7.5 dH: to 12°

This fish is a predator that has the same manners as *C. johanna*. Males are generally larger than females, with larger fins, the dorsal slightly more extended, and are darker in colour. To confuse things even more, there are several different colour forms of this fish.

Breeding
They spawn on the roof of caves and the female protects the eggs and fry while the male guards the territory.

Tank Set-up
As for *C. johanna*.

CRENICICHLA STRIGATA
(GUENTHER, 1862)

24–27°C
75–80°F

40 cm (16 in)

Family: CICHLIDAE

Common name: NONE

Distribution: Guyana, northern Brazil, Amazon river

Size: 40 cm (16 in) plus

Food: CARNIVOROUS. Meaty food, live and dead food

Temperature range: 24–27°C / 75–80°F

pH: 7.0 dH: to 20°

As it is impossible to tell male from female with very young fish, raise them as a shoal in a large aquarium. As they reach some 30 cm (12 in) or so in length, it is possible to tell the sexes on colour: females have a reddish-mauve belly.

Breeding
Reports of wild spawns state that they breed in caves, and eggs are suspended from the roof by adhesive threads. Both parents guard the eggs and fry.

Tank Set-up
Provide a large aquarium with plenty of caves and some large robust plants; subdued lighting; and good filtration.

CYNOTILAPIA AFRA
(GUNTHER, 1893)

23–26°C
73–79°F

12 cm (4½ in)

Family: CICHLIDAE

Common name: DOGTOOTH CICHLID

Distribution: Lake Malawi

Size: 12 cm (4½ in)

Food: CARNIVOROUS. Small live food

Temperature range: 23–26°C / 73–79°F

pH: 8.0–8.5 dH: to 15°

In the wild, these fish feed in open water on planktonic crustaceans. In captivity they need plenty of *Daphnia*, brine shrimp, etc in their diet. Males are a bright blue with darker vertical stripes and egg spots on the anal fin. Females are a plain blue grey. Keep several females with each male.

Breeding
They are mouthbrooders. The female takes care of the eggs and fry on her own.

Tank Set-up
Use a typical rocky Malawi aquarium with plenty of hiding places. Hardy plants, such as Java Fern, can be grown. Provide good filtration.

CYPHOTILAPIA FRONTOSA
(BOULENGER, 1906)

24–26°C
75–79°F

35 cm (14 in)

Family: CICHLIDAE

Common name: FRONTOSA CICHLID

Distribution: Lake Tanganyika

Size: 35 cm (14 in)

Food: CARNIVOROUS. Live food, takes flake and frozen food

Temperature range: 24–26°C / 75–79°F

pH: 8.0–9.0 dH: to 20°

Tolerant of others, if territorial at times. Difficult to tell the sexes except by observing their behaviour in the aquarium. Both sexes have a nuchal hump. In Africa they inhabit off-shore sloping lake bottoms, and as a food fish are considered a delicacy.

Breeding
Eggs are laid in a cave and immediately the female takes them into her mouth. Care of the eggs and fry may last for six weeks or so.

Tank Set-up
Provide plenty of stable rock work so that the fish have sufficient territories. Plants are not required but a sand substrate and good filtration are.

Family: CICHLIDAE	
Common name: NONE	
Distribution: Lake Tanganyika	
Size: 14 cm (5½ in)	
Food: OMNIVOROUS. Live, flake, frozen food	
Temperature range: 23–25°C / 73–77°F	
pH: 8.0–9.0 dH: to 20°	

A shoaling fish, it requires a lot of swimming space in the upper levels of the aquarium. It may be kept with other Cichlids as it is quite peaceful. The sexes are easily distinguished by colour: males are brownish with yellow tips to the pectoral fins, and have blue dorsal and anal fins; females are grey with some silver on the side of their heads.

Breeding
Spawning takes place near the surface. As an egg is expelled, the female turns and catches it in her mouth as it falls through the water. She may produce 50 eggs which hatch in three weeks. When released, the fry remain near the surface and both parents ignore them.

Tank Set-up
Provide a large aquarium with open water, the lower regions of which may be banked with rocks for other Cichlids. Keep the aquarium well covered as these fish jump. Good filtration is required.

CYPRICHROMIS LEPTOSOMA
(BOULENGER, 1898)

23–25°C 73–77°F   14 cm (5½ in)

CYPRICHROMIS NIGRIPINNIS
(BOULENGER, 1901)

23–25°C 73–77°F   10 cm (4 in)

Family: CICHLIDAE	
Common name: BLACK-FIN CICHLID	
Distribution: Lake Tanganyika	
Size: 10 cm (4 in)	
Food: CARNIVOROUS. Daphnia, etc, may take flake	
Temperature range: 23–25°C / 73–77°F	
pH: 7.5–8.5 dH: to 15°	

A pelagic fish, in the wild odd individuals are found in schools of C. microlepdotus. The only time the fish go down to the substrate is for breeding. The males are beautiful with an overall bronze coloration and fine electric-blue lines along the body, the edge of the dorsal and top and bottom edges of the caudal fin are edged in electric-blue. The anal fin is black. Females lack the fine blue lines on the body and their dorsal is edged in dark blue. The anal fin is yellow.

Breeding
Little is known. Eggs are laid on the substrate and taken up into the female's mouth.

Tank Set-up
As for C. microlepidotus.

DICROSSUS FILAMENTOSA
LADIGES, 1958

23–25°C 73–77°F   9 cm (3½ in)

Family: CICHLIDAE	
Common name: CHECKERBOARD CICHLID	
Distribution: Negro River, Orinoco basin (South America)	
Size: Males 9 cm (3½ in); females 6 cm (2½ in)	
Food: CARNIVOROUS. Predominantly small live food, occasionally flake	
Temperature range: 23–25°C / 73–77°F	
pH: 5.5–6.0 dH: to 5°	

A beautiful little Cichlid, it may be kept with some of the South American Characins in a planted aquarium. They claim territories and several females should be kept for each male. Great care is needed to maintain water quality otherwise the fish will suffer. Males have much larger and more colourful finnage. In females the fins are clear.

Breeding
Eggs are laid on plants or a flat rock and the female tends them and the fry. If the water is not soft enough, the eggs may grow fungus.

Tank Set-up
A well-planted, mature aquarium with a very efficient filtration system and regular water changes is required.

DIMIDIOCHROMIS COMPRESSICEPS
(BOULENGER, 1908)

Family: CICHLIDAE	
Common name: MALAWI EYE-BITER	
Distribution: Lake Malawi	
Size: To 25 cm (10 in)	
Food: CARNIVOROUS. Live, frozen food	
Temperature range: 22–27°C / 72–80°F	
pH: 8.0–8.5 dH: 10–15°	

This fish is predatory and is the only known predator to eat its prey tail first. Locals have witnessed this fish biting the eyes out of other fishes. Mature males are green-blue and have egg spots on the anal fin, females have a golden head.

22–27°C
72–80°F   To 25 cm (10 in)

Breeding
In water values as given above, they are mouthbrooders with the female taking charge of the brood.

Tank Set-up
A rocky set-up with an open sandy area and thickets of tall plants such as *Vallisneria*, allows the fish plenty of room and also many hiding places. Provide good filtration.

ERETOMODUS CYANOSTICTUS
BOULENGER, 1898

24–26°C
75–79°F   8 cm (3 in)

Family: CICHLIDAE	
Common name: STRIPED GOBY CICHLID	
Distribution: Lake Tanganyika	
Size: 8 cm (3 in)	
Food: CARNIVOROUS. Mostly live food	
Temperature range: 24–26°C / 75–79°F	
pH: 8.5–9.0 dH: 12–15°	

A fish of rocky shallows it is not easy to keep in captivity, as it places heavy demands on water quality. It is not easy to sex them, although the male's ventral fins may be longer. They form pairs and are best left to pair themselves by growing several individuals up together. Once paired they remain together.

Breeding
A flat surface is cleaned and the female lays up to 25 eggs on it. These are fertilised by the male before she takes them into her mouth for incubation. Both parents care for the fry.

Tank Set-up
Use plenty of rocks to give as many hiding places as possible. Do not use wood as this may acidify the water. Provide dense thickets of plants. Of greatest importance is the filtration system, it must be as efficient as possible and coupled with regular partial water changes of about a third every 7–10 days so that good water conditions are maintained.

ETROPLUS MACULATUS
BLOCH, 1795

Family: CICHLIDAE	
Common name: ORANGE CHROMIDE	
Distribution: Sri Lanka and western India	
Size: 8 cm (3 in)	
Food: OMNIVOROUS. Live, flake, frozen, green food	
Temperature range: 21–25°C / 70–77°F	
pH: 7.0–8.0 dH: to 15°	

These attractively coloured fish from fresh and brackish waters like some marine salt added to the water. It is hard to tell which is male and which is female unless you have seen them spawn. Females are usually drabber than males and males have a red edge to their fins. However, if the water conditions are not to their liking they may both lose colour.

Breeding
The 'stemmed' eggs are laid on a flat surface such as a piece of slate. Both parents guard the fry, herding them into pits.

Tank Set-up
A well-planned mature aquarium with a filtration system that can maintain good quality water is best. Use rocks to form hiding places.

21–25°C
70–77°F   8 cm (3 in)

ETROPLUS SURATENSIS
(BLOCH, 1790)

| 23–26°C | | To 46 cm (18 in) |
| 73–79°F | | |

| Family: CICHLIDAE |
| Common name: GREEN CHROMIDE, BANDED CHROMIDE |
| Distribution: India and Sri Lanka |
| Size: To 46 cm (18 in) |
| Food: OMNIVOROUS. Live, flake, frozen, green food |
| Temperature range: 23–26°C/73–79°F |
| pH: 8.0–8.5 dH: 20–25° |

It is a fish best kept in brackish water, but may be kept in freshwater provided they are acclimatised slowly. There is no visible difference between the sexes. They are aggressive, especially among themselves or when spawning. They eat soft plants.

Breeding
They lay their eggs on a flat surface either in the open or in a sheltered place. Both parents care for the eggs and fry.

Tank Set-up
Provide a brackish water aquarium with rocks to give shelter. Robust, hardy, salt tolerant plants may be used. Provide good filtration to maintain high quality water conditions.

| Family: CICHLIDAE |
| Common name: PEARL CICHLID |
| Distribution: Eastern Brazil |
| Size: 28 cm (11 in), usually smaller |
| Food: OMNIVOROUS. Live, flake, frozen food |
| Temperature range: 20–23°C/68–73°F |
| pH: 6.5–7.0 dH: to 10° |

Although territorial, it is fairly tolerant of other fishes. Males and females are difficult to tell apart unless they are breeding when you can see that the male's genital papilla is pointed and the female's rounded. These fish are best left to pair themselves as, if the pair is incompatible, they may keep eating the eggs.

Breeding
They choose a dark, secluded area in the aquarium and clean the spawning site. Some 700 eggs may be laid. The female tends the eggs and fry while the male protects his territory.

Tank Set-up
Use plants, wood and rocks to provide shelter and ensure there are some flat rocks which can be used as spawning sites. Provide efficient filtration.

GEOPHAGUS BRASILIENSIS
(QUOY & GAIMARD, 1824)

| 20–23°C | | 28 cm (11 in) |
| 68–73°F | | |

GEOPHAGUS SURINAMENSIS
(BLOCH, 1791)

| 22–25°C | | 30 cm (12 in) |
| 72–77°F | | |

| Family: CICHLIDAE |
| Common name: NONE |
| Distribution: Guyana southwards to the Amazon |
| Size: 30 cm (12 in) |
| Food: OMNIVOROUS. Live, frozen, flake food |
| Temperature range: 22–25°C/72–77°F |
| pH: 6.5–7.0 dH: to 10° |

Aggressive fish, when not squabbling with others, they spend their time digging in the substrate. The sexes are well nigh impossible to differentiate.

Breeding
The eggs are laid on a pre-cleaned rock but are not taken into the mouths of both parents until just prior to hatching or just after hatching.

Tank Set-up
Have a large aquarium with some rocks and wood to form caves. Use large, robust plants which can be potted and pebbles placed around the top of the pot to deter digging. A fine gravel or sand substrate is preferred so the fish do not damage their mouths when digging. Place a few flat stones on the substrate.

GUIANACARA GEAYI
(PELLEGRIN, 1902)

22–25°C	15 cm (6 in)
72–77°F	

Family: CICHLIDAE

Common name: NONE

Distribution: Guyana and northern Brazil

Size: Male 15 cm (6 in); female 13 cm (5 in)

Food: OMNIVOROUS. Live, frozen, flake

Temperature range: 22–25°C / 72–77°F

pH: 6.5–7.0 dH: to 12°

This is a territorial but generally peaceful fish, only causing conflict during breeding. Males are larger and have a more sharply angled forehead. The genital papilla is pointed and slopes to the back on males and is blunt and points forwards on females.

Breeding
The fish spawn in caves with the female guarding the eggs while the male defends the territory. Once hatched the fry is protected by both parents.

Tank Set-up
Best is a community aquarium with caves and hiding places, and a fine gravel substrate as they like to dig.

Family: CICHLIDAE

Common name: NONE

Distribution: Paraguay and Parana Rivers (South America)

Size: 20 cm (8 in)

Food: OMNIVOROUS

Temperature range: 22–27°C / 72–80°F

pH: 6.5–7.5 dH: to 15°

A quiet, peaceful, if territorial Cichlid. Although they dig, they do not usually damage plants. Mature males are easily recognisable, the dorsal and anal fins being much longer than those of the female, and they have a cranial hump.

Breeding
The female takes the eggs into her mouth some 30 hours after they are laid on a rock. She carries out the care of the fry.

Tank Set-up
A planted community aquarium with similar sized, peaceful fishes is adequate. Provide fine gravel or sand

GYMNOGEOPHAGUS BALZANII
(PERUGIA, 1891)

for the substrate and caves and hiding places among plants with rocks for spawning on. Good filtration is needed.

22–27°C	20 cm (8 in)
72–80°F	

GYMNOGEOPHAGUS GYMNOGENYS
(HENSEL, 1870)

Family: CICHLIDAE

Common name: SQUAREHEADED GEOPHAGUS

Distribution: Southern Brazil, Uruguay, Argentina

Size: 25 cm (10 in)

Food: OMNIVOROUS. Live, flake, frozen food

Temperature range: 21–24°C / 70–75°F

pH: 6.5–7.0 dH: to 10°

Typical Geophagines, they love to dig. Males are much larger than females. Can be territorial but do no real harm to like-sized fishes.

Breeding
Not known.

Tank Set-up
As for *Satanoperca daemon*.

21–24°C	25 cm (10 in)
70–75°F	

HEMICHROMIS BIMACULATUS
GILL, 1862

21–23°C
70–73°F

To 15 cm (6 in)

Family: CICHLIDAE	
Common name: JEWEL CICHLID	
Distribution: Central Liberia to southern Guinea	
Size: To 15 cm (6 in)	
Food: OMNIVOROUS. Live, frozen, flake	
Temperature range: 21–23°C / 70–73°F	
pH: 7.0 dH: to 12°	

These fish from forested regions are noted for their aggression when breeding. It is difficult to tell the sexes apart except at this time. Allow the fish to pair themselves because if they are not a compatible pair, the ensuing fighting may end in the death of one of the pair.

Breeding
These fish spawn on rocks and, when the fry hatch, they are moved to pits dug in the substrate in secluded areas of the aquarium. They are good parents. As many as 500 eggs may be produced.

Tank Set-up
Use a well-planted aquarium to give the fish shelter and give secluded areas for raising a family. Wood and rocks may also be used. Provide efficient filtration.

HEMICHROMIS LIFALILI
LOISELLE, 1979

22–24°C
72–75°F

10 cm (4 in)

Family: CICHLIDAE	
Common name: LIFALILI CICHLID	
Distribution: Zaire basin	
Size: 10 cm (4 in)	
Food: OMNIVOROUS. Live, frozen, flake	
Temperature range: 22–24°C / 72–75°F	
pH: 7.0 dH: to 12°	

This species is very similar to the Jewel Cichlid in manner. It differs from the Jewel externally, in coloration and the length of the snout, and internally by the shape of the lower pharyngeal bone.

Breeding
They are excellent parents, tending both the eggs, which are laid on rocks, and the fry.

Tank Set-up
Use a well-planted aquarium as for the Jewel Cichlid but pay more attention to the water quality and ensure that the water is well oxygenated.

HERICHTHYS CYANOGUTTATUM
(BAIRD & GIRARD, 1854)

20–24°C
68–75°F

To 30 cm (12 in)

Family: CICHLIDAE	
Common name: TEXAS CICHLID, RIO GRANDE PERCH	
Distribution: Texas (USA) and north-eastern Mexico	
Size: to 30 cm (12 in)	
Food: OMNIVOROUS. Live, flake, frozen food	
Temperature range: 20–24°C / 68–75°F	
pH: 7.0–6.5 dH: to 12°	

These territorial fish are quarrelsome amongst themselves and with others. It is difficult to tell the sexes but males are usually larger and more intensely coloured – this is most obvious when a pair have started courtship.

Breeding
A rock is picked clean prior to spawning and the eggs are laid on it. Although the parents guard the eggs and fry, they may eat them.

Tank Set-up
Provide a large aquarium with sandy or fine gravel substrate and rocks and plants arranged so the fish can have territories. Provide very good filtration to give a supply of well-oxygenated water and regular partial water changes every week.

HEROS SEVERUS
HECKEL, 1840

23–25°C
73–77°F

20 cm (8 in)

Family: CICHLIDAE	
Common name: SEVERUM, BANDED CICHLID	
Distribution: Northern and central South America	
Size: 20 cm (8 in)	
Food: CARNIVOROUS. Mostly live food, will take flake and frozen food	
Temperature range: 23–25°C / 73–77°F	
pH: 6.0–6.5 dH: to 7°	

A very gentle, peaceful Cichlid from weedy rivers that only becomes a little aggressive when spawning. They are best left to pick their own mates. Males have pointed fins and fine spots and markings on the head, females have a dark patch on the dorsal.

Breeding
The pair clean off a rock, and up to 1,000 eggs may be laid thereon. Both parents guard the eggs and fry. Feed young newly hatched brine shrimp.

Tank Set-up
Choose a large aquarium with flat rocks and large plants such as Amazon Sword plants. Regular water changes and very good filtration are needed to maintain water quality.

Family: CICHLIDAE	
Common name: NONE	
Distribution: Panama to Nicaragua	
Size: To 13 cm (5 in)	
Food: OMNIVOROUS. Live, flake, frozen, green food	
Temperature range: 22–25°C / 72–77°F	
pH: 7.0 dH: to 10°	

These fish are like chameleons, they change colour according to their mood. It is difficult to tell the sexes even though the male's fins tend to be pointed and longer. Only when about to spawn can you be certain because the short ovipositor of the female is visible.

Breeding

They produce many eggs, laying them on a clean rock. The female fans them with her fins to keep a current passing over them. The fry are herded to pits.

Tank Set-up

Provide a reasonable-sized aquarium, with fine gravel on the bottom, furnished with rocks, wood and some plants. Gentle filtration is necessary.

22–25°C
72–77°F
To 13 cm (5 in)

HEROTILAPIA MULTISPINOSA
(GUENTHER, 1866)

HOPLARCHUS PSITTACUS
(HECKEL, 1840)

24–27°C
75–80°F
35 cm (14 in)

Family: CICHLIDAE	
Common name: PARROT CICHLID	
Distribution: Brazil	
Size: 35 cm (14 in)	
Food: OMNIVOROUS. Live, frozen, flake, tablet food	
Temperature range: 24–27°C / 75–80°F	
pH: 5.5–6.0 dH: to 8°	

Juveniles of this species are relatively drab creatures with large eyes, but adult males especially are spectacular with a red belly and olive green and lighter green markings on their upper body and flanks. They are territorial, each fish needing its own area to live in and, as long as they have enough space, they can be kept with other fishes such as large Catfish. In males the genital papilla is pointed, in females it is blunt.

Breeding

LIttle is known – the broods are large and they like to spawn in the shelter of an overhang. Parental care is practised.

Tank Set-up

Decorate a very large aquarium with adequate large roots and rocks to give plenty of hiding places. Some plants may also be used. Give efficient filtration.

JULIDOCHROMIS DICKFELDI
STAECK, 1975

22–25°C
72–77°F
60 cm (24 in)

Family: CICHLIDAE	
Common name: BROWN JULIE	
Distribution: Lake Tanganyika, on the southwest shore	
Size: 60 cm (24 in)	
Food: OMNIVOROUS. Live, frozen, flake	
Temperature range: 22–25°C / 72–77°F	
pH: 8.0–9.0 dH: to 14°	

Living in transitional rocky areas of the lake shore it is very picky towards its own kind, but provided there is sufficient hiding places and space for males to stake territories there is no real damage done. Sexing is difficult, females may be larger.

Breeding

With water values as above but a few degrees warmer females will lay up to 300 eggs on the roof of a cave, which hatch in a little under three days at 27°C / 80°F. The parents tend the fry.

Tank Set-up

Use rocks built up to imitate their natural environment: this structure can reach to the surface. Use some plants such as *Vallisneria* and a sand substrate. Provide good filtration.

JULIDOCHROMIS MARLIERI
POLL, 1956

22–25°C
72–77°F

To 15 cm (6 in)

Family: CICHLIDAE	
Common name: NONE	
Distribution: Lake Tanganyika	
Size: To 15 cm (6 in)	
Food: OMNIVOROUS. Live, flake, frozen food	
Temperature range: 22–25°C / 72–77°F	
pH: 7.5–9.0 dH: to 15°	

From the same habitat as Brown Julie they are peaceable amongst themselves but only if they can each have their own territory. Any movement of rocks when cleaning the aquarium can result in squabbles breaking out. They are sexable when ready to breed by the difference in the genital papillae.

Breeding
They spawn in caves, producing, on average about 120 eggs. Both parents guard the fry.

Tank Set-up
As for *J. dickfeld*i.

Family: CICHLIDAE	
Common name: NONE	
Distribution: Lake Tanganyika	
Size: to 30 cm (12 in)	
Food: OMNIVOROUS. Live, frozen, flake	
Temperature range: 22–25°C / 72–77°F	
pH: 8.0–9.0 dH: to 15°	

Typical *Julidochromis*, intolerant of its own kind and territorial, this species also like to dig. When ready to spawn the genital papillae are the obvious sex distinctions.

Breeding
This is a typical cave spawner. The female guards the eggs, the male the territory, both share care of the fry. Females have sometimes been observed defending the territory.

Tank Set-up
Provide plenty of caves in rockwork that can reach the surface, a few robust plants, a fine substrate and good filtration.

JULIDOCHROMIS REGANI
POLL, 1942

22–25°C
72–77°F

To 30 cm (12 in)

Family: CICHLIDAE	
Common name: BLACK AND WHITE JULIE	
Distribution: Lake Tanganyika	
Size: 7 cm (3 in)	
Food: OMNIVOROUS. Live, flake, frozen food	
Temperature range: 22–25°C / 72–77°F	
pH: 8.0–9.0 dH: to 15°	

The smallest of the genus, it looks, at first glance, like *J. marlieri*, but it has two rows of spots instead of three. In temperament it is much like *J. marlieri*.

Breeding
Not very fecund, it may produce broods of only 30 eggs. It is a typical cave spawner.

Tank Set-up
As for *J. dickfeldi*.

22–25°C
72–77°F

7 cm (3 in)

JULIDOCHROMIS TRANSCRIPTUS
MATTHES, 1959

LABEOCHROMIS FUELLEBORNI

AHL, 1927

Family: CICHLIDAE

Common name: FUELLEBORN'S CICHLID

Distribution: Lake Malawi

Size: 15 cm (6 in)

Food: OMNIVOROUS. Live, flake, frozen food, algae

Temperature range: 22–25°C / 72–77°F

pH: 7.5–8.5 dH: to 15°

Pugnacious and territorial, several females should be kept with each male but ensure there are plenty of caves for them to hide in. They only pair off when spawning. There are several colour morphs of females. They like to graze over algae.

Breeding

The female spawns on a cleaned rock and immediately takes the eggs into her mouth, she then mouths the eggs spots

22–25°C
72–77°F 15 cm (6 in)

of the male's anal fin and, at the same time, he releases his milt which she takes into her mouth to fertilise the eggs.

Tank Set-up

Plant the aquarium with robust plants. Create plenty of caves but make sure you include some flattish rocks for the fish to spawn on. Provide good lighting to give some algae growth, and good filtration.

LABEOTROPHEUS TREWAVASAE

FRYER, 1956

Family: CICHLIDAE

Common name: TREWAVAS' CICHLID

Distribution: Lake Malawi

Size: 12 cm (4½ in)

Food: OMNIVOROUS. Live, frozen, flake food, algae

Temperature range: 21–24°C / 70–75°F

pH: 7.0–8.0 dH: to 15°

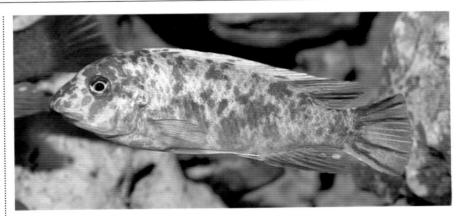

It is a very belligerent and territorial fish. Keep several females with each male. Males have conspicuous egg spots on their anal fins which may be very faintly visible on females or completely lacking. There are several colour variations including white, depending on which locality the fish originate from.

Breeding

Warmer temperatures are required for spawning. They breed in the same manner as *L. fuelleborni*, but the male should be removed after spawning or sufficient cover ensured for the female.

21–24°C
70–75°F 12 cm (4½ in)

Tank Set-up

Provide hardy plants such as Java Fern and plenty of rockwork. Algae growth is beneficial. Good filtration is needed.

LAETACARA CURVICEPS

(AHL, 1924)

Family: CICHLIDAE

Common name: FLAG CICHLID

Distribution: Amazon basin

Size: 9 cm (3½ in)

Food: OMNIVOROUS. Live, frozen, flake

Temperature range: 22–26°C / 72–79°F

pH: 6.0–7.0 dH: to 18°

Their natural habitat is a quiet stream but a pair may be kept in a community aquarium where they will do no harm unless they wish to breed. Males are larger and have extended dorsal and anal fins. The colouring of these fish is very variable.

Breeding

The fish will spawn in soft to medium-hard water, laying their eggs on a flat surface such as a stone or piece of slate. Both parents care for the fry whose first foods are newly hatched brine.

Tank Set-up

Provide a planted community aquarium with plenty of hiding places. Use wood and rocks for decor and sand or fine gravel for the substrate. The aquarium needs gentle filtration and regular water changes.

22–26°C
72–79°F 9 cm (3½ in)

MELANOCHROMIS AURATUS
(BOULENGER, 1897)

Family:	CICHLIDAE
Common name:	MALAWI GOLDEN CICHLID, AURATUS
Distribution:	Lake Malawi
Size:	Males 11 cm (4½ in); females 9 cm (3½ in)
Food:	OMNIVOROUS. Live, flake, frozen food, algae
Temperature range:	22–26°C / 72–79°F
pH:	7.0–8.5 dH: to 15°

Belligerent and territorial, one male and four or five females should be kept together in an aquarium where there are plenty of hiding places. Males and females differ in colour, the male has more black and has eggs spots on his ventral while the female is more yellow.

Breeding
A typical mouthbrooder, the female takes up the eggs which are fertilised orally. Her care lasts for about a week after the fry hatch.

Tank Set-up
Provide a standard Malawi aquarium with plenty of rockwork and good filtration.

22–26°C
72–79°F

11 cm (4½ in)

MESONAUTA FESTIVA
(HECKEL, 1840)

23–25°C
73–77°F

15 cm (6 in)

Family:	CICHLIDAE
Common name:	FESTIVUM
Distribution:	Guyana, the Amazon basin
Size:	15 cm (6 in)
Food:	OMNIVOROUS. Live, frozen, flake, some green food
Temperature range:	23–25°C / 73–77°F
pH:	6.5–7.5 dH: to 10°

Most of the fish we see today are commercially bred and will tolerate water around neutral. The fish are quiet and easily frightened. They are sensitive to nitrates and any deterioration in water quality. Do not keep with small fishes that may be eaten.

Breeding
Difficult to breed they need soft (5°) acidic (6.0–6.5) water that is warm (up to 28°/82°F). They lay their eggs on a flat surface, such as a leaf or rock, and both parents tend the eggs and fry.

Tank Set-up
A heavily planted aquarium with wood to provide hiding places is preferable. Ensure that some broad-leaved plants such as Amazon Swords are included and also some flat rocks as spawning sites. Very efficient filtration system and regular water changes will maintain water quality.

MICROGEOPHAGUS RAMIREZI
(MYERS & HARRY, 1948)

Family:	CICHLIDAE
Common name:	RAM, BUTTERFLY CICHLID
Distribution:	Colombia, Venezuela
Size:	7 cm (3 in)
Food:	OMNIVOROUS. Live, flake, frozen food
Temperature range:	22–26°C / 72–79°F
pH:	7.0 dH: to 10°

The majority of the Rams offered for sale have been bred commercially. Some strains are so inbred that the size and colour of the fish has deteriorated. It is suitable for the soft water community aquarium. Males have longer rays at the beginning of the dorsal fin. In females these are shorter and she will have a pinkish belly. They are not a long-lived fish, 3 years being considered quite old for a Ram.

Breeding
The eggs are laid on stones or in pits and both parents care for them and the fry. Feed the fry newly hatched brine shrimp.

22–26°C
72–79°F

7 cm (3 in)

Tank Set-up
Provide a well-planted, mature aquarium with some rocks and wood. Leave some open areas for the fish to display. Ensure the water quality is good as they are very sensitive to poor water conditions, chemicals and very fresh water.

NANDOPSIS FESTAE

(BOULENGER, 1899)

Family: CICHLIDAE

Common name: RED TERROR

Distribution: Ecuador

Size: 50 cm (20 in)

Food: CARNIVOROUS. Will take live and dead food

Temperature range: 26–28°C / 79–82°F

pH: 7.0–7.5 dH: to 12°

These fish have all the bad habits associated with Cichlids – they are aggressive, they dig and they are belligerent. On the plus side, they are beautiful, with almost irridescent shades of blue-green, pink and gold. Because of their temperament they are best suited to a species aquarium.

Breeding

These fish are very fecund. The eggs are laid on flat rocks. Part of the spawning ritual involves digging deep pits, and

after the eggs hatch the fry are transferred to these. The female guards the eggs while the male defends the territory. Once fry are free-swimming both parents share the guard duties. Feed fry newly hatched brine shrimp.

| 26–28°C 79–82°F | | 50 cm (20 in) |

Tank Set-up

Provide a large aquarium such as that for *N. managuense*. Good filtration and regular water changes are beneficial.

NANDOPSIS FRIEDRICHSTHALII

(HECKEL, 1840)

| 22–27°C 72–80°F | | To 25 cm (10 in) |

Family: CICHLIDAE

Common name: FRIEDRICHSTHAL'S CICHLID

Distribution: Central America

Size: To 25 cm (10 in)

Food: OMNIVOROUS. Live, frozen, flake

Temperature range: 22–27°C / 72–80°F

pH: 7.0–7.5 dH: to 15°

A more peaceful Central American Cichlid, it may be kept in an aquarium planted with a few large, robust plants provided there is plenty of open water. Males are usually larger and darker in colour. In the wild they feed almost

entirely on fish and other live food but in captivity they will take most foods offered.

Breeding

It spawns on rocks and when the eggs hatch the larvae are transferred to pits.

Tank Set-up

As for *N. managuense* but robust plants can also be included.

NANDOPSIS MANAGUENSE

(GUENTHER, 1866)

Family: CICHLIDAE

Common name: MANAGUA CICHLID

Distribution: Eastern Honduras, Nicaragua, Costa Rica

Size: To 30 cm (12 in), usually less

Food: OMNIVOROUS. Live, flake, frozen, tablet food

Temperature range: 23–25°C / 73–77°F

pH: 7.0–8.5 dH: to 15°

Belligerent fishes both to their own kind and to others, they are difficult to sex. Males are normally larger, more highly coloured and have pointed dorsal and anal fins. In their native land they are an important food fish.

Breeding

They are fecund, producing up to 5,000 yellow eggs. The female carries out most of the brood care.

| 23–25°C 73–77°F | | To 30 cm (12 in) |

Tank Set-up

A large aquarium with swimming space as well as sheltered areas is required. Place any rocks or wood on the base glass as these fish dig, also protect any plants against their excavations. Provide good filtration.

NANDOPSIS OCTOFASCIATUS
(REGAN, 1903)

22–25°C 72–77°F	20 cm (8 in)

Family: CICHLIDAE

Common name: JACK DEMPSEY

Distribution: Guatemala, Yucatan, Honduras

Size: 20 cm (8 in)

Food: OMNIVOROUS. Live, flake, frozen, green food

Temperature range: 22–25°C / 72–77°F

pH: 6.5–7.0 dH: to 12°

Pugnacious and intolerant these fish need a species aquarium. In males the dorsal and anal fins are pointed as is the genital papilla. In females the genital papilla is rounded.

Breeding
Easy to breed they pair readily and will produce up to 800 eggs which are laid on rocks. The pair share parental duties of guarding the fry which are kept in pits.

Tank Set-up
Provide plenty of caves and hollows to hide in – seat wood and rocks on the base glass for safety. As they eat plants, use either Java Fern attached to the wood or artificial plants. They need good filtration.

NANDOPSIS SALVINI
(GUENTHER, 1862)

Family: CICHLIDAE

Common name: NONE

Distribution: Southern Mexico, Guatemala, Honduras

Size: 15 cm (6 in)

Food: OMNIVOROUS

Temperature range: 22–26°C / 72–79°F

pH: 7.0 dH: to 10°

Although aggressive, it may be kept with other similar sized fishes. Its saving graces are that it is very attractively coloured, it does not dig and neither does it damage plants. Males are larger and more intensely coloured than females which have a dark patch in the dorsal and a spot on the lower part of the operculum.

Breeding
They breed readily on pre-cleaned rocks. Both parents care for the eggs and brood.

Tank Set-up
A planted aquarium with some hiding places and good filtration is ideal.

22–26°C 72–79°F	15 cm (6 in)

NANDOPSIS TETRACANTHUS
(CUVIER & VALENCIENNES, 1831)

Family: CICHLIDAE

Common name: CUBAN CICHLID

Distribution: Cuba

Size: 25 cm (10 in)

Food: OMNIVOROUS. Live, flake, frozen food

Temperature range: 21–26°C / 70–79°F

pH: 6.5–7.5 dH: to 15°

A territorial but not pugnacious fish of swamps, lakes, even brackish water, it may be kept with other Central American species and Catfish. Males are larger than females but, other than that there is no particular difference between the sexes unless they are breeding, at which time the female is velvety black in the ventral region and has vertical black stripes on a silvery white body.

Breeding
Good parents, they product about 500 eggs. It is a typical open spawner with the fry being transferred to pits.

21–26°C 70–79°F	25 cm (10 in)

Tank Set-up
Make sure there are plenty of hiding places, which can be created using rocks and wood. Some large, robust plants may be included as these help to define territories. Provide efficient filtration and regular water changes.

NANDOPSIS TRIMACULATUS
(GUNTHER, 1866)

23–30°C
73–86°F
36 cm (14 in)

Family: CICHLIDAE
Common name: THREE-SPOT CICHLID
Distribution: Central America
Size: Males 36 cm (14 in); females 25 cm (10 in)
Food: OMNIVOROUS. Live, frozen, flake, green food
Temperature range: 23–30°C / 73–86°F
pH: 7.0–8.0 dH: to 15°

Possibly one of the most pugnacious Cichlids, they need to be kept with others that are able to fend for themselves. Males are larger than females. Females are usually darker and during courtship display vertical bands. These fish are prone to digging and destroying plants.

Breeding
Use young pairs and they will breed in a manner typical of open spawners. Parental care is good.

Tank Set-up
Use a large aquarium with gravel substrate and plenty of hiding places. Seat rocks and wood on the base glass to avoid any disasters that may come about from the fish digging. Good filtration that can cope with the debris stirred up from their excavations is needed.

NANNACARA ANOMALA
REGAN, 1905

22–25°C
72–77°F
9 cm (3½ in)

Family: CICHLIDAE
Common name: GOLDEN DWARF ACARA
Distribution: Guyana
Size: Males 9 cm (3½ in); females 5 cm (2 in)
Food: CARNIVOROUS. Live food, flakes may be accepted
Temperature range: 22–25°C / 72–77°F
pH: 6.0–6.5 dH: to 10°

It may be kept in a community aquarium with other peaceful fishes. The only time they defend their territory is when spawning and, at this time, the other fishes may be relegated to quite a small section of the aquarium.

Males are more intensely coloured and larger.

Breeding
Females lay their eggs in caves and guard the brood. When the fry hatch they continue parental care. Research has shown that the jerky swimming movement of the female at this time is a signal to the fry that they should follow her.

Tank Set-up
A well-planted community aquarium with caves, sheltered areas and good filtration is required.

NEOLAMPROLOGUS BRICHARDI
POLL, 1974

22–25°C
72–77°F
10 cm (4 in)

Family: CICHLIDAE
Common name: FAIRY CICHLID, LYRETAIL LAMPROLOGUS
Distribution: Lake Tanganyika
Size: 10 cm (4 in)
Food: OMNIVOROUS. Live, frozen, flake
Temperature range: 22–25°C / 72–77°F
pH: 7.5–8.5 dH: to 20°

This beautiful little Cichlid from the rocky shores of the Lake, could at first glance be mistaken for a marine fish. It is difficult to tell the sexes, the dorsal and anal fins of the male are slightly more pointed than those of the female.

Keep as a group but provide sufficient space. Pairs form to spawn.

Breeding
Females guard the eggs which are laid in caves. There is little parental care for the fry. Several broods of different ages can be found in one 'community' and the older fry will help with the care and defence of young siblings.

Tank Set-up
Use plenty of rocky outcrops and a sandy substrate. Plants can be added. Good filtration is required.

NEOLAMPROLOGUS LELEUPI
POLL, 1956

24–26°C
75–79°F
10 cm (4 in)

Family: CICHLIDAE
Common name: LEMON CICHLID
Distribution: Lake Tanganyika
Size: 10 cm (4 in)
Food: CARNIVOROUS. Predominantly live food, will take flake
Temperature range: 24–26°C / 75–79°F
pH: 7.5–8.5 dH: to 15°

This attractive fish is relatively peaceful although males can become aggressive if there are more females around than he requires. They form pairs but it is hard to distinguish the sexes.

Breeding
Cave spawners, the female tends the brood while the male defends the territory. On average 100 eggs are laid. Maintain clean conditions as the fry are susceptible to bacterial infection.

Tank Set-up
Provide sand substrate with plenty of rock formations. Plants may be grown. Good filtration and regular water changes are needed to maintain the required water quality.

NIMBOCHROMIS LINNI
(BURGESS & AXELROD, 1975)

23–26°C
73–79°F

25 cm (10 in)

Family: CICHLIDAE
Common name: ELEPHANT-NOSE CICHLID
Distribution: Lake Malawi
Size: 25 cm (10 in)
Food: OMNIVOROUS. Live, frozen, flake, tablet food
Temperature range: 23–26°C / 73–79°F
pH: 8.0–8.5 dH: 10–15°

This fish's mouth gives away its lifestyle, the jaws open to engulf any small fish that will fit into them. Keep the fish with similar sized companions. Males are more intensely coloured with a red, yellow and white edge to the dorsal fin and they have egg spots on the anal fin.

Breeding
The female mouthbroods the eggs for up to a week and thereafter cares for the fry which may still retreat to her mouth in times of danger.

Tank Set-up
A typical Malawi set-up with plenty of rocks providing hiding places and some open sandy or gravel areas is best. Plants may be used. Good filtration is necessary.

NIMBOCHROMIS LIVINGSTONII
(GUENTHER, 1893)

24–27°C
75–80°F

20 cm (8 in)

Family: CICHLIDAE
Common name: NONE
Distribution: Lake Malawi
Size: 20 cm (8 in)
Food: OMNIVOROUS. Live, frozen, flake
Temperature range: 24–27°C / 75–80°F
pH: 8.0–8.5 dH: 10–15°

Peaceful with each other, they are territorial. Keep several females with each male. Males are more brightly coloured and have egg spots on the anal fin. Their natural habitat is inshore over sand and they have an intriguing method of preying on other fish: they

lie motionless on the bottom as if dead, and as an unsuspecting fish comes to pick at the 'corpse', the Cichlid lunges at them at the speed of light.

Breeding
The female collects the eggs after spawning and broods them in her mouth. Up to 100 fry may be produced.

Tank Set-up
Plenty of rock work to give caves and crevices, thus allowing the fish territories, is needed. Plants may be added. A fine gravel substrate and good filtration is necessary.

PARATHERAPS SYNSPILUM
HUBBS, 1935

24–27°C
75–80°

35 cm (14 in)

Family: CICHLIDAE
Common name: REDHEADED CICHLID
Distribution: Central America
Size: 35 cm (14 in)
Food: OMNIVOROUS. Live, frozen, flake, tablet, green food
Temperature range: 24–27°C / 75–80°F
pH: 7.0–7.5 dH: to 15°

Probably one of the most spectacular Central American Cichlids, it is territorial and reasonably peaceful towards other species. However, to its own kind it is very quarrelsome. Difficult to sex, old males develop a cephalic hump. If you want to try and breed them it is best to raise a group of youngsters and allow them to pair themselves. Vary the diet in order to get the best coloration on the fish.

Breeding
They lay a large number of eggs, over 1,000, which are laid on a pre-cleaned stone. They make good parents, guarding the eggs and fry.

Tank Set-up
In a large aquarium with rocks and wood, leave an open space for the fish to swim. Regular water changes and good filtration are beneficial.

PELVICACHROMIS HUMILIS
(BOULENGER, 1916)

24–26°C
75–79°F

12.5 cm (4½ in)

Family:	CICHLIDAE
Common name:	YELLOW KRIB
Distribution:	West Africa
Size:	Males 12.5 cm (4½ in); females 10 cm (4 in)
Food:	OMNIVOROUS. Live, frozen, flake
Temperature range:	24–26°C / 75–79°F
pH:	6.0–6.5 dH: to 8°

This pretty little fish occurs in three colour morphs depending on its locality. The dorsal, anal and ventral fins of males are pointed, and males are also larger than females. It is peaceable except when spawning, when they will defend their territory.

Breeding
Cave spawners, both parents play a part in raising the fry.

Tank Set-up
Have a well-planted, mature aquarium and ensure the water is very soft and acidic with very efficient filtration to maintain water quality.

Family:	CICHLIDAE
Common name:	KRIBENSIS, PURPLE CICHLID
Distribution:	Nigeria
Size:	10 cm (4 in)
Food:	OMNIVOROUS. Live, flake, frozen food
Temperature range:	24–25°C / 75–77°F
pH:	6.5–7.5 dH: to 12°

Like many other Cichlids, these fish are bred commercially in huge numbers and, as a result some strains have become small, poorly coloured and very weak. They may be kept in a community aquarium where little harm will be caused unless the fish are breeding. The male is the larger fish and he also has longer, pointed dorsal and anal fins. The female has rounded anal fins and bright coloration.

Breeding
Spawning takes place in caves – a flowerpot laid on its side makes an acceptable substitute. The females takes charge of the eggs while the male defends the territory. Both parents participate in shepherding the fry around. Keep the fry with the adults until the pair are ready to spawn again otherwise the male may bully the female if she is not ready to mate.

PELVICACHROMIS PULCHER
(BOULENGER, 1901)

Tank Set-up
Provide a planted community aquarium with caves and other hiding places and good filtration.

24–25°C
75–77°F

10 cm (4 in)

PELVICACHROMIS ROLOFFI
(THYS, 1968)

Family:	CICHLIDAE
Common name:	ROLOFF'S KRIBENSIS
Distribution:	West Africa
Size:	Males 8.5 cm (3½ in); females 6 cm (2½ in)
Food:	OMNIVOROUS. Live, flake, frozen food
Temperature range:	24–26°C / 75–79°F
pH:	6.0–7.0 dH: to 8°

This quiet little fish may be kept in a community aquarium. The only time they become territorial is when they are breeding. Males are larger with

24–26°C
75–79°F

8.5 cm (3½ in)

extensions to their dorsal, anal and ventral fins, they also have a dark band along their flanks. Females have a more rounded profile and their belly is pinkish.

Breeding
These fish have a long courtship before spawning in caves. Both parents share parental care.

Tank Set-up
As for *P. humilis*.

PLACIDOCHROMIS ELECTRA
(BURGESS, 1979)

24–26°C
75–79°F
16 cm (6 in)

Family: CICHLIDAE	
Common name: DEEPWATER HAP	
Distribution: Lake Malawi	
Size: to 16 cm (6 in)	
Food: OMNIVOROUS. Live, flake, frozen food	
Temperature range: 24–26°C / 75–79°F	
pH: 8.0–9.0 dH: to 18°	

This very innocuous Cichlid that lives over sand may be kept without problems with other peaceable Malawi fish. It does not bother plants. Males are much larger and more colourful than females. It will claim a territory and breed in the community aquarium.

Breeding
Females mouthbrood the eggs and take charge of the fry.

Tank Set-up
Use a typical Malawi set-up with plenty of rocks and some plants.

PROTOMELAS ANNECTENS
(REGAN, 1922)

24–26°C
75–79°F
20 cm (8 in)

Family: CICHLIDAE	
Common name: CHUNKY HAP	
Distribution: Lake Malawi	
Size: 20 cm (8 in)	
Food: OMNIVOROUS. Live, frozen, flake	
Temperature range: 24–26°C / 75–79°F	
pH: 7.5–9.0 dH: to 20°	

This peaceful Cichlid may be kept with others of the same genus or fish of a similar nature. Males have more blue on them than females and are generally larger. It likes to sift through mouthfuls of sand to find food but does not dig in the accepted sense and will not uproot plants.

Breeding
No details are available.

Tank Set-up
Use a set-up with rocky outcrops, thickets of plants, sand substrate and good filtration.

PSEUDOCRENILABRUS MULTICOLOR
(HILGENDORF, 1903)

20–24°C
68–75°F
8 cm (3 in)

Family: CICHLIDAE	
Common name: EGYPTIAN MOUTHBROODER	
Distribution: Lower Nile to Uganda and Tanzania	
Size: 8 cm (3 in)	
Food: OMNIVOROUS. Live, frozen, flake	
Temperature range: 20–24°C / 68–75°F	
pH: 6.5–7.5 dH: to 12°	

This small fish may be kept in a community aquarium without too much chaos being caused. Males are larger and generally more colourful (especially when breeding) than females.

Breeding
The eggs are deposited in a spawning pit and not taken into the female's mouth until after they have been fertilised by the male. They are brooded for some ten days.

Tank Set-up
Planted community aquarium with plenty of hiding places. Maintain good quality water and make regular water changes.

PSEUDOCRENILABRUS PHILANDER
(TREWAVAS, 1936)

21–24°C
70–75°F
11 cm (4½ in)

Family: CICHLIDAE	
Common name: COPPER MOUTHBROODER	
Distribution: Southern Africa	
Size: 11 cm (4½ in)	
Food: OMNIVOROUS. Live, frozen, flake	
Temperature range: 21–24°C / 70–75°F	
pH: 6.5–7.5 dH: to 12°	

They can be very aggressive and belligerent especially when breeding, at which time they also dig in the substrate. Keep only with other fish that can easily fend for themselves. Males are much more brightly coloured than females.

Breeding
Similar to *P. multicolor*.

Tank Set-up
Provide a planted aquarium but use robust plants and, if necessary, grow them in pots. Allow some rocks and wood arranged to give shelter. Provide good filtration.

PSEUDOTROPHEUS LOMBARDOI
BURGESS, 1977

Family: CICHLIDAE	
Common name: NONE	
Distribution: Lake Malawi	
Size: 15 cm (6 in)	
Food: OMNIVOROUS. Live, flake, frozen food	
Temperature range: 24–26°C / 75–79°F	
pH: 8.0–8.5 dH: to 18°	

Both males and females can be extremely quarrelsome with other fish, so much so that they can inflict wounds. Males and females differ in colour: males have a bright yellow anal fin with egg spots, females are pale blue with darker bands. Keep two females per male.

Breeding
Females mouthbrood the eggs and subsequent fry. The fry are easy to raise on newly hatched brine shrimp and fine flake food.

Tank Set-up
Use a typical Malawi set-up but, with this species, it is imperative that there is sufficient space for the fish to have territories, so the aquarium should be large and well stocked with rocky structures. Provide good filtration.

24–26°C 75–79°F	15 cm (6 in)

Family: CICHLIDAE	
Common name: EDUARD'S MBUNA	
Distribution: Lake Malawi	
Size: 12 cm (4½ in)	
Food: OMNIVOROUS. Live, flake, frozen food	
Temperature range: 24–26°C / 75–79°F	
pH: 8.0–8.5 dH: to 18°	

This peaceful creature is only defensive when breeding. The easiest way to tell the sexes is by the egg spots on the anal fin of the male.

Breeding
Typical mouthbrooders, the females brood the eggs and fry. Once released, brood care ceases.

Tank Set-up
Use a rocky Malawi set-up.

24–26°C 75–79°F	12 cm (4½in)

PSEUDOTROPHEUS SOCOLOFI
JOHNSON, 1974

PSEUDOTROPHEUS TROPHEOPS
REGAN, 1921

Family: CICHLIDAE	
Common name: GOLDEN TROPHEOPS	
Distribution: Lake Malawi	
Size: To 20 cm (8 in)	
Food: OMNIVOROUS. Live, flake, frozen, green food	
Temperature range: 24–26°C / 75–79°F	
pH: 8.0–8.5 dH: to 20°	

This fish is aggressive not only to its own kind but to every other fish as well. Males claim territories. Keep several females with each male. The male is larger, more colourful and has eggs spots on the anal fin. There are different colour forms of this fish.

Breeding
A typical mouthbrooder, the females produce about 40 eggs. The fry are guarded for just a short time after release.

Tank Set-up
Rocky Malawi set-up plus a few plants so that the fish can claim their territories.

24–26°C 75–79°F	To 20 cm (8 in)

PSEUDOTROPHEUS ZEBRA

(BOULENGER, 1899)

Family: CICHLIDAE

Common name: ZEBRA CICHLID, NYASSA BLUE CICHLID

Distribution: Lake Malawi

Size: 12 cm (4½ in)

Food: OMNIVOROUS. Live, flake, frozen, green food

Temperature range: 22–27°C / 72–80°F

pH: 8.0–9.0 dH: to 20°

An exceptionally belligerent fish, it requires plenty of space to form territories otherwise it will bully everything else in the aquarium. Keep several females with each male. The females may be seen swimming as a group. Males have eggs spots on the anal fin. Several colour morphs are available.

Breeding

A typical mouthbrooder, the female produces up to 60 eggs. Maternal care for the young fry after they are released from the mouth is usual.

Tank Set-up

Have plenty of rocky structures with caves and nooks and crannies also some plants to allow the fish to define territories.

| 22–27°C 72–80°F | 12 cm (4½ in) |

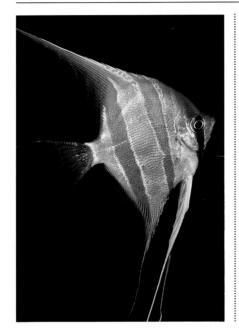

PTEROPHYLLUM ALTUM

PELLEGRIN, 1903

Family: CICHLIDAE

Common name: ALTUM ANGEL

Distribution: Orinoco basin

Size: 18 cm (7 in)

Food: OMNIVOROUS. Live, frozen, flake, green food

Temperature range: 28–30°C / 82–86°F

pH: 5.5–6.0 dH: to 8°

Only wild caught specimens of this fish are available. It is a very demanding fish as far as water quality is concerned and they also require high temperatures. Majestic to look at, they differ from *P. scalare* in that the dorsal profile is much steeper and they have a pronounced 'snout'. They have been crossed with *P. scalare* and the resultant hybrid has much higher finnage. A very peaceful fish that is best kept in a species aquarium.

Breeding

Have been bred but no details are available.

Tank Set-up

Use a deep aquarium, maybe 60 cm (24 in) from top to bottom, and plant with tall plants such as Amazon Swords. Add wood for decor. A very efficient filtration system is required to maintain the water quality.

| 28–30°C 82–86°F | 18 cm (7 in) |

PTEROPHYLLUM SCALARE

(LICHTENSTEIN, 1823)

Family: CICHLIDAE

Common name: ANGELFISH

Distribution: Central Amazon to Peru and Ecuador

Size: 15 cm (6 in)

Food: OMNIVOROUS. Live, frozen, flake, green food

Temperature range: 24–28°C / 75–82°F

pH: 6.5–7.5 dH: to 10°

Virtually all the fish offered in the trade are captive bred. Angels are bred in large numbers in the Far East, South Africa and the USA for the trade. Their ease of breeding has also led to the development of several different colour forms and some with elongated finnage. Some strains are of very poor quality, lacking colour and having stunted growth, through indiscriminate breeding. Other strains, which have been properly line bred are much stronger fish. Angels may be kept in the community aquarium but they may eat smaller fish such as Neon Tetras. The only conclusive method of checking the sexes is by the genital papillae: in males it is pointed; in females rounded.

Breeding

Spawning takes place on a cleaned leaf or rock and both parents tend the brood.

Tank Set-up

Use a large, mature aquarium with plenty of plants. Deeper tanks are best so the fish can display their finnage. They like warmth and need good, efficient filtration and regular water changes.

| 24–28°C 75–82°F | 15 cm (6 in) |

Family: CICHLIDAE
Common name: SPARKLING GEOPHAGUS
Distribution: Amazon basin
Size: 25 cm (10 in)
Food: OMNIVOROUS. Live, frozen, flake
Temperature range: 24–26°C / 75–79°F
pH: 6.5–7.0 dH: to 12°

A beautiful, non-aggressive Cichlid whose only drawback is that it likes to dig, it may be kept with other peaceful fishes. Males have extended dorsal and anal fins.

Breeding
The only report is from the turn of the century and this states that the fish spawn in the open and both parents care for the brood.

Tank Set-up
Use a large aquarium with rocks and wood to create hiding places. Well established, large plants can be used, but protect the area around the crown with pebbles to discourage the fish from digging up the plant. Provide good filtration.

SATANOPERCA ACUTICEPS
HECKEL, 1840

24–26°C
75–79°F
25 cm (10 in)

SATANOPERCA DAEMON
HECKEL, 1840

26–30°C
79–86°F
30 cm (12 in)

Family: CICHLIDAE
Common name: THREE-SPOTTED EARTHEATER
Distribution: Orinoco, Amazon and Negro Rivers (South America)
Size: 30 cm (12 in)
Food: OMNIVOROUS. Live, frozen, flake
Temperature range: 26–30°C / 79–86°F
pH: 6.0–6.5 dH: to 10°

Often confused with *S. acuticeps*, *S. daemon* has two spots on its flanks plus one at the base of the caudal fin, while *S. acuticeps* has three spots on its flanks plus one at the base of the caudal fin. They are reasonably peaceful. Mature males have extended rays on the dorsal fin.

Breeding
Not known.

Tank Set-up
Use a large aquarium with a sand or fine gravel substrate and well-established plants. Good filtration to cope with the debris stirred up when digging is necessary.

SATANOPERCA JURUPARI
HECKELL, 1840

24–26°C
75–79°F
25 cm (10 in)

Family: CICHLIDAE
Common name: EARTH-EATER, DEMON FISH
Distribution: Brazil, Guyana
Size: 25 cm (10 in), usually smaller
Food: OMNIVOROUS. Live, flake, frozen food
Temperature range: 24–26°C / 75–79°F
pH: 6.0–7.0 dH: to 10°

Although it is a large fish, it is quite peaceful unless breeding. The common name, Earth-eater, refers to its habit of digging. The amount of gravel they can move around an aquarium is amazing. Telling the sexes is virtually impossible unless the fish are breeding.

Breeding
Up to 400 eggs are laid on a flat surface, 24 hours later the female takes them into her mouth, keeping them in the front of the mouth and not in the throat sac as most other Cichlids do. Both parents share the care, taking it in turns to have the eggs and fry in their mouth.

Tank Set-up
Provide a large aquarium with sand or fine gravel and some rocks which should be placed on the base glass to avoid the fish undermining them when digging. Well-established plants are beneficial. Good filtration is necessary to cope with the amount of mulum these fish can stir up.

SPATHODUS MARLIERI
POLL, 1950

25–27°C
77–80°F

To 9 cm (3½ in)

Family: CICHLIDAE
Common name: PLAIN GOBY CICHLID
Distribution: Lake Tanganyika
Size: To 9 cm (3½ in)
Food: OMNIVOROUS. Live, flake, frozen food
Temperature range: 25–27°C / 77–80°F
pH: 7.5–8.5 dH: 10–20°

The fish is relatively peaceful provided there are plenty of nooks and crannies for it to slip into and over. It can be more quarrelsome when breeding. Males are larger and when they get older develop a cranial hump. Keep fish in pairs.

Breeding
After laying the eggs the female takes them into her mouth then she takes in the male's sperm. She broods the eggs and fry for 10–14 days before handing over responsibilities for the fry to the male.

Tank Set-up
The fish must be kept in relatively hard, alkaline water. Use fine sand as substrate and also piles of rocks to give cover. Plants may be used. Provide good filtration.

Family: CICHLIDAE
Common name: AFRICAN BLOCKHEAD
Distribution: Central Zaire
Size: Males 11 cm (4½ in); females 8 cm (3 in)
Food: OMNIVOROUS. Live, frozen, flake, tablet food
Temperature range: 24–28°C / 75–82°F
pH: 6.5–7.0 dH: to 18°

Considered ugly by some, the males have a very pronounced fatty lump on their forehead while in females this protruberance is smaller. Blockheads pair for life and, if one partner dies, the fish to not take on a replacement. They are belligerent. The fish do not swim about the aquarium but move sporadically around the bottom and over the rocks in a similar manner to Gobies.

Breeding
The fish spawn in caves, an overturned flowerpot is a good substitute, and tend the eggs and fry. Broods are small, usually between 20 and 60 eggs are laid.

24–28°C
75–82°F

 11 cm (4½ in)

STEATOCRANUS CASUARIUS
(POLL, 1939)

Tank Set-up
Rocks, wood and plants may be used in the aquarium. Create caves and hiding places and provide efficient filtration.

SYMPHYSODON AEQUIFASCIATUS
PELLEGRIN, 1903

Family: CICHLIDAE
Common name: GREEN DISCUS
Distribution: Amazon
Size: To 15 cm (6 in)
Food: CARNIVOROUS. Small live food, captive bred specimens will usually take flake and frozen food
Temperature range: 26–30°C / 79–86°F
pH: 6.5 dH: to 5°

A very peaceful fish, only becoming a little territorial when breeding. It is best kept in a species aquarium housing several individuals so they can pair themselves. The only thing which will

definitely distinguish the sexes is the genital papilla which is pointed on males and rounded on females.

Breeding
Warm, slightly acidic soft water is required. The pair will clean the spawning site and tend the eggs. When free swimming, the fry feed on a secretion produced from the parents' skin.

Tank Set-up
Use a large aquarium with plants and wood. Pay particular attention to water quality and carry out regular water changes.

26–30°C
79–86°F

 To 15 cm (6 in)

SYMPHYSODON DISCUS
HECKEL, 1840

26–30°C
79–86°F
20 cm (8 in)

Family: CICHLIDAE	
Common name: HECKEL DISCUS	
Distribution: Negro River (South America)	
Size: 20 cm (8 in)	
Food: CARNIVOROUS. Small live food, will also take flake and frozen food	
Temperature range: 26–30°C/79–86°F	
pH: 6.0–6.5 dH: to 5°	

The behaviour and sexual differences of this fish from quiet, weedy waters are as for *S. aequifasciatus*. There are many sorts and hybrids of *S. discus* that differ in colour, body shape and finnage or in a combination of these characteristics that have been manipulated by the breeders of *S. discus*.

Breeding
Much the same as for *S. aequifasciatus*, but it is much more difficult to induce *S. discus* to spawn.

Tank Set-up
Use as large a tank as possible, especially in depth with soft substrate and a few large plants and some wood for decor. Provide subdued lighting, warm summer temperatures around 27°C/80°F, dropping by about 3 degrees in winter and very efficient filtration to maintain optimum water quality.

TELEOGRAMMA BRICHARDI
POLL, 1959

20–23°C
68–73°F
12 cm (4½ in)

Family: CICHLIDAE	
Common name: NONE	
Distribution: Lower Zaire River	
Size: Males 12 cm (4½ in); females 9 cm (3½ in)	
Food: OMNIVOROUS. Live, frozen, flake	
Temperature range: 20–23°C/68–73°F	
pH: 6.5–7.0 dH: to 10°	

These fish require plenty of space as they claim large territories and are very intolerant of each other. Males have a wide white edge to the dorsal fin and this white extends into the top of the caudal fin. Females have a thinner

white edge.

Breeding
They breed in caves and the female drives the male away after spawning. She cares for the brood while the male defends the territory. Once free swimming the fry are all but disowned by the parents.

Tank Set-up
Use plenty of rocks to form caves and crevices and provide good filtration.

TELMATOCHROMIS BIFRENATUS
MYERS, 1936

24–26°C
75–79°F
6 cm (2½ in)

Family: CICHLIDAE	
Common name: TWO-BANDED CICHLID	
Distribution: Lake Tanganyika	
Size: 6 cm (2½ in)	
Food: OMNIVOROUS. Live, flake, frozen food	
Temperature range: 24–26°C/75–79°F	
pH: 9.0 dH: 12–15°	

One of the smallest of the Cichlids, they are peaceful and territorial, living on rocky shores. Males are larger and have longer finnage. Keep a male and two or three females together.

Breeding
A flowerpot on its side makes an acceptable cave for the female to spawn in. The eggs hatch in 10 days. The female tends the fry until they are free swimming when her interest in them wanes.

Tank Set-up
Provide plenty of rockwork which will give shelter, territories and good filtration.

TELMATOCHROMIS TEMPORALIS
BOULENGER, 1898

Family: CICHLIDAE	
Common name: TEMPORALIS CICHLID	
Distribution: Lake Tanganyika	
Size: 10 cm (4 in)	
Food: OMNIVOROUS. Live, flake, frozen food	
Temperature range: 25–27°C/77–80°F	
pH: 8.0–9.0 dH: 10–20°	

It is generally peaceful unless breeding. Males are larger than females and, as they get older, develop a cranial hump.

25–27°C
77–80°F
10 cm (4 in)

Breeding
They spawn in caves, laying their eggs on the roof. The female fans the egg and guards the fry when they hatch. Both parents guard the fry once they are free swimming.

Tank Set-up
Use plenty of rockwork in a typical Malawi aquarium.

THORICHTHYS MEEKI

BRIND, 1918

21–23°C
70–73°F

15 cm (6 in)

Family: CICHLIDAE	
Common name: FIREMOUTH	
Distribution: Guatemala, Yucatan	
Size: 15 cm (6 in)	
Food: OMNIVOROUS. Live, frozen, flake	
Temperature range: 21–23°C / 70–73°F	
pH: 7.0 dH: to 10°	

Although territorial, Firemouths rarely harm other fish unless they are in the process of spawning. Their defensive display of spreading their operculum and inflating their throat sac is majestic. Males are larger than females and have more colour, a red throat, with the colour extending along the belly and extended finnage.

Breeding
The pair clean a rock and the female deposits up to 500 eggs. Both parents tend the fry which are moved from pit to pit in the aquarium. Four or five broods may be produced in a year.

Tank Set-up
Provide a large, planted aquarium with other peaceful fishes. Leave some open areas for the fish to swim and display. Use rocks and wood to give cover. provide efficient filtration.

TILAPIA BUTTIKOFERI

(HUBRECHT, 1881)

Family: CICHLIDAE	
Common name: ZEBRA CICHLID	
Distribution: West Africa	
Size: 25 cm (10 in)	
Food: OMNIVOROUS. Live, frozen, flake, tablet, green food	
Temperature range: 22–25°C / 72–77°F	
pH: 6.5–7.0 dH: to 15°	

Young animals are gregarious but with age their temperament changes and they become more aggressive to the point of predating on anything small enough to be eaten. Their vertical black and cream bands make them very attractive. Males are larger than females. They may be kept with similar-sized fishes.

22–25°C
72–77°F

25 cm (10 in)

Breeding
Little is known – they are substrate spawners and practise brood care.

Tank Set-up
A large, spacious aquarium with rocks and some large, well-established, robust plants with good filtration is best.

TILAPIA MARIAE

BOULENGER, 1899

Family: CICHLIDAE	
Common name: NONE	
Distribution: Niger basin to Cameroon	
Size: To 35 cm (14 in)	
Food: OMNIVOROUS. Live, frozen, flake, tablet, green food	
Temperature range: 21–25°C / 70–77°F	
pH: 6.5–7.0 dH: to 10°	

As juveniles the fish have vertical black and yellowish stripes, and as they mature the bands break up to black blotches while the body becomes more yellow, but leaving a faint trace of the vertical markings. They can be belligerent. Males have longer finnage than females and a steep profile to the forehead. Of interest is the fact that wild-caught fishes have been found to have sand in their gut which helps to grind up their food.

Breeding
They spawn on rocks, but after the second day the eggs are transferred to a pit dug by the male in a sheltered spot under a rock. Both parents guard the eggs and resultant fry. Broods are large – up to 2,000 eggs.

Tank Set-up
Have a large aquarium with a sand substrate and use wood and flat stones for decor. Robust plants such a Java Fern may survive (these Cichlids eat plants) alternatively use artificial plants. Provide good filtration.

21–25°C
70–77°F

To 35 cm (14 in)

Family: CICHLIDAE	
Common name: ZILLI'S CICHLID	
Distribution: North Africa	
Size: To 30 cm (12 in)	
Food: OMNIVOROUS. Live, vegetable food, may not accept flake	
Temperature range: 21–23°C/70–73°F	
pH: 6.5–8.0 dH: to 18°	

Not often seen in the hobby, *T. zillii* is a territorial, belligerent fish. It loves to dig and also eats plants, neither characteristic making it particularly endearing. The best method of determining the sexes is the genital papillae: pointed in males; rounded in females.

Breeding
The female produces 1,000 or so eggs and lays them on cleaned rock. Both parents tend the eggs and fry.

Tank Set-up
Provide a large aquarium with a fine gravel or sand substrate. Use large rocks seated on the base glass of the aquarium. Water values are not critical but the filtration should be good enough to cope with all the detritus the fish stir up when digging.

TILAPIA ZILLII
(GERVAIS, 1848)

21–23°C 70–73°F	To 30 cm (12 in)

TROPHEUS BRICHARDI
NELISSEN & THYS, 1975

24–26°C 75–79°F	12 cm (4½ in)

Family: CICHLIDAE	
Common name: BLUE-EYED TROPHEUS	
Distribution: Lake Tanganyika	
Size: 12 cm (4½ in)	
Food: OMNIVOROUS. Live, frozen, flake, vegetable food	
Temperature range: 24–26°C/75–79°F	
pH: 7.0–9.0 dH: to 15°	

The fish needs plenty of secluded areas. It is peaceful with like-natured fishes. The sexes are indistinguishable. Specialised feeders, in the lake they feed on aufwuchs, therefore include vegetable matter in the diet.

Breeding
The fish is an open spawner and the eggs are mouthbrooded. The eggs are yellow in colour and large, 7 mm (¼ in) in diameter. At each spawning about ten young are produced.

Tank Set-up
Use a large aquarium with plenty of rock structures and open areas of sand. Provide bright light to encourage algae growth for feeding. Good filtration is beneficial.

TROPHEUS DUBOISI
MARLIER, 1959

24–26°C 75–79°F	12 cm (4½ in)

Family: CICHLIDAE	
Common name: WHITE-SPOTTED CICHLID	
Distribution: Lake Tanganyika	
Size: 12 cm (4½ in)	
Food: OMNIVOROUS. Live, frozen, flake, vegetable food	
Temperature range: 24–26°C/75–79°F	
pH: 8.5–9.0 dH: 10–12°	

These fish inhabit rocky zones in the lake, at a depth of 3–15 m (9–45 ft). Territorial, they are only aggressive towards their own kind. They are often seen swimming alone or in pairs. A specialised feeder, they prefer micro-organisms, and there should be a reasonable amount of vegetable matter

included in their diet. It is closely related to *T. moorii* but it is found in deeper waters in Lake Tanganyika and the fish also behave differently.

Breeding
Females lay some 5 to 15 eggs and take them into their mouth for brooding. They continue to care for the fry for about 7 days after releasing them. The fry have greyish spots over a dark grey-blue background.

Tank Set-up
Provide a typical rocky set-up with caves, crevices, etc. and good filtration.

Family: CICHLIDAE
Common name: NONE
Distribution: Lake Tanganyika
Size: 15 cm (6 in)
Food: OMNIVOROUS. Live, flake, frozen, vegetable food
Temperature range: 24–26°C / 75–79°F
pH: 7.0–9.0 dH: to 15°

The fish has a number of different colour forms depending on the locality it comes from. It is very difficult to distinguish the sexes so allow the fish to pair themselves. They are territorial but only tend to squabble among their own kind. Keep as a group rather than as individuals or pairs.

Breeding
They spawn in water, the female catching the eggs before they reach the ground. Maternal care is continued for a week after the fry are free swimming.

TROPHEUS MOORII
BOULENGER, 1898

Tank Set-up
Provide plenty of rocky structures but also some open water. Use strong lighting to encourage algae and give good filtration.

24–26°C
75–79°F

14 cm (6 in)

UARU AMPHICANTHIODES
HECKEL, 1840

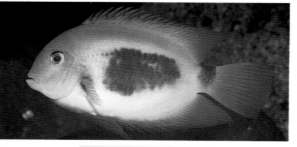

26–28°C
79–82°F

30 cm (12 in)

Family: CICHLIDAE
Common name: UARU, TRIANGLE CICHLID, WAROO
Distribution: Amazon river, Guyana
Size: to 30 cm (12 in)
Food: CARNIVOROUS. Live food predominantly, vegetable matter when young
Temperature range: 26–28°C / 79–82°F
pH: 6.0 dH: to 5°

A delicate fish but one that is well worth persevering with. Keep as a shoal and allow the fish to pair themselves. Young specimens require a large amount of vegetable matter in their diet. Coloration changes as the fish grow, young specimens are spotted

while the adults have a dusky area on the lower flanks.

Breeding
A challenge to breed. They spawn on rocks or plants and the fry are very delicate. Initially the fry feed on the body mucous of the parents and later should be fed micro-organisms.

Tank Set-up
Use a large aquarium with a gravel substrate and wood and rocks with a few robust plants such as Amazon Swords and Java Fern for decor. It is essential to maintain the water quality. Provide subdued lighting.

VIEJA MACULICAUDA
(REGAN, 1905)

22–26°C
72–79°F

30 cm (12 in)

Family: CICHLIDAE
Common name: BLACK BELT CICHLID
Distribution: Central America
Size: 30 cm (12 in)
Food: OMNIVOROUS. Vegetable matter, live, frozen, flake
Temperature range: 22–26°C / 72–79°F
pH: 6.5–7.5 dH: to 15°

Males are beautifully coloured whereas females are more drab. They are aggressive towards their own kind and other species. Ensure that you are feeding them plenty of vegetable foods

as these fish are predominantly herbivores, however, in captivity they eat whatever is offered them.

Breeding
They are open spawners with excellent parental care.

Tank Set-up
Use large rocks and pieces of wood to decorate the aquarium. Any plants should be artificial otherwise they will be eaten. Good filtration.

Cyprinids

Balitoridae
Cobitidae
Cyprinidae

Family: BALITORIDAE

Common name: SADDLED HILLSTREAM LOACH

Distribution: Indonesia, Thailand

Size: 12 cm (4½ in)

Food: OMNIVOROUS. Aufwuchs, bloodworms and the like

Temperature range: 20–24°C / 68–75°F

pH: 7.0 dH: to 10°

Very peaceable with other fish; with each other there may be mock fights but no damage is done. They spend much time grazing through algae and over flat rocks and leaves.

Breeding
Not known.

Tank Set-up
Mature aquarium with soft, neutral water. Broad-leaved plants and large flat stones for decor. Good filtration with a reasonable flow of well-oxygenated water. Regular water changes of about 20% every 10–14 days.

| 20–24°C 68–75°F | | 12 cm (4½ in) |

HOMALOPTERA ORTHOGONIATA
VAILLANT, 1902

HOMALOPTERA ZOLLINGERI
BLEEKER, 1853

Family: BALITORIDAE

Common name: NONE

Distribution: Southeast Asia

Size: 10 cm (4 in)

Food: OMNIVOROUS. Live food and algae preferred, takes flake as a last resort

Temperature range: 22–24°C / 72–75°F

pH: 6.0–6.5 dH: to 10°

A delicate fish, not often offered for sale, and difficult to acclimatise to aquarium conditions. It holds station in fast-flowing waters using suction produced by the expanded pectoral and ventral fins, which are forced down onto any surface by the water passing over them.

| 22–24°C 72–75°F | | 10 cm (4 in) |

Breeding
Not known.

Tank Set-up
Cool, clear, well-oxygenated, fast-flowing water. Very efficient filtration system. Plenty of algae.

BOTIA BERDMOREI
(BYTH, 1860)

Family: COBITIDAE

Common name: NONE

Distribution: Burma, Thailand

Size: 15 cm (6 in); in the wild 25 cm (10 in)

Food: OMNIVOROUS. Flake, frozen and live food

Temperature range: 22–26°C / 72–79°F

pH: 6.5–7.5 dH: to 15°

A boisterous fish, it can be aggressive to its own kind and others, preventing them from feeding and generally bullying them. When irate it may make

| 22–26°C 72–79°F | | 15 cm (6 in) |

clicking noises. Take care when handling any *Botia*, as the bifid spines beneath the eyes can get caught in the net. These spines are also used when fighting, and can inflict wounds and scratches on other fish.

Breeding
Not known.

Tank Set-up
Large aquarium with fine substrate. Pebbles and wood for decoration. Good filtration.

BOTIA LOHACHATA

CHAUDHURI, 1912

24–28°C
75–82°F
 7 cm (3 in)

Family: COBITIDAE

Common name: NONE

Distribution: North and northeastern India, Bangladesh

Size: 7 cm (3 in)

Food: OMNIVOROUS. Flake, frozen, live and tablet food

Temperature range: 24–28°C / 75–82°F

pH: 6.0–6.5 dH: to 8°

Active after dark, this loach can be aggressive. Although it looks as though it should feed from the substrate, it actually takes food from the surface, turning as it does so. There is wide variation in colour pattern.

Breeding
Not known.

Tank Set-up
Community aquarium with larger, robust species. Rocks, wood and plants for decor, with some caves for it to hide in. Soft substrate so it can dig. Efficient filtration.

BOTIA MACRACANTHUS

(BLEEKER, 1852)

Family: COBITIDAE

Common name: CLOWN LOACH

Distribution: India, Sumatra, Borneo

Size: 16 cm (6 in); in the wild to 30 cm (12 in)

Food: OMNIVOROUS. Flake, frozen, tablet and especially live foods (e.g. small worms)

Temperature range: 25–30°C / 77–86°F

pH: 6.0–6.5 dH: to 12°

A social Loach that should be kept in groups. It is active by day, and a worthy occupant for any community aquarium. The species is prone to White Spot. It is prized as a food fish in its countries of origin.

Breeding
Not bred in aquaria. In the wild it spawns in the rainy season in fast-flowing streams. The fry grow up in calmer waters.

Tank Set-up
Mature community aquarium that is not overstocked. Very good filtration to provide clean, clear water.

25–30°C
77–86°F
16 cm (6 in)

BOTIA SIDTHIMUNKI

KLAUSEWITZ, 1959

Family: COBITIDAE

Common name: CHAIN BOTIA, DWARF LOACH

Distribution: Northern India, northern Thailand

Size: 5 cm (2 in)

Food: OMNIVOROUS. Small live food, flake

Temperature range: 25–28°C / 77–82°F

pH: 6.0–6.5 dH: to 8°

A shoaling fish, keep a group of six or more in the community aquarium. They are very active, spending much of their time swimming, as a shoal, around the aquarium. When resting, they will often utilise the leaves of broad-leaved plants in preference to the substrate. No discernible differences between the sexes.

Breeding
Not known.

Tank Set-up
A well-maintained, mature community aquarium with plenty of plants including some broad-leaved specimens. Good filtration and regular water changes are essential.

25–28°C
77–82°F
 5 cm (2 in)

BOTIA STRIATA

RAO, 1920

Family: COBITIDAE	
Common name: ZEBRA LOACH	
Distribution: Southern India	
Size: 6 cm (2½ in); in the wild 10 cm (4 in)	
Food: OMNIVOROUS. Flake, frozen, live and tablet food	
Temperature range: 23–26°C/73–79°F	
pH: 6.5–8.0 dH: to 20°	

A sociable Loach that should be kept in groups. It is unaggressive, and may be housed in a community aquarium.

Breeding
Not known.

Tank Set-up
Soft substrate so it can burrow. Caves and tubes to hide in, plants, wood and pebbles for decor. Gentle filtration.

23–26°C
73–79°F
6 cm (2½ in)

22–24°C
72–75°F
8 cm (3 in)

LEPIDOCEPHALUS THERMALIS

(VALENCIENNES, 1846)

Family: COBITIDAE	
Common name: LESSER LOACH, INDIAN STONEBITER	
Distribution: India and Sri Lanka	
Size: 8 cm (3 in)	
Food: OMNIVOROUS. Very partial to small worms and other live food, but will also take flake, frozen and tablet food	
Temperature range: 22–24°C/72–75°F	
pH: 6.5–7.0 dH: to 6°	

A fish for the cooler community aquarium which has soft, slightly acidic water. Keep in groups. It is nocturnal, but will often be seen in the evening searching for food.

Breeding
Not known.

Tank Set-up
Soft substrate so it can burrow. Flat stones, and broad-leaved plants as it likes to rest on leaves. Good filtration to provide clean, clear water with a fast current.

MISGURNUS ANGUILLICAUDATUS

(CANTOR, 1842)

Family: COBITIDAE	
Common name: WEATHERLOACH, WEATHERFISH	
Distribution: Amur region (Siberia), China, Korea, Hainan, Japan	
Size: 50 cm (20 in)	
Food: OMNIVOROUS. Anything and everything from live food to vegetable matter	
Temperature range: 10–15°C/50–59°F	
pH: 6.0–8.0 dH: to 25°	

A very peaceful Loach, well suited to a community aquarium. However, plants should be well established, or they may be uprooted as it digs in the substrate. Sexing this species can be difficult, the second ray of the male's pelvic fin is generally thicker than that of the female.

10–15°C
50–59°F
50 cm (20 in)

Breeding
Has been bred but no details available.

Tank Set-up
Sand or mud substrate. Either potted or well-established plants. Wood and rocks for decor and to provide secluded areas. Very efficient filtration system, to cope with all the dirt and debris stirred up when the fish digs.

NOEMACHEILUS BARBATULUS
(LINNAEUS, 1758)

Family:	COBITIDAE
Common name:	COMMON LOACH, STONE LOACH
Distribution:	Europe
Size:	16 cm (6 in)
Food:	CARNIVOROUS. Small live foods such as *Daphnia* and *Tubifex*; flake food may be accepted
Temperature range:	10–18°C / 50–64°F
pH: 7.0–7.5 dH: to 15°	

These Loaches can be difficult to keep in the home aquarium, because the water temperature usually rises too high for them. Keep as a group. Males are slimmer than females, and have longer pectoral fins with a thickened second ray. May be kept with other peaceful fish which also require cool conditions.

Breeding
Spawns between March and May. Eggs are placed on stones or directly onto gravel, and may be guarded by the male. Hatching time, seven days. First foods: brine shrimp nauplii.

10–18°C 50–64°F		16 cm (6 in)

Tank Set-up
Large tank with gravel and stone substrate. Rocks and a few plants for cover. Clean, clear, cool, well-oxygenated water with a strong current.

Family:	CYPRINIDAE
Common name:	SILVER SHARK, BALA SHARK
Distribution:	Southeast Asia
Size:	35 cm (14 in)
Food:	OMNIVOROUS. Live, flake and vegetable food
Temperature range:	22–28°C / 72–82°F
pH: 6.5–7.0 dH: to 10°	

A very active shoaling species that requires a lot of swimming space. It is easily frightened and may jump. Sexing is only possible during the spawning season when females are generally fatter than males.

Breeding
Not accomplished in aquaria.

Tank Set-up
Large aquarium with large specimen plants and wood for decoration. Good filtration with a steady flow of water through the tank. Open water for the fish to swim in. Tight cover glass.

BALANTEOCHEILUS MELANOPTERUS
(BLEEKER, 1851)

22–28°C 72–82°F		35 cm (14 in)

BARBUS ARULIUS
(JERDON, 1849)

19–24°C 66–75°F		12 cm (4½ in)

Family:	CYPRINIDAE
Common name:	ARULIUS BARB
Distribution:	South and southeast India
Size:	12 cm (4½ in)
Food:	OMNIVOROUS. Live, flake and green food
Temperature range:	19–24°C / 66–75°F
pH: 6.0–7.0 dH: to 10°	

A classic Barb, often overlooked for the community aquarium because it does not reach its full colour potential until it is quite old. A hardy creature, mature males show more colour and have extensions to the rays of the dorsal fin. Females are more rounded. When ready to spawn, males have breeding tubercles around the snout.

Breeding
A large aquarium with bunches of plants or other spawning medium. After an active courtship they spawn over fine-leaved plants producing 80 or so eggs.

Tank Set-up
Community aquarium with other similar-sized fish. Broad-leaved plants (they may eat fine-leaved plants!) and wood for decor. Good filtration.

BARBUS BARILIOIDES
BOULENGER, 1914

22–25°C	5 cm (2 in)
70–77°F	

Family: CYPRINIDAE

Common name: BLUE-BANDED BARB, BLUE-BARRED BARB

Distribution: Southern Zaire, Zambia, northern Zimbabwe, Angola

Size: 5 cm (2 in)

Food: OMNIVOROUS. Live, flake and frozen food

Temperature range: 22–25°C / 70–77°F

pH: 6.0–6.5 dH: to 7°

Can be a very difficult fish to acclimatize to aquarium conditions. Water quality seems to be the key to success, plus keeping a shoal of 10 or more fish. They can be very shy and retiring. Males are slimmer than females.

Breeding
Requires a well-planted aquarium specially set up for the purpose. Use dense thickets of fine-leaved plants, as the fish will spawn in these. Remove the parents or they will eat the eggs. Hatching takes about 36–40 hours. First foods: infusoria and brine shrimp nauplii.

Tank Set-up
Calm community aquarium with plenty of plants. Mature water and an efficient filtration system.

Family: CYPRINIDAE

Common name: TWO-SPOT BARB

Distribution: Sri Lanka

Size: 7 cm (3 in)

Food: OMNIVOROUS. Live, frozen and flake

Temperature range: 22–24°C / 72–75°F

pH: 6.5–7.0 dH: to 15°

Classic shoaling fish that likes the company of its own kind. Kept in groups they will swim out in the open, but kept as solitary specimens or pairs they tend to retire to the darker recesses of the aquarium. Males are slimmer and have a reddish stripe along the body.

Breeding
Soft, slightly acidic water is required for spawning, and clumps of plants. Eggs are deposited among the plants a few at a time. Remove the parents or they will eat the eggs. Hatching in 24 hours or so, the fry should be fed brine shrimp nauplii. Keep the tank very clean as the fry are sensitive to any deterioration in water quality.

BARBUS BIMACULATUS
(BLEEKER, 1864)

Tank Set-up
Community aquarium, well planted to the sides and rear but with open water. Good filtration and a gentle current is beneficial.

22–24°C	7 cm (3 in)
72–75°F	

BARBUS BINOTATUS
VALENCIENNES, 1842

Family: CYPRINIDAE

Common name: SPOTTED BARB

Distribution: Philippines, Indonesia, Malaysia

Size: 12 cm (4½ in); in the wild 18 cm (7 in)

Food: OMNIVOROUS. Live, frozen and flake

Temperature range: 24–26°C / 75–79°F

pH: 6.0–7.0 dH: to 10°

A shoaling fish that may be kept with similar-sized species in the larger community aquarium. Males are slimmer than females.

24–26°C	12 cm (4½ in)
75–79°F	

Breeding
These fish usually spawn in the early morning, scattering their eggs over pebbles. Either use large pebbles or spawning mesh so that the parents cannot eat the eggs. The fry will take newly hatched brine shrimp.

Tank Set-up
Community aquarium with rocks, wood and plants for decoration. Good filtration and a flow of water is beneficial.

BARBUS CALLIPTERUS
BOULENGER, 1907

20–24°C	9 cm (3½ in)
68–75°F	

Family: CYPRINIDAE	
Common name: CLIPPER BARB	
Distribution: Niger to Cameroon	
Size: 9 cm (3½ in)	
Food: OMNIVOROUS. Flake, frozen, live and green food	
Temperature range: 20–24°C / 68–75°F	
pH: 6.5–7.5 dH: to 12°	

A undemanding fish that settles easily to aquarium life. It does jump, so use floating plants and also ensure the tank is well covered. Sexing this species is not easy, but what are presumed to be females are plumper at some times of the year.

Breeding
Not known.

Tank Set-up
Community aquarium with plants. Good filtration to give a current. Tight-fitting cover glass.

BARBUS CONCHONIUS
(HAMILTON, 1822)

18–22°C	8 cm (3 in)
64–72°F	

Family: CYPRINIDAE	
Common name: ROSY BARB	
Distribution: Northern India	
Size: 8 cm (3 in)	
Food: OMNIVOROUS. Flake, frozen and live food	
Temperature range: 18–22°C / 64–72°F	
pH: 6.5–7.5 dH: to 12°	

Widely bred for the tropical fish trade, this creature has been cultivated to produce a long-finned form. It is very peaceful and adapts well to life in an aquarium. The best colours are seen in cooler conditions: males have much red on their bodies and a golden back, while females are gold.

Breeding
Easy to breed using one male and two females. The eggs are scattered across plants and fall to the bottom. If necessary use a mesh across the bottom of the aquarium, so the eggs fall through and cannot be eaten by the parents. Hatching after 30 hours, the fry may be fed on newly hatched brine shrimp.

Tank Set-up
General community aquarium. Good filtration. Cool conditions.

BARBUS CUMINGI
(GUENTHER, 1868)

22–27°C	5 cm (2 in)
72–81°F	

Family: CYPRINIDAE	
Common name: CUMING'S BARB	
Distribution: Sri Lanka	
Size: 5 cm (2 in)	
Food: OMNIVOROUS. Live, frozen and vegetable food	
Temperature range: 22–27°C / 72–81°F	
pH: 6.5–7.5 dH: to 12°	

A popular fish in the hobby, it is now bred commercially in large numbers. In the wild the fish are now scarce. Males are slimmer and more intensely coloured.

Breeding
Can be difficult. Use a mature aquarium with plenty of plants and algae, soft water and a pH of 6.5–7.2.

Tank Set-up
Well-planted mature aquarium. Regular partial water changes. Good efficient filtration giving a flow of water. Subdued lighting, which can be achieved using some floating plants.

BARBUS EVERETTI
BOULENGER, 1894

24–29°C	10 cm (4 in)
75–84°F	

Family: CYPRINIDAE	
Common name: CLOWN BARB	
Distribution: Southeast Asia	
Size: 10 cm (4 in)	
Food: OMNIVOROUS. Flake, frozen, vegetable and live food	
Temperature range: 24–29°C / 75–84°F	
pH: 6.0–7.0 dH: to 12°	

A very peaceable Barb which requires warm conditions. Males are slimmer than females and have better colours. The males mature later (females are mature at a year, males at 18 months), and some of the difficulties in breeding these creatures have resulted from using males which are immature.

Breeding
Use warm water (28–29°C / 82–84°F), a large aquarium, and a mature pair of fish. Condition the parents well and they should spawn over fine-leaved plants. Raise fry on brine shrimp nauplii.

Tank Set-up
A roomy aquarium with open water for swimming. Keep the water temperature fairly high. Good filtration.

BARBUS FILAMENTOSUS
(VALENCIENNES, 1842)

Family: CYPRINIDAE	
Common name: FILAMENT BARB, BLACK-SPOT BARB	
Distribution: Southern India and Sri Lanka	
Size: 15 cm (6 in)	
Food: OMNIVOROUS. Live, flake, green and frozen food	
Temperature range: 20–24°C / 68–75°F	
pH: 6.0–6.5 dH: to 15°	

A very active Barb that needs a lot of space. A shoal of mature fish makes an attractive display. Males are smaller but more intensely coloured than females, and also have extensions to their dorsal fin.

20–24°C
68–75°F   15 cm (6 in)

Breeding
Spawning takes place between plants and the eggs hatch in about 40 hours. Fry are easy to raise on brine shrimp nauplii and fine flake.

Tank Set-up
Long aquarium, planted at the sides and rear. Good filtration.

BARBUS GELIUS
(HAMILTON, 1822)

Family: CYPRINIDAE	
Common name: DWARF BARB	
Distribution: Central India	
Size: 4 cm (1½ in)	
Food: OMNIVOROUS. Small live food, flake and algae	
Temperature range: 18–22°C / 64–72°F	
pH: 6.0–7.0 dH: to 10°	

Ideal for the smaller aquarium, this Barb can be kept with other small fishes. Males are slimmer and have a more coppery-coloured stripe than females. Best kept as a small shoal.

18–22°C
64–72°F   4 cm (1½ in)

Breeding
Spawns in shallow, soft, acidic water, placing the eggs on the undersides of leaves. Eggs hatch in 24 hours. Feed fry the finest of live foods.

Tank Set-up
Community aquarium with other small, peaceful species. Low growing plants, so the fish have something to swim over. Wood for decoration. Good filtration.

BARBUS HOLOTAENIA
BOULENGER, 1904

Family: CYPRINIDAE	
Common name: NONE	
Distribution: Cameroon to Zaire and Angola	
Size: 12 cm (4½ in)	
Food: OMNIVOROUS. Live and flake food, plus algae and green foods such as lettuce and peas	
Temperature range: 24–28°C / 75–82°F	
pH: 6.0–6.5 dH: to 10°	

A very active shoaling fish that combines well with other community fishes. Allow plenty of space in the aquarium for them to swim.

24–28°C
75–82°F   12 cm (4½ in)

Breeding
Not known..

Tank Set-up
Large aquarium with soft substrate. Roots and pebbles for decor. Plant the back and sides of the aquarium, and use low growing plants in the foreground. Good filtration.

BARBUS LATERISTRIGA
VALENCIENNES, 1842

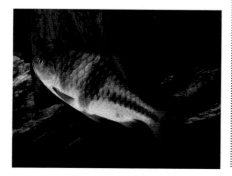

Family: CYPRINIDAE	
Common name: SPANNER BARB	
Distribution: Southeast Asia	
Size: 18 cm (7 in)	
Food: OMNIVOROUS	
Temperature range: 24–27°C / 75–81°F	
pH: 6.0–7.0 dH: to 12°	

Young fish are gregarious and boisterous but peaceful; adults tend to be loners. May be kept with other

24–27°C
75–81°F   18 cm (7 in)

species of similar disposition. Males are slimmer, and the red in their dorsal fin is more intense.

Breeding
About 100 eggs are produced and stick to plants. They hatch in about 24 hours and the fry will take brine shrimp nauplii.

Tank Set-up
Community aquarium with other fish of similar size and manner. Thickets of plants, some wood and rocks. Good filtration.

BARBUS LINEATUS

DUNCKER, 1904

Family: CYPRINIDAE	
Common name: STRIPED BARB	
Distribution: Malay Peninsula, parts of Indonesia	
Size: 12 cm (4½ in)	
Food: OMNIVOROUS. Live, frozen, flake and green food	
Temperature range: 21–24°C / 70–75°F	
pH: 6.0–6.5 dH: to 10°	

A very active shoaling fish that should be kept in groups of 10 or more. The lines on the male's body are more pronounced and he is slimmer than the female.

Breeding
Very soft, acid water (pH 5.5–6.0; dH to 5°) and dense vegetation. Eggs are deposited among the plants and hatch in about 24 hours. Remove the parents or they will eat the eggs. The fry are easily raised on newly hatched brine shrimp and powdered flake.

Tank Set-up
Well-planted community aquarium with some open water for the shoal to swim. Good filtration.

 21–24°C 70–75°F   12 cm (4½ in)

BARBUS NIGROFASCIATUS

GUENTHER, 1868

Family: CYPRINIDAE	
Common name: RUBY BARB	
Distribution: Sri Lanka	
Size: 6.5 cm (2½ in)	
Food: OMNIVOROUS. Flake, frozen and live food	
Temperature range: 20–26°C / 68–79°F	
pH: 6.0–7.0 dH: to 15°	

A Barb that may be kept in a community aquarium, or with other Barbs that have a similar pattern of vertical stripes. Males are larger than females, and during the breeding season have more intense coloration, being a ruby red – hence the common name.

20–26°C 68–79°F   6.5 cm (2½ in)

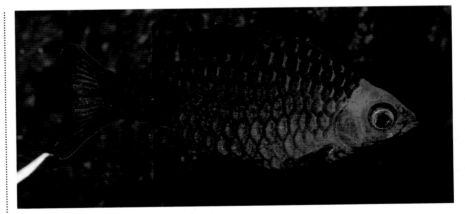

Breeding
These fish spawn in the morning, over and between plants. The eggs hatch after 24 hours and the fry take small, live foods.

Tank Set-up
Community aquarium with subdued lighting. (If lighting is too bright, the fish will hide away.) Provide plant cover to give them some security. Good filtration.

BARBUS OLIGOLEPIS

(BLEEKER, 1853)

20–24°C 68–75°F   15 cm (6 in)

Family: CYPRINIDAE	
Common name: CHECKER BARB, ISLAND BARB	
Distribution: Indonesia	
Size: 15 cm (6 in); usually smaller in aquaria	
Food: OMNIVOROUS. Live, flake, frozen and green food	
Temperature range: 20–24°C / 68–75°F	
pH: 6.0–6.5 dH: to 10°	

Often overlooked in dealers' tanks as they do not show their true colours, these fish are gems for the home aquarium. Males are exquisitely coloured, and though they appear to spar with each other, no damage is done. Keep a shoal of males and females to see them at their best.

Breeding
Soft, slightly acidic, warm water with clumps of fine-leaved plants that reach the surface. Place a pair in the breeding aquarium and they will spawn on the plants, near the surface. The eggs hatch in about 36 hours. Fine first foods.

Tank Set-up
Mature community aquarium with plenty of plants and wood. Regular partial water changes with aged water. Very efficient filtration.

BARBUS ORPHOIDES
VALENCIENNES, 1842

Family: CYPRINIDAE	
Common name: NONE	
Distribution: Southeast Asia	
Size: 25 cm (10 in)	
Food: OMNIVOROUS. Live, frozen, flake and vegetable food	
Temperature range: 22–25°C / 72–77°F	
pH: 6.0–6.5 dH: to 10°	

Young specimens make ideal shoaling fish for the larger aquarium because of their attractive coloration: silvery bodies with red fins, a black spot in the caudal peduncle, and black edges to the caudal fin. However, as large adults they demolish plants and lose the striking coloration, becoming a greyish green.

22–25°C
72–77°F   25 cm (10 in)

Breeding
Not known.

Tank Set-up
Large aquarium with very efficient filtration. Some tough plants and wood for decoration. Alternatively, use artificial plants.

BARBUS PENTAZONA
BOULENGER, 1894

Family: CYPRINIDAE	
Common name: FIVE-BANDED BARB	
Distribution: Southeast Asia	
Size: 5 cm (2 in)	
Food: OMNIVOROUS. Live, frozen and flake	
Temperature range: 22–26°C / 72–79°F	
pH: 6.0–6.5 dH: to 10°	

A somewhat shy Barb that requires very peaceful companions. They prefer the water to be at the warmer end of their temperature range. Males are smaller and slimmer than females.

22–26°C
72–79°F   5 cm (2 in)

Breeding
Use well-conditioned pairs of fish, but do not separate the pair to condition them. About 200 eggs may be produced and they hatch in 30 hours. First foods: newly hatched brine shrimp. Keep the tank scrupulously clean as the fry are susceptible to infection.

Tank Set-up
Mature, well-planted community aquarium. Gentle but efficient filtration. Subdued lighting.

BARBUS RHOMBOOCELLATUS
KOUMANS, 1940

Family: CYPRINIDAE	
Common name: NONE	
Distribution: Borneo (unconfirmed)	
Size: 5 cm (2 in)	
Food: OMNIVOROUS. Prefers live foods but takes flake	
Temperature range: 23–28°C / 73–82°F	
pH: 6.5–7.5 dH: to 10°	

Seldom imported, this fish is worth a try if available. It seems to do well in soft, slightly acidic water that has a good turnover (at least twice an hour). Any deterioration in water quality and the fish lose colour and do not feed. What appear to be males are slimmer in the body than females. When in good health and fed copious amounts of live foods these fish have an almost iridescent sheen on the body.

Breeding
Not known.

23–28°C
73–82°F   5 cm (2 in)

Tank Set-up
Mature community aquarium with plenty of plants. Wood for decor. Very efficient filtration and high water turnover, such as that provided by an external power filter.

BARBUS SCHWANEFELDI
BLEEKER, 1853

Family: CYPRINIDAE	
Common name: TINFOIL BARB, SCHWANEFELD'S BARB	
Distribution: Southeast Asia	
Size: 35 cm (14 in)	
Food: OMNIVOROUS. Live, flake, frozen and green food	
Temperature range: 22–25°C / 72–77°F	
pH: 6.5–7.0 dH: to 10°	

Although sold in great numbers for community aquaria, they are not really suited to this. They grow large and are very active, requiring a lot of room for swimming. They are ideal when kept as a shoal in very large display tanks.

Breeding
Not known.

Tank Set-up
Large aquarium with minimal planting. Soft substrate, as they like to dig, and very good filtration to cope with the amount of debris stirred up.

22–25°C 72–77°F		35 cm (14 in)

BARBUS TETRAZONA
(BLEEKER, 1855)

20–26°C 68–79°F		7 cm (3 in)

Family: CYPRINIDAE	
Common name: TIGER BARB	
Distribution: Indonesia, Borneo	
Size: 7 cm (3 in)	
Food: OMNIVOROUS. Flake, frozen, live and green food	
Temperature range: 20–26°C / 68–79°F	
pH: 6.5–7.5 dH: to 12°	

Often bought for the community aquarium as either a single fish or a pair, it will wreak havoc among the other occupants, nipping fins and generally harassing them. However, if kept in a shoal of eight or more individuals, they establish a pecking order amongst themselves and more or less leave the other fish alone. Males have more colour, and are slimmer and smaller than females. Ensure that you have both males and females in a shoal. Several colour varieties have been developed: black, green, and albino.

Breeding
Place a pair in the breeding aquarium with thickets of fine-leaved plants that reach the surface. After spawning raise the fry on newly hatched brine shrimp.

Tank Set-up
Community aquarium if keeping a large enough shoal, otherwise a species tank. Good filtration.

BARBUS TICTO
(HAMILTON, 1822)

Family: CYPRINIDAE	
Common name: TICTO BARB, TWO-SPOT BARB	
Distribution: India, Sri Lanka	
Size: 10 cm (4 in)	
Food: OMNIVOROUS. Live, flake and frozen food	
Temperature range: 19–22°C / 66–72°F	
pH: 6.5 dH: to 10°	

Ideally suited to a community aquarium, these fish are undemanding and a delight to watch. Males have a red stripe along the body and more spots on the dorsal fin. They can take cooler conditions in the winter, when you can allow the water to drop to 14 or 15°C / 57 or 59°F. Before doing this however, check that your other fish can tolerate such low conditions.

Breeding
One or two pairs in a breeding aquarium. Allow them to spawn over

Java Moss or breeding mesh – anything to keep the parents away from the eggs or they will be eaten. Hatching is in 24-36 hours. First food: brine shrimp nauplii.

19–22°C 66–72°F		10 cm (4 in)

Tank Set-up
Mature community aquarium.

BARBUS TITTEYA
(Deraniyagala, 1929)

23–26°C
73–79°F

5 cm (2 in)

Family: Cyprinidae	
Common name: Cherry Barb	
Distribution: Sri Lanka	
Size: 5 cm (2 in)	
Food: Omnivorous. Live, flake and frozen food	
Temperature range: 23–26°C / 73–79°F	
pH: 6.5–7.5 dH: to 12°	

A fish that likes to be kept as a pair, male and female. If more than this are kept they will each seek out their own space in the aquarium. Males are an intense cherry red when breeding, females are brownish red.

Breeding
They spawn on plants such as Java Moss, the eggs being attached to the plant by a thread. Hatching takes 24 hours and the fry may be fed on newly hatched brine shrimp.

Tank Set-up
Community aquarium with thickets of plants. Good filtration.

BARBUS VITTATUS
(Day, 1865)

20–24°C
68–75°F

6 cm (2½ in)

Family: Cyprinidae	
Common name: None	
Distribution: India, Sri Lanka	
Size: 6 cm (2½ in)	
Food: Omnivorous. Live, flake, green and frozen food	
Temperature range: 20–24°C / 68–75°F	
pH: 6.5 dH: to 10°	

The juveniles of this species are shoaling fish, but adults tend to be solitary, spending much time lurking in clumps of plants. Males are smaller and slimmer than females.

Breeding
There is a long and complex courtship after which about 300 eggs are laid. These hatch in about 24 hours and require very small foods.

Tank Set-up
Well-planted community aquarium with wood for decor. Good filtration.

BARBUS VIVIPARUS
Weber, 1897

22–24°C
72–75°F

6.5 cm (2½ in)

Family: Cyprinidae	
Common name: None	
Distribution: Southeast Africa	
Size: 6.5 cm (2½ in)	
Food: Omnivorous. Flake, frozen and live food	
Temperature range: 22–24°C / 72–75°F	
pH: 6.5–7.0 dH: to 12°	

Little is known about this Barb, except that it is undemanding and likes the company of its own kind. It is suitable for a community aquarium of similar-sized, peaceful fishes. Its specific name, viviparus, means "live-bearing", but this fish is in fact an egg-layer.

Breeding
Not known.

Tank Set-up
Community aquarium with plenty of open water. Plant the sides and rear of the tank. Good filtration to give a flow of water.

BRACHYDANIO ALBOLINEATUS
(Blyth, 1860)

21–25°C
70–77°F

6 cm (2½ in)

Family: Cyprinidae	
Common name: Pearl Danio	
Distribution: Southeast Asia	
Size: 6 cm (2½ in)	
Food: Omnivorous. Live and frozen food	
Temperature range: 21–25°C / 70–77°F	
pH: 6.5–7.0 dH: to 12°	

Often overlooked as a fish for the community aquarium, the Pearl Danio is a gem, provided it is kept as a shoal in the right water conditions. Single fish, or even groups of two or three individuals, never show their true potential. Females are much larger than males, but the males show the better colours.

Breeding
In shallow, fresh, warm water (26–30°C / 79–86°F), the fish spawn over clumps of plant. Remove the parents. Eggs hatch in about 36 hours. Feed fry the finest of foods.

Tank Set-up
Community aquarium with other similar-sized fishes.

BRACHYDANIO KERRI
(SMITH, 1931)

23–25°C	5 cm (2 in)
73–77°F	

Family: CYPRINIDAE	
Common name: NONE	
Distribution: Islands of Koh Yao Yai and Koh Yao Noi (Thailand)	
Habitat: Streams	
Size: 5 cm (2 in)	
Food: OMNIVOROUS. Live, frozen, flake and green food	
Temperature range: 23–25°C / 73–77°F	
pH: 6.5–7.0 dH: to 12°	

A delicately coloured fish, it combines well with other *Brachydanio* species in the community aquarium. Males are much slimmer than females.

Breeding
Shallow water. The eggs are scattered over the substrate. Use marbles, coarse gravel or spawning mesh on the bottom of the breeding aquarium, so that the parents cannot reach the eggs. Hatching in about 36 hours, the fry require fine live foods.

Tank Set-up
Community aquarium with similar-sized occupants. Regular water changes. Good filtration giving a reasonable flow of water.

BRACHYDANIO NIGROFASCIATUS
(DAY, 1869)

Family: CYPRINIDAE	
Common name: SPOTTED DANIO	
Distribution: Burma	
Size: 4.5 cm (2 in)	
Food: OMNIVOROUS. Live, frozen and flake	
Temperature range: 24–28°C / 75–82°F	
pH: 6.5–7.0 dH: to 12°	

These seem to prefer warmer waters than other *Brachydanio* species. Keep them as a shoal. Males are slimmer, and their anal fin has a dark brown edge which can show a golden glint as the light catches it. In females this edge is lighter coloured and without the gold glint.

Breeding
Warm water, up to 28°C / 82°F. Condition the fish well. Eggs are deposited in thickets of plants. After hatching, feed infusoria and brine shrimp nauplii.

Tank Set-up
Community aquarium with plenty of plants. A good turnover of water. Regular water changes.

24–28°C	4.5 cm (2 in)
75–82°F	

BRACHYDANIO RERIO
(HAMILTON, 1822)

18–24°C	6 cm (2½ in)
64–75°F	

Family: CYPRINIDAE	
Common name: ZEBRA DANIO, ZEBRA FISH	
Distribution: India	
Size: 6 cm (2½ in)	
Food: OMNIVOROUS. Flake and frozen food	
Temperature range: 18–24°C / 64–75°F	
pH: 6.5–7.0 dH: to 12°	

A very popular aquarium fish, it has been bred commercially to produce an albino strain and also a long-finned strain. Keep in groups rather than as solitary fish. Males are generally slimmer than females and they remain loyal to one partner: a male that has spawned with a female can seldom be persuaded to spawn with a different one.

Breeding
Using a pair of fish in a breeding aquarium with thickets of fine-leaved plants, some 300–400 eggs will be produced. These hatch in about 48 hours and the fry may be fed on fine foods.

Tank Set-up
Community aquarium with like fishes. Good water conditions are essential, as are regular water changes.

CHELA DADYBURJORI
MENON, 1952

Family: CYPRINIDAE	
Common name: NONE	
Distribution: Burma, Cochin (southwest India)	
Size: 4 cm (1½ in)	
Food: CARNIVOROUS. All sorts of small flies and insects	
Temperature range: 22–24°C / 72–75°F	
pH: 6.5–7.0 dH: to 12°	

22–24°C
72–75°F   4 cm (1½ in)

A delicate surface dweller that can be difficult to maintain in the aquarium. It requires copious amounts of live foods such as *Drosophila*, mosquito larvae, etc. Males are slimmer than females. In a well-established and well-maintained aquarium these fish are quite long lived, four years being not uncommon.

Breeding
Spawns in surface vegetation such as *Riccia* and other floating plants.

Tank Set-up
Mature aquarium, well planted and with very efficient filtration. Some floating plants, but leave much of the surface open for the fish to feed. Regular water changes of 20–25% to maintain water quality.

CHELA LAUBUCA
(HAMILTON, 1822)

Family: CYPRINIDAE	
Common name: INDIAN GLASS BARB	
Distribution: Southeast Asia	
Size: 6 cm (2½ in)	
Food: OMNIVOROUS. Flake, frozen, live and green food	
Temperature range: 24–26°C / 75–79°F	
pH: 6.5–7.0 dH: to 12°	

24–26°C
75–79°F   6 cm (2½ in)

A more unusual shoaling fish for the community aquarium. It feeds mainly from the surface and upper regions of the water column; any food falling to the substrate will be ignored. During the spawning season females are fatter than males.

Breeding
Use a breeding aquarium with thickets of plants. The male wraps himself around the female's body, and about 35 eggs are expelled among plants. Eggs hatch in 24 hours. Very fine first foods.

Tank Set-up
Planted community aquarium with good water conditions. Regular water changes of up to 25% every 10–14 days. Efficient filtration. Good cover glass – the fish may jump.

Family: CYPRINIDAE	
Common name: SIAMESE FLYING FOX	
Distribution: Southeast Asia	
Size: 14 cm (5½ in)	
Food: OMNIVOROUS. Predominantly plants but also worms	
Temperature range: 24–26°C / 75–79°F	
pH: 6.5–7.5 dH: to 15°	

A useful little fish, in as much as it will include thread algae and planarium worms in its diet. Although it likes vegetable matter it does not damage plants. It may be kept in a community aquarium and although it can be a little quarrelsome with its own kind no damage is usually done. It likes well-oxygenated water and does best in softer slightly acidic conditions.

Breeding
Not known.

Tank Set-up
Mature community aquarium with very efficient filtration providing clear, well-oxygenated water.

24–26°C
75–79°F   14 cm (5½ in)

CROSSOCHEILUS SIAMENSIS
(SMITH, 1931)

CTENOPHARYGODON IDELLA
(VALENCIENNES, 1844)

Family: CYPRINIDAE	
Common name: SILVER ORFE, GRASS CARP, WHITE AMUR	
Distribution: Middle and lower reaches of the River Amur, lowland rivers of China	
Size: 1 m (3 ft)	
Food: HERBIVOROUS	
Temperature range: 10–20°C / 50–68°F	
pH: 6.0–8.0 dH: to 25°	

A large fish that is best suited to the garden pond where it can survive cold winters. Its main drawback is that it consumes vast quantities of plant material and has been introduced to weed-choked waterways to help free them. Small specimens may be maintained in the coldwater aquarium. Commercially raised as a food fish because of its ease of feeding – it takes any green vegetable food, even grass cuttings.

Breeding
It spawns in warm (26–28°C / 79–82°F), flowing water. The pelagic eggs are washed downstream where they hatch. Unlikely to breed in the confines of a home aquarium or pond.

10–20°C
50–68°F

1 m (3 ft)

Tank Set-up
A large aquarium with good filtration. Plants may be provided but they will be eaten. It is best to use rocks, wood and artificial plants for decoration.

CYCLOCHEILICHTHYS APOGON
(VALENCIENNES, 1842)

24–26°C
75–79°F

To 50 cm (20 in)

Family: CYPRINIDAE	
Common name: NONE	
Distribution: Southeast Asia	
Size: To 50 cm (20 in); more usually 15–20 cm (6–8 in)	
Food: OMNIVOROUS. Flake, frozen and live food	
Temperature range: 24–26°C / 75–79°F	
pH: 6.5–7.5 dH: to 15°	

A large fish, it feeds from the substrate, sifting through sand and gravel for insect larvae and detritus. It is undemanding, and may be kept with larger, peaceful Catfishes.

Breeding
Not known.

Tank Set-up
Avoid extremes of water conditions. Good filtration to cope with the sediments stirred up. Some plants are beneficial.

CYCLOCHEILICHTHYS JANTHOCHIR
(BLEEKER, 1853)

Family: CYPRINIDAE	
Common name: NONE	
Distribution: Indonesia, Borneo	
Size: 20 cm (8 in)	
Food: OMNIVOROUS. Flake, frozen and live food	
Temperature range: 22–26°C / 72–79°F	
pH: 6.0–6.5 dH: to 8°	

An active fish, it likes plenty of space to swim in. Generally peaceful towards fishes of a similar size. It makes excellent companions for peaceful, bottom dwelling Catfish. Males appear to be slimmer than females.

Breeding
Unlikely in the aquarium.

Tank Set-up
A large aquarium with plenty of plants. Regular water changes and good filtration are essential.

22–26°C
72–79°F

20 cm (8 in)

DANIO AEQUIPINNATUS
(McClelland, 1839)

Family: CYPRINIDAE	
Common name: GIANT DANIO	
Distribution: India, Sri Lanka	
Size: 10 cm (4 in)	
Food: OMNIVOROUS. Flake, frozen, live and vegetable food	
Temperature range: 22–24°C / 72–75°F	
pH: 6.0–7.0 dH: to 12°	

An excellent fish for the larger community aquarium. Keep in shoals of males and females. Males are slimmer and more intensely coloured, and the blue stripe runs straight into the caudal fin. In the fatter females, the blue stripe bends upwards at the base of the caudal fin.

Breeding
Sunlight is a good stimulant for spawning. Up to 300 eggs may be produced. They hatch in about 30 hours and are relatively easy to raise.

22–24°C 72–75°F 10 cm (4 in)

Tank Set-up
Large community aquarium with plenty of open water. Regular water changes. Good filtration.

DANIO DEVARIO
(Hamilton, 1822)

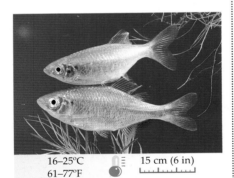

16–25°C 61–77°F — 15 cm (6 in)

Family: CYPRINIDAE	
Common name: BENGAL DANIO	
Distribution: Northern India, Bangladesh	
Size: 15 cm (6 in)	
Food: OMNIVOROUS. Flake, frozen, live and vegetable food	
Temperature range: 16–25°C / 61–77°F	
pH: 6.5–7.0 dH: to 12°	

Water conditions, especially temperature, are very critical for this fish. It does not like to be too warm unless it is breeding. Keep in a shoal, as individuals can be shy and retiring. Males are slimmer than females and show more colour.

Breeding
In warmer water, the fish spawn through plants. The fry are reasonably easy to raise on tiny live foods.

Tank Set-up
Community aquarium with efficient filtration. Regular 20% water changes are beneficial.

EIRMOTUS OCTOZONA
Schultz, 1959

Family: CYPRINIDAE	
Common name: EIGHT-BANDED FALSE BARB	
Distribution: Indonesia, Borneo	
Size: 5 cm (2 in)	
Food: OMNIVOROUS. Live, flake and green food	
Temperature range: 24–26°C / 75–79°F	
pH: 6.5–7.5 dH: to 12°	

Shoals of eight or so individuals are suited to a community aquarium. They are undemanding and retiring, so keep with fish of similar size and temperament. Males are slimmer than females and have reddish unpaired and ventral fins, whereas in females these fins are yellowish.

Breeding
Not known.

Tank Set-up
Quiet community aquarium with thickets of plants. Gentle filtration. Subdued lighting, or use floating plants to dim part of the aquarium.

24–26°C 75–79°F 5 cm (2 in)

EPALZEORHYNCHUS BICOLOR
(SMITH, 1931)

Family: CYPRINIDAE

Common name: RED-TAILED SHARK, RED-TAILED BLACK SHARK, RED-TAILED LABEO

Distribution: Thailand

Size: 12 cm (4½ in)

Food: OMNIVOROUS. Live, flake, frozen and green food

Temperature range: 22–26°C / 72–79°F

pH: 6.5–7.5 dH: to 15°

Although a favourite for the community aquarium, this fish can be aggressive to the point of terrorisation. Large specimens are not only quarrelsome amongst themselves, they will also pick on other fishes, so if you want to keep them be prepared for some belligerence in the aquarium. Males are supposed to have a more pointed dorsal fin, while in females the rear edge forms a right angle.

Breeding
Difficult because of their intolerant nature. One report states that they spawn in a hollow and the eggs hatch in 48 hours.

22–26°C
72–79°F 12 cm (4½ in)

Tank Set-up
Large, well-planted aquarium with rocks and roots, providing territories so that one fish cannot see another.

EPALZEORHYNCHUS FRENATUS
FOWLER, 1937

Family: CYPRINIDAE

Common name: RED-FINNED SHARK, RAINBOW SHARK, RUBY SHARK

Distribution: Thailand

Size: 15 cm (6 in)

Food: OMNIVOROUS. Flake, frozen, live and green food

Temperature range: 22–26°C / 72–79°F

pH: 6.5–7.5 dH: to 15°

Often kept as a novelty in the community aquarium, these fishes are loners. They can be aggressive towards each other, sometimes ripping each others' fins to shreds, but normally leave other occupants of the aquarium alone. Males are slimmer and have a black edge to the anal fin.

Breeding
Chance spawnings have occurred but no details are available.

Tank Set-up
Large community aquarium with other fish of similar size. Thickets of plants, rocks and wood to enable the fish to stake out territories. Good filtration.

22–26°C
72–79°F 15 cm (6 in)

EPALZEORHYNCHUS KALLOPTERUS
(BLEEKER, 1850)

24–26°C
75–79°F 15 cm (6 in)

Family: CYPRINIDAE

Common name: FLYING FOX

Distribution: Borneo, Indonesia, Thailand, India

Size: 15 cm (6 in)

Food: OMNIVOROUS. Live, frozen, flake and vegetable food

Temperature range: 24–26°C / 75–79°F

pH: 6.5–7.0 dH: to 10°

Primarily a loner, although several can be kept in an aquarium as long as there is sufficient space for them to have their own territories. They do not worry other fishes. Much time is spent resting on the leaves of broad-leaved plants or grazing through algae.

Breeding
Not known.

Tank Set-up
Community aquarium with broad-leaved plants and flat stones. Good filtration to give clean, clear, flowing water. Regular water changes of up to 25% every 10–14 days.

GARRA TAENIATA
SMITH, 1931

24–26°C	15 cm (6 in)
75–79°F	

Family: CYPRINIDAE
Common name: SIAMESE STONE-LAPPING FISH
Distribution: Thailand
Size: 15 cm (6 in)
Food: OMNIVOROUS. Flake, frozen, live and green food
Temperature range: 24–26°C / 75–79°F
pH: 6.5–7.0 dH: to 12°

When several are kept together they can be rather boisterous, stirring up the substrate and hollowing out areas beneath plants and wood. However, they do not harrass other tank mates.

Breeding
Not known.

Tank Set-up
Planted aquarium with wood and rocks. Broad-leaved plants and flat stones to provide resting places. Good filtration – they like to cavort in the return from a power filter. Regular water changes.

GOBIO GOBIO
(LINNAEUS, 1758)

10–18°C	20 cm (8 in)
50–64°F	

Family: CYPRINIDAE
Common name: GUDGEON
Distribution: Most of Europe
Size: 20 cm (8 in)
Food: OMNIVOROUS. Live foods predominantly but will take flake and tablet food
Temperature range: 10–18°C / 50–64°F
pH: 7.0–7.5 dH: to 20°

A coldwater fish, it is quite peaceful and may be kept with Minnows, Stone Loaches and the like. It is a food fish in some countries. Males have breeding tubercles in the breeding season.

Breeding
Captive breeding details not available.

Tank Set-up
Cool, clear, well-filtered water that is high in oxygen is essential. There should be a definite current of water through the aquarium. Sandy substrate with rocks and pebbles and some plants.

LABEO CHRYSOPHEKADION
(BLEEKER, 1849)

24–27°C	60 cm (2 ft)
75–81°F	

Family: CYPRINIDAE
Common name: BLACK SHARK, BLACK LABEO
Distribution: Southeast Asia
Size: 60 cm (2 ft)
Food: OMNIVOROUS. Live, flake, frozen and green food
Temperature range: 24–27°C / 75–81°F
pH: 6.5–7.5 dH: to 15°

A very large, boisterous and sometimes quarrelsome fish, not suited to the community aquarium. Include plenty of green food in its diet. In southeast Asia it is an important food fish and the flesh is considered a delicacy.

Breeding
Not known.

Tank Set-up
Large aquarium with rocks and wood for decoration. Very efficient filtration system and regular water changes. Good cover glass as this fish sometimes jumps.

LABEO FORSKALII
RUPPELL, 1853

Family: CYPRINIDAE
Common name: PLAIN SHARK
Distribution: Basin of the Nile and Blue Nile
Size: 35 cm (14 in); in captivity 20 cm (8 in)
Food: OMNIVOROUS. Live, flake, frozen and green food
Temperature range: 20–25°C / 68–77°F
pH: 6.5–7.5 dH: to 15°

Very quarrelsome with their own kind but not towards other fishes. As they get older and larger they become more and more territorial. The first and last rays of the dorsal fin are elongated in males.

Breeding
Not known.

20–25°C	35 cm (14 in)
68–77°F	

Tank Set-up
Large aquarium with other fish of similar size. Some rocks, plant and wood to provide cover and allow them to take up territories. Good filtration.

LABEO VARIEGATUS
PELLEGRIN, 1926

21–25°C
70–77°F

30 cm (12 in)

Family: CYPRINIDAE

Common name: HARLEQUIN SHARK, VARIEGATED SHARK

Distribution: Zaire

Size: 30 cm (12 in)

Food: OMNIVOROUS. Flake, frozen, tablet, live and green food

Temperature range: 21–25°C / 70–77°F

pH: 6.5–7.5 dH: to 18°

Small specimens are fairly peaceful with fish of a similar size, but with age they become more quarrelsome and even aggressive towards their companions.

Keep with fish that are capable of defending themselves. They are greedy feeders.

Breeding
Not known.

Tank Set-up
Large aquarium with rocks, wood and large plants. Good filtration.

LABIOBARBUS FESTIVUS
(HECKEL, 1843)

Family: CYPRINIDAE

Common name: FESTIVE APOLLO SHARK, DIAMOND SHARK, SIGNAL BARB

Distribution: Borneo

Size: 20 cm (8 in)

Food: OMNIVOROUS. Live, frozen, flake and green food

Temperature range: 22–25°C / 72–77°F

pH: 6.0–6.5 dH: to 10°

A retiring fish, it does best in a large, well-planted aquarium with other peaceful species. It is easily frightened and will jump when scared. Provide a good proportion of vegetable matter in the diet. It will also eat algae and Java Moss, but tends not to damage most plants. Regular water changes are essential to keep it in good health.

Breeding
Not known.

Tank Set-up
Large aquarium with roots and plants. Very efficient filtration to provide a good flow of water.

22–25°C
72–77°F

20 cm (8 in)

Family: CYPRINIDAE

Common name: RIVER BARB, RED-FINNED CIGAR SHARK

Distribution: Southeast Asia

Size: 50 cm (20 in)

Food: OMNIVOROUS. Live, frozen, flake and green food

Temperature range: 22–26°C / 72–79°F

pH: 6.5–7.5 dH: to 15°

An undemanding but very large fish, only juveniles are really suitable for the home aquarium. Very active, it jumps readily and may injure itself. Best kept in groups, it requires plenty of swimming space.

Breeding
Not known.

Tank Set-up
Large, spacious aquarium with some wood and large, robust plants. A flow of water is beneficial, and this can be provided by an external power filter.

LEPTOBARBUS HOEVENII
(BLEEKER, 1851)

22–26°C
72–79°F

50 cm (20 in)

LUCIOSOMA TRINEMA
BLEEKER, 1855

24–27°C	30 cm (12 in)
75–81°F	

Family: CYPRINIDAE

Common name: NONE

Distribution: Southeast Asia

Size: 30 cm (12 in)

Food: OMNIVOROUS. Live, frozen, flake and vegetable food

Temperature range: 24–27°C / 75–81°F

pH: 6.5–7.0 dH: to 10°

This large, shoaling surface-dweller makes a wonderful companion for medium-sized bottom-dwelling catfish. The generic name means 'pike-like body', a reference to its streamlined appearance. It also jumps, so ensure a good cover glass. It is believed to be possible to tell the sexes by the long, thread-like extensions to the pelvic fins.

Breeding
Not known.

Tank Set-up
A long tank is essential for these active creatures. Minimal planting. Good, heavy, tight-fitting cover glass – these large, boisterous fish will dislodge a lightweight cover. Efficient filtration.

NOCOMIS LEPTOCEPHALUS
(GIRARD, 1857)

Family: CYPRINIDAE

Common name: BLUEHEAD CHUB

Distribution: Atlantic Coast and Gulf coast streams of the USA

Size: 20 cm (8 in)

Food: OMNIVOROUS. Algae, small aquatic invertebrates

Temperature range: 10–20°C / 50–68°F

pH: 6.0–7.0 dH: to 10°

May be kept in a cold water aquarium. Young fish have a dark line along their flanks and a caudal spot. When breeding, males have breeding tubercules on a swollen crest between the eyes.

Breeding
Males construct a large, dome-shaped nest of stones during early summer. The nest may be up to 1 m (3 ft) wide.

Tank Set-up
A large aquarium with good filtration. Use pebbles and plants for decor but provide some open sandy areas.

10–20°C	20 cm (8 in)
50–68°F	

NOTOMIGONUS CRYSOLEUCAS
(MITCHILL, 1814)

10–20°C	30 cm (12 in)
50–68°F	

Family: CYPRINIDAE

Common name: GOLDEN SHINER

Distribution: Eastern North America from southern Canada to the Gulf Coast

Size: 30 cm (12 in)

Food: OMNIVOROUS. Small invertebrates, plant matter

Temperature range: 10–20°C / 50–68°F

pH: 6.5–7.5 dH: to 12°

A shoaling fish, small specimens may be kept in the aquarium. They are active fishes and require plenty of open water. Males in breeding condition have an orange tinge to their ventral and anal fins. Widely used as bait fish by anglers.

Breeding
Spawns in spring and early summer in shallow water.

Tank Set-up
A large, well-maintained aquarium with a sand or gravel substrate and rocks, wood and thickets of plants for decor. Gentle filtration.

NOTROPIS LUTRENSIS
(BAIRD & GIRARD, 1853)

Family: CYPRINIDAE	
Common name: SHINER	
Distribution: Midwest USA	
Size: 8 cm (3½ in)	
Food: OMNIVOROUS. Live, flake and frozen food	
Temperature range: 15–24°C / 59–75°F	
pH: 7.0–7.5 dH: to 18°	

A coldwater fish, it is becoming more and more popular for the aquarium. Males are far more colourful than females and have breeding tubercules during the spawning season. Keep as a shoal. In the wild they live in moderately flowing streams which have a gravel or sand substrate.

Breeding
Not reported in aquaria.

Tank Set-up
Coldwater aquarium with some plants and sand or gravel substrate. Good water flow provided by an efficient filtration system.

15–24°C
59–75°F
 8 cm (3½ in)

Family: CYPRINIDAE	
Common name: NONE	
Distribution: Northern Ghana	
Size: 15 cm (6 in)	
Food: CARNIVOROUS. Mostly small aquatic invertebrates and flies from the surface, but will take flake	
Temperature range: 22–24°C / 72–75°F	
pH: 6.5 dH: to 10°	

A very attractive fish but seldom imported, it should be kept in groups. A surface dweller, it will jump at the least provocation. The colours in sunlight are unbelievable.

Breeding
Not known.

Tank Set-up
Large aquarium with plants and open areas. Some floating plants for the fish to lurk beneath. Good filtration to provide the best quality water. Regular water changes. Other tank decor can include wood and pebbles.

OPSARISIUM CHRYSTYI
(BOULENGER, 1920)

22–24°C
72–75°F
15 cm (6 in)

OSTEOCHILUS HASSELTI
(VALENCIENNES, 1842)

22–24°C
72–75°F
30 cm (12 in)

Family: CYPRINIDAE	
Common name: NONE	
Distribution: Southeast Asia	
Size: 30 cm (12 in)	
Food: OMNIVOROUS. Flake, live, frozen and green food	
Temperature range: 22–24°C / 72–75°F	
pH: 6.5–7.0 dH: to 10°	

An attractive fish that is easy to keep and peaceful. Small specimens do well in a community aquarium, but be prepared to provide larger accommodation as the fish grows. It is fond of nibbling plants, but if sufficient Java Moss is present and some green foods are provided, it will concentrate on these and leave the other plants alone.

Breeding
Not known.

Tank Set-up
Planted community aquarium for small specimens; larger specimens may be kept with peaceful catfishes. Good filtration as they dislike poor quality water.

PARLUCIOSOMA CEPHALOTAENIA
(BLEEKER, 1852)

Family: CYPRINIDAE	
Common name: PORTHOLE RASBORA	
Distribution: Southeast Asia	
Size: 14 cm (5½ in)	
Food: OMNIVOROUS. Live, frozen and flake food	
Temperature range: 22–24°C / 72–75°F	
pH: 6.0–6.5 dH: to 15°	

Classic shoaling fish that is often overlooked for the aquarium. It should be kept in groups of six or more individuals. Males are slimmer than females.

Breeding
They breed in soft, slightly acidic, warm water. The eggs are laid in fine-leaved plants, and hatch in about 36 hours. The fry require very fine live foods such as infusoria, followed by brine shrimp nauplii.

Tank Set-up
Large community aquarium which need not be especially deep. Well planted to the sides and rear but with open water. Good filtration. Regular water changes are beneficial.

 22–24°C 72–75°F   14 cm (5½ in)

Family: CYPRINIDAE	
Common name: SOUTHERN REDBELLY DACE	
Distribution: Central USA	
Size: 7.5 cm (3 in)	
Food: OMNIVOROUS. Predominantly small live food, will take flake	
Temperature range: 10–20°C / 50–68°F	
pH: 6.5–7.0 dH: to 12°	

A fish for the cool water aquarium, it adapts well and is easy to keep. The males are most attractive, their flanks and belly may be bright red or even yellow. To see them at their best, keep both sexes.

Breeding
It spawns in spring and early summer in fast-flowing, shallow water.

Tank Set-up
An aquarium with a sandy substrate, small pebbles and some plants for decoration. Provide a good flow of water and efficient filtration.

PHOXINUS ERYTHROGASTER
(RAFINESQUE IN KIRTLAND, 1844)

 10–20°C 50–68°F   7.5 cm (3 in)

PIMEPHALES NOTATUS
(RAFINESQUE, 1820)

Family: CYPRINIDAE	
Common name: BLUNTNOSE MINNOW	
Distribution: Widespread through central USA	
Size: 10 cm (4 in)	
Food: OMNIVOROUS. Aquatic invertebrates	
Temperature range: 10–20°C / 50–68°F	
pH: 6.5–7.5 dH: to 12°	

A shoaling fish that adapts well to the confines of an aquarium provided they are kept as a group of at least six and the water is well maintained.

 10–20°C 50–68°F   10 cm (4 in)

Breeding
Males clear a small area beneath a flat rock. The eggs are placed on the underside of the rock; they and the subsequent fry are guarded by the male.

Tank Set-up
A well-established aquarium with good filtration. Provide plant cover, a fine substrate and flat rocks.

RASBORA BORAPETENSIS
SMITH, 1934

| 22–26°C | 5 cm (2 in) |
| 72–79°F | |

| Family: CYPRINIDAE |
| Common name: RED-TAILED RASBORA |
| Distribution: Thailand, western Malaysia |
| Size: 5 cm (2 in) |
| Food: OMNIVOROUS. Most small food but live preferred |
| Temperature range: 22–26°C / 72–79°F |
| pH: 6.0–6.5 dH: to 12° |

Classic peaceful, shoaling fish that may be kept with creatures of similar size and temperament. Males are slimmer than females, but this may only be apparent when the fish are ready to spawn.

Breeding
Shallow water with thickets of plants. The addition of some fresh water may trigger spawning. About six eggs are produced at a time, until some 36 or so have been released. They hatch in 36 hours. Feed fine foods. Remove parents after spawning or they will eat the eggs.

Tank Set-up
Community aquarium decorated with plants and wood. Gentle filtration. Subdued lighting.

RASBORA CAUDIMACULATA
VOLZ, 1903

| 20–25°C | 12 cm (4½ in) |
| 68–77°F | |

| Family: CYPRINIDAE |
| Common name: GREATER SCISSORTAIL |
| Distribution: Southeast Asia |
| Size: 12 cm (4½ in) |
| Food: OMNIVOROUS. Flake, green and live food |
| Temperature range: 20–25°C / 68–77°F |
| pH: 6.5–7.5 dH: to 12° |

Favoured as a show fish in bigger display aquaria, these large, active fish require plenty of open water for swimming. They also have a habit of jumping, so ensure the aquarium is well covered. Males are slimmer, their anal fin is yellowish, and the tips of their caudal fin lobes are white.

Breeding
Not known.

Tank Set-up
Large furnished aquarium with roots and pebbles for decor. Good water movement is essential, and may be supplied by an efficient external power filter.

RASBORA DANICONIUS DANICONIUS
(HAMILTON, 1822)

| Family: CYPRINIDAE |
| Common name: NONE |
| Distribution: Thailand, Burma, India, Sri Lanka |
| Size: 10 cm (4 in) |
| Food: OMNIVOROUS. Small live food for preference, will take flake and frozen |
| Temperature range: 24–26°C / 75–79°F |
| pH: 6.5–7.5 dH: to 15° |

An active shoaling fish that likes a well-planted aquarium. Keep them in a group of six or more individuals, as single specimens hide away and may even die. They are best seen in sunlight when the gold stripe along their body seems to glow. Males are slimmer and smaller, and their belly is reddish.

Breeding
Use a reasonable-sized aquarium, as any decaying milt or unfertilised eggs will pollute the water. Include clumps of fine-leaved plants that reach the surface, and the eggs will be deposited in these, close to the surface. Eggs hatch in about three days and the fry may be fed brine shrimp nauplii. Regular water changes are essential.

Tank Set-up
Community aquarium with like species. Good filtration.

| 24–26°C | 10 cm (4 in) |
| 75–79°F | |

RASBORA DORSIOCELLATA
DUNCKER, 1904

20–24°C	6.5 cm (2½ in)
68–75°F	

Family: CYPRINIDAE

Common name: HI-SPOT RASBORA

Distribution: Malay Peninsula, Sumatra

Size: 6.5 cm (2½ in)

Food: OMNIVOROUS. Live, flake and frozen food

Temperature range: 20–24°C / 68–75°F

pH: 6.0–6.5 dH: to 10°

A lively fish, it requires an aquarium with plenty of swimming space for the shoal to display. Males have a red tinge to their caudal fin, while in females it has a hint of yellow. Because of their small size, they require equally small companions.

Breeding
Set the tank up with clumps of fine-leaved plants (Java Moss is ideal). Place the female in the aquarium about 36 hours before you introduce the male. Eggs are deposited among the plants and they hatch in 24 hours. Feed fry on very fine live foods.

Tank Set-up
Well-planted and mature community aquarium. Gentle filtration.

RASBORA EINTHOVENII
(BLEEKER, 1851)

Family: CYPRINIDAE

Common name: LONG-BAND RASBORA

Distribution: Southeast Asia

Size: 8 cm (3 in)

Food: OMNIVOROUS. Live, flake and frozen food

Temperature range: 22–25°C / 72–77°F

pH: 6.0–6.5 dH: to 8°

A shoaling fish for the community aquarium. It is only possible to tell males and females apart during the breeding season. At this time males are smaller and slimmer, while females are fuller in the body with a convex lateral line.

Breeding
These fish spawn among plants. The eggs hatch in about 36 hours, and the fry are relatively easy to raise on newly hatched brine shrimp.

Tank Set-up
Well-planted community aquarium. Provide a tight-fitting cover glass as the fish jump. Good filtration.

22–25°C	8 cm (3 in)
72–77°F	

RASBORA ELEGANS
VOLZ, 1903

Family: CYPRINIDAE

Common name: TWO-SPOT RASBORA, ELEGANT RASBORA

Distribution: Southeast Asia

Size: 20 cm (8 in)

Food: OMNIVOROUS

Temperature range: 21–25°C / 70–77°F

pH: 6.0–6.5 dH: to 10°

Keep as a shoal in a mature system. It is a suitable companion for other medium-sized Barbs and Rasboras. The sexes are easiest to differentiate when ready to breed, females being fuller in the body than males.

Breeding
Very fecund, these creatures spawn over plants. Remove the parents or they will eat the eggs. Eggs hatch in about 36 hours. Feed fry newly hatched brine shrimp.

Tank Set-up
Mature, well-planted aquarium. Efficient filtration system. Regular water changes are beneficial, perhaps 20% every 10–14 days.

21–25°C	20 cm (8 in)
70–77°F	

Family: CYPRINIDAE	
Common name: ESPE'S RASBORA	
Distribution: Thailand	
Size: 4.5 cm (2 in)	
Food: OMNIVOROUS. Flake, frozen and live food – live preferred	
Temperature range: 23–27°C / 73–81°F	
pH: 6.0–6.5 dH: to 10°	

By day these active fish can be seen swimming around the aquarium, but at night they become solitary creatures and spend the hours of darkness resting on leaves. Males are slimmer and more highly coloured than females.

Breeding
Difficult. Requires shallow water with broad-leaved plants on which the eggs are placed. Eggs hatch in some 24 hours and the fry should be fed infusoria.

Tank Set-up
Mature community aquarium with other peaceful fish. Plenty of plants, especially broad-leaved species. Good filtration and regular water changes are essential.

23–27°C 73–81°F		4.5 cm (2 in)

RASBORA ESPEI
(MEINKEN, 1967)

RASBORA HETEROMORPHA
DUNCKER, 1904

22–25°C 72–77°F		4.5 cm (2 in)

Family: CYPRINIDAE	
Common name: HARLEQUIN, RED RASBORA	
Distribution: Southeast Asia	
Size: 4.5 cm (2 in)	
Food: OMNIVOROUS. Flake, frozen and, preferably, live food	
Temperature range: 22–25°C / 72–77°F	
pH: 6.0–6.5 dH: to 10°	

Probably one of the most popular aquarium fishes, it is seldom seen at its best. It should be kept in groups of at least eight individuals, in the company of other equally small and peaceful fishes. The markings on the fish distinguish the sexes: females have a straight edge to the black mark, while in males it is slightly rounded at the bottom and the tip is slightly extended.

Breeding
Not easy. Very soft acidic, warm shallow water. Use a young female with a two-year old male. They spawn on the undersides of broad leaves. Remove parents and keep the tank dark after spawning. Eggs hatch in 24 hours. Feed fry infusoria.

Tank Set-up
Well-established, planted community aquarium. Efficient filtration. Regular water changes.

RASBORA KALOCHROMA
(BLEEKER, 1850)

25–28°C 77–82°F		10 cm (4 in)

Family: CYPRINIDAE	
Common name: CLOWN RASBORA	
Distribution: Southeast Asia	
Size: 10 cm (4 in)	
Food: OMNIVOROUS. Live, flake and frozen food	
Temperature range: 25–28°C / 77–82°F	
pH: 6.0–6.5 dH: to 10°	

One of the larger rasboras, it is also one of the more difficult ones to keep. In the aquarium it does not shoal: the fish tend to take up station in different areas of the tank almost as if they have territories, but there does not seen to be any territorial defence. Males are more highly coloured and have a darker anal fin than females.

Breeding
Not known.

Tank Set-up
Community aquarium, but pay particular attention to water conditions. Some like to add salt to the water, but if you do this check the other inhabitants can tolerate it. Subdued lighting.

RASBORA MACULATA
DUNCKER, 1904

24–26°C
75–79°F

2.5 cm (1 in)

Family: CYPRINIDAE
Common name: PYGMY RASBORA, SPOTTED RASBORA
Distribution: Southeast Asia
Size: 2.5 cm (1 in)
Food: OMNIVOROUS. All kinds of small food
Temperature range: 24–26°C/75–79°F
pH: 6.0–6.5 dH: to 10°

Because of its small size – it is the smallest of the cyprinids – this fish is best kept in a species aquarium. Males are slimmer and more brightly coloured than females.

Breeding
Spawns in thickets of plants, producing up to 50 eggs. These hatch in 24–36 hours and the fry require the smallest of foods.

Tank Set-up
Small aquarium with plenty of fine-leaved plants. Gentle filtration.

Family: CYPRINIDAE
Common name: RED-LINE RASBORA
Distribution: Southeast Asia
Size: 7 cm (3 in)
Food: OMNIVOROUS. Has a preference for live food but takes flake and frozen
Temperature range: 22–25°C/72–77°F
pH: 6.0–6.5 dH: to 10°

Ideal for the community aquarium. Keep a group of eight or more as single individuals hide away. Males are slimmer than females.

Breeding
Let the fish pair themselves. Eggs are laid on fine-leaved plants and hatch in 36 hours. Feed fry fine live foods.

Tank Set-up
Well-planted community aquarium with plenty of open water. Good filtration and a gentle flow of water is beneficial. Regular water changes.

22–25°C
72–77°F

7 cm (3 in)

RASBORA PAUCIPERFORATA
WEBER & DE BEAUFORT, 1916

Family: CYPRINIDAE
Common name: NET RASBORA
Distribution: Sumatra
Size: 6 cm (2½ in)
Food: OMNIVOROUS. Live, frozen and flake
Temperature range: 22–26°C/72–79°F
pH: 6.0–6.5 dH: to 10°

A very attractive fish for the community aquarium, and compatible with other peaceable fishes of a similar size. Males are slimmer than females.

Breeding
They spawn among plants. Raise fry on newly hatched brine shrimp.

Tank Set-up
Large community aquarium with open water. Good cover glass as they may jump. Water change of 25 per cent every ten days. Efficient filtration.

RASBORA RETICULATA
WEBER & DE BEAUFORT, 1915

22–26°C
72–79°F

6 cm (2½ in)

RASBORA TAENIATA
AHL, 1922

22–24°C
72–75°F
7 cm (3 in)

Family: CYPRINIDAE
Common name: BLACK-LINE RASBORA
Distribution: Southeast Asia
Size: 7 cm (3 in)
Food: OMNIVOROUS. Live, flake, frozen and vegetable food
Temperature range: 22–24°C / 72–75°F
pH: 6.5–7.0 dH: to 10°

A shoal of these is very attractive. The males are slim with a yellowish-red caudal fin, the females are more rounded and have an orange caudal fin. They make ideal companions for other Rasboras and some small Barbs.

Breeding
They spawn in shallow water. Remove the parents after spawning or they will eat the eggs. These hatch in 36 hours and the fry may be fed infusoria followed by newly hatched brine shrimp.

Tank Set-up
Well-planted, mature community aquarium with efficient filtration system. Subdued lighting, or provide floating plants on part of the water surface. Regular water changes.

RASBORA TRILINEATA
STEINDACHNER, 1870

23–25°C
73–77°F
15 cm (6 in)

Family: CYPRINIDAE
Common name: SCISSOR-TAIL
Distribution: Malaysia, Sumatra, Borneo
Size: 15 cm (6 in)
Food: OMNIVOROUS. Flake, frozen and live food
Temperature range: 23–25°C / 73–77°F
pH: 6.0–6.5 dH: to 10°

A beautiful shoaling fish for a display aquarium, where they make an impressive sight. They may be kept with other peaceful fishes. The males are smaller and slimmer.

Breeding
Difficult. Use soft, acidic, shallow water. Eggs are laid against plants and hatch in 24 hours. The parents should be removed before they eat the eggs. Feed fry newly hatched brine shrimp.

Tank Set-up
Well-planted, mature community aquarium. The tank should be quite long, to allow the fish swimming space. Good filtration and regular water changes are essential.

RASBORA UROPHTHALMA
AHL, 1922

23–25°C
73–77°F
3.5 cm (1½ in)

Family: CYPRINIDAE
Common name: NONE
Distribution: Indonesia
Size: 3.5 cm (1½ in)
Food: OMNIVOROUS. Preferably small, live food but will take flake
Temperature range: 23–25°C / 73–77°F
pH: 6.0–6.5 dH: to 10°

A delicate little Rasbora that is best suited to a species aquarium, but may be kept with other fish of a similar size and nature. Males are smaller and slimmer; they also have a white area at the base of the dorsal and, above this, a black area.

Breeding
Warm water, up to 28°C / 82°F, that is also soft and slightly acidic. The fish spawn on the undersides of leaves, producing 40 or 50 eggs which hatch in 48 hours. Very small foods are required to feed the fry.

Tank Set-up
Mature aquarium with a selection of fine- and broad-leaved plants. Gentle but efficient filtration. Regular water changes of 10 per cent every seven days.

RASBORA VATERIFLORIS
DERANIYAGALA, 1930

25–28°C
77–82°F
4 cm (1½ in)

Family: CYPRINIDAE
Common name: SINGHALESE FIRE BARB, ORANGE-FINNED BARB
Distribution: Sri Lanka
Size: 4 cm (1½ in)
Food: OMNIVOROUS. Predominantly live food, but flake and vegetable food also taken
Temperature range: 25–28°C / 77–82°F
pH: 6.0–6.5 dH: to 5°

A fish for the specialist, particular attention needing to be paid to water quality. Best in a well-planted, mature aquarium with other very peaceful, warmth-loving fishes. Males are slimmer and have more colour than females.

Breeding
Difficult. Requires a well-planted breeding tank so the fish can spawn in amongst the plants. Drop the water level to about 15 cm (6 in) after spawning. The eggs will hatch in 36 hours and the fry require very fine food.

Tank Set-up
Mature, well-planted, well-filtered community or species aquarium, with some open water for swimming. Keep the water warm.

Family: CYPRINIDAE	
Common name: CREEK CHUB	
Distribution: Eastern North America	
Size: 30 cm (12 in)	
Food: OMNIVOROUS. Algae, aquatic invertebrates	
Temperature range: 10–20°C / 50--68°F	
pH: 6.5–7.5 dH: to 12°	

Young specimens may be kept in the aquarium, larger specimens are more suited to a pond. Fairly active fish that likes the company of its own kind.

Breeding
They spawn in spring, the male excavating a nest in the substrate. Once the eggs have been deposited in the nest they are covered with gravel and left to fend for themselves.

Tank Set-up
A good-sized aquarium with an efficient filtration system. Provide a sand / gravel substrate and rocks, wood and some thickets of plants for decor.

SEMOTILUS ATROMACULATUS
(MITCHILL, 1818)

10–20°C 50–68°F		30 cm (12 in)

TANICHTHYS ALBONUBES
LIN SHU-YEN, 1932

18–22°C 64–72°F		4 cm (1½ in)

Family: CYPRINIDAE
Common name: WHITE CLOUD MOUNTAIN MINNOW
Distribution: White Cloud Mountain, southern China
Size: 4 cm (1½ in)
Food: OMNIVOROUS. Live, flake and frozen food
Temperature range: 18–22°C / 64–72°F
pH: 6.5–7.5 dH: to 15°

A very undemanding fish, provided it is kept at low temperatures. Single specimens tend to lose their colour and hide away, but if kept in a group of eight or more they are both active and colourful. Males are slimmer and have more intense coloration than females. Captive breeding has produced a long-finned variety.

Breeding
In cool water, the fish spawn over plants. The eggs hatch in about 36 hours and the fry may be fed very fine food.

Tank Set-up
Community aquarium with other peaceful fishes. Efficient filtration. Low temperatures: these fish do not like much above 22°C / 72°F for any length of time.

25–28°C 77–82°F		27 cm (11 in)

GYRINOCHEILUS AYMONIERI
(TIRANT, 1883)

Family: GYRINOCHEILIDAE
Common name: SUCKING LOACH, CHINESE ALGAE EATER, INDIAN ALGAE EATER
Distribution: India, Thailand
Size: 27 cm (11 in)
Food: HERBIVOROUS. Likes green food, but will take flake, tablet and live food
Temperature range: 25–28°C / 77–82°F
pH: 6.0–8.0 dH: to 20°

Often purchased for its ability to eat algae, this fish soon outgrows its welcome, becoming boisterous and sometimes aggressive towards other occupants of the aquarium. As they get older they also become territorial. Mature fish have tubercles around the mouth, and it is presumed that these are more numerous on males.

Breeding
Not known.

Tank Set-up
Larger community aquaria. Provide rocks and wood for hiding places; also large plants, as the fish like to rest on the leaves. Efficient filtration is needed to cope with the sediment stirred up by this species.

Killifish

Aplocheilidae
Cyprinodontidae

APLOCHEILUS LINEATUS
(VALENCIENNES, 1846)

22–25°C
72–77°F

10 cm (4 in)

Family:	APLOCHEILIDAE
Common name:	NONE
Distribution:	Southern India
Size:	10 cm (4 in)
Food:	CARNIVOROUS. All live food from insect larvae to young fish; will take flake and frozen food
Temperature range:	22–25°C / 72–77°F
pH: 6.0–7.0	dH: to 12°

This fish can be aggressive, especially towards its own kind. Even so, it is suitable for a community of larger fish. It spends its time close to the surface, where it hunts for insects. Keep males as well as females if you wish to see them at their best, because the more colourful males will display to the females.

Breeding
Eggs are deposited on fine-leaved plants, or on spawning mops. Early morning sunlight seems to trigger spawning – and also shows off the true colours of this fish. Remove parents, or hatch eggs in a separate container. Hatching takes about 12 days. Feed fry on crumbled flake and small live food.

Tank Set-up
Thickets of plants, roots and rocks to provide cover. Some floating plants will give the fish a sense of security and reduce the risk of them jumping. Tight-fitting cover glass in case they do jump. A gentle current is beneficial.

Family:	APLOCHEILIDAE
Common name:	CAPE LOPEZ LYRETAIL
Distribution:	West Africa
Size:	6 cm (2½ in)
Food:	OMNIVOROUS. A preference for small live food, but will take flake, etc
Temperature range:	21–24°C / 70–75°F
pH: 5.5–6.5	dH: to 10°

One of the most frequently seen killies, and an excellent fish for the softwater community aquarium. Males are far more colourful than females, and have extended finnage. There are several colour forms available.

Breeding
Best bred in a specially set-up tank, for in a community aquarium few fry will survive. Use soft, slightly acidic water. The fish spawn on spawning mops or fine-leaved plants. Remove mops daily, and hatch in a separate container. Feed fry newly hatched brine shrimp.

Tank Set-up
Community aquarium with other small, very peaceful species. Thickets of fine-leaved plants. Soft, slightly acidic water, gentle filtration.

APHYOSEMION AUSTRALE
(RACHOW, 1921)

21–24°C
70–75°F

6 cm (2½ in)

APHYOSEMION BIVITATTUM
(LOENNBERG, 1895)

22–24°C
72–75°F

5 cm (2 in)

Family:	APLOCHEILIDAE
Common name:	RED APHYOSEMION
Distribution:	West Africa
Size:	5 cm (2 in)
Food:	CARNIVOROUS. Prefers live food, but will take frozen bloodworm and *Daphnia*, and sometimes flake
Temperature range:	22–24°C / 72–75°F
pH: 6.0–6.5	dH: to 10°

There are several colour variations of this species. Males have extended finnage, the top and bottom of their caudal fin is extended to a point, and they are also more colourful than females.

Breeding
May be spawned in a small aquarium with plenty of Java Moss or some spawning mops. Use peat for the substrate. Subdued lighting. Eggs hatch in about three weeks. First foods should be very fine.

Tank Set-up
Best kept in a species aquarium. Set up much as for breeding. Regular water changes.

APHYOSEMION CALLIURUM

(BOULENGER, 1911)

Family: APLOCHEILIDAE	
Common name: RED-SEAM KILLIE	
Distribution: West Africa	
Size: 5 cm (2 in)	
Food: CARNIVOROUS. Live food but will take frozen and flake	
Temperature range: 24–26°C / 75–79°F	
pH: 6.5–7.0 dH: to 15°	

Males can be quarrelsome with other males of their own kind. Females are plain in comparison with the highly coloured males.

Breeding
Plant or bottom spawner. Use one male to two females. If spawning over peat, store the eggs for three to four weeks. If

using mops, the eggs hatch in two to three weeks. Feed fry on newly hatched brine shrimp.

24–26°C
75–79°F

5 cm (2 in)

Tank Set-up
Can be kept in a well-planted community aquarium and removed for breeding purposes. Medium hard, slightly acidic water. Gentle filtration.

APHYOSEMION CINNAMOMEUM

CLAUSEN, 1963

Family: APLOCHEILIDAE	
Common name: CINNAMON KILLIE	
Distribution: West Africa	
Size: 5 cm (2 in)	
Food: CARNIVOROUS. Live food but will take flake and frozen	
Temperature range: 22–24°C / 72–75°F	
pH: 6.5–7.0 dH: to 15°	

Easy to keep, the only problem can be the aggressive nature of adult males. Males are more colourful than females.

Breeding
Typical *Aphyosemion*: eggs are laid on spawning mops or fine-leaved plants. After hatching, feed fry on brine shrimp nauplii.

Tank Set-up
Well-planted aquarium, with other fishes able to hold their own. Regular water changes are beneficial.

22–24°C
72–75°F

5 cm (2 in)

Family: APLOCHEILIDAE	
Common name: BLACKTAIL KILLIE	
Distribution: West Africa	
Size: 4.5 cm (2 in)	
Food: CARNIVOROUS. Live food for preference, will take frozen	
Temperature range: 20–24°C / 68–75°F	
pH: 6.0–6.5 dH: to 15°	

Males are very attractive, predominantly yellow in colour, but may have a green tint to the body, which is overlain with red spots. Females are greyish in colour. Very peaceful fish, they are best kept in a species tank.

Breeding
Although they will breed either on mops and plants or in the substrate, the better method is on mops. Use one male and two females. Feed fry on newly hatched brine shrimp.

APHYOSEMION CONGICUM

(AHL, 1924)

Tank Set-up
Small, well-planted aquarium. Regular water changes. Monitor the water regularly, as these fish are susceptible to any deterioration in quality.

20–24°C
68–75°F

4.5 cm (2 in)

APHYOSEMION FALLAX
AHL, 1935

Family: APLOCHEILIDAE	
Common name: NONE	
Distribution: Southwestern Cameroon	
Size: 9 cm (3½ in)	
Food: CARNIVOROUS. Aquatic invertebrates	
Temperature range: 22–26°C / 72–79°F	
pH: 6.5 dH: to 10°	

This species is closely related to *A. sjoestedi*, and it is reported that intermediate forms have been found. In the aquarium it may be kept with other fishes. However, it can be aggressive towards its own kind (females not ready to spawn and other males) if kept under cramped conditions. Males are highly coloured with extended finnage. Females by contrast have only a few red spots on the body and their fins are much smaller.

Breeding

A substrate spawner, so set up the aquarium with a peat base. Observe the spawning and remove the female if the male becomes too aggressive.

Tank Set-up

Quiet community aquarium with plenty of plants for cover.

 22–26°C 72–79°F 9 cm (3½ in)

APHYOSEMION GARDNERI
(BOULENGER, 1911)

Family: APLOCHEILIDAE	
Common name: STEEL-BLUE APHYOSEMION	
Distribution: Nigeria, western Cameroon	
Size: 6 cm (2½ in)	
Food: CARNIVOROUS. Predominantly insect larvae, etc, will take flake	
Temperature range: 22–25°C / 72–77°F	
pH: 6.0–6.5 dH: to 8°	

A very attractive killi, whose coloration can vary depending on their original source. They can be quarrelsome, especially the males, not only with other fish but also among themselves. Best kept in a species aquarium. Males are more highly coloured than females.

Breeding

Spawns on fine-leaved plants or spawning mops. Eggs hatch in two to three weeks. Fry will take brine shrimp.

Tank Set-up

May be kept in a small tank, say 50 cm (20 in) x 30 cm (12 in) x 30 cm (12 in). Dark substrate, fine-leaved plants (Java Moss is ideal), soft, slightly acidic water. Very gentle filtration.

 22–25°C 72–77°F 6 cm (2½ in)

APHYOSEMION GERYI
(LAMBERT, 1958)

Family: APLOCHEILIDAE	
Common name: NONE	
Distribution: West Africa	
Size: 5 cm (2 in)	
Food: CARNIVOROUS. Live food, will accept flake and frozen	
Temperature range: 22–26°C / 72–79°F	
pH: 5.5–6.5 dH: to 10°	

East to keep, this attractive fish may be placed in a community aquarium. Males are more colourful than females. However, different populations have differing degrees of coloration.

Breeding

As for genus *Aphyosemion*: eggs are laid on plants or spawning mops. Fry may be raised on brine shrimp.

Tank Set-up

Soft, acidic water, plenty of plants and regular water changes will maintain this fish in good health.

 22–26°C 72–79°F 5 cm (2 in)

APHYOSEMION MIRABILE
RADDA, 1970

Family: APLOCHEILIDAE	
Common name: NONE	
Distribution: Cameroon (M'byo district)	
Size: 7 cm (3 in)	
Food: CARNIVOROUS. Small live food, particularly mosquito larvae	
Temperature range: 22–25°C / 72–77°F	
pH: 6.0–6.5 dH: to 6°	

A fish for the specialist; keep in a species aquarium. Males are more attractive than females. Four subspecies have been described: *A. mirabile mirabile*, *A. m. moense*, *A. m. intermittens*, and *A. m. traudae*.

Breeding

Soft, acidic water. Subdued lighting. Plenty of Java Moss or several spawning mops. Use one male with two or three females. Hatch eggs separately. Feed fry on fine food.

Tank Set-up

Well-planted aquarium with subdued lighting and plenty of hiding places. Peat substrate. Regular water changes are essential.

22–25°C 72–77°F 7 cm (3 in)

Family: APLOCHEILIDAE	
Common name: SCHMITT'S KILLIE	
Distribution: Liberia	
Size: 6 cm (2½ in)	
Food: CARNIVOROUS. All small live food	
Temperature range: 22–24°C / 72–75°F	
pH: 6.0–6.5 dH: to 8°	

These are peaceful fish that may be kept with others of a similar nature. Males are exceedingly colourful, whereas females are brown with faint red spots.

Breeding
Eggs are stuck all over spawning mops, and can be collected and raised separately. Fry will feed on newly hatched brine shrimp.

Tank Set-up
Planted aquarium with soft, acidic water. Very gentle filtration.

22–24°C 72–75°F		6 cm (2½ in)

APHYOSEMION SCHMITTI
(ROMAND, 1979)

APHYOSEMION SJOESTEDTI
(LOENNBERG, 1895)

Family: APLOCHEILIDAE	
Common name: GOLDEN PHEASANT	
Distribution: Ghana to western Cameroon	
Size: 12 cm (4½ in)	
Food: CARNIVOROUS. Live food of all kinds, including the fry of other fish; will take flake and frozen food	
Temperature range: 23–26°C / 73–79°F	
pH: 6.0–6.5 dH: to 15°	

An active fish, well able to hold its own in the community aquarium. Males can be aggressive. They are larger and more colourful than females.

Breeding
Set up the spawning tank with a deep peat base and some clumps of Java Moss. Use soft, slightly acidic water with a temperature of about 23°C/73°F. The eggs are buried in the peat. After spawning, remove the substrate and squeeze out the excess water. Store for six weeks in a plastic bag at about

23–26°C 73–79°F		12 cm (4½ in)

18°C/64°F. Ensure the peat remains damp. To hatch, add water. Feed fry newly hatched brine shrimp.

Tank Set-up
Large tank with plenty of plants, roots and rocks to provide cover. Gentle filtration. Soft, slightly acidic water.

APHYOSEMION STRIATUM
(BOULENGER, 1911)

22–23°C 72–73°F		5 cm (2 in)

Family: APLOCHEILIDAE	
Common name: NONE	
Distribution: Gabon	
Size: 5 cm (2 in)	
Food: CARNIVOROUS. Live food but will take frozen	
Temperature range: 22–23°C / 72–73°F	
pH: 6.0–6.5 dH: to 10°	

A striking fish, the males have red stripes running the length of their bodies. Females, in contrast, are much plainer. Best kept in a species aquarium.

Breeding
Easy to spawn and raise. Use soft, slightly acidic water. The fish spawn on Java Moss or spawning mops, a pair producing up to 30 eggs per day over a period of about a fortnight. The eggs hatch in about 12 days. Feed fry newly hatched brine shrimp.

Tank Set-up
Small aquarium with plenty of fine-leaved plants, plus some floating plants for cover as this fish jumps. Good cover glass. Regular water changes.

APLOCHEILUS DAYI
(STEINDACHNER, 1892)

Family: APLOCHEILIDAE	
Common name: CEYLON KILLIE	
Distribution: Sri Lanka, southern India	
Size: 10 cm (4 in)	
Food: CARNIVOROUS. Small live food, will take flake	
Temperature range: 21–25°C / 70–77°F	
pH: 6.0–7.0 dH: to 15°	

With this species, dominant fish will harass others of their kind unless there is plenty of cover in the aquarium. Males are more colourful and have larger fins than females. Females have a black spot on the base of the dorsal fin.

Breeding
Spawns on plants or spawning mops. About 10 eggs are produced each day,

21–25°C
70–77°F

 10 cm (4 in)

and hatch within two weeks. Fry grow rapidly.

Tank Set-up
Well-planted tank, to permit smaller fish to avoid aggressive larger ones. Good cover glass, as these surface dwellers will jump. Gentle filtration.

CYNOLEBIAS BOITONEI
(DE CARVALHOI, 1959)

Family: APLOCHEILIDAE	
Common name: BRAZILIAN PEARLFISH	
Distribution: Brazil	
Size: 4 cm (1½ in)	
Food: CARNIVOROUS. Small live food	
Temperature range: 20–24°C / 68–75°F	
pH: 6.5–7.5 dH: to 15°	

A killie that likes the company of its own kind. Keep in groups in a species aquarium. Males have larger fins and are more colourful than females.

Breeding
A substrate spawner. After the eggs have been deposited, remove the peat and store damp for about eight weeks.

Tank Set-up
Peat substrate and clumps of plants. Regular water changes.

20–24°C
68–75°F

 4 cm (1½ in)

EPIPLATYS GRAHAMI
(BOULENGER, 1911)

23–27°C
73–81°F

6 cm (2½ in)

Family: APLOCHEILIDAE	
Common name: GRAHAM'S PANCHAX	
Distribution: West Africa	
Size: 6 cm (2½ in)	
Food: CARNIVOROUS. Small live food, flake also taken	
Temperature range: 23–27°C / 73–81°F	
pH: 7.0 dH: to 15°	

A surface-dwelling species that is good at jumping! It is quite at home in the community aquarium. Males are beautifully coloured, with metallic grey-green bodies with rows of red dots. Depending on their mood, they may also show slanting cross bars. Females are deeper in the body and less intensely coloured, with clear fins.

Breeding
Best bred in a separate aquarium. Eggs are laid on plants or mops. Remove eggs, and hatch and rear in shallow water. Fry need plenty of space to grow. Feed fry newly hatched brine shrimp.

Tank Set-up
Well-planted community aquarium, with some floating plants and open areas for swimming. Tight-fitting cover glass. Gentle filtration.

RIVULUS XIPHIDIUS
HUBER, 1979

Family: APLOCHEILIDAE	
Common name: BLUE-STRIPE RIVULUS	
Distribution: Surinam, French Guiana	
Size: 4 cm (1½ in)	
Food: CARNIVOROUS. Live food	
Temperature range: 22–25°C / 72–77°F	
pH: 6.0–6.5 dH: to 6°	

22–25°C
72–77°F

4 cm (1½ in)

Definitely a fish for the specialist, it is sensitive to water conditions and can be difficult to feed. It is a small, timid fish, which thrives best in a species aquarium. However, it can be combined with very small, peaceful Characins or *Corydoras*. Males are highly coloured whereas females are smaller and drab.

Breeding
Eggs are placed on spawning mops or Java Moss. Use pairs or one male and two females. Eggs hatch in about two weeks. Young are tiny and require infusoria followed by brine shrimp nauplii.

Tank Set-up
Species aquarium with fine-leaved plants and soft, acidic water. Regular water changes are essential to maintain these creatures.

APHANIUS DISPAR
(RÜPPELL, 1828)

Family: CYPRINODONTIDAE	
Common name: MOTHER OF PEARL KILLIE	
Distribution: Coastal areas of Somalia, non-Mediterranean Middle East, vicinity of the Kutch (western India)	
Size: 7 cm (3 in)	
Food: OMNIVOROUS. Flake, frozen and live food and algae	
Temperature range: 16–25°C / 61–77°F	
pH: 7.5–8.5 dH: to 30°	

16–25°C
61–77°F
7 cm (3 in)

These fish are best kept with salt in the water, as they are extremely salt tolerant; the degree of salinity will depend on the origins of the fish. Males are wonderfully coloured, with bright yellow bars in the caudal fin. Females are much less brilliant and the caudal lacks the yellow bars. Keep in shoals. Adults can be quarrelsome, but provided there is sufficient cover and the tank is large enough, it is unlikely that problems will occur.

Breeding
Warm water, about 27°C / 81°F. Eggs are placed on spawning mops or fine-leaved, salt-tolerant plants. Fry should be fed newly hatched brine shrimp.

Tank Set-up
Use either plastic plants or salt-tolerant live plants. Good filtration.

APLOCHEILICHTHYS KATANGAE
(BOULENGER, 1912)

Family: CYPRINODONTIDAE	
Common name: KATANGA LAMPEYE	
Distribution: Southern central and southern Africa	
Size: 4 cm (1½ in)	
Food: CARNIVOROUS. Small live food, will take flake and frozen if there is nothing else	
Temperature range: 20–28°C / 68–82°F	
pH: 6.5–7.5 dH: to 12°	

20–28°C
68–82°F
4 cm (1½ in)

A shoaling fish, this does best when kept in a species aquarium. Males have more colour than females, their fins are yellowish, and the black line is more pronounced.

Breeding
These fish will spawn on spawning mops or plants. Collect the eggs, and hatch and rear fry apart from the parents. Fry require very fine foods initially, followed by brine shrimp nauplii.

Tank Set-up
Planted aquarium, but with plenty of open water for swimming. Soft, slightly acidic water. Gentle current seems beneficial.

CUBANICHTHYS CUBENSIS
(EIGENMANN, 1902)

Family: CYPRINODONTIDAE	
Common name: CUBAN KILLIE, CUBAN MINNOW	
Distribution: Western Cuba	
Size: 4 cm (1½ in)	
Food: OMNIVOROUS. Flake and frozen food but live food is preferred	
Temperature range: 23–27°C / 73–81°F	
pH: 7.0 dH: to 15°	

23–27°C
73–81°F

4 cm (1½ in)

Peaceful and should be kept in small shoals. Males are very colourful, having rows of stripes and dots along their flanks. Females are plainer, with a single dark longitudinal strip.

Breeding
Will breed successfully in a community aquarium provided there is sufficient plant cover for the fry to hide. The adhesive eggs hatch in about 10 days. First foods: *Paramecium* followed by newly hatched brine shrimp.

Tank Set-up
Well-planted community aquarium with other small peaceful fish. Efficient filtration.

FUNDULUS LINEOLATUS
(AGASSIZ, 1854)

18–23°C
64–73°F
7 cm (3 in)

Family: CYPRINODONTIDAE
Common name: LINE TOPMINNOW
Distribution: Florida to North Carolina (USA)
Size: 7 cm (3 in)
Food: OMNIVOROUS. Live food preferred but will take flake and frozen
Temperature range: 18–23°C / 64–73°F
pH: 6.5–7.5 dH: to 12°

Shy and retiring, this fish is suited to a species aquarium. Juveniles school together while adults form pairs. Males have 11–15 vertical bars on the flanks, females 7–8 longitudinal stripes, with the vertical bars only faintly apparent.

Breeding
Easy to spawn on mops or plants. Collect the light-sensitive eggs and hatch separately, or parents may eat them. Fry hatch in about two weeks and will take newly hatched brine shrimp.

Tank Set-up
Heavily planted at the back of the aquarium, with open water for juveniles to shoal. Gentle filtration. Cooler temperatures in the winter months are beneficial.

Family: CYPRINODONTIDAE
Common name: GREEN LAMPEYE
Distribution: West Africa
Size: 6 cm (2½ in)
Food: CARNIVOROUS. Small live food, may accept flake
Temperature range: 24–26°C / 75–79°F
pH: 7.0 dH: to 12°

A shoaling fish, and if it is to be maintained for any length of time, it should be kept as such. It is sensitive to poor water conditions. Males have a beautiful blue metallic sheen on the body and the fins are tinged with red. Females are smaller, less colourful and have transparent finnage.

Breeding
These fish spawn in crevices, laying their eggs in cracks in wood, slots in filter baskets, etc. Eggs hatch in two weeks. Fry should be fed fine live food. Growth is slow.

Tank Set-up
A community aquarium, provided it is not overstocked. An efficient filtration system and regular water changes are essential.

24–26°C
75–79°F
6 cm (2½ in)

PROCATOPUS ABERRANS
AHL, 1927

PROCATOPUS SIMILIS
AHL, 1927

24–26°C
75–79°F
7 cm (3 in)

Family: CYPRINODONTIDAE
Common name: NIGERIAN LAMPEYE
Distribution: Nigeria and western Cameroon
Size: 7 cm (3 in)
Food: CARNIVOROUS. Live food, will also take flake and frozen
Temperature range: 24–26°C / 75–79°F
pH: 6.5–7.5 dH: to 15°

The male has a bluish-green body with a metallic sheen, and yellowish fins sometimes with red dots and marks. The female is smaller and less colourful. Kept in shoals they are peaceful, but lone males can sometimes become belligerent.

Breeding
Can be difficult to breed. Eggs hatch in 12–14 days and the fry accept brine shrimp nauplii.

Tank Set-up
Community aquarium with open water. Good filtration with a gentle flow of water.

Livebearers

Anablepidae
Goodeidae
Hemirhamphidae
Poeciliidae

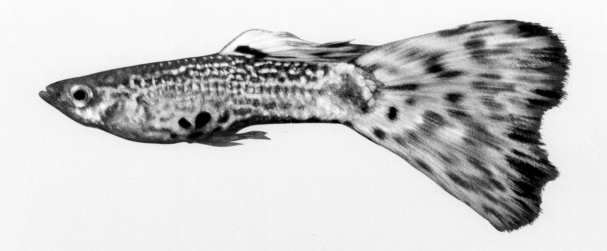

ANABLEPS ANABLEPS

(LINNAEUS, 1756)

Family: ANABLEPIDAE	
Common name: STRIPED FOUR-EYED FISH	
Distribution: Central and northern South America	
Size: Males 18 cm (7 in); females 24 cm (9½ in)	
Food: CARNIVOROUS. Insect larvae, worms, will take flake	
Temperature range: 23–28°C / 73–82°F	
pH: 7.0–8.5 dH: 20–35°	

Very active fish, prone to jumping, so ensure the aquarium is well covered. Keep in shoals. The fish cruise the surface with half their eyes protruding above the water. The cornea, pupil and retina are divided in half, the lower part allowing the fish to see below the water surface while the upper part lets them keep watch for aerial predators. They are sexually mature when half grown, and the male possesses a gonopodium.

23–28°C
73–82°F
18 cm (7 in)

Breeding
Shallow tanks and warm, brackish water. the young are about 2.5 cm (1 in) long when born.

Tank Set-up
Shallow aquarium with a large surface area. Warm, brackish water for preference. Use brackish water plants such as *Sagitteria*, planted in sand substrate. Gentle filtration.

AMECA SPLENDENS

MILLER & FITZSIMONS, 1971

21–24°C
70–75°F
7 cm (3 in)

Family: GOODEIDAE	
Common name: BUTTERFLY GOODEID	
Distribution: Mexico	
Size: Males 7 cm (3 in); females 10 cm (4 in)	
Food: OMNIVOROUS. Predominantly algae and vegetable matter, but will also take live food, flake, etc	
Temperature range: 21–24°C / 70–75°F	
pH: 7.0–7.5 dH: to 15°	

A fairly peaceful species that may be kept in the community aquarium. Males have a modified anal fin and a larger dorsal fin, together with black and yellow bars on the edge of the caudal fin.

Breeding
Gestation is about eight weeks and up to 30 young may be produced. At birth they are about 2 cm (1 in) long, and have an 'umbilical cord' which falls away in about 24 hours.

Tank Set-up
High light levels for good algae growth. Thickets of plants and some rocks. Good filtration system to give a high turnover of water.

Family: GOODEIDAE	
Common name: RAINBOW GOODEID	
Distribution: Mexico	
Size: Males 3.5 cm (1½ in); females 5 cm (2 in)	
Food: OMNIVOROUS. Include plenty of live food in the diet	
Temperature range: 20–24°C / 68–75°F	
pH: 7.0–7.5 dH: 8–30°	

A pretty fish which may be kept with other small species. Males are smaller and more highly coloured, and have longer ventral fins. Almost extinct in the wild, so captive breeding is essential.

Breeding
Not prolific: 15 or so young are produced every eight weeks. The sex ratio of the broods is usually five males to one female. Raise on small live food and algae.

CHARACODON LATERALIS

GÜNTHER, 1866

Tank Set-up
Brightly lit aquarium with a dark substrate and a dense growth of algae. Good filtration.

20–24°C
68–75°F
 3.5 cm (1½ in)

ILYODON WHITEI
(MEEK, 1904)

Family: GOODEIDAE	
Common name: WHITE'S ILYODEN	
Distribution: Mexico	
Size: Males 6 cm (2½ in); females 10 cm (4 in)	
Food: OMNIVOROUS. Predominantly algae and live food, but will take flake and frozen	
Temperature range: 21–24°C / 70–77°F	
pH: 7.0–8.0 dH: 8–30°	

A rare fish in the hobby. It may be included in a community aquarium but, given this rarity, is better kept in a species tank. Males are significantly more colourful than females, and have a copulatory organ.

Breeding
About 25 to 30 young will be produced every couple of months. Feed young on algae and small food. They are sexually mature at about five months old.

Tank Set-up
Clumps of plant and rocks. Good plant growth. Gentle filtration.

21–24°C
70–77°F

6 cm (2½ in)

XENOTOCA EISENI
(RUTTER, 1896)

Family: GOODEIDAE	
Common name: RED-TAILED GOODEID	
Distribution: Mexico	
Size: Males 6 cm (2½ in); females 7 cm (3 in)	
Food: OMNIVOROUS. Algae, live food, flake, frozen food	
Temperature range: 16–26°C / 61–78°F	
pH: 7.0–8.0 dH: 8–30°	

An undemanding fish, as far as tank conditions are concerned. It occasionally nibbles the fins of other fish, but otherwise is quite peaceful. Males are more colourful than females.

Breeding
Will breed in the community aquarium, and some fry will survive provided there is a partial cover of floating plants for them to hide among. Females give birth every eight weeks or so, and larger females may produce 45 or so young.

Tank Set-up
Community aquarium with good filtration providing a rapid turnover of water and high oxygen levels.

16–26°C
61–78°F
6 cm (2½ in)

XENOTOCA VARIATA
(BEAN, 1887)

Family: GOODEIDAE	
Common name: JEWELLED GOODEID	
Distribution: Mexico	
Size: Males 6 cm (2½ in); females 7 cm (3 in)	
Food: OMNIVOROUS. All types of green food and some small live food	
Temperature range: 21–24°C / 70–74°F	
pH: 7.0–8.0 dH: 8–30°	

A peaceful species, so it may be kept with other small fishes. Females have a dark lateral stripe which is less pronounced in males. The male's caudal fin has a yellow edge.

Breeding
Gestation eight weeks. Some 30 or so fry are produced and these should be raised on live food and flake.

Tank Set-up
Plenty of plant growth. Use plants with tough leaves, such as Java Fern, because softer plants will be eaten if there is insufficient green food. Good, strong filtration with plenty of water movement.

21–24°C
70–74°F

6 cm (2½ in)

DERMOGENYS PUSILLUS

VAN HASSELT, 1823

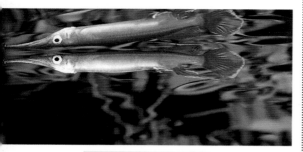

20–30°C	7 cm (3 in)
68–86°F	

Family: HEMIRHAMPHIDAE
Common name: NONE
Distribution: Southeast Asia
Size: 7 cm (3 in)
Food: CARNIVOROUS. Mainly live aquatic invertebrates but will take flake
Temperature range: 20–30°C / 68–86°F
pH: 7.0–7.5 dH: 10–20°

A nervous fish, they are best kept in a species aquarium. Much of their time is spent swimming near the water surface and, if startled they will jump or crash into the side of the aquarium, the resultant injuries to the body or, more probably snout, can lead to death.

Males have a red patch on the dorsal and a copulatory modification to the anal fin.

Breeding
A livebearer, gestation is 20–60 days and up to 30 fry may be produced. Fry are often born dead but the addition of vitamin D to their diet can help prevent this.

Tank Set-up
Use a shallow aquarium with a sand substrate and plants around the edges, leaving plenty of open water and have gentle filtration.

HEMIRHAMPHODON POGONOGNATHUS

BLEEKER, 1853

Family: HEMIRHAMPHIDAE
Common name: LONG-SNOUTED HALFBEAK
Distribution: Southeast Asia
Size: Males 9 cm (3½ in); females 6 cm (2½ in)
Food: OMNIVOROUS. Live, flake and frozen food
Temperature range: 22–27°C / 72–80°F
pH: 7.0–7.5 dH: to 10°

A surface dwelling fish ,they can be very aggressive towards each other, this aggressive behaviour is especially prevalent among males. Keep one male and several females together in a large aquarium. Males are much larger than females and the rear part of the anal fin is modified into a copulatory organ.

Breeding
These livebearers produce up to five young every day for about two weeks. Young can be fed newly hatched brine shrimp.

Tank Set-up
A large, but not necessarily deep aquarium is best with plenty of plants including a few floating. Cover the tank as these fish will jump. Have good filtration.

22–27°C	9 cm (3½ in)
72–80°F	

NOMORHAMPHUS LIEMI

VOGT, 1978

Family: HEMIRHAMPHIDAE
Common name: CELEBES HALFBEAK
Distribution: Sulawesi
Size: Males 6 cm (2½ in); females 9 cm (3½ in)
Food: CARNIVOROUS. Live food (insect larvae, etc), may be persuaded to take flake
Temperature range: 24–26°C / 75–79°F
pH: 6.8–7.5 dH: to 12°

Keep in small shoals. The finnage on males is highly coloured, and the modified anal fin is a genital organ: they also have black fleshy lobes on the lower jaw. Females have smaller fleshy lobes which may be red or uncoloured, and less coloration in the finnage. Celebes Halfbeaks are very active, so cover the tank well.

Breeding
Shallow tanks with soft, slightly acidic water and a temperature of about 25°C / 77°F. Gestation is about six to eight weeks. Few fry are produced (about 10) and they are some 1.8 cm (¾ in) when born.

Tank Set-up
Shallow aquarium with some plants and plenty of hiding places – use rocks to form caves or include pieces of wood. Good filtration.

24–26°C	6 cm (2½ in)
75–79°F	

ALFARO CULTRATUS
(REGAN, 1908)

Family: POECILIIDAE

Common name: KNIFE LIVEBEARER

Distribution: Nicaragua to western Panama

Size: Males 6 cm (2½ in); females 8 cm (3 in)

Food: CARNIVOROUS. Live food predominantly but will accept flake and frozen

Temperature range: 24–28°C / 75–82°F

pH: 6.5–7.5 dH: 4–30°

May be kept with other small peaceable species. Males have a gonopodium, and their elongated ventral fins are used to stimulate the female when breeding. Their common name is derived from the two rows of overlapping scales that form a keel, or 'knife-edge', on the rear lower edge of the body.

Breeding
Gestation is about four weeks and up to 50 young are produced. They are susceptible to bacterial infection, so cleanliness is all important. Feed fry on newly hatched brine shrimp.

Tank Set-up
Shallow tank with thickets of plants and some open water. Very efficient filtration and a good current of water. Regular water changes every seven days will help prevent bacterial infection.

 24–28°C 75–82°F   6 cm (2½ in)

Family: POECILIIDAE

Common name: BISHOP BRACHY

Distribution: Central America

Size: Males 3.5 cm (1½ in); females 5 cm (2 in)

Food: CARNIVOROUS. Predominantly small live food, sometimes frozen food but seldom flake

Temperature range: 24–26°C / 75–79°F

pH: 7.0–8.0 dH: 4–20°

A beautiful little livebearer, but very difficult to maintain for any length of time in captivity. It is susceptible to disease, so aquarium hygiene is all important. The males are more colourful and have a gonopodium.

Breeding
Use a well-planted tank as the parents will canibalise the fry. Gestation is four weeks. On average 15 young are produced. They are difficult to raise, requiring aufwuchs in their diet; brine shrimp is not sufficient.

Tank Set-up
Well-planted species aquarium with very efficient filtration. Pay particular attention to water quality and carry out regular water changes.

BRACHYRHAPHIS EPISCOPI
(STEINDACHNER, 1878)

 24–26°C 75–79°F   3.5 cm (1½ in)

CNESTERODON CARNEGIEI
HASEMAN, 1911

Family: POECILIIDAE

Common name: CARNEGIE'S LIVEBEARER

Distribution: Brazil, Uruguay, Argentina

Size: Males 2 cm (1 in); females 3.5 cm (1½ in)

Food: OMNIVOROUS. Flake, small live and frozen food, algae

Temperature range: 19–25°C / 66–77°F

pH: 6.5–8.0 dH: to 25°

A very undemanding fish that is ideal for a community of other small peaceful fishes. Males are smaller and have a gonopodium.

Breeding
A small aquarium with plenty of plants and some algae. Anything up to 15 tiny fry will be produced after only 24 days gestation. They require the smallest of food. The parents do not chase the fry.

Tank Set-up
A small aquarium with lots of plants and plenty of light to produce reasonable algae growth. Gentle filtration.

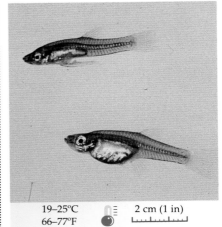

19–25°C 66–77°F   2 cm (1 in)

FLEXIPENIS VITTATA
HUBBS, 1926

24–27°C	4.5 cm (1¾ in)
75–81°F	

Family: POECILIIDAE
Common name: BLACKLINE MOSQUITO FISH
Distribution: Mexico
Size: Males 4.5 cm (1¾ in); females 5.5 cm (2 in)
Food: OMNIVOROUS. Flake, frozen, live and green food
Temperature range: 24–27°C/75–81°F
pH: 7.0–8.0 dH: to 20°

Peaceful fish which may be kept with others of a similar nature. Males have a gonopodium and are more colourful, females have a gravid patch.

Breeding
Gestation is four weeks. As many as 30 young may be produced. They are easy to raise on newly hatched brine shrimp and fine flake food, and should be fed several times a day.

Tank Set-up
Planted aquarium with a very efficient filtration system, as this fish likes clean, clear water with a reasonable flow.

Family: POECILIIDAE
Common name: WESTERN MOSQUITOFISH
Distribution: Texas (USA)
Size: Males 4 cm (1½ in); females 6.5 cm (2½ in)
Food: CARNIVOROUS. flake and frozen food, but really loves live mosquito larvae, *Daphnia*, etc
Temperature range: 18–24°C/64–75°F
pH: 6.0–8.0 dH: to 30°°

A gregarious and undemanding fish which may be kept with other similar fishes. Males have a gonopodium and are smaller than the females, which show a gravid patch. Its almost insatiable appetite for mosquito larvae has lead to this fish being widely used for malaria control.

Breeding
As many as 50 or 60 fry may be born after a gestation period of about four weeks. Parents will eat the young, so provide plenty of dense plant cover. Feed fry newly hatched brine shrimp, fine flake, etc

Tank Set-up
Well-planted aquarium with good filtration.

GAMBUSIA AFFINIS
(BAIRD & GIRARD, 1853)

18–24°C	4 cm (1½ in)
64–75°F	

GAMBUSIA REGANI
HUBBS, 1926

Family: POECILIIDAE
Common name: ELEGANT MOSQUITOFISH
Distribution: Mexico
Size: Males 3 cm (1 in); females 4 cm (1½ in)
Food: OMNIVOROUS. Flake and live food
Temperature range: 21–27°C/70–81°F
pH: 6.5–7.5 dH: to 25°

A delicately coloured little fish. Both sexes are similarly coloured, but males have a gonopodium. Best kept in a species aquarium. Feed small amounts frequently, say five to six times a day.

21–27°C	3 cm (1 in)
70–81°F	

Breeding
On average, 30 fry are produced every three to four weeks. Raise the fry on small live food such as brine shrimp nauplii.

Tank Set-up
Planted aquarium with little water movement and gentle filtration.

GIRARDINUS FALCATUS
(EIGENMANN, 1903)

Family: POECILIIDAE

Common name: YELLOW BELLY

Distribution: Western Cuba

Size: Males 4.5 cm (2 in); females 7 cm (3 in)

Food: OMNIVOROUS. Flake, frozen, live and green food

Temperature range: 24–29°C / 75–84°F

pH: 6.0–8.0 dH: to 25°

Very tolerant of most water conditions, this fish may be kept with other peaceful fishes. Its name refers to the sickle-shaped gonopodium of the males.

Breeding
Easy to breed and rear, especially if kept in a well-planted species aquarium. As many as 40 young may be produced every three to four weeks. Feed them newly hatched brine shrimp and green food.

Tank Set-up
Well-planted aquarium, but allow some free areas for swimming. Good filtration to give a flow of water.

| 24–29°C 75–84°F | | 4.5 cm (2 in) |

GIRARDINUS METALLICUS
POEY, 1854

Family: POECILIIDAE

Common name: METALLIC TOPMINNOW

Distribution: Costa Rica, Cuba

Size: Males 5 cm (2 in); females 9 cm (3½ in)

Food: OMNIVOROUS

Temperature range: 22–26°C / 72–79°F

pH: 6.5–7.5 dH: to 25°

Ideal for the community aquarium, these are peaceful and easy to feed. Males are much smaller than females and may have a black gonopodium.

Breeding
Females will produce batches of up to 100 small fry, about 6 mm (¼ in) long, every three to four weeks. Provide dense thickets of fine-leaved plants and some floating plants as cover for the fry, and separate them for growing on or they will be eaten.

Tank Set-up
Well-planted aquarium. Good filtration to provide gentle water movement.

| 22–26°C 72–79°F | | 5 cm (2 in) |

HETERANDRIA BIMACULATA
(HECKEL, 1848)

| 20–27°C 68–81°F | | 7 cm (3 in) |

Family: POECILIIDAE

Common name: COMMON TWIN SPOT LIVEBEARER

Distribution: Mexico to Honduras

Size: Males 7 cm (3 in); females 15 cm (6 in)

Food: CARNIVOROUS. Will take flake, live and frozen food

Temperature range: 20–27°C / 68–81°F

pH: 7.0–8.0 dH: 8–30°

Because of the wide range of habitats this fish is found in, the water values given are averages in which most specimens should survive. If possible, ascertain the actual origin of your fish (e.g. brackish lagoon) so that you can provide more exact conditions. Coloration also varies, those from lowlands being more colourful than those from mountain areas. Males have a gonopodium. May be kept with other fish of a similar size – but they are not averse to eating smaller fishes!

Breeding
Young are produced every four weeks or so, and large females may produce 100 fry. Remove the adults from the breeding tank or they will eat the fry. Even the fry can be cannibalistic as they grow on, so remove larger fish to prevent them eating the smaller ones. Maintain cleanliness as the fry are susceptible to bacterial infection.

Tank Set-up
Large aquarium with plant cover and some open areas. Good filtration.

HETERANDRIA FORMOSA
AGASSIZ, 1853

Family: POECILIIDAE	
Common name: DWARF TOPMINNOW	
Distribution: USA (South Carolina)	
Size: Males 2 cm (1 in); females 4.5 cm (2 in)	
Food: OMNIVOROUS. Small aquatic invertebrates, flake, etc	
Temperature range: 17–26°C / 62–79°F	
pH: 6.5–7.5 dH: to 25°	

One of the smallest fishes in the world, this creature is best suited to a species aquarium. Males have a gonopodium

17–26°C 62–79°F		2 cm (1 in)

and are smaller than females. They are partial to mosquito larvae and have been introduced to many places in an attempt to control this insect.

Breeding
Easy to breed. Fry are produced over a two-week period.

Tank Set-up
Densely planted small aquarium with gentle water movement.

Family: POECILIIDAE	
Common name: BLACK-BELLY LIMIA	
Distribution: Jamaica, Haiti	
Size: Males 4 cm (1½ in); females 6.5 cm (2½ in)	
Food: OMNIVOROUS. Algae, small aquatic invertebrates, flake, etc	
Temperature range: 22–28°C / 72–82°F	
pH: 7.5–8.5 dH: 20–30°	

Although rarely kept, this undemanding, attractive livebearer deserves more recognition. Males are more highly coloured than females and have a gonopodium. Females show a gravid patch.

Breeding
Easy to breed provided adequate live food is included in the diet.

Tank Set-up
Use plants tolerant of hard water conditions such as Java Fern and *Vallisneria*. Combine them with rocks and pebbles to decorate the aquarium but leave the fish some swimming space. A good flow of water is beneficial.

LIMIA MELANOGASTER
GUENTHER, 1866

22–28°C 72–82°F		4 cm (1½ in)

LIMIA NIGROFASCIATA
(REGAN, 1913)

22–25°C 72–77°F		4.5 cm (2 in)

Family: POECILIIDAE	
Common name: HUMPBACK LIMIA	
Distribution: Haiti	
Size: Males 4.5 cm (2 in); females 7 cm (3 in)	
Food: OMNIVOROUS. Predominantly vegetarian, but will also take small aquatic invertebrates, flake, etc	
Temperature range: 22–25°C / 72–77°F	
pH: 7.0–8.5 dH: 10–30°	

A species that thrives in hard water, it makes an ideal community fish. Make sure there is plenty of green food in the diet. Males have an arched back (the arching increases with age). They also

have a gonopodium, and a wedge-shaped caudal fin.

Breeding
Easy to breed. About 25 fry are produced each time. Females will eat the young.

Tank Set-up
Well-maintained and planted community aquarium.

Family: POECILIIDAE
Common name: CUBAN LIMIA
Distribution: Cuba
Size: 12 cm (4½ in)
Food: OMNIVOROUS. Algae, small aquatic invertebrates, flake, etc
Temperature range: 22–25°C / 72–79°F
pH: 7.5–8.5 dH: 8–30°

An excellent fish for the hard water community aquarium. Males are more colourful, with black and gold spangles on the dorsal and caudal fins. Females have less intense coloration and lack a gonopodium.

Breeding
Females produce up to 50 fry every four weeks or so.

Tank Set-up
Plants, rocks and wood may be used to decorate the aquarium. Salt may be added to the water provided the other occupants and plants will tolerate it. Good filtration system. The species is sensitive to fresh water, so take care when carrying out water changes.

LIMIA VITTATA
GUENTHER, 1866

 22–25°C 72–77°F   12 cm (4½ in)

LIMIA ZONATA
(NICHOLS, 1915)

22–25°C 72–77°F   6 cm (2½ in)

Family: POECILIIDAE
Common name: STRIPED LIMA
Distribution: Dominican Republic
Size: Males 6 cm (2½ in); females 8 cm (3 in)
Food: OMNIVOROUS. Flake, frozen and live food, plus large amounts of algae and other green food
Temperature range: 22–25°C / 72–77°F
pH: 6.5–7.5 dH: 10–20°

A peaceful fish for a community or species aquarium. Males have a gonopodium.

Breeding
They produce up to 30 young every four weeks or so. These are easily raised on the normal fry food.

Tank Set-up
Well-planted community aquarium with good filtration. Regular water changes are essential.

PHALLICHTHYS AMATES
(MILLER, 1907)

Family: POECILIIDAE
Common name: MERRY WIDOW
Distribution: Guatemala, Panama to Honduras
Size: Males 3 cm (1 in); females 6 cm (2½ in)
Food: OMNIVOROUS. Algae, small aquatic invertebrates, flake, etc
Temperature range: 23–28°C / 73–82°F
pH: 6.5–7.5 dH: to 25°

Will do well in a peaceful community aquarium. Males are much smaller than females and have a gonopodium.

Breeding
Females produce up to 80 fry every four weeks. Remove the parents before the fry are eaten, or else use a spawning tank with a slatted false bottom that the fry can drop through. Some fry will survive in a well-planted community tank.

Tank Set-up
Typical, well-maintained community aquarium, with some thickets of plants as cover for newly born fry. The species is susceptible to water conditions, so try to maintain these within the given tolerances.

 23–28°C 73–82°F   3 cm (1 in)

PHALLOCEROS CAUDIMACULATUS
(Hensel, 1868)

Family: Poeciliidae	
Common name: The Caudo	
Distribution: Central Brazil, Paraguay, Uruguay	
Size: Males 3 cm (1 in); females 4.5 cm (2 in)	
Food: Omnivorous. Algae, small aquatic invertebrates, flake, etc	
Temperature range: 23–28°C / 73–82°F	
pH: 6.5–8.0 dH: 4–20°	

These may be kept with other small, quiet fishes. Males are smaller and have

23–28°C 73–82°F		3 cm (1 in)

a gonopodium. Also their operculum is more brightly coloured and has a black edge.

Breeding
Make sure the breeding tank is clean with no debris on the bottom. When the fry are born they fall to the bottom, and do not become free-swimming for about an hour. Females produce up to 40 fry.

Tank Set-up
Well maintained community aquarium with clumps of plants for cover.

POECILIA CAUCANA
(Steindachner, 1880)

Family: Poeciliidae	
Common name: Caucon Molly	
Distribution: Panama, Colombia, Venezuela	
Size: Males 4 cm (1½ in); females 6 cm (2½ in)	
Food: Omnivorous. Small live food and plenty of green food	
Temperature range: 23–28°C / 73–82°F	
pH: 7.0–7.5 dH: 10–25°	

23–28°C 73–82°F		4 cm (1½ in)

A peaceful fish for the community aquarium. Males have a gonopodium.

Breeding
Use an aquarium with plenty of plant cover. Females produce about 20 young at a time. Feed on small live food.

Tank Set-up
Community aquarium with medium-hard water and good filtration. Good plant cover but some open waters, as the fish like to shoal in a gentle current.

POECILIA LATIPINNA
(LeSueur, 1821)

Family: Poeciliidae	
Common name: Sailfin Molly	
Distribution: Southern USA (southern Virginia, Carolina, Florida, Texas)	
Size: Males 10 cm (4 in); females 12 cm (4½ in)	
Food: Omnivorous. Algae, plant material, plus small live food and flake	
Temperature range: 20–28°C / 68–82°F	
pH: 7.5–8.5 dH: 10–30°	

A species which has been cultivated to produce various colour forms. Suitable for a hardwater community aquarium, but best kept in brackish or marine water. Males have a dorsal fin and a gonopodium.

Breeding
Use a heavily planted aquarium or a large spawning trap. Up to about 50 young are produced every four weeks or so. Include some live food in their diet.

Tank Set-up
Hardwater community aquarium with robust species. Plants need to be able to withstand the occasional nibble (Java Fern is tough enough to tolerate this treatment). Very efficient filtration is essential.

20–28°C 68–82°F	10 cm (4 in)

Family: POECILIIDAE
Common name: GUPPY, MILLIONSFISH
Distribution: Central America to Brazil
Size: 6 cm (2½ in)
Food: OMNIVOROUS. Small aquatic invertebrates, flake, etc
Temperature range: 18–27°C / 64–81°F
pH: 7.0–8.5 dH: 4–30°

A highly adaptable fish that is a firm favourite among novices. Males are more highly coloured, with larger finnage and a gonopodium. Females are dull coloured, but usually with some coloration in the caudal fin, and also show a gravid patch. Bred by the millions in fish farms, Guppies have been hybridised to give larger finnage on males, different caudal fin shapes, and improved colour. However, the wild fish has a charm all of its own and is well worth trying to keep, though it is more sensitive to water conditions.

18–27°C
64–81°F

6 cm (2½ in)

POECILIA RETICULATA
PETERS, 1859

Breeding
Guppies mature early, females at three months, males even sooner. Broods are usually of about 30 fry.

Tank Set-up
Well-maintained and planted community aquarium.

POECILIA SPHENOPS
VALENCIENNES, 1846

18–28°C
64–82°F
6 cm (2½ in)

Family: POECILIIDAE
Common name: MEXICAN MOLLY
Distribution: Mexico to Colombia
Size: 6 cm (2½ in)
Food: OMNIVOROUS. Algae, peas, flake, etc
Temperature range: 18–28°C / 64–82°F
pH: 7.0–8.5 dH: 12–30°

Wild fish will live quite happily at the lower end of the temperature range, but the various hybrids – Black, Lyretail, etc – are more often offered for sale in retail outlets. These hybrids are far more delicate (and more prone to disease). They require high temperatures, and

adding a small amount of salt to the aquarium is also beneficial. Males have larger finnage and a gonopodium.

Breeding
Prolific, and very easy to breed. Provide plenty of plant cover in the aquarium and a good proportion of fry will survive.

Tank Set-up
Hard-water community aquarium, well-maintained and planted. Keep the hybrids with other fish and plants that can tolerate higher temperatures and a little salt.

POECILIA VELIFERA
(REGAN, 1914)

25–28°C
77–82°F
12 cm (4½ in)

Family: POECILIIDAE
Common name: YUCATAN MOLLY
Distribution: Mexico, Yucatan
Size: Males 12 cm (4½ in); females 18 cm (7 in)
Food: HERBIVOROUS. Predominantly green food, but will also take insect larvae, flake, etc
Temperature range: 25–28°C / 77–82°F
pH: 7.5–8.5 dH: 20–35°

A beautiful fish if given the right conditions. Not for the community aquarium, it should be kept in a species tank to see it at its best. Can be acclimatised to marine aquaria, indeed it is often used to mature marine tanks. Must have copious amounts of green food, especially algae. Males have a beautiful, large dorsal fin which is used in displaying to females. Hybrids between *P. laipinna* and this species are often offered for sale. These may be

black, red, mottled, etc, and are more hardy than the green non-hybrid fish. The species can be differentiated by the number of dorsal fin rays: 18–19 for *P. velifera* and 14 for *P. latipinna*.

Breeding
Difficult to breed. The young should be fed mainly on live food with additional green food. They require a lot of swimming space, otherwise the dorsal fin of the males does not develop to its full potential.

Tank Set-up
Large, hard-water aquarium with fish such as Archers and Scats. Salt may be added. Maintain the hardness with dolomite or similar. Provide a good flow of water via a very efficient filtration system.

Family: POECILIIDAE	
Common name: ONE SPOT MOLLY	
Distribution: West Venezuela to Argentina and some offshore islands	
Size: Males 5 cm (2 in); females 7 cm (3 in)	
Food: OMNIVOROUS. Flake, frozen, green and live food	
Temperature range: 264–28°C / 74–82°F	
pH: 7.0–8.0 dH: 10–35°	

Gregarious, peaceful fish for the community aquarium. Males have a black spot at the base of the dorsal and a gonopodium.

Breeding
Gestation is four weeks. Large numbers of fry (up to 100) may be produced. These are easily reared on commercial fry foods.

Tank Set-up
Shallow, sparsely planted aquarium with little water movement.

POECILIA VIVIPARA
(BLOCH & SCHNEIDER, 1801)

 24–28°C 74–82°F   5 cm (2 in)

POECILIOPSIS GRACILIS
(HECKEL, 1848)

24–28°C 75–82°F   3.5 cm (1½ in)

Family: POECILIIDAE	
Common name: PORTHOLE LIVEBEARER	
Distribution: Central America	
Size: Males 3.5 cm (1½ in); females 6 cm (2½ in)	
Food: OMNIVOROUS. Wide variety of food	
Temperature range: 24–28°C / 75–82°F	
pH: 6.5–7.5 dH: 8–30°	

Very attractive little fish that is suited to community aquaria with other peaceful species. Males are smaller and have a gonopodium.

Breeding
Best bred in a densely planted species tank which has plenty of plants. On average 30 fry are produced at a time. Sexually mature in three months.

Tank Set-up
Community aquarium with some broad-leaved plants for the fish to shelter under and some floating vegetation. Efficient filtration system with a high turnover rate.

Family: POECILIIDAE	
Common name: MAYON BLUE-EYE	
Distribution: Mexico	
Size: Males 3–5 cm (1–2 in); females 5 cm (2 in)	
Food: OMNIVOROUS. All manner of small live food, but will take standard and vegetable flake	
Temperature range: 24–27°C / 75–81°F	
pH: 6.5–7.2 dH: 8–20°	

Best kept in a densely planted species tank as they are very timid. Males are thinner and have a gonopodium.

Breeding
Condition the fish well on live food, especially mosquito larvae. Ripe females may be placed in a breeding trap until they give birth. Feed fry on small live food.

Tank Set-up
Large aquarium with a good flow of water. Some thickets of plants, but plenty of open water for swimming. Good filtration and regular water changes.

PRIAPELLA COMPRESSA
ALVAREZ, 1948

 24–27°C 75–81°F   3–5 cm (1–2 in)

PRIAPELLA INTERMEDIA
ALVAREZ, 1952

24–26°C	5 cm (2 in)
75–79°F	

Family: POECILIIDAE

Common name: OAXACAN BLUE-EYE

Distribution: Coatzacoalcos river (Mexico)

Size: Males 5 cm (2 in); females 7 cm (3 in)

Food: OMNIVOROUS. Small aquatic invertebrates, flake, etc

Temperature range: 24–26°C / 75–79°F

pH: 7.0–7.5 dH: 10–20°

Best kept in a species aquarium where a steady temperature can be maintained, as this fish is sensitive to fluctuations. In its native habitat, there is little temperature change.

Breeding

Small broods of up to 20 fry from mature females, produced every five weeks or so. Raise the young on brine shrimp.

Tank Set-up

Clean, clear water with a good flow. Maintain an even temperature. Use floating plants to cut down the light.

QUINTANA ATRIZONA
HUBBS, 1934

24–28°C	2 cm (1 in)
75–82°F	

Family: POECILIIDAE

Common name: BLACK-BARRED LIVEBEARER

Distribution: Cuba

Size: Males 2 cm (1 in); females 4 cm (1½ in)

Food: OMNIVOROUS. Grindal worms, microworms, vegetable flake, brine shrimp

Temperature range: 24–28°C / 75–82°F

pH: 6.5–7.5 dH: 4–18°

A shy, peaceful fish for the species aquarium. Males are smaller and have a gonopodium. When feeding offer very small amounts up to three times a day.

Breeding

Java Moss and *Riccia* for cover. Gestation is five to six weeks, and about 25 young are produced. Newly imported fish are relatively easy to breed, subsequent generations become more difficult.

Tank Set-up

Species aquarium with fine-leaved plants. Minimal filtration and water movement.

Family: POECILIIDAE

Common name: GREEN SWORDTAIL

Distribution: Central America

Size: Males 10 cm (4 in); females 12 cm (4½ in)

Food: OMNIVOROUS. Small aquatic invertebrates, flake, etc

Temperature range: 20–26°C / 68–79°F

pH: 7.0–8.0 dH: 8–35°

A popular community fish, Green Swordtails are easy to keep and breed. This ease of reproduction has led to the trade developing several different colour forms and finnage shapes. Only the males have the long, swordlike extension to the lower part of the caudal fin that gives rise to their common name. They are not born with this extension, the 'sword' develops as the fish matures. Females lack the sword and gonopodium but do show a gravid patch. Males may bicker between themselves.

Breeding

Up to 80 fry may be produced by a full-grown female. Provide plenty of plant cover to protect the fry, or use a spawning trap.

Tank Set-up

A large aquarium with plenty of plants and lots of swimming space.

20–26°C	10 cm (4 in)
68–79°F	

XIPHOPHORUS HELLERI
HECKEL, 1848

XIPHOPHORUS MACULATUS

(GUENTHER, 1866)

Family: POECILIIDAE

Common name: SOUTHERN PLATY

Distribution: Eastern coast of Mexico and Guatemala and into northern Honduras

Size: Males 10 cm (4 in); females 12 cm (4½ in)

Food: OMNIVOROUS. Small aquatic invertebrates, flake, etc

Temperature range: 22–26°C / 72–79°F

pH: 7.0–8.0 dH: 8–35°

The ideal community fish, peaceful and fecund. Its young will even grow to maturity in a community tank. Males are smaller than females and have gonopodium. Bred in large numbers by the trade, many variant colour forms have been produced.

Breeding

Broods are not large and, provided there is plenty of cover, some will survive in a community tank.

Tank Set-up

Any well-maintained community aquarium.

22–26°C
72–79°F
10 cm (4 in)

XIPHOPHORUS MILLERI

ROSEN, 1960

Family: POECILIIDAE

Common name: CATEMACO PLATY

Distribution: Lake Catemaco (Mexico)

Size: Males 3 cm (1 in); females 4 cm (1½ in)

Food: OMNIVOROUS. Flake, frozen, live and green food

Temperature range: 24–27°C / 75–81°F

pH: 7.5 dH: 4–30°

Ideal for a community aquarium. Males are smaller, with a gonopodium, and the rear lower portion of the body is speckled. Females have a gravid patch.

24–27°C
75–81°F
3 cm (1 in)

Breeding

Difficult. The water has to be perfect, with no nitrates. Not prolific, the maximum number of fry is 50. Raise them on *Artemia*.

Tank Set-up

Well-oxygenated and filtered water with a high turnover (twice an hour). Very dense plant growth. Check water quality regularly.

XIPHOPHORUS PYGMAEUS

HUBBS & GORDON, 1943

Family: POECILIIDAE

Common name: SLENDER PYGMY SWORDTAIL

Distribution: Axtla river (Mexico)

Size: 4 cm (1½ in)

Food: OMNIVOROUS. Small aquatic invertebrates, flake, etc

Temperature range: 24–28°C / 75–82°F

pH: 7.0–8.5 dH: 10–30°

This species may be kept in a community aquarium provided the other occupants are peaceful. Males have a gonopodium; females are larger and deeper in the body. Males show only a hint of a sword on the bottom of the tail.

Breeding

Small broods. The parents may well chase the fry or eat them. Use a spawning trap or similar and provide plant cover.

Tank Set-up

Provide clean, clear, well-oxygenated water. Use wood, plants and rocks to provide shelter. A few floating plants are beneficial.

24–28°C
75–82°F
4 cm (1½ in)

XIPHOPHORUS VARIATUS
(MEEK, 1904)

Family: POECILIIDAE	
Common name: VARIABLE PLATY	
Distribution: Southern Mexico	
Size: Males 5.5 cm (2 in); females 7 cm (3 in)	
Food: OMNIVOROUS. Small aquatic invertebrates, flake, etc	
Temperature range: 15–25°C / 59–77°F	
pH: 7.0–8.0 dH: 8–35°	

A classic community fish. It can even be kept at low temperatures in an unheated aquarium, provided it is acclimatised to these conditions slowly. Under these conditions they show more colour. Males have a gonopodium, females a gravid patch.

Breeding
Females are best removed to a spawning tank to give birth. Provide plants for cover. Fry are easy to raise on flake, live food, etc.

Tank Set-up
Any good, well-kept community aquarium of peaceful fish.

 15–25°C 59–77°F   5.5 cm (2 in)

Family: POECILIIDAE	
Common name: SPIKETAIL PLATY	
Distribution: Mexico	
Size: Males 4 cm (1½ in); females 5 cm (2 in)	
Food: OMNIVOROUS. Algae, small aquatic invertebrates, flake, etc	
Temperature range: 22–25°C / 72–77°F	
pH: 7.0–8.0 dH: 8–30°	

Best kept as a large shoal in a species aquarium, these fish are sensitive to poor water conditions. Males have a short sword.

Breeding
Low brood numbers, about 20 fry at most. Provide copious amounts of brine shrimp for food.

Tank Set-up
Efficient filtration system to maintain low nitrite levels. Bright lighting to promote plant growth.

 22–25°C 72–77°F   4 cm (1½ in)

XIPHOPHORUS XIPHIDIUM
(HUBBS & GORDON, 1932)

Rainbowfish

Atherinidae
Melanotaeniidae
Pseudomugilidae

BEDOTIA GEAYI
PELLEGRIN, 1907

Family: ATHTERINIDAE	
Common name: MADAGASCAN RAINBOW	
Distribution: Madagascar	
Size: 15 cm (6 in)	
Food: OMNIVOROUS. Algae, small aquatic invertebrates, flake, etc	
Temperature range: 20–24°C / 68–75°F	
pH: 7.0 dH: above 10°	

Peaceful fish which should be kept in a shoal if you are to succeed with them. They are sensitive to water conditions, preferring it to be medium to hard and neutral to slightly alkaline. Males have far brighter colours and their first dorsal comes to a point. Females are more yellowish in colour and deeper in the body.

20–24°C 68–75°F	15 cm (6 in)

Breeding
Spawn over fine-leaved plants, the eggs hanging by a thread. Can also spawn using spawning mops. Fry are very difficult to raise. Use infusoria followed by newly hatched brine shrimp.

Tank Set-up
Give the fish plenty of swimming space as they are very active. Partial water changes of say 25% should be carried out each week. Good, powerful filtration to maintain water quality and give a good flow.

TELMATHERINA LADIGESI
AHL, 1936

Family: ATHTERINIDAE	
Common name: CELEBES RAINBOW	
Distribution: Sulawesi	
Size: 7.5 cm (3 in)	
Food: OMNIVOROUS. Algae, small aquatic invertebrates, flake, etc	
Temperature range. 22–27°C / 72–81°F	
pH: 7.0 dH: in excess of 12°	

These may be kept in the community aquarium with other peaceful fish. Males have extended rays on the second dorsal and anal fins, and are highly coloured; females are drabber. They show their colours best in natural light.

Breeding
Eggs are laid among plants or on spawning mops. They hatch in about 10 days. Feed fry on commercially prepared live foods and newly hatched brine shrimp.

Tank Set-up
An active fish, so give them plenty of room. The water should be neutral and medium hard; salt may be added if the companion fish will tolerate it. Carry out a water change every week. Do not attempt to transfer these fish straight from hard to softer water as they are very sensitive to change. Acclimatise them slowly in either direction, although they cope better with a change from soft to hard water. Good filtration using a power filter is beneficial.

22–27°C 72–81°F	7.5 cm (3 in)

Family: MELANOTAENIIDAE	
Common name: AXELROD'S RAINBOW	
Distribution: Yungkiri Stream, a tributary of the Pual River (Papua New Guinea)	
Size: Males 9 cm (3½ in); females 7 cm (3 in)	
Food: OMNIVOROUS. Takes flake, frozen and live food	
Temperature range: 25–28°C / 77–82°F	
pH: 7.0–8.0 dH: to 12°	

An active fish which displays well when kept as a shoal of males and females. Males are more colourful than females.

Breeding
Eggs are produced a few at a time over a period of days. Remove spawning media from main tank and hatch separately. Feed fry on newly hatched brine shrimp.

Tank Set-up
Planted community aquarium with plenty of open water.

CHILATHERINA AXELRODI
ALLEN, 1980

25–28°C 77–82°F	9 cm (3½ in)

*C*HILATHERINA BLERHERI
ALLEN, 1985

Family: MELANOTAENIIDAE	
Common name: BLEHER'S RAINBOW	
Distribution: Lake Holmes (Irian Jaya)	
Size: 10 cm (4 in)	
Food: OMNIVOROUS. Live, flake and frozen food; mosquito larvae are relished	
Temperature range: 23–27°C / 73–81°F	
pH: 7.0–7.5 dH: to 15°	

Males have a wonderful red rear half of the body with a dark lateral stripe. Females are plain coloured, sometimes also showing the dark lateral stripe.

Breeding
Spawn readily on mops and fine-leaved plants. Stimulated by sunlight falling on the tank. Hatch eggs separately. Feed fry on newly hatched brine shrimp.

Tank Set-up
Well-planted, large aquarium with plenty of open water. Efficient filtration with a good flow of water.

23–27°C		10 cm (4 in)
73–81°F		

*C*HILATHERINA *FASCIATA*
(WEBER, 1913)

Family: MELANOTAENIIDAE	
Common name: BARRED RAINBOW	
Distribution: Northern New Guinea	
Size: Males 11 cm (4½ in); females 10 cm (4 in)	
Food: OMNIVOROUS. Prefers live food	
Temperature range: 27–30°C / 81–86°F	
pH: 7.0–8.0 dH: to 10°	

A rather attractive rainbow, it likes brightly lit conditions, being found in areas of streams where sunlight falls. Males are larger and more colourful than females.

Breeding
Typically for rainbows, it deposits its eggs over a number of days on Java Moss or spawning mops. Raise fry on small live food.

Tank Set-up
Roots and plants for cover but open water as well. Bright lighting or sunlight. Good filtration with a gentle flow of water.

27–30°C		11 cm (4½ in)
81–86°F		

Family: MELANOTAENIIDAE	
Common name: SENTANI RAINBOW	
Distribution: Lake Sentani (Irian Jaya)	
Size: Males 10 cm (4 in); females 8.5 cm (3½ in)	
Food: OMNIVOROUS. Include algae in the diet as well as insect larvae; will take flake and frozen food	
Temperature range: 24–28°C / 75–82°F	
pH: 6.5–7.5 dH: to 15°	

This shoaling fish is very active and needs a lot of space. Males are slimmer and more highly coloured than females.

Breeding
Bred on spawning mops hung in the community aquarium. Only a few eggs are produced at a time. Raise fry in separate tanks. First foods: newly hatched brine shrimps.

Tank Set-up
Clumps of fine-leaved plants, leaving plenty of open water. Good filtration system as these fish react adversely to poor water conditions.

*C*HILATHERINA *SENTANIENSIS*
(WEBER, 1908)

24–28°C		10 cm (4 in)
75–82°F		

GLOSSOLEPIS INCISUS
WEBER, 1908

Family:	MELANOTAENIIDAE
Common name:	RED RAINBOW
Distribution:	Lake Sentani (Irian Jaya)
Size:	Males 12 cm (4½ in); females 10 cm (4 in)
Food:	OMNIVOROUS. Prepared food plus plenty of live food
Temperature range:	24–26°C / 75–79°F
pH: 7.0	dH: to 15°

Probably the best known rainbow fish, because of the intense red coloration of the males. It is tempting just to keep males because the females are plain and silvery, but the males show their best colours when there are females to display to.

24–26°C
75–79°F
12 cm (4½ in)

Breeding
Spawns over a number of days on mops or Java Moss. Hatch the eggs and raise fry separately. Fry require very small first food such as *Paramecium* and newly hatched brine shrimp.

Tank Set-up
Large aquarium, as these are active fish and need swimming space. Maintenance of good water conditions is paramount. They like gentle water movement.

Family:	MELANOTAENIIDAE
Common name:	SPOTTED RAINBOW
Distribution:	Tributary of the Omsis River (Papua New Guinea)
Size:	5 cm (2 in)
Food:	OMNIVOROUS. Flake and frozen food, will also eat some algae
Temperature range:	24–26°C / 75–79°F
pH: 7.5	dH: to 12°

One of the smaller rainbow fish, they may be combined with other peaceful fish. Keep them in shoals and pay careful attention to water quality. The spots along the flanks only become apparent when the fish are two to three months old.

Breeding
Use clumps of Java Moss or spawning mops. Only a few eggs are produced each day and they hatch eight to ten days. Feed fry on newly hatched brine shrimp.

Tank Set-up
Good, efficient filtration. Dense clumps of plants.

24–26°C
75–79°F
5 cm (2 in)

GLOSSOLEPIS MACULOSUS
ALLEN, 1981

GLOSSOLEPIS MULTISQUAMATUS
(WEBER & DE BEAUFORT, 1922)

Family:	MELANOTAENIIDAE
Common name:	SEPIK RAINBOW
Distribution:	Papua New Guinea, Irian Jaya
Size:	Males 12 cm (4½ in); females 10 cm (4 in)
Food:	OMNIVOROUS. Flake and frozen food taken, but live food preferred
Temperature range:	26–29°C / 79–84°F
pH: 6.5	dH: to 10°

A fish for the larger community aquarium. Males are larger and more colourful than females.

Breeding
Will spawn on mops in the community aquarium or in a breeding tank set up with soft, slightly acidic water and clumps of Java Moss and / or spawning mops. A few eggs are laid each day. Hatch separately and raise fry on very fine food.

Tank Set-up
Well-established aquarium with plenty of plants and not too much water movement. Decorate with wood.

26–29°C
79–84°F
12 cm (4½ in)

GLOSSOLEPIS WANAMENSIS
ALLEN & KAILOLA, 1979

Family: MELANOTAENIIDAE	
Common name: LAKE WANAM RAINBOW	
Distribution: Lake Wanam (Papua New Guinea)	
Size: Males 9 cm (3½ in); females 8.5 cm (3½ in)	
Food: OMNIVOROUS. Will take prepared food but does best on live	
Temperature range: 25–28°C / 77–82°F	
pH: 7.0–8.0 dH: to 15°	

25–28°C / 77–82°F   9 cm (3½ in)

One of the most majestic of the rainbows, the extended finnage of the males makes them a worthy addition to any aquarium. Females do not have the extended finnage or intense coloration.

Breeding
Not too easy to breed. Use water of a neutral pH and hardness of about 10°. Eggs are laid on spawning mops or Java Moss and hatch in about ten days. The fry require very small live food to thrive.

Tank Set-up
Well-planted aquarium with open areas where the males may display to the females. Good filtration is essential to maintain these fish for any length of time.

IRIATHERINA WERNERI
MEINKEN, 1974

Family: MELANOTAENIIDAE	
Common name: THREADFIN RAINBOW	
Distribution: Irian Jaya	
Size: Males 3.5 cm (1½ in); females 3 cm (1 in)	
Food: OMNIVOROUS. Takes prepared food but prefers small live food	
Temperature range: 24–27°C / 75–81°F	
pH: 5.5–6.5 dH: to 10°	

24–27°C / 75–81°F   3.5 cm (1½ in)

A very attractive fish, but not for the community aquarium as it will be harassed and may have its fins nibbled. Best kept in a species aquarium where males can be seen displaying to females. Males have thread-like extensions on their dorsal and anal fins, hence the common name.

Breeding
The fish will spawn on large clumps of Java Moss. Remove the parents and let the eggs hatch; this takes about eight days. Feed fry very tiny live food such as *Paramecium*, followed by newly hatched brine shrimp.

Tank Set-up
Well-planted aquarium. Very gentle water movement but efficient filtration. Wood may also be used to decorate the tank.

MELANOTAENIA AFFINIS
(WEBER, 1908)

Family: MELANOTAENIIDAE	
Common name: NORTH NEW GUINEA RAINBOW	
Distribution: North of the central dividing range in New Guinea	
Size: Males 11.5 cm (4½ in); females 10 cm (4 in)	
Food: OMNIVOROUS. Will take most food	
Temperature range: 21–29°C / 70–84°F	
pH: 7.0–7.5 dH: to 10–15°	

21–29°C / 70–84°F   11.5 cm (4½ in)

A widespread rainbow fish, there can be colour variations. Males are deeper in the body and more colourful than females.

Breeding
Easy to breed given the water values above. The eggs will be stuck on Java Moss or mops and hatch in about a week. The fry feed on newly hatched brine shrimp. Remove parents or they will eat the young. Alternatively remove plants / mops and raise fry separately.

Tank Set-up
Large aquarium with open spaces. Efficient filtration and gentle water flow.

MELANOTAENIA BOESEMANI
ALLEN & CROSS, 1980

Family: MELANOTAENIIDAE	
Common name: BOESEMAN'S RAINBOW	
Distribution: Ajamaru Lakes (Irian Jaya)	
Size: Males 9 cm (3½ in); females 7 cm (3 in)	
Food: OMNIVOROUS. Takes flake, frozen and live food	
Temperature range: 27–30°C / 81–86°F	
pH: 6.5–7.0 dH: to 10°	

A sought-after fish because of the striking coloration of the males. However, the intensity of colour seems

 27–30°C / 81–86°F   9 cm (3½ in)

to degenerate with each generation of captive-bred fish. Kept as a shoal of both sexes they make a good focal point for the larger furnished aquarium.

Breeding
Spawns on Java Moss or spawning mops over several days. Fry are hard to rear and require the finest of food.

Tank Set-up
Large aquarium with plenty of swimming space. Efficient filtration but not too much water movement.

MELANOTAENIA HERBERTAXELRODI
ALLEN, 1981

Family: MELANOTAENIIDAE

Common name: LAKE TEBERA RAINBOW

Distribution: Lake Tebera basin (Papua New Guinea)

Size: 8.5 cm (3½ in)

Food: OMNIVOROUS. Flake, frozen and live food

Temperature range: 21–25°C / 70–77°F

pH: 7.5–8.0 dH: 10–15°

A peaceful shoaling fish. Males are deeper in the body and more colourful than females. The best colours are shown in sunlight.

Breeding
As for the other *Melanotaenia* spp. The eggs hatch in about seven days and the fry will take newly hatched brine shrimp.

Tank Set-up
A large aquarium with thickets of plants around the edges and open water. Good filtration and a gentle current is beneficial. Site the tank where morning sunlight can fall on it to see the fish at their best and trigger spawning.

21–25°C 70–77°F | 8.5 cm (3½ in)

MELANOTAENIA LACUSTRIS
MUNRO, 1964

Family: MELANOTAENIIDAE

Common name: LAKE KUTUBU RAINBOW

Distribution: Lake Kutubu (Papua New Guinea)

Size: 10 cm (4 in)

Food: OMNIVOROUS. Flake, frozen and live food

Temperature range: 24–26°C / 75–79°F

pH: 7.0–7.5 dH: about 12°

Very eyecatching, these fish make a wonderful focal point in an aquarium. Males have the more intense blue coloration. Unfortunately this colour fades slightly with successive captive-bred generations.

Breeding
Given natural lighting, they spawn in the early morning just after dawn. The eggs are placed on Java Moss or mops. Fry hatch in about eight days and may be fed on newly hatched brine shrimp.

Tank Set-up
Plenty of open water as they are quite active. They appreciate regular water changes and a reasonable flow of water.

24–26°C 75–79°F | 10 cm (4 in)

MELANOTAENIA MACCULLOCHI
OGILBY, 1915

24–30°C 75–86°F | 6 cm (2½ in)

Family: MELANOTAENIIDAE

Common name: MCCULLOCH'S RAINBOW

Distribution: Southern Papua New Guinea; Queensland, Australia (Cape York Peninsula and coastal regions south of Cairns)

Size: 6 cm (2½ in)

Food: OMNIVOROUS. Frozen, flake and live food

Temperature range: 24–30°C / 75–86°F

pH: 5.5–7.5 dH: to 12°

One of the smaller rainbows, there are two distinct populations with colour variations. In the fish found in Queensland, Australia between Cairns and Cardwell, the stripes are interrupted or very faint. They do share the neon nuptual stripe with the McIvor-Daintree population, a feature lacking in those fish from the Jardine river and southwest Papua New Guinea.

Breeding
They are sexually mature when about 3 cm (1 in). Eggs are placed in Java Moss or on mops and hatch in about a week. Feed fry very fine live foods.

Tank Set-up
Well-planted aquarium with very good filtration and a gentle current. Acid water is a must to maintain these creatures in good health.

MELANOTAENIA NIGRANS
(RICHARDSON, 1843)

24–28°C
75–82°F
7 cm (3 in)

Family: MELANOTAENIIDAE

Common name: BLACK-BANDED RAINBOW, DARK AUSTRALIAN RAINBOW

Distribution: Northern part of Northern Territory and north tip of Cape York Peninsula (Australia)

Size: Males 7 cm (3 in); females 6 cm (2½ in)

Food: OMNIVOROUS. Flake, frozen live food

Temperature range: 24–28°C / 75–82°F

pH: 5.5–6.0 dH: 10–12°

A undemanding fish that makes an excellent addition to the community aquarium if the acidic water conditions can be met. Keep in shoals. Avoid sudden drops in temperature.

Breeding
Will spawn on mops in the community aquarium. These can be removed and the eggs hatched separately. Alternatively use a fairly large breeding aquarium with mops and Java Moss. Raise fry on newly hatched brine shrimp.

Tank Set-up
Community aquarium with plants and roots or wood for cover and open water. Gentle flow of water.

MELANOTAENIA PARKINSONI
ALLEN, 1980

Family: MELANOTAENIIDAE

Common name: PARKINSON'S RAINBOW

Distribution: Southeast of Port Moresby (Papua New Guinea)

Size: Males 11 cm (4½ in); females 9 cm (3½ in)

Food: OMNIVOROUS. Prefers live food but accepts flake and frozen

Temperature range: 26–29°C / 79–84°F

pH: 7.5–8.0 dH: 8–15°

Keep these active fishes in a shoal. These are one of the easier rainbows to keep, and they breed readily in the community aquarium.

Breeding
Typical of the rainbows, they utilise mops and Java Moss. Hang mops in the community aquarium. Remove when full of eggs and raise fry separately.

Tank Set-up
Plenty of open space, with thickets of plants at the sides and rear of the aquarium. Efficient filtration.

26–29°C
79–84°F
11 cm (4½ in)

MELANOTAENIA SPLENDIDA SPLENDIDA
(PETERS, 1866)

Family: MELANOTAENIIDAE

Common name: SPLENDID RAINBOW

Distribution: Queensland (Australia)

Size: Males 11 cm (4½ in); females 10 cm (4 in)

Food: OMNIVOROUS. Flake, frozen and live food

Temperature range: 21–28°C / 70–82°F

pH: 6.5–7.5 dH: 10–12°

There are many subspecies of M. splendida and they vary in range, size and colour. All make excellent fish for the home aquarium.

Breeding
Typical of the rainbows. The fry are relatively easy to rear.

Tank Set-up
Well-planted community aquarium with good filtration.

21–28°C
70–82°F
11 cm (4½ in)

MELANOTAENIA TRIFASCIATA
(RENDAHL, 1922)

22–28°C
72–82°F

11 cm (4½ in)

Family: MELANOTAENIIDAE
Common name: BANDED RAINBOW
Distribution: Northern Territory and Cape York Peninsula (Australia)
Size: Males 11 cm (4½ in); females 9.5 cm (4 in)
Food: OMNIVOROUS. Flake, frozen, live food
Temperature range: 22–28°C / 72–82°F
pH: 6.0–7.5 dH: 10–12°

A very colourful rainbow, the different populations exhibit differing intensity of colour. Depending on the population some require harder water (those from the Goyder River), while others like it soft and acidic.

Breeding
Breeds very readily. A water change and sunlight will help trigger them. The fry can be raised on newly hatched brine shrimp.

Tank Set-up
Planted community aquarium with good filtration. Regular partial water changes are essential.

PSEUDOMUGIL FURCATUS
(NICHOLS, 1955)

24–26°C
75–79°F

5.5 cm (2 in)

Family: PSEUDOMUGILIIDAE
Common name: FORKTAILED RAINBOW
Distribution: Papua New Guinea
Size: Males 5.5 cm (2 in); females 4.5 cm (1¾ in)
Food: OMNIVOROUS. Live food preferred
Temperature range: 24–26°C / 75–79°F
pH: 7.5–8.0 dH: 12–15°

A delicate little fish that will provide a challenge to keep and breed. Males have a longer first dorsal fin and are more colourful than females. Best kept in a species aquarium.

Breeding
Use a small aquarium with clumps of Java Moss. Either pairs of fish or a small group can be used for breeding. The eggs take two to three weeks to hatch and the fry require the finest of live food.

Tank Set-up
Densely planted aquarium with some floating plants such as Water Lettuce or, better still, *Riccia*.

Family: PSEUDOMUGILIIDAE
Common name: AUSTRALIAN BLUE-EYE
Distribution: Northern and eastern Queensland (Australia)
Size: 4.5 cm (2 in)
Food: OMNIVOROUS. Algae, small aquatic invertebrates, flake, etc
Temperature range: 23–27°C / 73–81°F
pH: 7.0 dH: to 15°

A colourful shoaling fish which may be kept in the community aquarium but does better in a species tank. Males are generally larger and more colourful than females, but when breeding the females have a red anal fin.

Breeding
Spawns on fine-leaved plants or spawning mops. The water should have a neutral pH and a hardness of about 12–14°. It takes about 14 days for the large eggs to hatch. First foods: newly hatched brine shrimp. Early morning sunlight falling on the tank will often trigger them into spawning.

Tank Set-up
Give the fish plenty of open space but include some plants.

23–27°C
73–81°F

4.5 cm (2 in)

PSEUDOMUGIL SIGNIFER
KNER, 1864

Miscellaneous

Acipenseridae	Mastacembelidae
Amiidae	Monodactylidae
Apteronotidae	Mormyridae
Badidae	Nandidae
Belonidae	Notopteridae
Catostomidae	Oryziatidae
Centrachidae	Osteoglossidae
Ceratotidae	Pantodontidae
Chandidae	Percidae
Channidae	Percichthyidae
Clupeidae	Phractolaemidae
Cottidae	Polyodontidae
Electrophoridae	Polypteridae
Eleotridae	Potamotrygonidae
Esocidae	Protopteridae
Gasterosteidae	Rhamphichthyidae
Gobiidae	Scatophagidae
Gymnotidae	Soleidae
Lepidosirenidae	Sygnathidae
Lepisosteidae	Synbranchidae
Lobotidae	Tetraodontidae
Luciocephalidae	Toxotidae
	Umbridae

ACIPENSER RUTHENUS

LINNAEUS, 1758

Family: ACIPENSERIDAE

Common name: STERLET

Distribution: Europe to Siberia

Size: 100 cm (40 in)

Food: CARNIVOROUS. Insect larvae, snails, small fish, etc

Temperature range: 10–18°C / 50–64°F

pH: 7.0–7.5 dH: to 10°

A coldwater fish, small specimens may be kept in aquaria, larger ones require a pond. Very peaceful despite their potential size but do not keep with small fish. Their common name refers to the small bony plates on their flanks which look like stars.

Breeding

Improbable in aquaria because of their size. In the wild they breed in early summer, spawning over gravel beds. Up to 135,000 eggs may be produced. These hatch in about five days.

Tank Set-up

Use a large aquarium with very clean, clear, cold, well-oxygenated water with a good flow, and a sandy substrate. Well-maintained Koi pools are ideal for these fish.

10–18°C 50–64°F   100 cm (40 in)

ACIPENSER STURIO

LINNAEUS, 1758

10–18°C 50–64°F   600 cm (20 ft)

Family: ACIPENSERIDAE

Common name: ATLANTIC STURGEON

Distribution: Europe, North America

Size: 600 cm (20 ft)

Food: CARNIVOROUS. Small fish, worms, invertebrates

Temperature range: 10–18°C / 50–64°F

pH: 7.0–7.5 dH: to 20°

A very large fish only suited to ponds or very large aquaria and even then only young fish should be kept. The roe is used for caviar, the swimbladder provides isinglass and the flesh is edible. Large specimens live around the coasts of Europe and the Atlantic coast of North America, entering rivers in late winter and early spring to spawn in freshwater.

Breeding

Not in aquaria. In the wild they spawn over gravel beds producing up to 250,000 eggs.

Tank Set-up

Provide cold, clear water with a good flow, very efficient filtration and sand substrate.

HUSO HUSO

(LINNAEUS, 1758)

Family: ACIPENSERIDAE

Common name: BELUGA

Distribution: From the Adriatic through the Black and Caspian Seas to the Volga

Size: 900 cm (29 ft)

Food: CARNIVOROUS. Aquatic invertebrates, snails, worms, small fish, etc

Temperature range: 10–18°C / 50–64°F

pH: 7.0–7.5 dH: to 20°

Again only small fish are suitable for the aquarium where they spend much of their time swimming just above the substrate, their barbels barely in contact with the sand, searching for food. These fish can weigh over a 1,000 kg (2,204 lb) and it is from them that the famed Beluga caviar comes, the roe of one female can produce up to 100 kg (220 lb).

10–18°C 50–64°F   900 cm (29 ft)

Breeding

Not possible in aquaria.

Tank Set-up

Use a large aquarium with a sand substrate. Cold, clear, well-filtered water is essential.

SCAPHIRHYNCHUS PLATORYNCHUS
(RAFINESQUE, 1820)

Family: ACIPENSERIDAE	
Common name: SHOVELNOSED STURGEON	
Distribution: Ohio, Mississippi, Missouri Rivers; Mobile Bay drainage, Rio Grande	
Size: 100 cm (39 in)	
Food: CARNIVOROUS: Small fish, aquatic invertebrates	
Temperature range: 10–18°C / 50–64°F	
pH: 7.0 dH: to 18°	

The smallest and most common of the North American Sturgeons, this fish is one of the mainstays of the commercial fishing industry on the Missouri and Mississippi rivers. Its habitat is large, turbid, moderately flowing rivers with sand or gravel substrate.

Breeding
Not known in aquaria. In the wild they spawn over gravel beds between mid-spring and early summer.

Tank Set-up
A large aquarium with cool, clean, clear, well-oxygenated and well-filtered water is needed.

10–18°C 50–64°F		100 cm (39 in)

AMIA CALVA
LINNAEUS, 1766

13–19°C 55–66°F		50 cm (20 in)

Family: AMIIDAE	
Common name: BOWFIN	
Distribution: Drainages of the Mississippi and Lakes Huron and Erie (USA)	
Size: Males 50 cm (20 in); females 75 cm (30 in)	
Food: CARNIVOROUS. Fish, crustaceans, etc	
Temperature range: 13–19°C / 55–66°F	
pH: 7.0 dH: to 10°	

Very predatory so only keep with creatures it cannot swallow, or keep it alone. They are voracious feeders. The Bowfin can breath air if the water conditions deteriorate. Males are smaller and have a black spot surrounded with a ring of yellow at the base of the caudal fin; females are larger and lack the ocellus.

Breeding
In the wild they construct nests of pieces of plants. They spawn at night, producing up to 70,000 eggs which hatch in about a week. The male guards the nest and resultant fry until they reach about 10 cm (4 in) in length.

Tank Set-up
Create a large aquarium with plenty of hiding places, gravel or sand substrate and thickets of plants. Ensure cold, well-filtered water.

Family: APTERONOTIDAE	
Common name: NONE	
Distribution: Northern South America	
Size: 50 cm (20 in)	
Food: OMNIVOROUS. Live, flake, frozen food	
Temperature range: 23–27°C / 73–80°F	
pH: 6.5–7.0 dH: to 10°	

Although a timid fish, it can be aggressive towards its own kind. They possess a weak electric organ in the caudal peduncle which they use to locate food. They can be long-lived in captivity – there is one report of a fish living for 16 years. May be kept with large peaceful fishes.

Breeding
Not known.

Tank Set-up
Create a planted aquarium with wood and rocks arranged to give the fish

APTERONOTUS ALBIFRONS
LINNAEUS, 1758

plenty of cover. Ensure good filtration as they react adversely to poor water conditions.

23–27°C 73–80°F		50 cm (20 in)

BADIS BADIS BADIS
(HAMILTON, 1822)

Family: BADIDAE	
Common name: BADIS	
Distribution: India	
Size: 8 cm (3 in)	
Food: CARNIVOROUS. Small live food, small pieces of meat	
Temperature range: 23–26°C / 73–79°F	
pH: 6.5–7.5 dH: to 15°	

These stillwater fish can be territorial and are best kept in a species tank. They form family groups headed by the male. Males are more brightly coloured than females and their ventral line is concave whereas the female's is convex. There is another subspecies, the red coloured *B. b. burmanicus*, which as its name suggests, comes from Burma and differs from the blue *B. b. badis* in coloration only.

Breeding
They breed in caves (flowerpots are a good substitute), the male guards the eggs and fry. Remove parents when the fry are free swimming. Feed fry newly hatched brine shrimps and other small live food.

 23–26°C 73–79°F   8 cm (3 in)

Tank Set-up
Use a planted aquarium with caves and hollows. Good but gentle filtration and regular water changes are beneficial.

Family: BELONIDAE	
Common name: NEEDLEFISH	
Distribution: Asia	
Size: 32 cm (13 in)	
Food: CARNIVOROUS. Fish, frogs, will take dead food eventually	
Temperature range: 22–27°C / 72–80°F	
pH: 7.0 dH: to 20°	

A skittish fish that is very easily frightened, even by something as simple as the aquarium lights being turned on. Very prone to jumping, especially when scared. Keep as a shoal. Males usually have a black edge to the dorsal and anal fins.

Breeding
Up to 15 eggs are produced each day. These are hung on the vegetation by a thread about 20 mm (1 in) long. The eggs are 3.5 mm (⅛ in) in diameter and

22–27°C 72–80°F   32 cm (13 in)

XENENTODON CANCILA
(HAMILTON, 1822)

hatch after ten days. On hatching, the fry are 10–12 mm (⅜–½ in) long. The problem with feeding the fry is that they require live food such as the fry of other fishes.

Tank Set-up
A large aquarium, not very deep, say 30 cm (12 in) of water is sufficient. Use dense planting around the edges but with open areas for swimming, and ensure good filtration.

HYPENTELIUM NIGRICANS
(LeSUEUR, 1817)

Family: CATOSTOMIDAE	
Common name: NORTHERN HOG SUCKER	
Distribution: Eastern and central North America	
Size: 60 cm (24 in)	
Food: OMNIVOROUS. Small invertebrates, algae	
Temperature range: 6–15°C / 42–59°F	
pH: 6.5–7.5 dH: to 12°	

Although potentially a large fish, small specimens are fairly peaceful. They feed by taking invertebrates from amongst the stones on the bottom or by grazing over algae-covered rocks. They have toothless jaws (but do have pharygeal teeth) and use their thick, fleshy, bristle-covered lips and a sucking action to remove the algae.

Breeding
Spawning occurs in early summer.

Tank Set-up
A well-maintained aquarium with a gravel substrate and rocks, and thickets of plants for decor. Efficient filtration is essential as they are intolerant of any deterioration in water quality.

 6–15°C 42–59°F   60 cm (24 in)

ICTIOBUS BUBALUS
(RAFINESQUE, 1818)

Family: CATOSTOMIDAE

Common name: SMALLMOUTH BUFFALO

Distribution: Mississippi basin and Gulf coast drainages of the USA

Size: 90 cm (35 in)

Food: OMNIVOROUS. Small invertebrates, algae

Temperature range: 6–15°C / 42–59°F

pH: 6.5–7.5 dH: to 12°

A large, bottom-dwelling, deep-bodied fish with a humped back. Its size and humped back give rise to its common name. It is fished commercially, though rarely as a sport fish, in the Mississippi and some of the large lakes; large specimens can weigh up to 16 kg (35 lb). Small specimens may be kept in the aquarium.

Breeding
Spawning occurs in early summer.

Tank Set-up
A large aquarium with a gravel substrate and rocks, and thickets of plants for decor but leave plenty of room for the fish to swim. Efficient filtration.

6–15°C 42–59°F		90 cm (35 in)

ELASSOMA EVERGLADEI
JORDAN, 1884

Family: CENTRARCHIDAE

Common name: PIGMY SUNFISH, FLORIDA PIGMY SUNFISH, EVERGLADES PIGMY SUNFISH

Distribution: North Carolina to Florida (USA)

Size: 3.5 cm (1½ in)

Food: OMNIVOROUS. Live food, flake and algae

Temperature range: 10–30°C / 50–86°F

pH: 7.0–7.5 dH: to 10°

This small creature should be maintained as a group in a species aquarium. When in spawning condition the fins on males are black while on females they remain clear.

Breeding
Keep cool over winter to encourage the fish to spawn the following spring. Some 50 or so eggs are produced and they hatch in two to three days. First food needs to be small.

Tank Set-up
You will need a mature, planted aquarium with a sand substrate. Include some rocks and roots so the fish can stake out territories, and give gentle filtration.

10–30°C 50–86°F		3.5 cm (1½ in)

ENNEACANTHUS CHAETODON
(BAIRD, 1854)

Family: CENTRARCHIDAE

Common name: BLACK-BANDED SUNFISH

Distribution: New York, New Jersey, Maryland (USA)

Size: 10 cm (4 in)

Food: CARNIVOROUS. Small live food preferred

Temperature range: 4–20°C / 39–68°F

pH: 7.0 dH: 10–20°

A very quiet, peaceful fish of slow moving streams that requires companions of a similar nature. Keep them as a small shoal and let them pair themselves for breeding. They need lots of small live food and will only rarely accept flake or frozen food.

Breeding
The male digs a spawning pit in which the female lays her eggs. The male guards both the eggs and fry.

Tank Set-up
A planted aquarium with a fine sand substrate to which wood and rocks can be added to enable the fish to claim territories is best. The water needs to be clean, clear and very well-oxygenated, any deterioration in water quality means the fish suffer. They are intolerant of fluctuations in temperature (unless it is very gradual), major water changes and chemicals.

4–20°C 39–68°F		10 cm (4 in)

ENNEACANTHUS GLORIOSUS
(HOLBROCK, 1855)

Family:	CENTRACHIDAE
Common name:	BLUE-SPOTTED SUNFISH
Distribution:	New York down the eastern seaboard of Florida (USA)
Size:	8 cm (3 in)
Food:	OMNIVOROUS. Live, frozen and flake food
Temperature range:	10–20°C / 50–68°F
pH:	7.0–7.5 dH: to 10°

A shoaling fish that is not aggressive unless it is breeding, at which time the male will take on all-comers. It has a black spot on the operculum. The dark bands on the body fade with age. They are sensitive to changes in pH, this is especially so when moving them from

acid to alkaline conditions. At such time the fish becomes susceptible to fungal attack, so take care when doing water changes.

Breeding
Pit spawner with the male guarding the eggs and fry. To encourage spawning keep at cooler temperatures over the winter.

Tank Set-up
A well-planted aquarium with plenty of hiding places, a fine gravel substrate and very good filtration to maintain water quality is needed.

10–20°C
50–68°F

8 cm (3 in)

ENNEACANTHUS OBESUS
(GIRARD, 1854)

Family:	CENTRACHIDAE
Common name:	DIAMOND SUNFISH, LITTLE SUNFISH
Distribution:	Eastern seaboard from New England to Florida (USA)
Size:	10 cm (4 in)
Food:	OMNIVOROUS. Live, flake and frozen food
Temperature range:	10–20°C / 50–68°F
pH:	7.0–7.5 dH: to 12°

A shoaling species but males take up territories especially when breeding. They sometimes bury themselves in the substrate until only their eyes are

showing. Sensitive to changes in pH, take care when moving the fish or when doing water changes.

Breeding
Pit spawners, the male carries out the parental duties of guarding the nest and fry.

Tank Set-up
Provide a mature, well-planted aquarium with rocks and wood and efficient filtration to maintain the water quality.

10–20°C
50–68°F

10 cm (4 in)

LEPOMIS CYANELLUS
RAFINESQUE, 1819

Family:	CENTRACHIDAE
Common name:	GREEN SUNFISH
Distribution:	Canada to Mexico, east of the Rockies (USA)
Size:	20 cm (8 in)
Food:	OMNIVOROUS. Live, flake and frozen food
Temperature range:	15–22°C / 59–72°F
pH:	7.0–7.5 dH: to 15°

Generally a peaceful fish unless it is spawning. Makes good companions for other fish of a similar temperament. They prefer warmer conditions than most of the Sunfish although they can

be overwintered at 10°C / 50°F and will survive down to 4°C / 39°F.

Breeding
Pit spawner with the male guarding the eggs and fry.

Tank Set-up
Provide a planted aquarium with some open areas, gravel substrate and efficient filtration to ensure good water quality.

15–22°C
59–72°F
20 cm (8 in)

LEPOMIS GIBBOSUS
(LINNAEUS, 1758)

Family:	CENTRACHIDAE
Common name:	PUMPKINSEED SUNBASS, KIVER
Distribution:	Great Lakes east to New England and south to Texas and Florida (USA)
Size:	20 cm (8 in)
Food:	CARNIVOROUS. Live food but takes frozen and flake
Temperature range:	5–21°C / 41–70°F
pH:	7.0–7.5 dH: to 15°

A larger fish, it needs plenty of space, especially when breeding. Tolerant of most other fishes, the only time they become a little defensive is when breeding. Overwinter at cool

temperatures (10°C / 50°F or less) if you want to try and breed them.

Breeding
A large pit some 25–30 cm (10–12 in) is dug by the male. After spawning he guards the eggs and fry. In the confines of an aquarium, remove the female or she may be killed.

Tank Set-up
Have a well-planted aquarium with a gravel substrate and leave open water for swimming. Efficient filtration is needed.

5–21°C
41–70°F
20 cm (8 in)

LEPOMIS MACROCHIRUS
RAFINESQUE, 1819

Family: CENTRACHIDAE	
Common name: BLUEGILL	
Distribution: Ohio valley south to Arkansas and Kentucky (USA)	
Size: 213cm (5 in)	
Food: CARNIVOROUS. Live food	
Temperature range: 4–21°C / 39–70°F	
pH: 7.0–7.5 dH: to 15°	

A rare creature, its steel grey-blue colour alone makes it desirable for the aquarium. Peaceful unless defending a territory. Only rarely will they accept flake or frozen food.

Breeding
Not known.

Tank Set-up
A tank set-up and maintained similar to that for *L. gibbosus* is ideal.

 4–21°C 39–70°F   13 cm (5 in)

LEPOMIS MEGALOTIS
(RAFINESQUE, 1820)

10–20°C 50–68°F   23 cm (9 in)

Family: CENTRARCHIDAE	
Common name: LONGEAR SUNFISH	
Distribution: USA; southern Quebec and Manitoba down through the Mississippi drainage and along the Gulf Coast drainages	
Size: 23 cm (9 in)	
Food: CARNIVOROUS. Small invertebrates, crustaceans and fish	
Temperature range: 10–20°C / 50–68°F	
pH: 6.5–7.5 dH: to 12°	

A colourful creature that adapts well to aquarium life provided you give it enough space because, although youngsters are tolerant of each other, adults can be quarrelsome. In its native lands it is prized as a sport fish and has been widely introduced outside its natural range.

Breeding
Spawning occurs in early summer. Males excavate a nest and guard the eggs and fry.

Tank Set-up
A large aquarium with a gravel substrate, rocks, wood, and thickets of plants for decor. Efficient filtration.

NEOCERATODUS FORSTERI
(KREFFT, 1870)

Family: CERATOTIDAE	
Common name: AUSTRALIAN LUNGFISH	
Distribution: Queensland (Australia)	
Size: 180 cm (6 ft)	
Food: CARNIVOROUS. Fish and aquatic invertebrates, will take dead food	
Temperature range: 22–28°C / 72–82°F	
pH: 7.0 dH: to 15°	

A large and impressive creature, it is a protected species in its native country and thus is unlikely to be offered for sale. However, they are seen in public aquaria and, should they be bred commercially could become available. Only small specimens are suited to the aquarium. Although their African and South American counterparts practise aestivation, *Neoceratodus* does not. It also differs in that it does not use its capacity for breathing air to the same extent as its African and Asian cousins.

Breeding
Reports of spawnings in the wild state are of eggs laid on water plants, which are about 7 mm (¼ in) in diameter and covered in a gelatinous substance like that of frogs' eggs. When they hatch, the fry do not have external gills.

 22–28°C 72–82°F   180 cm (6 ft)

Tank Set-up
The fish needs a large aquarium with gravel substrate and efficient filtration. Use smooth large rocks or wood for decor.

POMOXIS NIGROMACULATUS
(LeSueur in Cuvier & Valenciennes, 1829)

Family: CENTRARCHIDAE	
Common name: BLACK CRAPPIE	
Distribution: Eastern and central North America	
Size: 40 cm (16 in)	
Food: CARNIVOROUS. Small invertebrates, algae	
Temperature range: 10–20°C / 50–68°F	
pH: 6.5–7.5 dH: to 12°	

Small specimens are fairly peaceful and suited to the aquarium. Youngsters feed on invertebrates and crustaceans but as they grow, they will take fish. It will feed at any time but is most active at dusk. It is a popular sport fish.

Breeding
Spawning occurs in early summer. Males excavate a nest and guard the eggs and fry.

Tank Set-up
A good-sized aquarium with a gravel substrate and rocks, and thickets of plants for decor. Efficient filtration.

 10–20°C 50–68°F   40 cm (16 in)

CHANDA COMMERSONII
(Cuvier & Valenciennes, 1828)

Family: CHANDIDAE	
Common name: COMMERSON'S GLASSFISH	
Distribution: Africa, Asia, north Australia	
Size: 10 cm (4 in)	
Food: CARNIVOROUS. Mostly live food, flake reluctantly accepted	
Temperature range: 22–26°C / 72–79°F	
pH: 7.0–8.0 dH: to 20°	

A fish that is best kept in brackish water. It is a peaceful shoaling species that may be kept in a species aquarium or with others of the same genus. On males the tip of the dorsal fin and caudal fin are black. It differs from *C. ranga* in its elongated body and fewer soft rays in the dorsal and anal fins.

Breeding
To instigate spawning it is necessary to keep the fish in marine water and gradually reduce the salinity. Many small eggs are laid. Feed fry brine shrimp nauplii.

Tank Set-up
Add marine salt to the water to create brackish or even marine conditions and use plenty of roots, rocks, etc to provide hiding places. Efficient filtration is needed.

 22–26°C 72–79°F   10 cm (4 in)

CHANDA RANGA
(Hamilton-Buchanan, 1822)

Family: CHANDIDAE	
Common name: INDIAN GLASSFISH	
Distribution: India, Burma, Thailand	
Size: 8 cm (3 in)	
Food: CARNIVOROUS. All small live food	
Temperature range: 20–30°C / 68–86°F	
pH: 7.0 dH: to 12°	

Very peaceful fish that is probably best kept in a species aquarium although it will live with other small, peaceful fishes. They can be territorial. The diet should be predominantly live food, and although they will take flake, it is not sufficient by itself.

Breeding
Spawning is induced by increasing temperatures, a change of water and morning sunlight. Eggs are laid over plants and they hatch in 24 hours. The fry are hard to raise.

Tank Set-up
Provide a very mature, planted aquarium with lots of hiding places, and gentle filtration.

 20–30°C 68–86°F   8 cm (3 in)

CHANDA WOLFFII
(BLEEKER, 1851)

Family: CHANDIDAE
Common name: GLASSFISH
Distribution: Thailand, Sumatra, Borneo
Size: 20 cm (8 in); in the aquarium maybe 8 cm (3 in)
Food: CARNIVOROUS. Predominantly live food
Temperature range: 18–24°C / 64–75°F
pH: 7.0–7.5 dH: to 12°

Sometimes territorial, it can nevertheless be kept with other similarly sized peaceful fishes. Keep as

a shoal and feed on live food. They will take flake but will not survive on this alone.

Breeding
Not known.

Tank Set-up
Provide similar to the set-up for *C. ranga*.

18–24°C 64–75°F		20 cm (8 in)

Family: CHANNIDAE
Common name: SPOTTED SNAKEHEAD
Distribution: China
Size: 100 cm (39 in)
Food: CARNIVOROUS. Live and dead food
Temperature range: 15–22°C / 59–72°F
pH: 7.0 dH: to 12°

A potentially large fish, it is best kept alone or with equally large companions if the aquarium and its filtration system are large enough to cope with them.

Breeding
A report from the wild states that a nest is constructed and is guarded by the male. The eggs float and hatch in 36 hours in relatively warm water (23–25°C / 73–77°F). Once the fry are free-swimming the male ceases parental duties.

15–22°C 59–72°F		100 cm (39 in)

CHANNA ARGUS
(CANTOR, 1842)

Tank Set-up
Use a large well-filtered aquarium with wood, rocks and robust plants for decor, and plenty of open water for swimming. A heavy cover glass is needed.

Family: CHANNIDAE
Common name: NONE
Distribution: India to Southern China
Size: 100 cm (39 in)
Food: CARNIVOROUS. Mostly live fish but will take dead food
Temperature range: 24–28°C / 75–82°F
pH: 6.5–7.5 dH: to 15°

Predatory but is peaceful and may be kept with similar sized fishes. They are large, powerful fishes that will jump at the slightest provocation. In their native lands they are highly prized as food fish.

Breeding
Not known.

Tank Set-up
A large, planted aquarium with hiding places, a heavy cover glass, and good filtration is needed.

CHANNA MARULIA
(HAMILTON, 1822)

24–28°C 75–82°F		100 cm (39 in)

CHANNA MICROPELTES
(CUVIER & VALENCIENNES, 1831)

Family: CHANNIDAE
Common name: RED SNAKEHEAD
Distribution: India, Burma, Thailand, Vietnam, Malaysia
Size: 100 cm (39 in)
Food: CARNIVOROUS. Mostly live fish, will take dead meaty food
Temperature range: 25–28°C / 77–82°F
pH: 6.5–7.5 dH: to 15°

A warmth-loving fish, it is fairly undemanding as far as water conditions are concerned, but will not tolerate low temperatures. Feed well, but take care not to overfeed.

Breeding
Unlikely in aquaria.

25–28°C
77–82°F

100 cm (39 in)

Tank Set-up
Use a large aquarium with an equally large filtration system. Provide wood and plants for cover, including some floating plants, and a tight cover glass.

CHANNA OBSCURA
(GUNTHER, 1861)

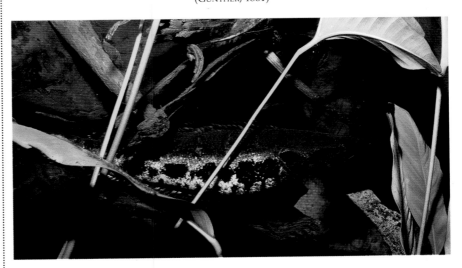

Family: CHANNIDAE
Common name: NONE
Distribution: West Africa
Size: 35 cm (14 in)
Food: CARNIVOROUS. Mostly fish, will rarely take dead food
Temperature range: 26–28°C / 79–82°F
pH: 6.5–7.5 dH: to 15°

A nasty piece of work, they are cannabalistic if several are kept together. Keep alone. Females are deeper bodied than males when ready to breed.

Breeding
The male guards the eggs and fry. Up to 3,000 eggs may be produced. The young are cannibalistic.

Tank Set-up
Use a well-planted aquarium with wood for decoration and to provide hiding places. A good cover glass and efficient filtration are necessary.

26–28°C
79–82°F

35 cm (14 in)

CHANNA ORIENTALIS
BLOCH & SCHNEIDER, 1801

23–26°C
73–79°F

30 cm (12 in)

Family: CHANNIDAE
Common name: NONE
Distribution: Sri Lanka, Afghanistan through China
Size: 30 cm (12 in), more usually 15–20 cm (6–8 in)
Food: CARNIVOROUS. Live food – insect larvae, worms, fish, etc
Temperature range: 23–26°C / 73–79°F
pH: 6.5–7.5 dH: to 18°

An interesting Snakehead and one that is small enough to be bred in the aquarium. Interestingly, the Sri Lankan population may occur with or without ventral fins. It adapts well to aquarium conditions and may become hand tame.

Breeding
The pair embrace in a similar manner to Labyrinth Fishes. After expulsion the eggs float to the surface and the male gathers them in his mouth. Hatching time can vary: in fish with ventral fins it is three to four days and some 200 fry may be produced; those without ventral fins take nine to ten days and produce at most 40 fry.

Tank Set-up
Use a well-planted aquarium with plenty of hiding places. The fish jump so a good heavy cover glass is essential. Have gentle filtration.

CHANNA STRIATA
(BLOCH, 1797)

23–27°C
73–80°F

90 cm (35 in)

Family: CHANNIDAE
Common name: STRIPED SNAKEHEAD
Distribution: Sri Lanka, Thailand to the Philippines and Moluccas
Size: 90 cm (35 in)
Food: CARNIVOROUS. Mostly live food
Temperature range: 23–27°C / 73–80°F
pH: 7.0–8.0 dH: to 10°

Widespread in its natural range, this fish has been introduced in Hawaii and has become established there. Very predatory, it will eat any fish it can fit in its mouth. They are an important food fish throughout their range. Provided their skin remains damp, they can survive the dry season buried in bogs.

Breeding
The male guards the floating eggs and subsequent fry. The parents may eat the young.

Tank Set-up
Provide a heavily planted aquarium with a fine substrate. Good, efficient filtration is essential as these fish produce copious amounts of waste.

ALOSA PSEUDOHARENGUS
(WILSON, C.1811)

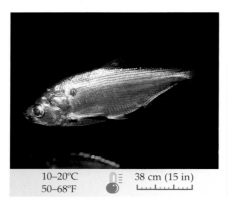

10–20°C
50–68°F

38 cm (15 in)

Family: CLUPEIDAE
Common name: ALEWIFE
Distribution: Eastern seaboard and into the Great Lakes of North America
Size: 38 cm (15 in)
Food: CARNIVOROUS. Small invertebrates, plankton
Temperature range: 10–20°C / 50–68°F
pH: 6.5–8.5 dH: to 20°

The Alewife is a member of the Herring family and can be found in marine, brackish and fresh waters. An active shoaling fish, young specimens may be kept in the aquarium. The locality the specimen was caught in will determine the water conditions it needs. Some populations have established themselves in freshwater lakes and do not enter the sea at all.

Breeding
Lake populations breed in the lake; marine and brackish water populations make spawning runs up freshwater rivers to spawn.

Tank Set-up
A good-sized aquarium with a gravel substrate and rocks. Water salinity should be matched to the requirements of the fish you have. Good filtration. Tight fitting cover glass.

Family: COTTIIDAE
Common name: BULLHEAD, MILLER'S THUMB
Distribution: Europe
Size: 15 cm (6 in)
Food: OMNIVOROUS. Small invertebrates – in captivity happily takes flake, frozen and live food
Temperature range: 10–20°C / 50–68°F
pH: 7.0–7.5 dH: to 10°

COTTUS GOBIO
LINNAEUS, 1758

A bottom-dwelling fish that occurs in the riffles in streams and rivers where the oxygen levels are fairly high. It adapts well to life in the aquarium and will breed. The common name, Millar's Thumb, refers to its resemblance to that part of a miller's anatomy.

Breeding
Spawns in spring and early summer, creating a nest beneath a flat stone, in shallow water.

Tank Set-up
Provide a mature aquarium and maintain good water quality. The substrate should be of sand and shingle with some flat rocks.

10–20°C
50–68°F

15 cm (6 in)

ELECTROPHORUS ELECTRICUS
(Linnaeus, 1766)

Family: Electrophoridae

Common name: Electric Eel

Distribution: Amazon, Brazil, Peru, Venezuela, Guyana

Size: 230 cm (90 in)

Food: Carnivorous. Fish, will take dead food

Temperature range: 23–27°C / 73–80°F

pH: 6.5–7.5 dH: to 15°

A large and potentially dangerous fish. A discharge from a mature specimen is capable of paralysing a horse, so handle with care. Keep alone in the aquarium. They can become hand tame and feed from the hand but this takes time and

23–27°C 73–80°F 230 cm (90 in)

patience and is not recommended. Small specimens can squabble amongst themselves, larger ones are more peaceful.

Breeding
Not known.

Tank Set-up
A large aquarium with roots and large rocks to provide hiding places, good filtration and subdued lighting is necessary.

BUTIS BUTIS
(Hamilton, 1822)

Family: Eleotridae

Common name: Crazy Fish, Bony-snouted Gudgeon

Distribution: Indo-Pacific

Size: 15 cm (6 in)

Food: Carnivorous. Live food

Temperature range: 22–28°C / 72–82°F

pH: 7.0–8.0 dH: to 20°

These creatures are crepuscular, hunting out unsuspecting prey they cruise the aquarium after dark. Feed copious amounts of live food. Depending on the location from where the fish originates, they may be kept in fresh, brackish or marine water and, with careful acclimatisation, fish can be transferred from one type of water to another. It has one alarming habit, that of floating upside down in the water as if it is dead (hence the common name). Why it should do this is unknown. They are best kept in a species aquarium.

22–28°C 72–82°F 15 cm (6 in)

Breeding
Not known.

Tank Set-up
Use a good sized aquarium with rocks, wood and plants to give plenty of hiding places. Ensure efficient filtration to give well-oxygenated water.

DORMITATOR MACULATUS
(Bloch, 1785)

Family: Eleotridae

Common name: Striped Sleeper Goby, Spotted Goby

Distribution: Atlantic coast of tropical South America

Size: 25 cm (10 in)

Food: Carnivorous. Live and frozen food

Temperature range: 22–24°C / 72–75°F

pH: 7.5–8.5 dH: to 25°

A brackish water fish that will not adapt to fresh water. It is predatory and is best kept in a species aquarium. Males are darker and more spotted.

Breeding
The eggs are laid in rows on a flat surface such as a rock. They hatch in 24 hours and growth of the fry is rapid.

Tank Set-up
Ensure there are plenty of caves and hollows for the fish to hide in. Use sand on the bottom as they like to dig. Provide efficient filtration and regular water changes.

22–24°C 72–75°F 25 cm (10 in)

HYPSELEOTRIS COMPRESSA
(KREFFT, 1864)

Family: ELEOTRIDAE	
Common name: EMPIRE GUDGEON, EMPIRE GOBY	
Distribution: Australia and New Guinea	
Size: 11 cm (4½ in)	
Food: OMNIVOROUS. Live, frozen, flake food	
Temperature range: 12–28°C / 53–82°F	
pH: 7.0 dH: to 15°	

An undemanding fish, it is very attractive even when not in full spawning dress. Males are more colourful than females. May be kept in brackish water as well as freshwater but make the transition either way gradually.

Breeding
These have been spawned in captivity. The males guard the eggs and fry. Problems arise with feeding the very small fry, and green water has been suggested as a solution.

Tank Set-up
You need a planted aquarium with rocks and stones and efficient filtration.

 12–28°C 53–82°F   11 cm (4½ in)

MOGURNDA MOGURNDA
(RICHARDSON, 1844)

Family: ELEOTRIDAE	
Common name: PURPLE-STRIPED GUDGEON	
Distribution: Australia, New Guinea	
Size: 17 cm (7 in)	
Food: OMNIVOROUS. Live, flake, frozen food	
Temperature range: 24–26°C / 75–79°F	
pH: 7.0 dH: to 8°	

These territorial little fishes can be quite aggressive towards each other, but they are best kept as a group so that no single individual is permanently picked upon. Males are generally smaller than females.

Breeding
Cave spawners, the eggs are usually attached to the roof of the cave and guarded by the male. The eggs hatch in about three days and the male continues his guard duties until the fry are free swimming. Feed newly hatched brine shrimp to the fry.

Tank Set-up
Use wood, rocks and plant to form caves and give shelter, a fine substrate and good filtration.

 24–26°C 75–79°F   17 cm (7 in)

OXYELEOTRIS MARMORATUS
(BLEEKER, 1853)

Family: ELEOTRIDAE	
Common name: MARBLED SLEEPER GOBY	
Distribution: Southeast Asia	
Size: 50 cm (20 in)	
Food: CARNIVOROUS. Eats most things but prefers live food	
Temperature range: 22–27°C / 72–80°F	
pH: 7.0 dH: to 15°	

A predatory fish, it spends much of the day hiding in caves and crevices or buried in the substrate. It may be kept with similar sized fishes. Males have a higher second dorsal, longer anal fin and conical genital papillae; females are more uniformly coloured and have a cylindrical genital papillae.

 22–27°C 72–80°F   50 cm (20 in)

Breeding
Not known.

Tank Set-up
Have a well-planted aquarium with plenty of hiding places; soft substrate; subdued lighting; good filtration but only a very gentle flow of water through the aquarium.

TATEURNDINA OCELLICAUDA
NICHOLS, 1955

22–26°C	7.5 cm (3 in)
72–79°F	

Family: ELEOTRIDAE
Common name: PEACOCK GOBY
Distribution: New Guinea
Size: 7.5 cm (3 in)
Food: OMNIVOROUS. Small live aquatic invertebrates, flake and frozen food
Temperature range: 22–26°C / 72–79°F
pH: 7.0 dH: to 8°

A softwater fish of streams and ponds, it is ideally suited to the community aquarium because of its beautiful colours and peaceful temperament. It is one of the smallest of the Sleeper Gobies. Males have a straight ventral profile and lighter-coloured dorsal and anal fins. Females have a more rounded ventral profile when ready to spawn, a yellowish belly and more yellow on the edge of the dorsal and anal fins.

Breeding
The pair prepare a spawning site, usually a cave or crevice. The male guards the spawn. The fry take newly hatched brine shrimp.

Tank Set-up
Provide a well-planted, peaceful community aquarium with plenty of hiding places; and good filtration.

ESOX AMERICANUS
GMELIN, 1788

Family: ESOCIDAE
Common name: REDFIN PICKEREL
Distribution: Eastern and central North America
Size: 60 cm (24 in)
Food: CARNIVOROUS. Predominantly fish
Temperature range: 10–20°C / 50–68°F
pH: 6.5–7.5 dH: to 12°

A loner, this predator lurks amongst plants in wait for prey. Small specimens may be kept in the aquarium with other fish, provided the companion fish are large enough not to be eaten.

Breeding
Spawns in spring among plants.

Tank Set-up
A large, well-maintained aquarium with thickets of plants for decor. Gentle filtration. Good cover glass as these fish may jump if frightened.

10–20°C	60 cm (24 in)
50–68°F	

ESOX NIGER
LESUEUR, 1818

Family: ESOCIDAE
Common name: CHAIN PICKEREL
Distribution: Eastern North America from Nova Scotia through New Brunswick, Maine, New York and south to the Gulf States and the Mississippi River
Size: 80 cm (31 in)
Food: CARNIVOROUS. Predominantly fish
Temperature range: 10–20°C / 50–68°F
pH: 6.5–7.5 dH: to 12°

A predator, small specimens are suited to the aquarium provided they are not kept with anything that is bite sized! Spends much of its time lurking amongst weeds waiting to lunge at prey. Although they prefer live food, it is possible to wean them onto pieces of fish or meat.

Breeding
Spawns in spring and early summer amongst weeds.

Tank Set-up
A large, well-maintained aquarium with thickets of plants for decor. Gentle filtration.

10–20°C	80 cm (31 in)
50–68°F	

GASTEROSTEUS ACULEATUS
LINNAEUS, 1758

Family:	GASTEROSTEIDAE
Common name:	THREE-SPINED STICKLEBACK
Distribution:	Europe, northern Asia, North America
Size:	12 cm (4½ in)
Food:	CARNIVOROUS. Small live aquatic invertebrates, will sometimes take flake
Temperature range:	4–18°C/39–64°F
pH: 6.5–7.5 dH: to 15°	

A shoaling fish that is well worth keeping to observe its breeding behaviour. It lives in fresh and brackish waters. When ready to breed, males are much more colourful with red bellies and bluish green backs while the females are greenish grey with a silvery belly. Males can be territorial so ensure there is room in the aquarium for each male to stake his claim to a territory and he will defend this against all-comers. Keep several females for each male.

Breeding
Keep cool in winter if you are going to attempt to spawn them. Males will construct a nest of plant material in their territory and lure a female to it. She pushes through the nest and deposits her eggs, he then follows and fertilises them. He repeats this procedure with several females until there are up to 50 or so eggs in the nest. He then guards the eggs and resultant fry.

Tank Set-up
A well-planted aquarium with plenty of caves and hiding places so the fish can claim territories is best. Good filtration must be provided.

4–18°C 39–64°F		12 cm (4½ in)

PUNGITUS PUNGITUS
(LINNAEUS, 1758)

10–18°C 50–64°F		7 cm (3 in)

Family:	GASTEROSTEIDAE
Common name:	TEN-SPINED STICKLEBACK
Distribution:	Europe, North America, northern Asia
Size:	7 cm (3 in)
Food:	CARNIVOROUS. Aquatic invertebrates, only rarely will it accept flake
Temperature range:	10–18°C/50–64°F
pH: 6.5–7.5 dH: to 18°	

A shoaling fish that behaves in a similar manner to the Three-spined Stickleback. Males are more colourful, when breeding they have a black throat and orange red pectoral fins. Keep several females with each male.

Breeding
As for the Three-spined Stickleback but the nest is constructed above the substrate rather than on it.

Tank Set-up
Ensure a well-planted aquarium with plenty of hiding places and good filtration.

Family:	GOBIIDAE
Common name:	BUMBLEBEE GOBY
Distribution:	Thailand, south Vietnam
Size:	4.5 cm (2 in)
Food:	CARNIVOROUS. Small live food of all kinds
Temperature range:	25–30°C/77–86°F
pH: 7.5–8.5 dH: 15–30°	

Very often sold for the community aquarium, this fish is best kept in a species aquarium so that its demands on water conditions may be met. From fresh and brackish waters they like hard, alkaline water with the addition of a little salt and this is not acceptable to the majority of community fish. However, Bumblebee Gobies may be kept with other species that require similar water conditions. Feeding can pose problems as they are often reluctant to accept flake food. When ready to breed, females are fuller in the body and the ovipositor can be seen.

25–30°C 77–86°F		4.5 cm (2 in)

BRACHYGOBIUS XANTHOZONA
(BLEEKER, 1849)

Breeding
Eggs are laid in caves or beneath stones and are guarded by the male. They hatch in about four days and the male continues his parental duties.

Tank Set-up
Best is a species aquarium with plenty of wood and rocks to create hiding places. Some plants are beneficial. Good filtration is ideal.

Family: GOBIIDAE

Common name: MUDSKIPPER

Distribution: Africa, Madagascar, Southeast Asia, Australia

Size: 15 cm (6 in)

Food: CARNIVOROUS. Live food such as worms

Temperature range: 25–30°C / 77–86°F

pH: 8.0–8.5 dH: to 25°

Brackish water fish that needs to leave the water. They can be territorial and are best kept in a species tank. Their natural habitat is the shoreline of mangrove swamps.

Breeding
Not known.

Tank Set-up
Provide an environment that imitates mangrove swamps – muddy substrate onto which the fish can crawl from out of the water, tree roots and a very humid atmosphere.

PERIOPHTHALMUS BARBARUS
(LINNAEUS, 1766)

25–30°C 77–86°F		15 cm (6 in)

PERIOPHTHALMUS PAPILIO
BLOCH & SCHNEIDER, 1801

Family: GOBIIDAE

Common name: BUTTERFLY MUDSKIPPER

Distribution: West Africa

Size: 25 cm (10 in)

Food: CARNIVOROUS. Live food, mostly worms

Temperature range: 26–30°C / 79–86°F

pH: 7.0–8.0 dH: to 20°

Brackish water fish, they are for the specialist who is willing to maintain them in a species aquarium. They can be territorial. They need to be able to come out of the water and rest on mud flats or roots, their natural habitat being mangrove swamps.

Breeding
Not known.

Tank Set-up
Create a shore-like environment with a beach area onto which the fish can crawl from out of the water. Sand or mud is best for the substrate and use roots that come out of the water. Good filtration.

26–30°C 79–86°F		25 cm (10 in)

STIPHODON ELEGANS
(STEINDACHNER, 1879)

24–27°C 75–80°F		4.5 cm (2 in)

Family: GOBIIDAE

Common name: EMERALD RIVER GOBY

Distribution: Southeast Asia

Size: 4.5 cm (2 in)

Food: OMNIVOROUS. Flake, frozen, live and green food, especially algae

Temperature range: 24–27°C / 75–80°F

pH: 7.0 dH: to 12°

The body shape of this fish gives an indication of its habitat. It lives in fast flowing streams and holds station against the current by using its fused ventral fins as a suction pad. They have a poorly developed swimbladder. They can be kept with other small peaceful fishes and are very active in the aquarium. They spend time resting on leaves or stones.

Breeding
They have been bred with limited success but details are not yet available.

Tank Set-up
A planted aquarium with a sandy substrate and pebbles is best. Very efficient filtration system that also creates a good current of well-oxygenated water in the aquarium is required.

STIGMATOGOBIUS SADANUNDIO
(HAMILTON, 1822)

Family:	GOBIIDAE
Common name:	NONE
Distribution:	Southeast Asia
Size:	8.5 cm (3½ in)
Food:	OMNIVOROUS. Mostly live food but also algae
Temperature range:	20–26°C / 68–79°F
pH: 7.5–8.0 dH: to 25°	

Very peaceful with other fishes although they can be territorial especially when breeding. Under no circumstances attempt to keep them in, or acclimatise them to, soft water. They also like a diurnal fluctuation in water temperature of a few degrees, higher

20–26°C 68–79°F   8.5 cm (3½ in)

during the day, lower at night. Males have larger finnage. Females are smaller and are yellowish in colour.

Breeding
Eggs are placed on the roof of caves. Up to 1,000 eggs may be produced. Both eggs and fry are guarded by the parents.

Tank Set-up
A sandy substrate with plenty of rocks and wood arranged to form caves and hollows, is needed. Some salt may be added to the water. If using plants, choose those which are salt tolerant. Have good filtration.

GYMNOTUS CARAPO
LINNAEUS, 1758

Family:	GYMNOTIDAE
Common name:	BANDED KNIFEFISH
Distribution:	Central and South America
Size:	60 cm (24 in)
Food:	CARNIVOROUS. All live food, will take dead meaty food
Temperature range:	22–27°C / 72–80°F
pH: 6.0–7.5 dH: to 15°	

22–27°C 72–80°F   60 cm (24 in)

An undemanding fish, it should be kept with other species of a similar size or larger as it is intolerant of its own kind. It is nocturnal. It may take some time to encourage it to take dead food so be prepared to feed live food at first.

Breeding
Not known.

Tank Set-up
A well-planted aquarium with wood and rocks arranged to provide shelter, and good filtration is best.

LEPIDOSIREN PARADOXA
FITZINGER, 1836

Family:	LEPIDOSIRENIDAE
Common name:	SOUTH AMERICAN LUNGFISH
Distribution:	Brazil, Paraguay
Size:	125 cm (49 in)
Food:	CARNIVOROUS. Fish, shrimps, worms, snails, etc, will take dead meat or fish
Temperature range:	23–28°C / 73–82°F
pH: 6.5–7.5 dH: to 15°	

A fish of swamps for the specialist because, although small specimens can be kept without too much trouble, large ones can be difficult. They are large, strong, powerful fish and escape easily but despite this are relatively peaceful and may be kept with other large, peaceful species. The smooth body is easily damaged by sharp objects. Juveniles are mottled yellow on black but this patterning fades to grey as the fish matures. In the wild they aestivate when conditions become too harsh.

Breeding
In the wild eggs are laid in tunnels and they and the resultant fry are guarded by the male. On hatching the young have feathery external gills for breathing.

Tank Set-up
Use a large aquarium with smooth rocks and wood. Some robust broad-leaved plants are beneficial. Provide a heavy cover glass and good filtration.

23–28°C 73–82°F   125 cm (49 in)

LEPISOSTEUS OCULATUS
(WINCHELL, 1864)

Family: LEPISOSTEIDAE
Common name: SPOTTED GAR
Distribution: Great Lakes, Mississippi and the Gulf Coast from Corpus Christi to western Florida (USA)
Size: 120 cm (47 in)
Food: CARNIVOROUS. Fish, will take dead food eventually
Temperature range: 12–18°C / 53–64°F
pH: 7.0 dH: 10–15°

A large predatory fish that spends much of its time lurking among roots and plants to lunge at passing prey. Best kept on their own or with fishes large enough not to eaten. Will jump if frightened.

Breeding
In the wild they spawn in the spring in shallow water, scattering the adhesive eggs over plants. The hatchlings have an adhesive pad on the upper jaw which allows them to attach themselves to plants.

Tank Set-up
Use a large, heavily planted aquarium with open regions for swimming. You will need very good filtration as these fish like clean, clear, well-oxygenated water.

12–18°C
53–64°F   120 cm (47 in)

LEPISOSTEUS OSSEUS
(LINNAEUS, 1758)

Family: LEPISOSTEIDAE
Common name: LONGNOSED GAR
Distribution: Great Lakes, St. Lawrence drainage, south from Vermont to the Rio Grande (USA)
Size: 160 cm (63 in)
Food: PISCIVOROUS. Live fish, will take dead food
Temperature range: 12–18°C / 53–64°F
pH: 7.0 dH: 10–15°

A predator of the first degree, this solitary animal prefers live food for which it lurks in wait beneath floating plants or camouflaged in thickets of plants. In the heat of summer, Longnosed Gars are often seen floating motionless on the surface of still water in rivers, lakes and creeks. Although it is a sport fish it is seldom eaten because the roe is poisonous.

Breeding
Adhesive eggs are scattered over plants.

Tank Set-up
In a large aquarium, plant the sides and rear. Have very efficient filtration providing cold, clean, well-oxygenated water.

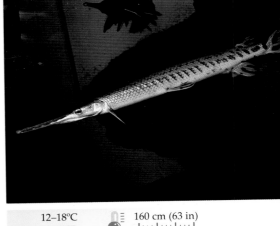

12–18°C
53–64°F   160 cm (63 in)

LEPISOSTEUS PLATOSTOMUS
RAFINESQUE, 1920

Family: LEPISOSTEIDAE
Common name: SHORTNOSED GAR, SPOTNOSED GAR
Distribution: Mississippi drainage
Size: 60 cm (24 in)
Food: CARNIVOROUS. Any meaty live food, worms, fish, etc, will take dead food eventually
Temperature range: 10–18°C / 50–64°F
pH: 7.0 dH: 10–15°

More suited to aquaria because of its smaller potential size. It is a hunter that lurks to ambush its prey. The median fins are located at the rear of the fish to give good initial thrust from a standing start enabling the fish to lunge at prey.

Breeding
Not in captivity. In the wild they scatter adhesive eggs over plants.

Tank Set-up
A large aquarium decorated with roots and thickets of plants to provide cover is best. Cool, clean, clear water and a good filtration system are essential.

10–18°C
50–64°F   60 cm (24 in)

LEPISOSTEUS TRISTOECHUS
(BLOCH & SCHNEIDER, 1801)

Family: LEPISOSTEIDAE

Common name: ALLIGATOR GAR

Distribution: Southern USA to northern Mexico and Cuba

Size: 300 cm (118 in)

Food: PISCIVOROUS. Live fish, will accept dead meaty food

Temperature range: 18–27°C/64–80°F

pH: 7.0–7.5 dH: to 15°

18–27°C
64–80°F

300 cm (118 in)

A Gar that likes warmer waters, it too is a lurking predator that lives in fresh and sometimes brackish and marine waters. Small specimens may be kept in aquaria.

Breeding
Egg scatterer. Breeds in the spring.

Tank Set-up
Create a large aquarium with good filtration and water quality. Plant the edges and back of the tank allowing the fish some swimming space. If kept in cramped conditions they often damage themselves, the aquarium or the decorations when lunging at prey.

DATNOIDES MICROLEPIS
BLEEKER, 1853

Family: LOBOTIDAE

Common name: SIAMESE TIGER

Distribution: Thailand, Cambodia, Borneo, Sumatra

Size: 40 cm (16 in); smaller in captivity

Food: CARNIVOROUS. Live food, can be trained to take frozen food

Temperature range: 22–26°C/72–79°F

pH: 7.0–7.5 dH: to 20°

A predator, it will stalk anything it can swallow. They are tolerant of other similar sized, peaceful species. Initially they will often only take live food but, once settled in they can be offered alternatives such as pieces of prawn.

Breeding
Not known.

Tank Set-up
Use a large aquarium with plenty of plants to give them hiding places. The fish are sensitive to poor water conditions so ensure that the filtration system is able to cope. Provide regular water changes, and subdued lighting.

22–26°C
72–79°F

40 cm (16 in)

DATNOIDES QUADRIFASCIATUS
(SEVASTIANOV, 1809)

Family: LOBOTIDAE

Common name: SIAMESE TIGER

Distribution: Widespread from the Ganges in India through Burma, Thailand, Malaysia and into the Indo-Australian Archipelago

Size: 30 cm (12 in)

Food: CARNIVOROUS. Live food of all kinds

Temperature range: 22–26°C / 72–79°F

pH: 7.0–8.0 dH: to 18°

From brackish regions, this species is harder to maintain than *D. microlepis*. It seems more sensitive to water conditions. Otherwise its manner is the same. Juveniles may be recognised by the black patch on the operculum and the three stripes radiating from the eye.

22–26°C
72–79°F
 30 cm (12 in)

Breeding
Not known.

Tank Set-up
Provide the same as for *D. microlepis* but the addition of some sea salt is advised.

LUCIOCEPHALUS PULCHER
(GRAY, 1830)

Family: LUCIOCEPHALIDAE

Common name: NONE

Distribution: Southeast Asia

Size: 18 cm (7 in)

Food: CARNIVOROUS. Will only take live food such as insects

Temperature range: 22–24°C / 72–75°F

pH: 6.0 dH: 8°

A notoriously delicate fish of fast flowing waters that is hard to maintain in captivity for any length of time. Feeding is difficult as they will only take live food either from the surface or just above it, and sometimes smaller fishes. Any food below the first few centimetres of water is ignored. They hunt like Pike (*Esox lucius*), lurking and darting out for their prey. They have a labyrinth organ but lack a swimbladder.

Breeding
Not known

Tank Set-up
Use a planted aquarium but leave plenty of surface area free. Very well-filtered, highly oxygenated water with a good flow is necessary.

22–24°C
72–75°F
 18 cm (7 in)

AFROMASTACEMBELUS PLAGIOSTOMUS
(MATTHES, 1962)

Family: MASTACEMBELIDAE

Common name: NONE

Distribution: Lake Tanganyika

Size: 35 cm (14 in)

Food: CARNIVOROUS. Live food of all kinds

Temperature range: 25–28°C / 77–82°F

pH: 7.5–8.0 dH: to 25°

Best kept alone, this creature is somewhat intolerant of others. Feeding can be a problem as it is reluctant to take tablet, flake or frozen food.

Breeding
Not known.

Tank Set-up
A reasonable-sized aquarium with a sandy substrate to allow the fish to bury; rocks for cover and good filtration is required.

25–28°C
77–82°F
 35 cm (14 in)

MACROGNATHUS ACULEATUS

(BLOCH, 1788)

Family: MASTACEMBELIDAE	
Common name: NONE	
Distribution: Southeast Asia	
Size: 35 cm (14 in)	
Food: CARNIVOROUS. Live food, invertebrates and fish	
Temperature range: 24–28°C / 75–82°F	
pH: 7.0–7.5 dH: to 30°	

A loner, this fish likes hard, slightly alkaline waters. It will tolerate larger companions but, other than when breeding, it is quarrelsome with others of the same species. It is difficult to acclimatise to dead food.

Breeding
This fish has been spawned in the aquarium. Over 1,000 clear eggs of 1.2 mm (⅕ in) in diameter were produced. They hatched in three days, and the fry were fed brine shrimp nauplii.

Tank Set-up
Provide sandy substrate with wood and rocks to create hiding places; good filtration; heavy cover glass.

24–28°C
75–82°F   35 cm (14 in)

Family: MASTACEMBELIDAE	
Common name: SPINY EEL	
Distribution: Southeast Asia	
Size: 75 cm (30 in)	
Food: CARNIVOROUS. Live worms, insect larvae, etc, sometimes tablet food	
Temperature range: 22–28°C / 72–82°F	
pH: 7.0 dH: to 15°	

A nocturnal fish, it is a predator and thus should only be kept with fishes large enough not to be considered food. They dig and bury themselves in the substrate so may uproot plants or undermine rockwork. Females are fatter when ready to breed.

Breeding
Not known.

22–28°C
72–82°F   75 cm (30 in)

MASTACEMBELUS ARMATUS

GUNTHER, 1861

Tank Set-up
Provide a reasonable-sized aquarium with a soft substrate and plenty of hiding places. Because the fish dig, ensure that all rockwork and wood is seated on the base glass of the aquarium. Good filtration and a tight fitting cover glass is needed.

MASTACEMBELUS CIRCUMCINCTUS

HORA, 1924

Family: MASTACEMBELIDAE	
Common name: NONE	
Distribution: Southeast Thailand	
Size: 16 cm (6 in)	
Food: CARNIVOROUS. Mostly live food but will eventually take frozen food	
Temperature range: 24–26°C / 75–79°F	
pH: 7.0 dH: to 15°	

Although peaceful with other large fishes, they can be quarrelsome amongst themselves. Feed after the tank lights are switched off as this creature will only eat at night.

Breeding
Not known.

Tank Set-up
Provide a good-sized aquarium with a soft substrate to allow the fish to bury itself if frightened. Any rockwork or wood should be seated on the base glass to avoid it being undermined by the fish. Also provide good filtration, and a tight cover glass. Some floating plant is beneficial.

24–26°C
75–79°F   16 cm (6 in)

MASTACEMBELUS ERYTHROTAENIA
BLEEKER, 1850

24–28°C
75–82°F
100 cm (39 in)

Family: MASTACEMBELIDAE	
Common name: FIRE EEL	
Distribution: Southeast Asia	
Size: 100 cm (39 in)	
Food: CARNIVOROUS. Live food of all types, will take tablet food	
Temperature range: 24–28°C / 75–82°F	
pH: 7.0 dH: to 15°	

Commonly available in the trade, this is probably the most difficult of the mastacembelids to keep as it is susceptible to injury and attack by parasitic ciliates. A large fish, it is intolerant of most other fishes and so should be kept alone. When ready to breed, females are fatter than males.

Breeding
Not known.

Tank Set-up
A large aquarium with rocks and wood arranged to provide secluded areas for the eel is best. Seat rocks and wood on the base glass and use sand substrate to allow the fish to bury. Provide efficient filtration.

MONODACTYLUS ARGENTEUS
(LINNAEUS, 1758)

Family: MONODACTYLIDAE	
Common name: MONO	
Distribution: Eastern coast of Africa and through Indonesia	
Size: 25 cm (10 in)	
Food: OMNIVOROUS. Live, green, flake and frozen food	
Temperature range: 24–28°C / 75–82°F	
pH: 7.0–8.0 dH: to 18°	

A very active shoaling fish that may be kept with others which require the same water conditions and are of a similar size – Monos are not averse to eating smaller fish. As juveniles their colours are quite bright but they fade as the fish matures.

Breeding
Not known.

Tank Set-up
Keep in a brackish water aquarium and take great care over maintaining the water quality. A very efficient filtration system is required to provide clean well-oxygenated water and a protein skimmer can also be employed. Use coral sand for substrate and plants tolerant of salt.

24–28°C
75–82°F
25 cm (10 in)

PSETTUS SEBAE
(CUVIER & VALENCIENNES, 1831)

Family: MONODACTYLIDAE	
Common name: SEBA MONO	
Distribution: Coast of Senegal to Zaire	
Size: 20 cm (8 in)	
Food: OMNIVOROUS. Live food and small fish, will take frozen, green and tablet food	
Temperature range: 24–28°C / 75–82°F	
pH: 7.5–8.5 dH: to 25°	

A brackish to marine water fish that only rarely enters fresh waters. To maintain them for any length of time they should be kept in a brackish aquarium with other similar species such as *M. argenteus*. They are peaceful if a little timid.

Breeding
Not known.

Tank Set-up
Provide a brackish water aquarium with plants and roots. Use coral sand or add crushed shell to gravel for the substrate. Ensure efficient filtration.

24–28°C
75–82°F
20 cm (8 in)

GNATHONEMUS PETERSII
(GUNTHER, 1862)

22–28°C
72–82°F
23 cm (9 in)

Family: MORMYRIDAE	
Common name: PETER'S ELEPHANTNOSE	
Distribution: Nigeria, Cameroons, Zaire	
Size: 23 cm (9 in)	
Food: OMNIVOROUS. Prefers live food but will take frozen and flake	
Temperature range: 22–28°C / 72–82°F	
pH: 6.0–7.0 dH: to 12°	

This is one of the electric fishes. The weak electric organ is used for location and contact. When happy with their surroundings they normally emit 800 pulses per minute. They have been used to monitor water supply systems because, when the water purity drops, the fish become stressed and the number of pulses increases.

Breeding
Not known.

Tank Set-up
Provide plenty of hiding places. Use a soft substrate so the snout is not damaged when rooting for food. Good filtration and regular water changes are essential.

GNATHONEMUS SCHILTHUISIAE
BOULENGER, 1899

Family: MORMYRIDAE

Common name: SCHILTHUIS' ELEPHANTNOSE

Distribution: Middle Congo River

Size: 10 cm (4 in)

Food: OMNIVOROUS. Live, flake and frozen food

Temperature range: 24–28°C / 75–82°F

pH: 7.0 dH: to 15°

24–28°C 75–82°F		10 cm (4 in)

These are shoaling fish that need a large aquarium so that they are not disturbed by each other's electrical pulses. They are one of the smaller Elephantnoses and may be kept with other peaceful fishes.

Breeding
Not known.

Tank Set-up
Use a soft sand substrate, plants, wood and rocks for decor, and have efficient filtration. Regular water changes are beneficial.

GNATHONEMUS TAMANDUA
(GUENTHER, 1862)

Family: MORMYRIDAE

Common name: NONE

Distribution: Niger, Volta, Zaire

Size: 43 cm (17 in)

Food: CARNIVOROUS. All live food but with a preference for worms

Temperature range: 23–27°C / 73–80°F

pH: 6.0–8.0 dH: to 20°

A more difficult fish to keep than *G. petersii*, it may be housed in a community aquarium of larger, peaceful fishes. If kept with its own kind there develops a definite pecking order, the smaller, weaker fishes often being denied access to food.

Breeding
Not known.

Tank Set-up
Provide a large aquarium with thickets of plants and plenty of hiding places, sandy substrate, very efficient filtration and a good flow of water.

23–27°C 73–80°F		43 cm (17 in)

MARCUSENIUS BRACHYISTIUS
GILL, 1862

Family: MORMYRIDAE

Common name: NONE

Distribution: West Africa

Size: 18 cm (7 in)

Food: CARNIVOROUS. Small live food

Temperature range: 25–28°C / 77–82°F

pH: 7.0 dH: to 10°

This crepuscular fish has a weak electrical organ which it uses for location purposes. Several can be kept together in a species aquarium provided it is quite large, otherwise they become very stressed by the interaction of their electrical discharges.

Breeding
Not known.

Tank Set-up
Use a large, planted aquarium with some open areas and good filtration.

25–28°C 77–82°F		18 cm (7 in)

MARCUSENIUS LONGIANALIS
BOULENGER, 1901

25–28°C
77–82°F
15 cm (6 in)

Family: MORMYRIDAE
Common name: SLENDER ELEPHANTNOSE
Distribution: Nigeria and Cameroon
Size: 15 cm (6 in)
Food: OMNIVOROUS. Small live food, algae, detritus
Temperature range: 25–28°C / 77–82°F
pH: 7.0 dH: to 10°

This may be kept with other fishes although its constant pulsing may upset some fishes. It is most active from dusk

to dawn; can be quarrelsome with its own kind; and spends much time picking over the substrate.

Breeding
Not known.

Tank Set-up
Best in a species aquarium with a sand substrate. Provide robust, broad-leaved plants, rocks and wood for shelter; good filtration and warmth which this fish likes.

MARCUSENIUS MACROLEPIDOTUS
(PETERS, 1852)

22–26°C
72–79°F
25 cm (10 in)

Family: MORMYRIDAE
Common name: LARGE-SCALED ELEPHANTNOSE
Distribution: Southeast Africa
Size: 25 cm (10 in)
Food: CARNIVOROUS. Small live food
Temperature range: 22–26°C / 72–79°F
pH: 7.0 dH: to 10°

Kept in a species aquarium so that they are able to get sufficient food, they have tiny mouths and hence require equally tiny live food. If this is fed in a community aquarium everyone else

gets the food before the Elephantnose. They are most active by night.

Breeding
Not known.

Tank Set-up
Provide a planted aquarium with wood and rocks and efficient, but gentle, filtration – make sure you are feeding sufficient food as much of the food may be taken out by the filter system.

PETROCEPHALUS BOVEI
(VALENCIENNES, 1846)

23–26°C
73–79°F
12 cm (4½ in)

Family: MORMYRIDAE
Common name: NONE
Distribution: Lower Nile, Senegal and Gambia rivers
Size: 12 cm (4½ in)
Food: CARNIVOROUS. Small live food
Temperature range: 23–26°C / 73–79°F
pH: 6.5–7.5 dH: to 15°

These are best kept in a species aquarium and then only a few specimens, otherwise their electrical impulses aggravate each other. They are more tolerant of other species than their own. These fish are most active between dusk and dawn.

Breeding
A report of a chance spawning tells of the discovery of a nest in a dark part of the aquarium. It contained eggs and young in various stages of development and was constructed of plant material and algae. Infusoria was used as a first food.

Tank Set-up
Use soft sand substrate and wood and rocks for decor. Plants may also be used. Very efficient filtration is necessary.

MONOCIRRHUS POLYACANTHUS
HECKEL, 1840

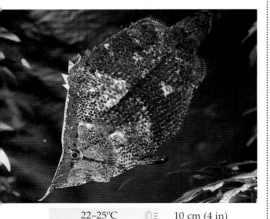

22–25°C
72–77°F
10 cm (4 in)

Family: NANDIDAE
Common name: SOUTH AMERICAN LEAF FISH
Distribution: Peruvian Amazon
Size: 10 cm (4 in)
Food: CARNIVOROUS. Only live food
Temperature range: 22–25°C / 72–77°F
pH: 6.0–6.5 dH: to 7°

From still and slow moving waters these are very demanding fish for the specialist, that are difficult to acclimatise to aquarium conditions. They will only eat live food and require copious amounts – adults will eat half their body weight in food each day and fry will eat their body weight in the same period. Fry will take insect larvae, etc, but the adults are mainly piscivorous. They hunt by drifting

almost motionless in the water towards the prey which is sucked into the cavernous mouth. Females are larger, deeper bodied fish.

Breeding
The eggs are laid on plant leaves, stones or other flat surfaces and guarded by the male. Up to 300 may be produced and they hatch in four days. Fry can be cannibalistic.

Tank Set-up
Provide a very well-planted mature aquarium with wood added, and very soft, acidic water. The filtration system must be extremely efficient as these fish react adversely to a drop in water quality. Provide regular water changes and very, very slow water movement.

NANDUS NANDUS
(HAMILTON, 1822)

Family: NANDIDAE	
Common name: NANDUS	
Distribution: Thailand, Burma, India	
Size: 20 cm (8 in)	
Food: CARNIVOROUS. Insect larvae, fish, etc, will sometimes take frozen food	
Temperature range: 22–26°C / 72–79°F	
pH: 7.0–8.0 dH: 10–20°	

This is a very attractive fish but be careful, it is predatory and will prey on smaller companions. The mouth is large and they can take fish up to half their size. Males are more colourful and have larger fins than females.

Breeding
The eggs are small and scattered over

 22–26°C 72–79°F   20 cm (8 in)

the substrate. They hatch in two days and the fry require quite small live food. There is no parental care.

Tank Set-up
Provide a good-sized aquarium with plenty of plants. Add rocks and wood for additional decor. Use clean, clear, hard water.

NANDUS NEBULOSUS
(GRAY, 1830)

Family: NANDIDAE	
Common name: CLOUDY NANDID, FOG NANDUS	
Distribution: Southeast Asia	
Size: 12 cm (4½ in)	
Food: CARNIVOROUS. Meaty food, insect larvae, etc	
Temperature range: 22–25°C / 72–77°F	
pH: 7.0 dH: 10–15°	

22–25°C 72–77°F   12 cm (4½ in)

This predator is most active at dawn and dusk. They are, in the main, loners. Do not keep with fishes small enough to be eaten. *N. nebulosus* can be differentiated from *N. nadus* by the number of scales in the lateral line: *N. nebulosus* 34; *N. nandus* 46–57.

Breeding
Not known.

Tank Set-up
A well-planted aquarium with wood and rock for decor and efficient filtration is best.

POLYCENTRUS SCHOMBURGKI
MUELLER & TROSCHEL, 1848

Family: NANDIDAE	
Common name: SCHOMBURGK'S LEAF FISH	
Distribution: Trinidad, Venezuela, Guyana	
Size: 10 cm (4 in)	
Food: CARNIVOROUS. Live food only, insect larvae, small fishes, etc	
Temperature range: 21–25°C / 70–77°F	
pH: 6.0–7.0 dH: to 15°	

Voracious predators, it is seldom that they can be tempted to take anything other than live food. They are best kept in a species aquarium or with fishes they cannot swallow. Most of their time is spent lurking among thickets of plants or roots. Males are darker and smaller bodied than females.

Breeding
They spawn in caves or on the undersides of leaves. Some 600 eggs will be produced. They hatch in three days. Feed fry with copious amounts of small live food. The male guards the eggs and fry.

Tank Set-up
Use a well-planted aquarium with some open water. Use wood, roots and stones for decor. Provide subdued lighting and good filtration.

 21–25°C 70–77°F   10 cm (4 in)

NOTOPTERUS CHITALA

(HAMILTON, 1822)

Family: NOTOPTERIDAE	
Common name: CLOWN KNIFEFISH	
Distribution: Southeast Asia	
Size: 100 cm (39 in)	
Food: OMNIVOROUS. Voracious feeders on anything meaty	
Temperature range: 24–28°C / 75–82°F	
pH: 6.0–6.5 dH: to 10°	

Can be belligerent and are best kept alone. They are most active between dusk and dawn when they will prey on other resting fishes. They will also take dead food. In their native lands they, too, are preyed upon – by the local people – and are considered a delicacy.

Breeding

They spawn on a hard surface and the eggs are guarded by the male. They hatch in about a week after which the male continues to guard the fry.

Tank Set-up

Provide a large aquarium decorated with rocks and wood to which Java Fern may be attached. Arrange these to provide hiding places but avoid sharp

edges on the rocks as the fish can easily damage their bodies. Floating plants may also be used. Provide good filtration.

24–28°C 75–82°F		100 cm (39 in)

NOTOPTERUS NOTOPTERUS

(PALLAS, 1769)

24–27°C 75–80°F		35 cm (14 in)

Family: NOTOPTERIDAE	
Common name: ASIAN KNIFEFISH	
Distribution: Southeast Asia	
Size: 35 cm (14 in)	
Food: CARNIVOROUS. Aquatic invertebrates, worms, fish, etc	
Temperature range: 24–27°C / 75–80°F	
pH: 6.0°6.5 dH: to 8°	

This nocturnal fish is intolerant of others so is best kept alone or with other large fishes, but only if the aquarium is large enough. It is very similar in appearance to its African counterpart, *Xenomystus nigri*, but may be distinguished by its dorsal fin which is lacking in *X. nigri*.

Breeding

Reports state that eggs are dropped on the substrate and are guarded and fanned by the male. They hatch after two weeks. The young can be fed newly hatched brine shrimp.

Tank Set-up

Provide a large aquarium with plenty of open water into which rocks, wood and hardy plants may be incorporated. Provide good filtration.

XENOMYSTUS NIGRI

(GUENTHER, 1868)

22–27°C 72–80°F		30 cm (12 in)

Family: NOTOPTERIDAE	
Common name: AFRICAN KNIFEFISH	
Distribution: Upper reaches of the Nile, Zaire, Gabon, Niger, Liberia	
Size: 30 cm (12 in)	
Food: CARNIVOROUS. Voracious predator – fish, worms, crustaceans, etc, plus dead meaty food	
Temperature range: 22–27°C / 72–80°F	
pH: 6.0–6.5 dH: to 8°	

Young specimens may be kept together but as they mature they become more quarrelsome and are then best kept alone. They will tolerate other companion fishes.

Breeding

Little is known. In the wild up to 200 eggs may be produced. They are 2 mm (½ in) in diameter.

Tank Set-up

Provide a large aquarium with other peaceful large fishes, roots and plants to provide cover and efficient filtration.

ORYZIAS LATIPES
(TEMMINCK & SCHLEGEL, 1850)

18–23°C
64–73°F

3.5 cm (1½ in)

Family: ORYZIATIDAE

Common name: JAPANESE RICE FISH, MEDAKA

Distribution: Japan, China, South Korea

Size: 3.5 cm (1½ in)

Food: OMNIVOROUS. Live, flake and frozen food

Temperature range: 18–23°C/64–73°F

pH: 6.5–7.5 dH: to 15°

This small fish is suited to the community aquarium as long as its companions are of a similar size and nature. Males are slimmer and the anal fin is larger and slightly pointed. There are different colour morphs of this fish. In the most frequently seen white and orange the males have more silvery scales on the rear of the body than females.

Breeding

Females can be seen with a cluster of eggs hanging around their anal area after spawning. The eggs are eventually wiped off onto plants. They hatch in about 10 days. The fry are easy to raise.

Tank Set-up

Use a well-planted community aquarium with clean, clear water and good filtration to provide a gentle current of water.

ARAPAIMA GIGAS
(CUVIER, 1829)

24–28°C
75–82°F

300 cm (118 in)

Family: OSTEOGLOSSIDAE

Common name: ARAPAIMA, PIRARUCÚ

Distribution: Amazon drainage

Size: 300 cm (118 in)

Food: CARNIVOROUS. Mostly fish but anything live accepted

Temperature range: 24–28°C/75–82°F

pH: 6.0–6.5 dH: to 10°

Only small specimens are suited to aquaria and these can be quite aggressive towards each other. Adult fishes are usually loners. They do jump. The largest true freshwater fish, it is an endangered species and not imported other than a few specimens for public aquaria.

Breeding

Eggs are deposited in shallow pits and guarded by the male. He continues brood care for some 12 weeks or so after hatching and, during this time, the female also participates.

Tank Set-up

Provide a very large aquarium with sand substrate, robust plants, some floating plants and a very efficient filtration system. Good cover glass is necessary.

OSTEOGLOSSUM BICIRRHOSUM
VANDELLI, 1829

24–28°C
75–82°F

120 cm (47 in)

Family: OSTEOGLOSSIDAE

Common name: AROWANA

Distribution: Amazon basin

Size: 120 cm (47 in)

Food: CARNIVOROUS. Lived fish, etc, will sometimes take dead food

Temperature range: 24–28°C/75–82°F

pH: 6.0–6.5 dH: to 8°

A large fish that soon outgrows the aquaria of most aquarists hence it is most often seen in public aquaria. They do jump, usually to catch prey. Arowana are able to breath air by using their swimbladder.

Breeding

The eggs are large, 1.6 cm (½ in) in diameter, and are brooded in the mouth of the male until they hatch some 60 days later. The young remain in the male's mouth until the yolk sac is absorbed.

Tank Set-up

Use a very large aquarium with plenty of open space. Soft, acidic, very well filtered water is preferred. A sand substrate with some robust plants such as Echinodorus species or Java Fern attached to wood could be used. A good heavy cover glass is essential.

OSTEOGLOSSUM FERREIRAI
KANAZAWA, 1966

24–30°C
75–86°F

100 cm (39 in)

Family: OSTEOGLOSSIDAE

Common name: BLACK AROWANA

Distribution: Negro River (South America)

Size: 100 cm (39 in)

Food: CARNIVOROUS. Live food, fish but also frogs, large insects, etc

Temperature range: 24–30°C/75–86°F

pH: 6.0–6.5 dH: to 8°

A very beautiful fish, it is only for the specialist because of the size it can attain. It is a jumper, so ensure the aquarium is well covered.

Breeding

The male mouthbroods the eggs and resultant fry until they are about 10 cm (4 in) long.

Tank Set-up

Provide a very large aquarium with a sandy substrate, wood and robust plants for decor. Use good cover glass and efficient filtration.

SCLEROPAGES FORMOSUS
(MÜLLER & SCHLEGEL, 1844)

Family:	OSTEOGLOSSIDAE
Common name:	ASIAN AROWANA, DRAGON FISH
Distribution:	Southeast Asia, Australia
Size:	100 cm (39 in)
Food:	CARNIVOROUS. Live food, fish, insect larvae, etc, will accept dead frozen food
Temperature range:	24–30°C / 75–86°F
pH:	6.0–6.5 dH: to 10°

A majestic fish that is supposed to bring good fortune to its owner, especially if it is a red fish. The silver and green colour forms are less highly prized. Until recently it was not possible to import them, but, with a captive breeding programme in the Far East,

this has changed. The Dragon Fish spends much of its time cruising the surface of calm weedy rivers, jumping to take insects if the opportunity arises. This habit of leaping out of the water may lead to them dislodging scales and harming themselves when kept in the confines of an aquarium, so be careful that they are not frightened by any sudden movements in the vicinity of the aquarium.

Breeding
Females mouthbrood the eggs and young.

Tank Set-up
Provide a large aquarium with plenty of open water for swimming and a very efficient filtration system as they are

24–30°C 75–86°F		100 cm (39 in)

susceptible to any deterioration in water quality. Decorate the aquarium with wood with Java Fern attached to it. Use a good cover glass.

Family:	OSTEOGLOSSIDAE
Common name:	NORTHERN SPOTTED BARRAMUNDI, GULF SARATOGA BARRAMUNDI
Distribution:	Jardine River westward to the head waters of the Adelaide River
Size:	90 cm (35 in); more usually 65 cm (26 in)
Food:	CARNIVOROUS. Fish, insects, etc
Temperature range:	24–30°C / 75–86°F
pH:	6.5 dH: to 10°

Another protected species, S. jardini is probably one of the most attractive of the genus with many small red spots on each scale. In its natural environment it is very vulnerable because of over-fishing. Its habits and manners are similar to the other two species in the genus.

Breeding
Little is known, but in the wild they breed in late autumn and early winter.

Tank Set-up
As for S. formosus, but this fish is less easily frightened.

24–30°C 75–86°F		90 cm (35 in)

SCLEROPAGES JARDINI
SAVILLE-KENT, 1892

SCLEROPAGES LEICHARDTI
(GUNTHER, 1864)

Family:	OSTEOGLOSSIDAE
Common name:	SPOTTED BARRAMUNDI
Distribution:	Southern New Guinea and the tropical areas of northern Australia
Size:	80 cm (31 in)
Food:	CARNIVOROUS. All kinds of live food
Temperature range:	25–30°C / 77–86°F
pH:	6.0–6.5 dH: to 10°

It is forbidden to import this species so the only live specimens you are likely to encounter are in public aquaria. However, with the successful captive

breeding of the Asian Arowana, there is always a chance that the same could be done for this fish.

Breeding
Breeding takes place in mid autumn. Males are reported to incubate the eggs in their mouths.

Tank Set-up
Similar requirements to S. formosus.

25–30°C 77–86°F		80 cm (31 in)

PANTODON BUCHHOLZI
PETERS, 1876

23–30°C
73–86°F

10 cm (4 in)

Family: PANTODONTIDAE	
Common name: BUTTERFLYFISH	
Distribution: West Africa	
Size: 10 cm (4 in)	
Food: CARNIVOROUS. fish, insects, worms, etc, will take frozen, flake and pelleted food	
Temperature range: 23–30°C/73–86°F	
pH: 6.0–6.5 dH: to 10°	

A surface-dwelling predator that may be kept with other fishes provided they occupy the mid and lower levels of the aquarium. They will jump at the slightest provocation although some plant or a piece of cork bark floating on the surface helps to discourage this. The anal fin of males is convex and the central rays form a tube. In females the anal fin has a straight edge.

Breeding
Some 200 eggs may be produced. They float and are transparent when laid but darken to a dark brown or even black over the following nine hours. Hatching in 36 hours, the fry are very difficult to raise, needing small flying insects as well as brine shrimp.

Tank Set-up
In a planted aquarium with a large surface area use some floating plant or cork bark on the surface. Use a tight-fitting cover glass. Ensure good filtration.

ETHEOSTOMA CAERULEUM
STORER, 1845

6–15°C
42–59°F

7 cm (3 in)

Family: PERCIDAE	
Common name: RAINBOW DARTER	
Distribution: Eastern North America predominantly in the northern Mississippi basin	
Size: 7 cm (3 in)	
Food: CARNIVOROUS. Small invertebrates	
Temperature range: 6–15°C/42–59°F	
pH: 6.5–7.5 dH: to 12°	

Very attractive fishes, these bottom dwellers really need to be kept in a species aquarium because they are very susceptible to any deterioration in water quality. Males are more colourful than females. They get their common name from their method of locomotion, they use their caudal and pectoral fins to dart about the substrate.

Breeding
They spawn in spring and early summer in riffles over a gravel bed. Up to 800 eggs may be produced.

Tank Set-up
A very well-maintained aquarium with a gravel substrate and rocks, and thickets of plants for decor. Regular water changes and very efficient filtration are essential to maintain this species for any length of time.

GYNOCEPHALUS CERNUA
(LINNAEUS, 1758)

8–20°C
46–68°F

25 cm (10 in)

Family: PERCIDAE	
Common name: RUFFE, BLACKTAIL	
Distribution: Europe, Asia	
Size: 25 cm (10 in)	
Food: CARNIVOROUS. Live food of any sort	
Temperature range: 8–20°C/46–68°F	
pH: 7.0 dH: to 12°	

A rather attractive coldwater fish that may be kept with other fishes large enough not to be eaten. Ruffe are shoaling fish and should be kept as such. It eats predominantly live food in the diet but may, on rare occasions, be persuaded to accept flake food. In the wild they are noted for eating fish spawn.

Breeding
In the wild they breed from early to late spring, placing the eggs on plants and rocks near the shore. The fry hatch out in about two weeks.

Tank Set-up
Use a good-sized aquarium with clean, clear, well-oxygenated water. Plants, wood and pebbles may be used for decoration.

PERCA FLUVIATILIS
LINNAEUS, 1758

8–20°C
46–68°F

45 cm (18 in)

Family: PERCIDAE	
Common name: PERCH	
Distribution: Europe	
Size: 45 cm (18 in)	
Food: CARNIVOROUS. Live food, especially aquatic invertebrates	
Temperature range: 8–20°C/46–68°F	
pH: 7.0 dH: to 10°	

An attractive fish, when young they shoal but, as they mature, become loners. They may be kept with other like-sized, cold water fishes. Males have more colour and are slimmer than females.

Breeding
It spawns between early spring and early summer, laying strings of eggs across rocks and plants. Hatching time is about three weeks.

Tank Set-up
Have a large aquarium, with a good filtration system to provide clean, clear water and plenty of plants for fish to lurk in. Keep the water temperature down.

PERCINA CAPRODES
(RAFINESQUE, 1818)

6–15°C 42–59°F	18 cm (7 in)

Family: PERCIDAE
Common name: LOGPERCH
Distribution: Eastern North America predominantly in the northern Mississippi basin
Size: 18 cm (7 in)
Food: CARNIVOROUS. Small invertebrates
Temperature range: 6–15°C/42–59°F
pH: 6.5–7.5 dH: to 12°

The most widespread member of the genus, the Logperch inhabits lakes as well as the pools and riffles of large, clear, unpolluted streams. It has an interesting method of feeding; it flips over stones with its snout to find insects. Males have a modified scale on the midline of their belly and they use this to stimulate the female during spawning.

Breeding
Spawning takes place in riffles over a gravel bed during early summer.

Tank Set-up
Efficient filtration providing a good flow of cool, clear water and a well-maintained aquarium with a gravel substrate with rocks, wood, and thickets of plants for decor are essential to maintain this species for any length of time.

STIZOSTEDION VITREUM
(MITCHILL, 1818)

4–15°C 39–59°F	1 m (3 ft)

Family: PERCIDAE
Common name: WALLEYE
Distribution: Widespread in central USA from the Hudson drainage down through the Great Lakes to Mississippi drainage
Size: 1 m (3 ft)
Food: CARNIVOROUS. Anything from invertebrates to fish
Temperature range: 4–15°C/39–59°F
pH: 6.5–7.5 dH: to 12°

The largest of the North American Perches, it is best known as a food and sport fish. Average specimens attain some 5 kg (11 lb) in weight (although there are reports of specimens much larger – up to 11 kg (24 lb) and would be about 15 years old. Small specimens may be kept in the aquarium but, take note, it is a voracious predator that will eat any companions it can swallow. In the wild it is found in fairly deep water down to 10 m (30 ft).

Breeding
They spawn in spring and early summer depending on their location.

Tank Set-up
A large, well-maintained aquarium with a substrate of flat stones and some areas of gravel with thickets of plants for decor. Allow plenty of swimming space. Regular water changes and efficient filtration.

Family: PERCICHTHYIDAE
Common name: WHITE BASS
Distribution: Eastern and central North America
Size: 45 cm (18 in)
Food: CARNIVOROUS. Small invertebrates, algae
Temperature range: 10–20°C/50–68°F
pH: 6.5–7.5 dH: 12°

Young specimens may be kept in the aquarium. They are active, shoaling fishes and require a large aquarium with plenty of open water. Because of their popularity as sport fish, they have been widely introduced outside their normal range.

Breeding
Spawning occurs in spring and early summer.

Tank Set-up
A large aquarium with a gravel substrate and rocks, and thickets of plants for decor but ensure there is plenty of free swimming space. Efficient filtration.

10–20°C 50–68°F	45 cm (18 in)

MORONE CHRYSOPS
(RAFINESQUE, 1820)

PHRACTOLAEMUS ANSORGEI
BOULENGER, 1901

Family: PHRACTOLAEMIDAE

Common name: NONE

Distribution: West Africa

Size: 15 cm (6 in)

Food: CARNIVOROUS. Small live food, chopped meat and worms

Temperature range: 25–30°C / 77–86°F

pH: 6.0–8.0 dH: to 24°

A warmth-loving, peaceful creature from muddy, weedy waters, it burrows into the substrate or hides amongst vegetation. There is a white lump on the head of mature males and also two rows of spiky growths on the caudal peduncle.

 25–30°C 77–86°F 15 cm (6 in)

Breeding
Not known.

Tank Set-up
A mature, planted aquarium with a soft substrate such as mud or sand is preferred. Warm conditions are essential as is good but gentle filtration.

POLYODON SPATHULA
(WALBAUM, 1792)

Family: POLYODONTIDAE

Common name: PADDLEFISH

Distribution: Mississippi drainage, Lake Erie

Size: 200 cm (79 in)

Food: CARNIVOROUS. Plankton feeder, copious amounts of *Daphnia* are required

Temperature range: 10–18°C / 50–64°F

pH: 7.0 dH: to 15°

Although offered for sale this is really a fish for the dedicated specialist or public aquaria. Its demands with regard to food are stringent: a plentiful supply of *Daphnia* throughout the year is needed and a large fish will consume equally large amounts. At feeding time they must literally be swimming with their mouths wide open in a *Daphnia* 'soup'. The *Daphnia* is caught in the gill rakers and swallowed. The snouts of these fish are easily damaged both in transit and in the aquarium. The fish

10–18°C 50–64°F 200 cm (79 in)

are fished commercially, can weigh up to 90 kg (198 lb) and live for 30 years.

Breeding
They spawn in shallow water over sand or gravel beds between late winter and mid spring, depending on their range.

Tank Set-up
Use a very large aquarium, preferably circular to avoid damaging the snout. It needs well filtered cool, clear water and sand substrate. Use rounded pebbles and / or wood for decor – avoid anything that the fish could damage itself on.

ERPETOICHTHYS CALABARICUS
(J. A. SMITH, 1865)

Family: POLYPTERIDAE

Common name: REED FISH, SNAKE FISH

Distribution: West Africa

Size: 40 cm (16 in)

Food: CARNIVOROUS. Live and dead meaty food

Temperature range: 22–28°C / 72–82°F

pH: 6.5–7.0 dH: to 10°

Very peaceful even with its own kind, however, if keeping it in a community aquarium do not keep it with fish small enough to be eaten by the Reed Fish. They escape through the smallest of openings so ensure the cover glass fits well. They spend much time in caves and hollows and will sometimes bury in the substrate.

Breeding
Not known.

22–28°C 72–82°F 40 cm (16 in)

Tank Set-up
Use a large aquarium with a soft sandy substrate; a few large, robust plants but mostly rockwork and wood for decoration; good filtration; and a tight-fitting cover glass.

POLYPTERUS DELHEZI
BOULENGER, 1899

Family: POLYPTERIDAE	
Common name: ARMOURED BICHIR	
Distribution: Upper and middle Zaire	
Size: 35 cm (14 in)	
Food: CARNIVOROUS. Fish, worms, crustaceans, etc	
Temperature range: 26–28°C / 79–82°F	
pH: 6.5–7.0 dH: to 10°	

Very belligerent with their own kind, to the point of biting each other, this fish is compatible with other similar sized fish, but is highly predatory and a voracious feeder.

Breeding
Not known.

Tank Set-up
A large aquarium with sandy substrate, large plants and some rocks and wood should be provided. A very efficient filtration system and tight-fitting cover glass is necessary.

26–28°C
79–82°F
35 cm (14 in)

POLYPTERUS ORNATIPINNIS
BOULENGER, 1902

26–28°C
79–82°F
40 cm (16 in)

Family: POLYPTERIDAE	
Common name: ORNATE BICHIR	
Distribution: Central Africa	
Size: 40 cm (16 in)	
Food: CARNIVOROUS. Live fish, dead meaty food	
Temperature range: 26–28°C / 79–82°F	
pH: 6.5–7.5 dH: to 12°	

Probably the most attractive of the Birchirs, these creatures are not usually aggressive towards their companions provided there are sufficient hiding places. It is believed that males have larger anal fins than females and females have larger heads than males.

Breeding
Virtually the same as for *P. palmas* but the eggs are put on clumps of vegetation.

Tank Set-up
Best is a large community aquarium with plenty of caves and crevices; good filtration; and a tight cover glass.

POLYPTERUS PALMAS
AYERS, 1850

26–28°C
79–82°F
30 cm (12 in)

Family: POLYPTERIDAE	
Common name: MARBLED BICHIR	
Distribution: Zaire, Liberia, Sierra Leone, Guinea	
Size: 30 cm (12 in)	
Food: CARNIVOROUS. Shrimps, worms, fish, etc	
Temperature range: 26–28°C / 79–82°F	
pH: 7.0 dH: to 10°	

Although peaceful with other fishes, it can be quarrelsome with its own kind. Keep with fishes it cannot swallow, as it is a predator. In males the anal fin is almost twice as wide as that of the female.

Breeding
After a courtship dance the male wraps his anal fin against the anal fin and opening of the female to catch the eggs as they are expelled from the female. He produces sperm at the same time. The eggs are then dropped to the substrate where they hatch about four days later. Feed young on brine shrimp nauplii.

Tank Set-up
Use a community aquarium of larger fish with plenty of wood and rocks to provide hiding places. Ensure reasonable filtration.

POLYPTERUS SENEGALUS
CUVIER, 1829

Family: POLYPTERIDAE

Common name: SENEGAL BICHIR

Distribution: White Nile to Lake Albert, Lakes Rudolf and Chad, Senegal, Gambia, Niger

Size: 30 cm (12 in)

Food: CARNIVOROUS. Fish, invertebrates, etc

Temperature range: 25–27°C / 77–80°F

pH: 6.5–7.5 dH: to 12°

Very quarrelsome with each other although this can be overcome to some extent by ensuring there are sufficient hiding places in the aquarium for each fish to have its own. Relatively peaceful with larger fishes. Great escape artists so ensure the aquarium is well covered.

25–27°C 77–80°F — 30 cm (12 in)

Breeding
Not known.

Tank Set-up
A community aquarium with larger fishes should have caves made from rocks and wood and a sandy substrate. Good filtration is needed. A tight cover glass is necessary.

POTAMOTRYGON LATICEPS
(GARMAN, 1913)

Family: POTAMOTRYGONIDAE

Common name: FRESHWATER STINGRAY

Distribution: Brazil, Paraguay, Uruguay, Argentina

Size: 70 cm (27 in)

Food: CARNIVOROUS. Live worms, shrimps, etc, will also take frozen food

Temperature range: 23–25°C / 73–77°F

pH: 6.5–7.0 dH: to 10°

Best kept in a spacious species aquarium. Take care when handling the fish or carrying out tank maintenance as they have a barb on the tail which can inflict a nasty and painful wound. The fish spend some time buried in the substrate.

Breeding
Not known.

Tank Set-up
Have a large, shallow aquarium with a sand substrate in which floating plants

may be used. Pebbles and wood make suitable decor. Very efficient filtration system is required as these Stingrays are very sensitive to any deterioration in water quality.

23–25°C 73–77°F — 70 cm (27 in)

POTAMOTRYGON MOTORO
(MÜLLER & HENLE, 1841)

24–26°C 75–79°F — 30 cm (12 in)

Family: POTAMOTRYGONIDAE

Common name: OCELLATED FRESHWATER STINGRAY

Distribution: Brazil, Paraguay, Uruguay

Size: 30 cm (12 in)

Food: CARNIVOROUS. Worms, chopped beefheart, shrimps, etc

Temperature range: 24–26°C / 75–79°F

pH: 6.5 dH: to 10°

A fish for the specialist, it is best kept in a species aquarium. Take care when handling them or doing routine tank maintenance. Males have claspers, females do not. Their method of feeding is strange. They place themselves over the food and direct a jet of water down onto it, stirring up the sand as well as

the food. This mixture is then sucked up, the food removed and the sand expelled.

Breeding
Not known.

Tank Set-up
Use a shallow aquarium with a deep substrate, say 10 cm (4 in) in depth to allow the fish to bury themselves in the sand. One or two plants and some pebbles may be used for decor thus giving them swimming space. Have good filtration.

PROTOPTERUS AETHIOPICUS
HECKEL, 1851

Family: PROTOPTERIDAE
Common name: ETHIOPIAN LUNGFISH
Distribution: Eastern Africa including the Nile
Size: 200 cm (79 in)
Food: CARNIVOROUS. Fish, etc
Temperature range: 25–30°C / 77–86°F
pH: 6.5–7.5 dH: to 20°

Bad tempered towards each other and other tank mates, these creatures are best kept alone. They have a powerful set of jaws and will snap at anything including your fingers and hands so take care when dealing with them. In Africa they are regarded as a delicacy and during the dry season the cocoons of the aestivating Lungfish are sought after.

Breeding
They breed when the dry season breaks. The eggs are laid in a U-shaped channel and guarded by the male.

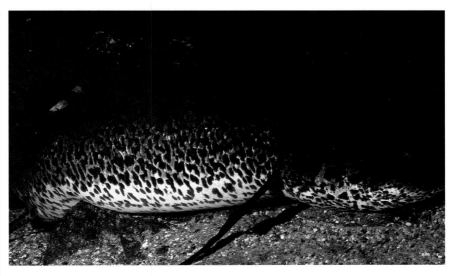

Tank Set-up
Have a large aquarium with an equally large filtration system, mud or sand substrate, wood and/or rocks for decor and a heavy, tight-fitting cover glass.

25–30°C 77–86°F   200 cm (79 in)

PROTOPTERUS ANNECTENS
(OWEN, 1839)

Family: PROTOPTERIDAE
Common name: AFRICAN LUNGFISH
Distribution: Widespread in Africa
Size: 70 cm (27 in)
Food: CARNIVOROUS. Most meaty food, live and dead
Temperature range: 25–30°C / 77–86°F
pH: 6.5–7.5 dH: to 20°

Undemanding as far as water conditions are concerned. It is very belligerent and should be kept alone. Its natural habitat is swamp and to survive the dry season it buries in the mud,

rolls into a ball, secretes a cocoon and aestivates until conditions improve.

Breeding
Little known. The male guards the eggs.

Tank Set-up
In a large aquarium, only a shallow depth of water is required. Have soft substrate, efficient filtration and a good, heavy cover glass.

25–30°C 77–86°F   70 cm (27 in)

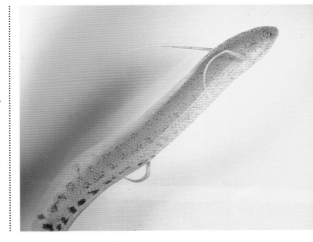

PROTOPTERUS DOLLOI
BOULENGER, 1900

Family: PROTOPTERIDAE
Common name: LUNGFISH
Distribution: Lower Zaire
Size: 85 cm (33 in)
Food: CARNIVOROUS. Eats anything and everything meaty
Temperature range: 25–30°C / 77–86°F
pH: 6.5–7.5 dH: to 20°

A large and powerful fish, it attacks anything, including hands, so beware when doing tank maintenance or moving the fish. These fish can survive the dry season by aestivating. They bury into the mud, wrap themselves

into a ball and secrete a mucus which hardens to form a cocoon. In this state they live out the dry season.

Breeding
Not known in aquaria. In the wild the male guards the eggs.

Tank Set-up
Use a large aquarium with soft mud or sand substrate and provide efficient filtration to cope with the debris they can stir up.

25–30°C 77–86°F   85 cm (33 in)

EIGENMANNIA VIRESCENS
(VALENCIENNES, 1849)

Family: RHAMPHICHTHYIDAE

Common name: NONE

Distribution: Tropical South America

Size: Males 35 cm (14 in); females 20 cm (8 in)

Food: CARNIVOROUS. Live food

Temperature range: 22–27°C / 72–80°F

pH: 6.0–7.0 dH: to 10°

Kept as a group in a species tank these fish form a social pecking order but no harm actually comes to any of them. Males are noticeably bigger than females. These fish lack both dorsal and caudal fins. They are sensitive to water conditions, especially water changes, so use well aged or conditioned water for this purpose.

22–27°C 72–80°F   35 cm (14 in)

Breeding
They have been bred in captivity. The adhesive eggs are laid a few at a time on floating plants.

Tank Set-up
A very mature, well-planted aquarium is required. Use wood and rocks to create hiding places. Maintain good filtration and a gentle flow of water through the aquarium.

STEATOGENES ELEGANS
(STEINDACHNER, 1880)

Family: RHAMPHICHTHYIDAE

Common name: NONE

Distribution: Northeastern South America

Size: 80 cm (31 in)

Food: CARNIVOROUS. Small live food

Temperature range: 22–26°C / 72–79°F

pH: 6.0–6.5 dH: to 10°

This peaceable creature may be kept with similar-sized and like-tempered fish. It is sensitive to water changes so avoid carrying out large ones. Of special interest is the fact that it is toothless – all the other Knifefish have teeth.

Breeding
Not known.

Tank Set-up
A well-matured aquarium with plenty of plants, rock and wood; subdued lighting; and very efficient filtration is required.

22–26°C 72–79°F 80 cm (31 in)

SCATOPHAGUS ARGUS
(LINNAEUS, 1766)

Family: SCATOPHAGIDAE

Common name: SCAT

Distribution: Indian and Pacific Oceans – Indonesia, Philippines

Size: 30 cm (12 in)

Food: OMNIVOROUS. Live, frozen, flake, tablet, green food

Temperature range: 22–28°C / 72–82°F

pH: 7.5–8.5 dH: to 25°

The habitat of these adaptable fish, is fresh, brackish and marine water and it seems to do well in captivity if kept in brackish water when young but moving to marine water as it matures. It is peaceful but will eat plants so use very robust plant species. The fish are active and require a lot of swimming space. Keep as a group.

Breeding
Not known.

Tank Set-up
Provide a large aquarium with an efficient filtration system as young fish will not tolerate any build up of nitrates. Decorate with rocks and tough plants or use plastic plants.

22–28°C 72–82°F   30 cm (12 in)

SCATOPHAGUS TETRACANTHUS
(LACEPEDE, 1880)

Family: SCATOPHAGIDAE	
Common name: AFRICAN SCAT	
Distribution: East African coast	
Size: 40 cm (16 in)	
Food: OMNIVOROUS. Live, frozen, flake, tablet, green food	
Temperature range: 23–30°C/73–86°F	
pH: 7.5–8.5 dH: to 25°	

This large, peaceful, shoaling fish, has one drawback in its preponderance for ripping plants to shreds. It is seldom imported.

Breeding
Not known.

Tank Set-up
Set up as for *S. argus*.

23–30°C
73–86°F   40 cm (16 in)

BRACHIURUS SALINARUM
OGILBY, 1911

Family: SOLEIDAE	
Common name: SALT-PAN SOLE	
Distribution: Australia	
Size: 15 cm (6 in)	
Food: OMNIVOROUS. Live, flake and tablet food	
Temperature range: 22–28°C/72–82°F	
pH: 7.0 dH: to 15°	

This bottom-dwelling fish is very peaceful. During the day it spends most of its time hiding semi-buried in the substrate or resting on rocks and is active by night. Feed just before turning the lights out. May be kept with other peaceful species but make sure the aquarium is not over-stocked.

Breeding
Not known.

Tank Set-up
Use a fine sand substrate with rocks, wood and plant for decor, an efficient filtration and a gentle flow of water.

22–28°C
72–82°F   15 cm (6 in)

ENNEACAMPUS ANSORGII
BOULENGER, 1910

Family: SYGNATHIDAE	
Common name: AFRICAN FRESHWATER PIPEFISH	
Distribution: West Africa	
Size: 15 cm (6 in)	
Food: CARNIVOROUS. Small live food	
Temperature range: 24–28°C/75–82°F	
pH: 7.0–8.5 dH: 12–18°	

Totally harmless, this fish is probably best kept in a species aquarium or with other very peaceful fish. The male has a ridge along his stomach which becomes the breeding pouch. When they feed, they just suck in the prey. Feed only small, live food such as *Daphnia*, mosquito larvae or the fry of other fishes, they will not take flake.

Breeding
The female spawns above the male's brood pouch and the eggs stick to the back of the male's anal opening. Two folds of skin enclose the eggs and form the pouch.

24–28°C
75–82°F   15 cm (6 in)

Tank Set-up
Use a planted aquarium with mature water and gentle filtration.

SYNBRANCHUS MARMORATUS
BLOCH, 1795

Family: SYNBRANCHIDAE	
Common name: MARBLED EEL	
Distribution: Central and South America	
Size: 100 cm (39 in) plus	
Food: CARNIVOROUS. Live and dead meat	
Temperature range: 20–22°C / 68–72°F	
pH: 6.5–7.5 dH: to 18°	

Voracious feeders, these Eels will consume large amounts of food and it is advisable to feed them every other or even every third day. They are also great escape artists so make sure the aquarium is well covered. Keep alone or with other very large fishes, as they can be belligerent.

20–22°C / 68–72°F   100 cm (39 in)

Breeding
Not known.

Tank Set-up
Use a shallow aquarium with mud or sand substrate, rocks, wood and large plants to give hiding places and good filtration.

TETRAODON FLUVIATILIS
(HAMILTON, 1822)

24–28°C / 75–82°F 17 cm (7 in)

Family: TETRAODONTIDAE	
Common name: GREEN PUFFER	
Distribution: Southeast Asia	
Size: 17 cm (7 in)	
Food: OMNIVOROUS. Live, frozen food	
Temperature range: 24–28°C / 75–82°F	
pH: 7.5–8.5 dH: to 20°	

As youngsters they are fairly tolerant but as they mature so their aggressiveness increases. They will pick on their own kind as well as other fishes. They will also attack plants. These fish are famed for their ability to inflate themselves in an attempt to avoid predation. Their flesh is poisonous to humans and animals, and even cooking does not remove the toxins.

Breeding
They have been spawned in brackish water. They spawn on the substrate, the male guarding the brood.

Tank Set-up
Give plenty of cover from rocks, wood and robust plants but leave open swimming space. Use a gravel substrate and efficient filtration.

TETRAODON LORTETI
TIRANT, 1885

Family: TETRAODONTIDAE	
Common name: NONE	
Distribution: Eastern India and Thailand	
Size: 6.5 cm (2½ in)	
Food: CARNIVOROUS. Invertebrates, shellfish, worms, sometimes tablet food	
Temperature range: 24–28°C / 75–82°F	
pH: 6.5 dH: to 10°	

In this softwater fish, the sexes are readily distinguishable: the male has a reddish belly and dorsal fin; while the belly of the female is pale grey with spots and stripes. Very aggressive, it will defend its territory against all comers.

Breeding
After courtship, the eggs are laid over plants such as Java Moss and they hatch in 30 hours. The fry are hard to raise even with large amounts of small live food.

24–28°C / 75–82°F   6.5 cm (2½ in)

Tank Set-up
Plants, rocks and wood should be used to create caves and territories. Regular water changes and efficient filtration are needed. Do not add salt to the water.

TETRAODON MBU
BOULENGER, 1899

Family: TETRAODONTIDAE
Common name: GIANT PUFFER
Distribution: Middle and lower Congo river
Size: 75 cm (30 in)
Food: CARNIVOROUS. All live food, will take frozen
Temperature range: 24–26°C / 75–79°F
pH: 7.0 dH: 10–15°

This freshwater fish is a typical Puffer; it is quarrelsome and so is best kept alone. They grow large and can reach a weight of 6.5 kg (14 lb) – not a fish to be argued with! Vary the diet, shellfish are particularly relished.

Breeding
Not known.

Tank Set-up
As for *T. fahaka*.

24–26°C
75–79°F 75 cm (30 in)

TETRAODON MIURUS
BOULENGER, 1902

24–28°C
75–82°F 15 cm (6 in)

Family: TETRAODONTIDAE
Common name: CONGO PUFFER
Distribution: Middle and lower Congo river
Size: 15 cm (6 in)
Food: CARNIVOROUS. Most live food
Temperature range: 24–28°C / 75–82°F
pH: 7.0 dH: 10–15°

A more manageable-sized Puffer but one with an equally bad temperament as its larger relatives, and for this reason they should be kept alone. The eyes of this creature are placed high on the head, and it has an upturned mouth. These features allow it to ambush its prey by burying itself in the sand with only its eyes showing.

Breeding
Not known.

Tank Set-up
In the aquarium use deep, fine sand substrate, plants and large pebbles for decor, and good filtration.

TETRAODON SCHOUTEDINI
PELLEGRIN, 1926

Family: TETRAODONTIDAE
Common name: NONE
Distribution: Central Africa
Size: 10 cm (4 in)
Food: CARNIVOROUS. Snails, shellfish, worms, etc
Temperature range: 22–26°C / 72–79°F
pH: 7.0 dH: to 20°

The most tolerant of the Puffers, they do little damage to their companions although members of the same species may have sparring matches. It may attack plants but only to remove the snails thereon. Most of the body is covered with tiny spines. Males are smaller than females.

Breeding
The eggs are laid on leaves and guarded by the male. The fry are hard to raise because it is difficult to find the right type of food.

Tank Set-up
Use a planted aquarium with plenty of hiding places. Provide regular water changes and good filtration.

22–26°C
72–79°F 10 cm (4 in)

TETRAODON STEINDACHNERI
DECKERS, 1975

Family: TETRAODONTIDAE

Common name: PUFFER

Distribution: Southeast Asia

Size: 6 cm (2½ in)

Food: OMNIVOROUS. Predominantly live food, but will also take oxheart, liver and lettuce

Temperature range: 22–26°C / 72–79°F

pH: 7.0 dH: to 12°

Intolerant of other fishes, they feed on snails and in so doing rip plants as they take snails off the leaves.

Breeding
Not known.

Tank Set-up
As for *T. fluviatilis* but do not add salt.

22–26°C 72–79°F		6 cm (2½ in)

Family: TOXOTIDAE

Common name: NONE

Distribution: Asia

Size: 27 cm (11 in)

Food: CARNIVOROUS. Flies, insects, etc, taken from the surface

Temperature range: 25–30°C / 77–86°F

pH: 7.0 dH: to 15°

This shoaling fish may be kept with others of a similar size. It feeds only from the surface and will jump to take flies. It should be kept in brackish conditions. It is a fish found mainly in estuaries.

Breeding
Not known.

Tank Set-up
A roomy aquarium with a clear surface so that the fish can feed easily is best. Plants, wood and rocks are acceptable as decor. Provide good filtration.

TOXOTES CHATAREUS
(HAMILTON, 1822)

25–30°C 77–86°F		27 cm (11 in)

TOXOTES JACULATRIX
(PALLAS, 1766)

25–30°C 77–86°F		24 cm (9 in)

Family: TOXOTIDAE

Common name: ARCHER FISH

Distribution: Widespread from Gulf of Aden along the coast of India and southeast Asia through to Australia

Size: 24 cm (9 in)

Food: CARNIVOROUS. Insects and the like

Temperature range: 25–30°C / 77–86°F

pH: 7.0–8.5 dH: to 20°

Living in fresh, brackish and salt waters the Archer Fish is famed for its ability to shoot down insects with a jet of water. It feeds only from the surface. This particular species is particularly warmth-loving and quickly goes off its food and sulks if kept in cool conditions. They are peaceful if kept in a shoal of like-sized specimens otherwise large ones will pick on smaller ones.

Breeding
Not known.

Tank Set-up
Good sized aquarium with an open top (if you want to see the fish shoot down flies!). Some vegetation either growing out of the water or falling into it so the flies, etc, have something to land on. Brackish water seems to suit them and it needs to be well filtered and mature. Take care when doing water changes as they do not like large amounts of fresh water.

TOXOTES LORENTZI
(WEBER, 1911)

Family: TOXOTIDAE
Common name: PRIMITIVE ARCHER FISH
Distribution: Australia and New Guinea
Size: 23 cm (9 in)
Food: CARNIVOROUS. Mostly flying insects
Temperature range: 24–30°C / 75–86°F
pH: 7.0–7.5 dH: to 15°

Best kept as a small shoal in a species aquarium. Keeping as a group cuts down the amount of aggression between individuals. Their diet consists mainly of flying insects and they will only take food from the water surface. They live in fresh water.

Breeding
Not known.

Tank Set-up
Use a densely planted aquarium with open water. The fish cruise mainly just below the surface, they like warmth and good filtration.

24–30°C
75–86°F 23 cm (9 in)

UMBRA LIMI
(KIRTLAND, 1840)

Family: UMBRIDAE
Common name: CENTRAL MUDMINNOW
Distribution: From Quebec, Canada through the Great Lakes into the Ohio river (USA)
Size: Males 11 cm (4½ in); females 15 cm (6 in)
Food: CARNIVOROUS. Small aquatic live food including fish eggs
Temperature range: 17–21°C / 62–70°F
pH: 6.0–6.5 dH: to 6°

A quiet, peaceful fish that likes cool conditions. Only when breeding is there any territorial aggression. Make sure that the fish can reach the water surface as they can breath through their swimbladder and, if unable to take in air from the surface they will die. Males are smaller than females which are yellowish in colour when ready to breed.

Breeding
They spawn in the spring in pits in the substrate. It takes 12 days for the eggs to hatch during which time the nest is guarded by the female.

Tank Set-up
Use a planted coldwater community aquarium with like-sized fishes.

17–21°C
62–70°F 11 cm (4½ in)

UMBRA PYGMAEA
(DE KAY, 1842)

Family: UMBRIDAE
Common name: EASTERN MUDMINNOW
Distribution: Long Island south to the Neuse river, North Carolina, eastern USA
Size: Males 12 cm (4½ in); females 15 cm (6 in)
Food: CARNIVOROUS. All small live food, will take flake
Temperature range: 17–23°C / 62–73°F
pH: 6.0–6.5 dH: to 8°

Very similar in all respects to *U. limi*, they are undemanding fish and make a useful addition to the cold water aquarium provided they are kept with suitable quiet companions. Males are smaller than females. They are found in shallow rivers and swamps.

Breeding
They spawn in depressions in the substrate and the female guards the nest and eggs.

17–23°C
62–73°F 12 cm (4½ in)

Tank Set-up
Use a planted cold water aquarium.

Marine

Entries for the marine section are slightly different to those from the freshwater section. The species kept in aquaria are mainly reef fish and as such, the aquarium set-up with the tufa rock to emulate a reef will remain constant. Likewise the salinity, temperature requirements and pH will be the same for all.

In the main, invertebrates are not included because they require very specialised care to keep them at their best for any length of time. The only exception to this is with the Clown Fish where an anemone or two is essential for the well being of the fish.

One problem area is breeding because so little is known of the reproductive behaviour of marine fish, either in captivity or in the wild. Where details could be found, these are given as aquarium observations or as observations in the wild. However, for others no reference could be found. With new information coming to light all the time, this situation could change.

Acanthuridae
Balistidae
Callionymidae
Centriscidae
Chaetodontidae
Cirrhitidae
Diodontidae
Gobiidae
Grammidae
Holocentridae
Labridae
Microdesmidae
Monocentridae

Opistognathidae
Ostraciidae
Platacidae
Plesiopidae
Plotosidae
Pomacanthidae
Pomacentridae
Pseudochromidae
Scorpaenidae
Serranidae
Siganidae
Syngnathidae

ACANTHURUS ACHILLES
SHAW, 1803

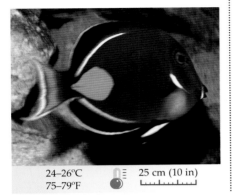

24–26°C
75–79°F

25 cm (10 in)

Family: ACANTHURIDAE	
Common name: ACHILLES TANG, RED-TAILED SURGEON	
Distribution: Pacific	
Size: 25 cm (10 in)	
Food: Plenty of green food – algae, lettuce, etc, plus live brine shrimp, frozen *Mysis*, etc	
Temperature range: 24–26°C / 75–79°F	
pH: 8.4 Salinity: 1.023–1.027	

In the main a peaceful if delicate fish, needing a large, mature aquarium. In the wild they live in shoals but in the aquarium, especially if it is too small, they can be a little quarrelsome among themselves. This is seen mostly as threat displays which rarely result in actual bodily harm. They will browse on any algae growing in the tank and this should be supplemented with plenty of green food. Adults develop more intense coloration than juveniles. There is no noticeable difference between the sexes, sometimes the male is larger, sometimes the female.

Breeding
Not known.

Tank Set-up
Provide algae, on which fish may browse.

ACANTHURUS COER'ULEUS
BLOCH & SCHNEIDER, 1801

24–26°C
75–79°F

30 cm (12 in)

Family: ACANTHURIDAE	
Common name: BLUE TANG	
Distribution: Western Atlantic	
Size: 30 cm (12 in)	
Food: Mostly algae	
Temperature range: 24–26°C / 75–79°F	
pH: 8.4 Salinity: 1.023–1.027	

An interesting fish in that its colour changes dramatically from juvenile to adult. Young fish are bright yellow with a trace of blue around the eye and a fine blue edge to the dorsal, anal and ventral fins. As they mature the head and body become blue but the caudal remains yellow, as if the blue is spreading from the fin edges across the body. Fully adult fish are completely blue, and the intensity of colour can vary with the mood of the fish, from powder blue to a deep, almost purple, blue. In the aquarium, young fish can be very domineering but this dominance seems to lessen as the fish matures. Their distribution is interesting: they are most common around Florida, the Bahamas and in the Caribbean but they have also been reported as far north as New York.

Breeding
Not known.

ACANTHURUS LEUCOSTERNON
(BENNETT, 1932)

Family: ACANTHURIDAE	
Common name: POWDER BLUE SURGEON	
Distribution: Indo-Pacific	
Size: 25 cm (10 in)	
Food: Frozen food, *Mysis*, etc, green food	
Temperature range: 24–26°C / 75–79°F	
pH: 8.4 Salinity: 1.023–1.027	

A very popular fish in the hobby because of its striking coloration, which does not seem to change from juvenile to adult. It is demanding both of water conditions and space. Keep only a single specimen as two will fight. Provide plenty of green food in the form of algae and lettuce in the diet. Males are generally larger than females.

Breeding
Not known.

Tank Set-up
Provide good water conditions, plenty of space and algae in the tank.

24–26°C
75–79°F

25 cm (10 in)

ACANTHURUS SOHAL
(FORSSKÅL, 1775)

24–26°C
75–79°F
25 cm (10 in)

Family: ACANTHURIDAE	
Common name: MAJESTIC SURGEON, ZEBRA SURGEON	
Distribution: Red Sea	
Size: 25 cm (10 in)	
Food: Algae, green food	
Temperature range: 24–26°C / 75–79°F	
pH: 8.4 Salinity: 1.023–1.027	

Not often offered for sale, the Majestic or Zebra Surgeon is a very imposing fish. It derives one of its common names from the white lines on a dark, sometimes black, background on its body. Young specimens are very argumentative with each other even in a very large aquarium and, therefore, only one specimen should be kept. The spine on the caudal peduncle, a characteristic of all Acanthurids, is marked in orange. Algae is a very important part of this fish's diet.

Breeding
Not known.

Tank Set-up
Provide algae.

NASO LITURATUS
(BLOCH & SCHNEIDER, 1801)

24–26°C
75–79°F
50 cm (20 in)

Family: ACANTHURIDAE	
Common name: LIPSTICK TANG, LIPSTICK SURGEON, SMOOTHHEAD UNICORN FISH	
Distribution: Indo-Pacific	
Size: 50 cm (20 in)	
Food: Green food, frozen *Mysis*, etc	
Temperature range: 24–26°C / 75–79°F	
pH: 8.4 Salinity: 1.023–1.027	

A peaceful fish which makes an attractive addition to the larger aquarium. The common names Lipstick Tang and Lipstick Surgeon refer to the red around the mouth of the fish. The 'Unicorn' of the other common name refers to a 'horn' that develops on the forehead of some species. On the caudal peduncle there are two razor sharp spines, so take care when handling this fish as it can inflict severe wounds. The coloration varies a little depending on locality: those fish from Hawaiian waters have a black dorsal fin and those from the Indian Ocean have orange in the dorsal fin.

Breeding
Not known.

PARACANTHURUS HEPATUS
LINNAEUS, 1766

24–26°C
75–79°F
25 cm (10 in)

Family: ACANTHURIDAE	
Common name: REGAL TANG, BLUE SURGEON FISH	
Distribution: Indo-Pacific	
Size: 25 cm (10 in)	
Food: Green food, frozen *Mysis*, etc	
Temperature range: 24–26°C / 75–79°F	
pH: 8.4 Salinity: 1.023–1.027	

An easy fish to recognise by the blue and black markings on the body coupled with the striking yellow caudal fin. Provided the aquarium is large enough, a small shoal of these fish may be kept. Acclimatise a group of youngsters which, although they may be a little quarrelsome at first, will usually settle down after a few days. Provide copious amounts of green food. In the wild they are found at depths of 10–40 m / 30–140 ft.

Breeding
Not known.

Tank Set-up
A large aquarium is required for a small shoal, with plenty of algae.

ZEBRASOMA FLAVESCENS
(BENNETT, 1828)

Family: ACANTHURIDAE	
Common name: YELLOW TANG	
Distribution: Pacific	
Size: 20 cm (8 in)	
Food: Green food	
Temperature range: 24–26°C / 75–79°F	
pH: 8.4 Salinity: 1.023–1.027	

A brilliant yellow fish, it is sometimes confused with young specimens of *Acanthurus coeruleus*. However, the Yellow Tang lacks any trace of blue coloration around the eye or in the finnage, and the head shape is different. A territorial fish, it should either be kept in a large shoal of six or more individuals in a very large aquarium or as a single specimen. It is predominantly an algal feeder and, as such should be offered plenty of green food.

Breeding
Not known.

Tank Set-up
Algae should be grown in the tank.

24–26°C
75–79°F

20 cm (8 in)

BALISTOIDES CONSPICILLUM
BLOCH & SCHNEIDER, 1801

24–26°C
75–79°F

50 cm (20 in)

Family:	BALISTIDAE
Common name:	CLOWN TRIGGER
Distribution:	Indo-Pacific
Size:	50 cm (20 in)
Food:	Molluscs, crustaceans
Temperature range:	24–26°C/75–79°F
pH: 8.4	Salinity: 1.023–1.027

An aggressive fish that soon asserts itself in the aquarium. Avoid keeping it with smaller species. They have the powerful jaws needed for feeding on molluscs and crustaceans. When feeding on sea urchins, they blow jets of water at the urchin to turn it over so they can feed on the exposed underbelly. Their common name comes from their ability to lock the first dorsal fin ray using a second ray. This aids against predation by increasing the size of the fish and making them a very prickly meal.

Breeding
Not known.

ODONUS NIGER
(RUPPELL, 1922)

Family:	BALISTIDAE
Common name:	BLACK TRIGGERFISH
Distribution:	Indo-Pacific, Red Sea
Size:	50 cm (20 in)
Food:	OMNIVOROUS
Temperature range:	24–26°C/75–79°F
pH: 8.4	Salinity: 1.023–1.027

A fish that adapts well to aquarium life, it is relatively peaceful. In the wild it eats sponges but, in captivity it takes just about anything. It is found over a wide area and its coloration can vary from blue to green and dark, almost black. The red teeth are quite distinctive. The scaling is interesting in that it gives the fish an intriguing diamond-shaped patterning across the body. Swimming is accomplished mainly by undulating the finnage rather than movements of the body. Adult specimens may jump.

Breeding
Not known.

24–26°C
75–79°F

50 cm (20 in)

SYNCHIROPUS PICTURATUS
(PETERS, 1876)

24–26°C
75–79°F

10 cm (4 in)

Family:	CALLIONYMIDAE
Common name:	PSYCHEDELIC FISH
Distribution:	Pacific
Size:	10 cm (4 in)
Food:	Algae, small crustaceans, etc
Temperature range:	24–26°C/75–79°F
pH: 8.4	Salinity: 1.023–1.027

These fish adapt well to living in the aquarium. They may be kept as pairs if the aquarium is big enough, otherwise they should be kept as single individuals as they are fairly intolerant of others of their species. They need quiet companions and much of their time is spent resting on rocks or hiding in crevices, sometimes even buried in the substrate. Males have more intense coloration and extended dorsal and anal fin rays.

Breeding
Little is known, although some species are believed to practise internal fertilisation. The eggs are pelagic, that is they float in water. Eggs have been produced under aquarium conditions but no fry resulted.

Tank Set-up
Rocks, stones, pebbles and sand should be provided for resting and 'hideaway' places.

SYNCHIROPUS SPLENDIDUS
(HERRE, 1927)

Family:	CALLIONYMIDAE
Common name:	MANDARIN FISH
Distribution:	Pacific
Size:	10 cm (4 in)
Food:	Algae, small crustaceans, etc
Temperature range:	24–26°C/75–79°F
pH: 8.4	Salinity: 1.023–1.027

Though far more colourful than *S. picturatus*, this species, too, is shy and retiring and requires the same aquarium conditions. Sexing is the same. It is said that the skin of the Mandarin Fish is poisonous. This fish is more often offered for sale than *S. picturatus*.

Breeding
See comments for *S. picturatus*.

24–26°C
75–79°F

10 cm (4 in)

AEOLISCUS STRIGATUS

(GUENTHER, 1860)

Family: CENTRISCIDAE	
Common name: SHRIMPFISH	
Distribution: Indo-Pacific	
Size: 10 cm (4 in)	
Food: OMNIVOROUS. Frozen and live food	
Temperature range: 24–26°C / 75–79°F	
pH: 8.4 Salinity: 1.023–1.027	

An oddity, these fish have the dorsal fin at the end of their body, just where you would expect the caudal to be. The body is covered with plates. Shrimpfish swim, head down, in shoals, working their way over a surface in search of food and this pattern of swimming has also been observed in caves. Some observers note that they have been seen in amongst the spines of sea urchins where the dark band along their body affords them camouflage amongst the long, black spines of the urchin. They can be difficult to acclimatise to aquarium conditions and may refuse to feed. Offer live *Mysis* and brine shrimps in the first instance.

Breeding
Not known.

24–26°C
75–79°F

10 cm (4 in)

OXYMONACANTHUS LONGIROSTRIS

(BLOCH & SCHNEIDER, 1801)

Family: CENTRISCIDAE	
Common name: LONG-NOSED FILEFISH, BEAKED LEATHERJACKET	
Distribution: Indo-Australian archipelago, Pacific Islands (excluding Hawaii)	
Size: 10 cm (4 in)	
Food: CARNIVOROUS. Frozen and live food	
Temperature range: 24–26°C / 75–79°F	
pH: 8.4 Salinity: 1.023–1.027	

24–26°C
75–79°F

10 cm (4 in)

A peaceful fish, its striking coloration makes it highly desirable for the home aquarium. The fish feeds by poking its long, pointed snout into the reef to feed on coral polyps. However, in the aquarium it will take brine shrimp. They inhabit shallow areas of the reef in amongst branched coral heads so be sure to provide similar structures in the aquarium. Because of its pernickity feeding habits it is a fish for the specialist. Without due care and attention it will not survive for any length of time in captivity.

Breeding
Not known.

CHAETODON ACULEATUS

(POEY, 1860)

Family: CHAETODONTIDAE	
Common name: LONGSNOUT BUTTERFLYFISH, CARIBBEAN LONGSNOUT BUTTERFLYFISH	
Distribution: Southern Florida, Caribbean, Bahamas, Gulf of Mexico	
Size: 10 cm (4 in)	
Food: Small invertebrates	
Temperature range: 24–26°C / 75–79°F	
pH: 8.4 Salinity: 1.023–1.027	

A small, solitary fish, although youngsters may form groups of ten or so, it is found close to or on the steep drop off zone of reefs, it feeds by foraging in the crevices in the reef wall and will also pick bits off the spines of sea urchins. Normally it is found at depth of 20–50 m / 66–164 ft, but the deepest recorded sighting was at 91 m / 298 ft. If frightened it retreats to caves and hollows. Relatively hardy, it is not too difficult to maintain in aquaria. The trade name 'Ross Butterflyfish' is sometimes applied to it.

24–26°C
75–79°F

10 cm (4 in)

Breeding
Not known.

Tank Set-up
Provide plenty of rocks and crevices as feeding and hiding places.

Family: CHAETODONTIDAE
Common name: THREADFIN BUTTERFLYFISH
Distribution: Indo-Pacific, Red Sea
Size: 18 cm (7 in)
Food: Crustaceans, algae and coral polyps
Temperature range: 24–26°C / 75–79°F
pH: 8.4 Salinity: 1.023–1.027

A peaceful but retiring fish that does
well in the aquarium, transferring quite
easily to feeding on commercially
available frozen food. The young fish
have a thread-like extension to the
dorsal fin, hence the common name. Its
preponderance for eating coral polyps
negates it from being kept in with
invertebrates. Some scientists recognise
two sub-species, *C. a. auriga* from the
Red Sea, which loses the dark spot on
the dorsal fin as it ages, and *C. a. setifer*
from the Indo-Pacific.

Breeding
Not known.

24–26°C
75–79°F
18 cm (7 in)

CHAETODON AURIGA
FORSSKÅL, 1775

CHAETODON COLLARE
BLOCH, 1787

Family: CHAETODONTIDAE
Common name: PAKISTANI BUTTERFLYFISH,
COLLARE BUTTERFLYFISH
Distribution: Indian Ocean
Size: 15 cm (6 in)
Food: Coral polyps, invertebrates, green food
Temperature range: 24–26°C / 75–79°F
pH: 8.4 Salinity: 1.023–1.027

Although often found in shoals in the
wild, this species can sometimes be
intolerant of its own kind and others, in
the confines of an aquarium. Opinion
differs as to the difficulty of keeping
this fish in an aquarium, some say it is
difficult, others that it is easy but both
factions agree that it is not a fish for the
beginner. Feeding is relatively simple
but offer your fish a variety of food as
fish from different localities have
different feeding patterns.

Breeding
Not known.

24–26°C
75–79°F

15 cm (6 in)

CHAETODON DECUSSATUS
CUVIER, 1831

Family: CHAETODONTIDAE
Common name: INDIAN VAGABOND BUTTERFLYFISH
Distribution: Sri Lanka through the Indo-Malay
Archipelago
Size: 20 cm (8 in)
Food: Algae, coral polyps
Temperature range: 24–26°C / 75–79°F
pH: 8.4 Salinity: 1.023–1.027

The bulk of these fish for the trade
come from Sri Lankan waters. They
acclimatise well to aquarium life once
they have been persuaded to feed. Even
though they eat algae and coral polyps
in the wild, it is not long before they
will accept commercially available
frozen and flake food.

Breeding
Not known.

24–26°C
75–79°F
20 cm (8 in)

CHAETODON FALCULA
BLOCH, 1793

Family: CHAETODONTIDAE

Common name: SADDLEBACK BUTTERFLYFISH,
DOUBLE-SADDLE BUTTERFLYFISH, PIG-FACED
BUTTERFLYFISH

Distribution: Indian Ocean

Size: 15 cm (6 in)

Food: Algae, invertebrates, etc

Temperature range: 24–26°C / 75–79°F

pH: 8.4 Salinity: 1.023–1.027

An aggressive fish that will not tolerate the companionship of like species in the aquarium. On reefs it is seen swimming about in small groups or in pairs at depths of 3–15 m / 9–45 ft. Once acclimatised in a mature aquarium, it does well in captivity but it is not a fish for the newcomer to marine fish-keeping.

Breeding
Not known.

Tank Set-up
A mature aquarium is required.

24–26°C
75–79°F

15 cm (6 in)

24–26°C
75–79°F

13 cm (5 in)

CHAETODON MILIARIS
QUOY & GAIMARD, 1824

Family: CHAETODONTIDAE

Common name: LEMON BUTTERFLYFISH

Distribution: Indo-Pacific

Size: 13 cm (5 in)

Food: Plankton, invertebrates, fish eggs

Temperature range: 24–26°C / 75–79°F

pH: 8.4 Salinity: 1.023–1.027

Probably one of the hardiest fishes to keep in the marine aquarium, the only drawback seems to be that the beautiful yellow coloration fades under aquarium conditions. It is not known whether particular foods, water conditions or perhaps a combination of both help the fish to maintain its colour. Indeed, it could be something else entirely. The fish have been observed at depths of 1 m / 3 ft down to below 250 m / 800 ft, sometimes forming large shoals when feeding and often raiding the nests of other fish such as Damsels to eat the eggs.

Breeding
They have a definite breeding season, and the young are seen in inshore waters of the Indo-Pacific during April, May and June.

CHAETODON VAGABUNDUS
LINNAEUS, 1758

Family: CHAETODONTIDAE

Common name: VAGABOND BUTTERFLYFISH,
CRISS-CROSS BUTTERFLYFISH

Distribution: Indo-Pacific

Size: 20 cm (8 in)

Food: Algae, corals, invertebrates

Temperature range: 24–26°C / 75–79°F

pH: 8.4 Salinity: 1.023–1.027

This species is considered the Butterflyfish for beginners, but it should be noted that this means the new marine aquarist and not the new aquarium. These fish need a mature set up with good water conditions. They are peaceful, causing no problems in the aquarium and feeding is simple. Offered frozen, flake and green food, they will become tame enough to feed from your hand.

Breeding
Not known.

24–26°C
75–79°F

20 cm (8 in)

Tank Set-up
A mature aquarium with good water conditions.

CHELMON ROSTRATUS

(LINNAEUS, 1758)

Family: CHAETODONTIDAE

Common name: COPPER-BAND BUTTERFLYFISH, BEAKED BUTTERFLYFISH

Distribution: Indo-Pacific, Red Sea

Size: 17 cm (7 in)

Food: Algae, invertebrates

Temperature range: 24–26°C / 75–79°F

pH: 8.4 Salinity: 1.023–1.027

A popular aquarium fish, it can be very aggressive towards its own kind so they are best kept as solitary individuals. They can be difficult to feed, preferring small live food although once established, they will take commercially available frozen food. Above all, maintain the water quality in the aquarium, should it start to deteriorate the Copper-band will succumb.

Breeding
Not known.

Tank Set-up
Maintain good water quality.

| 24–26°C 75–79°F | | 17 cm (7 in) |

FORCIPIGER FLAVISSIMUS

JORDAN & McGREGOR, 1898

Family: CHAETODONTIDAE

Common name: LONG-NOSED BUTTERFLYFISH

Distribution: Indo-Pacific, Red Sea

Size: 20 cm (8 in)

Food: Invertebrates, algae

Temperature range: 24–26°C / 75–79°F

pH: 8.4 Salinity: 1.023–1.027

These fish acclimatise well to aquarium conditions and once they have settled in they will feed on flake and frozen food. On the reefs it is found in areas where there are a lot of coral growths, it feeds by picking invertebrates from between the corals with its long snout. There is an eye-spot on the anal fin while the real eye is camouflaged by the black marking on the head. An all black version of this fish has been reported from Australia.

Breeding
Not known.

| 24–26°C 75–79°F | | 20 cm (8 in) |

Family: CHAETODONTIDAE

Common name: BIG LONG-NOSED BUTTERFLYFISH

Distribution: Indo-Pacific

Size: 19 cm (7 in)

Food: Algae, invertebrates

Temperature range: 24–26°C / 75–79°F

pH: 8.4 Salinity: 1.023–1.027

Closely related to *F. flavissimus*, *F. longirostris*, as its name suggests, has a much longer snout, and has 10–11 dorsal spines whereas *F. flavissimus* has 12. Maintenance in the aquarium is as for *F. flavissimus*. Black forms of this fish have also been recorded off Hawaii, Great Barrier Reef, Comore Islands and Christmas Island with one black individual occurring in about every hundred yellow. In the aquarium, the black form may revert to yellow, going through a dusky black and yellow stage. *F. longirostris* and *F. flavissimus* occur together in the wild.

FORCIPIGER LONGIROSTRIS

(BROUSSONET, 1782)

Breeding
Not known.

| 24–26°C 75–79°F | | 19 cm (7 in) |

HENIOCHUS ACUMINATUS
(LINNAEUS, 1758)

Family: CHAETODONTIDAE

Common name: LONG-FIN BANNERFISH, WIMPLEFISH, PENNANT CORALFISH, POOR MAN'S MOORISH IDOL

Distribution: Indo-Pacific, Red Sea

Size: 18 cm (7 in)

Food: OMNIVOROUS

Temperature range: 24–26°C / 75–79°F

pH: 8.4 Salinity: 1.023–1.027

A good fish for the aquarium, it is easy to keep and easy to feed as well as being very peaceable so two or three specimens may be kept in a large aquarium. If it goes off its food, check the water conditions and make sure the aquarium is not overcrowded as it likes plenty of swimming space and good quality water. The coloration changes little from juvenile to adult but the dorsal fin extends with age. Young fish act as cleaner fish.

Breeding
Not known.

Tank Set-up
Ensure good quality water and plenty of space for swimming.

 24–26°C 75–79°F 18 cm (7 in)

HENIOCHUS CHRYSOSTOMUS
CUVIER, 1831

Family: CHAETODONTIDAE

Common name: PENNANT BANNERFISH, HORNED CORALFISH

Distribution: Indo-Pacific

Size: 15 cm (6 in)

Food: Algae and corals

Temperature range: 24–26°C / 75–79°F

pH: 8.4 Salinity: 1.023–1.027

Rarely imported for the aquarium trade. In the wild it is often seen swimming with *Heniochus varius* in areas where there is plenty of coral. Juveniles are frequently found in shallow waters amongst the coral at about 1 m / 3 ft, adults venture down to 15 m / 45 ft.

Breeding
Not known.

 24–26°C 75–79°F 15 cm (6 in)

HENIOCHUS VARIUS
CUVIER, 1829

Family: CHAETODONTIDAE

Common name: HUMPHEAD BANNERFISH

Distribution: Indo-Pacific

Size: 18 cm (7 in)

Food: Tiny invertebrates

Temperature range: 24–26°C / 75–79°F

pH: 8.4 Salinity: 1.023–1.027

The heads of adults are quite distinctive, with two 'horns' above the eyes and a lump on the forehead. In the wild they prefer the shelter afforded by caves to the open reef. In the aquarium it is quite delicate and very difficult to feed. Youngsters require copious amounts of brine shrimp several times a day but, to complicate this, the brine shrimp should have been feeding on algae so that the fish benefits from this as well. Exported to the USA, it is rarely seen in Europe.

Breeding
Not known.

Tank Set-up
Prefer less light. Provide shaded conditions where the fish can shelter.

 24–26°C 75–79°F 18 cm (7 in)

OXYCIRRHITES TYPUS
(Bleeker, 1857)

Family: CIRRHITIDAE	
Common name: LONGNOSED HAWKFISH	
Distribution: Indian Ocean	
Size: 10 cm (4 in)	
Food: Omnivorous	
Temperature range: 24–26°C / 75–79°F	
pH: 8.4 Salinity: 1.023–1.027	

Settles in to aquarium life well, spending much of its time sitting in

24–26°C
75–79°F   10 cm (4 in)

corals until food floats past when it dashes out to grab it. Small, live and frozen food are taken with equal relish. They are peaceful and several specimens may be kept together. Males are smaller than females and have a deeper-red lower jaw.

Breeding
In the wild they spawn at dusk. Scanty reports of aquarium spawnings indicate that the eggs are adhesive and laid in groups.

DIODON HOLACANTHUS
(Linnaeus)

Family: DIODONTIDAE	
Common name: LONG-SPINED PORCUPINE FISH; BALLOON FISH	
Distribution: Worldwide in the tropics	
Size: 15 cm (6 in)	
Food: CARNIVOROUS. Frozen and live food	
Temperature range: 24–26°C / 75–79°F	
pH: 8.4 Salinity: 1.023–1.027	

Porcupine fish grow quite large and require an equally large species aquarium and, as they are messy feeders, ensure the filtration system is

24–26°C
75–79°F   15 cm (6 in)

able to cope with this. These fish are famed, like the Puffers (Tetraodontidae), for their ability to inflate their bodies which causes their spines to stand up. This affords them protection from predators. Avoid the temptation to provoke the fish into inflating itself as a party piece because this is very stressful for it. These fish are bold and may become tame enough to feed from your hand. Their diet consists of meaty food, shrimp, cockles and the like, so do not keep them in a community aquarium with invertebrates.

Breeding
Not known.

GOBIODON CITRINUS
(Ruppel, 1838)

Family: GOBIIDAE	
Common name: LEMON GOBY	
Distribution: Indo-Pacific	
Size: 3 cm (1 in)	
Food: OMNIVOROUS	
Temperature range: 24–26°C / 75–79°F	
pH: 8.4 Salinity: 1.023–1.027	

24–26°C
75–79°F   3cm (1 in)

An easy fish to keep whether you are a beginner or an experienced aquarist. It is peaceful but should not be kept with very large fishes for obvious reasons. Once settled it will accept most food but has a preference for live food. Much of its time is spent sitting on rocks or resting in amongst corals. The body mucus is said to be poisonous but there are not reports of it causing any problems in the aquarium.

Breeding
Not known.

LYTHRYPNUS DALLI
(Gilbert, 1891)

Family: GOBIIDAE	
Common name: CATALINA GOBY, BLUE-BANDED GOBY	
Distribution: Pacific coast of California	
Size: 6 cm (2½ in)	
Food: Invertebrates	
Temperature range: 20–22°C / 68–72°F	
pH: 8.4 Salinity: 1.023–1.027	

A cool water fish, this Goby may be kept in a relatively small aquarium with other small, peaceful fishes. It is

20–22°C
68–72°F   6 cm (2½ in)

territorial but provided there are sufficient rocks the fish will all establish their own areas and live together peacefully. Use a sand substrate as the fish like to dig burrows. It is not very long lived. Although it will accept frozen food, it has a preference for small live food, indeed these are essential if you try and breed them.

Breeding
The eggs are laid in caves, hollows or burrows and the male guards them. Fry are difficult to raise because of their small size.

GRAMMA LORETO
POEY, 1868

Family: GRAMMIDAE
Common name: ROYAL GRAMMA, FAIRY BASSLET
Distribution: Western Atlantic
Size: 13 cm (5 in)
Food: OMNIVOROUS
Temperature range: 24–26°C/75–79°F
pH: 8.4 Salinity: 1.023–1.027

These fish are found in caves and dark recesses so ensure there are such structures in the aquarium. Once acclimatised it will venture out even if the lighting is bright. Can be aggressive towards its own kind but, if the aquarium is large enough, two may be kept together. Will take most food offered. Males are reported to be larger than females.

Breeding
There are conflicting reports of aquarium spawnings, in one the male lined a cave with algae and was later seen mouthbrooding eggs. In the other algae was used to line a pit in which the eggs were laid and then guarded by what was presumed to be the male. The eggs hatched by the fry were not raised.

24–26°C 75–79°F		13 cm (5 in)

MYRIPRISTIS JACOBUS
CUVIER & VALENCIENNES

Family: HOLOCENTRIDAE
Common name: SQUIRRELFISH, BLACKBAR SOLDIERFISH
Distribution: Caribbean; northern Florida to Brazil
Size: 17 cm (7 in)
Food: CARNIVOROUS. Frozen and live food
Temperature range: 24–26°C/75–79°F
pH: 8.4 Salinity: 1.023–1.027

A nocturnal fish, their large eyes allow them to make the most of any light that is available. They spend much of the day hiding in caves and crevices, however, in captivity, they can often be tempted out with food such as shrimps, chopped meat or fish and with time, they can even be persuaded to accept flake food. Their one distinguishing feature is a black bar behind the operculum. Take care when netting these fish as they have spines on the gillcovers.

24–26°C 75–79°F		15 cm (6 in)

Breeding
Not known.

BODIANUS PULCHELLUS
(POEY, 1860)

Family: LABRIDAE
Common name: CUBAN HOGFISH, SPOTFIN HOGFISH
Distribution: Western Atlantic
Size: 25 cm (10 in)
Food: Crustaceans
Temperature range: 24–26°C/75–79°F
pH: 8.4 Salinity: 1.023–1.027

This fish goes through three colour phases. Juveniles are yellow with a black spot in the front of the dorsal fin, then there is an intermediate phase when the front part of the fish is dark, grey-black while the rear of the body and the caudal fin are yellow until, finally the fish reaches its red and yellow adult coloration. In the wild these fish act as cleaners to other, larger species. In the aquarium they are quite peaceful except with very small fish. Feed meaty food.

Breeding
Not known.

24–26°C 75–79°F		25 cm (10 in)

BODIANUS RUFUS
(LINNAEUS, 1758)

Family: LABRIDAE
Common name: SPANISH HOGFISH
Distribution: Western Atlantic
Size: 60 cm (24 in)
Food: Crustaceans, shellfish meat
Temperature range: 24–26°C / 75–79°F
pH: 8.4 Salinity: 1.023–1.027

Peaceful in the aquarium. Juveniles are yellow with blue-purple on the head and upper body and as the fish mature the blue-purple and eventually red area is just seen on the front part of the upper body. The coloration may vary depending on the locality of the fish. Juveniles act as cleaner fish to larger species.

Breeding
Not known.

24–26°C 75–79°F 60 cm (24 in)

CIRRHILABRUS RUBRIVENTRALIS
SPRINGER & RANDALL, 1974

Family: LABRIDAE
Common name: DWARF PARROT WRASSE, SEA FIGHTER
Distribution: Indian Ocean
Size: 7 cm (3 in)
Food: Omnivorous
Temperature range: 24–26°C / 75–79°F
pH: 8.4 Salinity: 1.023–1.027

A peaceful fish that is easy to acclimatise to aquarium conditions provided the water conditions are excellent. As for feeding, it will take live, frozen and flake food and should be given a good varied diet. Very colourful, the males have more intense coloration than females and they also have an extension to the leading edge of the dorsal fin. These fish may be kept in groups provided the aquarium is large enough and the male will then be seen displaying to the females.

Breeding
Not known.

24–26°C 75–79°F 7 cm (3 in)

CORIS GAIMARD
(QUOY & GAIMARD, 1824)

Family: LABRIDAE
Common name: CLOWN WRASSE, RED LABRID
Distribution: Indo-Pacific
Size: 30 cm (12 in)
Food: Crustaceans
Temperature range: 24–26°C / 75–79°F
pH: 8.4 Salinity: 1.023–1.027

Young fish may be kept in community aquaria but larger, older specimens can cause problems. They can be quarrelsome amongst themselves.

24–26°C 75–79°F 30 cm (12 in)

Youngsters are attractively coloured, being bright orange with white blotches edged in black. As they mature their take on their full adult coloration: orange head, dark body with blue speckles, red dorsal and anal fins and a yellow caudal fin. Feed chopped shrimp and similar food.

Breeding
Not known.

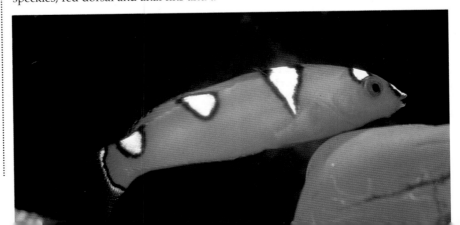

GOMPHOSUS VARIUS
LACEPÈDE, 1801

Family: LABRIDAE	
Common name: BIRDMOUTH WRASSE	
Distribution: Indo-Pacific	
Size: 25 cm (10 in)	
Food: Invertebrates	
Temperature range: 24–26°C / 75–79°F	
pH: 8.4 Salinity: 1.023–1.027	

24–26°C 75–79°F — 25 cm (10 in)

A peaceful fish, it is easy to tell males from females. Males are bright peacock-green in colour, while females are brown. They adapt well to aquarium life and thrive on a diet of *Mysis* shrimp, chopped up prawn and other fine food plus some green food. Young specimens may act as cleaner fish. The common name is derived from their long, beak-like jaws.

Breeding
Not known.

LABROIDES DIMIDIATUS
(VALENCIENNES, 1839)

Family: LABRIDAE	
Common name: CLEANER WRASSE	
Distribution: Indo-Pacific	
Size: 10 cm (4 in)	
Food: Skin parasites	
Temperature range: 24–26°C / 75–79°F	
pH: 8.4 Salinity: 1.023–1.027	

One of the most useful fish for the marine aquarium, it cleans larger fishes, ridding them of any unwanted skin parasites. They will not survive on these alone, in captivity, so feed finely chopped prawn. The Wrasse service other fish at 'Cleaner Stations', the larger fish knowing where to go on the reef to obtain the services of the Wrasse. The mouth of the Cleaner Wrasse is terminal, i.e. at the very tip of the snout, differentiating it from the False Cleaner Wrasse, *Aspidontus taeniatus*, which looks to all intents and purposes like

24–26°C 75–79°F — 10 cm (4 in)

the Cleaner but goes around taking chunks out of the larger fish.

Breeding
Not known.

NOVACULICHTHYS TAENIORUS
(LACEPÈDE, 1802)

Family: LABRIDAE	
Common name: DRAGON WRASSE	
Distribution: Indo-Pacific	
Size: 20 cm (8 in)	
Food: Meaty food	
Temperature range: 24–26°C / 75–79°F	
pH: 8.4 Salinity: 1.023–1.027	

24–26°C 75–79°F — 20 cm (8 in)

A very peaceful, attractive little fish. The juveniles have an olive-green coloration with white blotches and darker lines. As the fish reaches maturity the green fades to brown but it still looks just as attractive. Keep in the company of other similar-sized fishes or they may just hide away and not feed. They feed from the substrate so ensure that sufficient food falls to the bottom for them.

Breeding
Not known.

THALASSOMA LUNARE
(LINNAEUS, 1758)

Family: LABRIDAE	
Common name: LYRETAIL WRASSE, GREEN PARROT WRASSE, MOON WRASSE	
Distribution: Indo-Pacific	
Size: 33 cm (13 in)	
Food: Meaty food	
Temperature range: 24–26°C / 75–79°F	
pH: 8.4 Salinity: 1.023–1.027	

A boisterous fish, it needs a large, spacious aquarium. During the day it is constantly on the move and may

24–26°C 75–79°F — 33 cm (13 in)

disturb some fishes. Once established in the aquarium it will attack any new introductions regardless of their size. Feed plenty of meaty food, chopped prawn, frozen Lance-fish, etc, and make sure enough falls to the bottom to satisfy this fish's appetite. Adults lose the black blotches of juveniles and can be easily recognised by the central yellow section of the caudal fin and the greeny blue top and bottom sections which give the fish the appearance of having a lyretail.

Breeding
Not known.

NEMATELEOTRIS MAGNIFICA
FOWLER, 1938

Family: MICRODESMIDAE
Common name: FIREFISH
Distribution: Indo-Pacific
Size: 6 cm (2½ in)
Food: Small invertebrates
Temperature range: 24–26°C / 75–79°F
pH: 8.4 Salinity: 1.023–1.027

A bottom-dwelling fish, the Firefish
needs a deep sandy substrate to allow it
to burrow. Unless there are burrows
and hollows for the fish to retreat to, it
never really settles down in the
aquarium. Once established it is
peaceful and easy to feed. Initially it
may require live food but will soon take
frozen *Mysis* and the like. The extended
dorsal fin seems to be used as a signal
to other fish as it is often flicked back
and forth. The common name is derived
from the fiery coloration of the rear of
the body. Use a tight-fitting cover glass
as these fish are prone to jumping if
frightened.

Breeding
Details sketchy, some species have been
spawned but no reports of fry or details
of which species.

24–26°C
75–79°F

6 cm (2½ in)

PTERELEOTRIS EVIDES
JORDAN & HUBBS, 1925

Family: MICRODESMIDAE
Common name: SCISSORTAIL
Distribution: Indo-Pacific
Size: 12 cm (4½ in)
Food: Meaty food
Temperature range: 24–26°C / 75–79°F
pH: 8.4 Salinity: 1.023–1.027

Provide a deep sandy substrate for this
fish as it inhabits burrows. When in
search of food they hover just above the
substrate, never very far from the safety
of their burrow. They readily accept
frozen meaty food such as chopped
shrimp, brine shrimp and the like.
Catching these creatures can be quite a
challenge as they are very fast in
returning to their boltholes.

Breeding
Not known.

24–26°C
75–79°F

12 cm (4½ in)

MONOCENTRUS JAPONICUS
(HOUTTUYN)

24–26°C
75–79°F

15 cm (6 in)

Family: MONOCENTRIDAE
Common name: PINECONE FISH
Distribution: Indo-Pacific
Size: 15 cm (6 in)
Food: CARNIVOROUS: Frozen and live food
Temperature range: 24–26°C / 75–79°F
pH: 8.4 Salinity: 1.023–1.027

Just to look at them, Pinecone Fish are
peculiar. Their body is encased in a
rigid case formed by the fusion of the
large scales. As if this wasn't enough
protection, each scale has a large, sharp
spine at its centre. Pinecone Fish have

two luminous organs situated just
below the jaw and these are believed to
be used to attract prey. The organs
luminesce because of symbiotic bacteria
which live therein. In the wild Pinecone
Fish are found down to 182 m (600 ft)
where they cruise over the seabed. In
the aquarium they settle quite well in a
species tank and will accept a diet of
chopped meat and fish. They are
commercially raised as food fish in
Japan.

Breeding
Not known.

OPISTOGNATHUS AURIFRONS
(JORDAN & THOMPSON, 1905)

24–26°C
75–79°F

12 cm (4½ in)

Family:	OPISTOGNATHIDAE
Common name:	YELLOW-HEADED JAWFISH
Distribution:	Southern Florida, Bahamas, Caribbean
Size:	12 cm (4½ in)
Food:	Meaty food
Temperature range:	24–26°C / 75–79°F
pH: 8.4	Salinity: 1.023–1.027

A very peaceful little fish that minds its own business in the aquarium. Several specimens may be kept in the same aquarium provided there is enough room for each to have its own burrow and small territory. Usually they are seen hovering near their burrow and, if frightened, they rapidly retreat into the burrow tail first, quite a remarkable feat. The entrance to the burrow is covered with a pebble or shell at night. Use a tight-fitting cover glass as they are excellent jumpers. Feeding is not a problem as they take most finely chopped or small meaty food.

Breeding
Little known, the male incubates the eggs in his mouth.

LACTORIA CORNUTA
(LINNAEUS)

24–26°C
75–79°F

40 cm (16 in)

Family:	OSTRACIIDAE
Common name:	HORNED COWFISH
Distribution:	Indo-Pacific
Size:	40 cm (16 in)
Food:	OMNIVOROUS. Live food and algae, will accept frozen food
Temperature range:	24–26°C / 75–79°F
pH: 8.4	Salinity: 1.023–1.027

The body of this fish is encased in rigid bony plates, they propel themselves slowly through the water by moving their fins and caudal peduncle. The bony projections on the front and rear of this creature make them a difficult, if not impossible, meal for any predators. Feed regularly as these fish can easily be starved; the body starts to develop a concave look and, by this time, it is often too late for the fish to recover. Boxfish release poisons into the water when threatened and this can be fatal to the Boxfish and to any companion fish, especially in the confines of a transportation container or even aquarium.

Breeding
Not known.

PLATAX PINNATUS
(LINNAEUS)

Family:	PLATACIDAE
Common name:	RED-FACED BATFISH
Distribution:	Indo-Pacific
Size:	45 cm (18 in)
Food:	CARNIVOROUS. Frozen and live food
Temperature range:	24–26°C / 75–79°F
pH: 8.4	Salinity: 1.023–1.027

A beautiful fish for the marine aquarium, as a juvenile it is strikingly coloured, the red giving the fish a very dramatic appearance. As the fish matures it loses some of this coloration. It is, however, very difficult to keep because it needs a large, deep aquarium

and excellent water conditions. Juveniles are easier to acclimatise to captive conditions but you need to be prepared to take time and pander to their whims as far as feeding is concerned. Once established it grows quickly. Take care with companions and avoid any that may nip its fins or be so boisterous that the Batfish is prevented from feeding. A fish for the experienced aquarist.

Breeding
Not known.

24–26°C
75–79°F

45 cm (18 in)

CALLOPLESIOPS ALTIVELIS
(STEINDACHNER, 19031)

24–26°C
75–79°F

15 cm (6 in)

Family:	PLESIOPIDAE
Common name:	MARINE BETTA, COMET GROUPER, BLUE-SPOTTED LONGFIN
Distribution:	Indo-Pacific
Size:	15 cm (6 in)
Food:	Carnivorous
Temperature range:	24–26°C / 75–79°F
pH: 8.4	Salinity: 1.023–1.027

One of the most beautiful of the marine fishes, the false eye at the back of the dorsal fin is the first thing that you notice about it, the business end of the fish, the mouth and eyes go completely unseen, camouflaged among the small white spots. This false eye spot is passive defence, if a predator tries to take this fish, all it gets is a mouthful of finnage and the Betta can escape and regrow the lost fin. They are carnivores, and hunt head down, drifting through the water thus, so companions for Marine Bettas should be large enough not to be eaten.

Breeding
Not known.

CALLOPLESIOPS ARGUS
FOWLER & BEAN, 1930

Family: PLESIOPIDAE
Common name: MARINE BETTA
Distribution: Western Pacific
Size: 12 cm (4½ in)
Food: CARNIVOROUS
Temperature range: 24–26°C / 75–79°F
pH: 8.4 Salinity: 1.023–1.027

C. argus has much finer white spots scattered across its body than

C. altivelis, but it still has the eye-spot in the rear of the dorsal fin. Its maintenance in captivity is much the same as C. altivelis but it is far less frequently imported. Initially it may require live food to settle it down but will later accept dead meaty food.

Breeding
Not known.

24–26°C
75–79°F
12 cm (4½ in)

PLOTOSUS LINEATUS
(THUNBERG, 1787)

Family: PLOTOSIDAE
Common name: SALTWATER CATFISH
Distribution: Indo-Pacific
Size: 30 cm (12 in)
Food: CARNIVOROUS. Frozen and live food
Temperature range: 24–26°C / 75–79°F
pH: 8.4 Salinity: 1.023–1.027

Plotosus lineatus is not everyone's favourite fish for the home aquarium because, although the young are colourful, gregarious and very active, as the fish mature they become loners and their colour fades until they look quite drab. Young fish should be kept as a shoal; individual specimens do not fair well and often pine away. The other drawback is the poisonous spine on the dorsal and anal fins, so care is needed when handling this fish. If you should have the misfortune to be "stung", the wound is painful but bathing the area in hot water can help to alleviate this. In all other respects they are easy to keep and feed.

Breeding
The male guards the eggs and fry.

24–26°C
75–79°F
30 cm (12 in)

APOLEMICHTHYS TRIMACULATUS
(LACEPÈDE, in Cuvier, 1831)

Family: POMACANTHIDAE
Common name: THREE-SPOT ANGELFISH, FLAGFIN ANGELFISH
Distribution: Indo-Pacific
Size: 25 cm (10 in)
Food: Algae and other green food
Temperature range: 24–26°C / 75–79°F
pH: 8.4 Salinity: 1.023–1.027

One of the more difficult angelfishes to maintain in the aquarium, they should be kept as single specimens as they can be territorial. They require optimum water conditions and suffer if the water deteriorates. Offer different food including plenty of vegetable food and commercially prepared sponge-based food as well as Mysis, brine shrimp, etc. It is also beneficial to have algae growing in the aquarium so that the fish may graze on it. Their common name is derived from the three spots on the head.

Breeding
Not known.

24–26°C
75–79°F
25 cm (10 in)

CENTROPYGE ACANTHOPS
(NORMAN, 1922)

Family: POMACANTHIDAE

Common name: AFRICAN PYGMY ANGELFISH, FIREBALL ANGELFISH

Distribution: Indian Ocean, east African coast

Size: 7 cm (3 in)

Food: Green and meaty food

Temperature range: 24–26°C / 75–79°F

pH: 8.4 Salinity: 1.023–1.027

 24–26°C 75–79°F   7 cm (3 in)

This fish is found in small shoals of 8–10 individuals at depths of 8 to 40 m (26–31 ft) where there is coral rubble. A small, peaceful fish, it makes a welcome addition to the marine aquarium so long as it is kept with creatures of a similar disposition. Several may be kept provided the aquarium is large enough. Make sure you offer it a variety of food.

Breeding
Not known.

CENTROPYGE ARGI
WOODS & KANAZAWA, 1951

Family: POMACANTHIDAE

Common name: CHERUB PYGMY ANGELFISH, PYGMY ANGELFISH, CHERUBFISH, PURPLE FIREBALL

Distribution: Western Atlantic

Size: 7 cm (3 in)

Food: Green and meaty food

Temperature range: 24–26°C / 75–79°F

pH: 8.4 Salinity: 1.023–1.027

In the wild, these fish are usually found at depths of 30 m / 95 ft or more in regions where there is plenty of rubble and debris to provide hiding places. They are usually seen in pairs or small shoals. However, in the southern Caribbean they can be seen swimming in and out of corals in much shallower waters. They acclimatise well to aquarium life, feeding on a variety of food which should include a good deal

of vegetable matter. May be kept in pairs.

Breeding
Not known.

 24–26°C 75–79°F   7 cm (3 in)

CENTROPYGE BICOLOR
(BLOCH, 1787)

Family: POMACANTHIDAE

Common name: BICOLOR ANGELFISH, BICOLOR CHERUB, ORIOLE ANGEL

Distribution: Pacific

Size: 12 cm (4½ in)

Food: Algae and meaty food

Temperature range: 24–26°C / 75–79°F

pH: 8.4 Salinity: 1.023–1.027

A typical pygmy Angel, it likes to graze on algae. Additionally, feed it green food and a variety of small meaty offerings. Youngsters are found in shallow waters but adults retreat to deeper areas some 10 m / 30 ft down. They occur either in pairs or in groups of one male and several females. Interestingly, should the male die, one of the females will change sex and become male to take his place. In the aquarium they are very peaceful and may be kept in pairs or a small group.

Breeding
Not known.

24–26°C 75–79°F   12 cm (4½ in)

Family: POMACANTHIDAE·
Common name: TWO-SPINED ANGELFISH, CORAL BEAUTY
Distribution: Indo-Pacific
Size: 12 cm (4½ in)
Food: Meaty food, green food
Temperature range: 24–26°C / 75–79°F
pH: 8.4 Salinity: 1.023–1.027

The colour on this fish varies with its location. It ranges from a deep purple with the body having red bars across it to a dark blue with golden yellow. Philippine's fish have more red and purple than the Australasian fish. A much sought after fish by aquarists, they may be kept in pairs or groups. Ensure there are plenty of hiding places in the aquarium.

Breeding
Not known.

CENTROPYGE BISPINOSUS
(GÜNTHER, 1860)

24–26°C
75–79°F

12 cm (4½ in)

CENTROPYGE EIBLI
KLAUSEWITZ, 1963

Family: POMACANTHIDAE
Common name: EIBL'S ANGELFISH
Distribution: Indo-Pacific
Size: 15 cm (6 in)
Food: OMNIVOROUS
Temperature range: 24–26°C / 75–79°F
pH: 8.4 Salinity: 1.023–1.027

24–26°C
75–79°F

15 cm (6 in)

Frequently imported, C. eibli adapts well to life in the aquarium. It will eat most small food and likes to graze on algae. It is one of the larger dwarf Angels, in the wild it is found on coral reefs at depths of up to 20 m / 63 ft. A wide-ranging fish, its coloration varies with locality.

Breeding
Not known.

CENTROPYGE LORICULUS
(GÜNTHER, 1860)

Family: POMACANTHIDAE
Common name: FLAME ANGELFISH
Distribution: Pacific
Size: 10 cm (4 in)
Food: OMNIVOROUS
Temperature range: 24–26°C / 75–79°F
pH: 8.4 Salinity: 1.023–1.027

A very popular fish, it is easy to maintain in captivity and its coloration makes it a striking addition to the home aquarium. It is peaceable. Offer a wide variety of food including green food. Ensure that the filtration system is efficient as this fish does react adversely to any deterioration in water quality.

Breeding
Not known.

24–26°C
75–79°F

10 cm (4 in)

CENTROPYGE POTTERI
JORDAN & METZ, 1912

Family: POMACANTHIDAE
Common name: POTTER'S PYGMY ANGELFISH
Distribution: Hawaiian Islands
Size: 10 cm (4 in)
Food: Green and meaty food
Temperature range: 24–26°C / 75–79°F
pH: 8.4 Salinity: 1.023–1.027

This species is only found in the Hawaiian archipelago at the depths of more than 3 m / 10 ft. It ranges over areas of rocks and coral rubble. A very popular fish because of its colour and markings, it can be difficult to acclimatise to aquarium conditions and may require to be fed on live food in the first instance. Ensure that there is algae available for it to graze over. More than one specimen may be kept in the aquarium. The water quality must be good.

Breeding
Not known.

24–26°C
75–79°F

10 cm (4 in)

24–26°C
75–79°F

22 cm (9 in)

CHAETODONTOPLUS DUBOULAYI
(GÜNTHER, 1867)

Family: POMACANTHIDAE
Common name: SCRIBBLED ANGELFISH
Distribution: Pacific
Size: 22 cm (9 in)
Food: OMNIVOROUS
Temperature range: 24–26°C / 75–79°F
pH: 8.4 Salinity: 1.023–1.027

A much sought-after aquarium fish, it is relatively peaceful. Feeding poses no problems, it will accept invertebrates and there should be algae for it to graze on. In the wild, they supplement their diet by feeding on coral polyps. The markings on this fish change little with age. Good quality nitrate-free water is essential.

Breeding
Not known.

Family: POMACANTHIDAE
Common name: BLACK VELVET ANGELFISH
Distribution: Indonesia
Size: 18 cm (7 in)
Food: Invertebrates and green food
Temperature range: 24–26°C / 75–79°F
pH: 8.4 Salinity: 1.023–1.027

As adults these fish have a yellowish tinge to their head, a grey-white area extends back across the body and the rear and fins of the fish are velvet black. The rear of the dorsal caudal and anal fins are edged in yellow. Young fish are dark with a curved yellow band extending from just in front of the dorsal fin, going down the body to end just behind the ventral fins. It is sometimes kept in aquaria and settles in quickly to life in captivity.

Breeding
Not known.

24–26°C
75–79°F

18 cm (7 in)

CHAETODONTOPLUS MELANOSOMA
(BLEEKER, 1853)

EUXIPHIPOPS NAVARCHUS
(CUVIER, 1831)

Family: POMACANTHIDAE	
Common name: BLUE-GIRDLED ANGELFISH, MAJESTIC ANGELFISH	
Distribution: Pacific	
Size: 25 cm (10 in)	
Food: OMNIVOROUS	
Temperature range: 24–26°C / 75–79°F	
pH: 8.4 Salinity: 1.023–1.027	

Young specimens of this fish adapt well to living in an aquarium, they are far easier to acclimatise than adults. Ensure there is algae for them to feed on and offer small meaty food such as chopped shrimp, *Mysis*, etc, and once established they will even take flake. Juveniles are dark blue to black with vertical fine blue lines. These youngsters withstand the rigours of transportation far better than the adults.

Breeding
Not known.

24–26°C
75–79°F

25 cm (10 in)

EUXIPHIPOPS SEXSTRIATUS
(CUVIER, 1831)

Family: POMACANTHIDAE	
Common name: SIX-BANDED ANGELFISH	
Distribution: Pacific	
Size: 45 cm (18 in)	
Food: OMNIVOROUS	
Temperature range: 24–26°C / 75–79°F	
pH: 8.4 Salinity: 1.023–1.027	

24–26°C
75–79°F

45 cm (18 in)

Like most Angelfish, these differ greatly in colour from juvenile to adult. Young fish are dark with white vertical stripes each with a very fine blue line in between. In the wild they are found in relatively shallow waters only 2–5 m / 6–16 ft deep. They can also make a sound like a loud grunt when aggravated. Young specimens are suitable for aquaria but adult specimens are far too large for all except public aquaria.

Breeding
Not known.

EUXIPHIPOPS XANTHOMETAPON
(BLEEKER, 1853)

Family: POMACANTHIDAE	
Common name: YELLOW-FACED ANGELFISH, BLUE-FACED ANGELFISH, BLUE-MASKED ANGELFISH	
Distribution: Indo-Pacific	
Size: 38 cm (15 in)	
Food: OMNIVOROUS	
Temperature range: 24–26°C / 75–79°F	
pH: 8.4 Salinity: 1.023–1.027	

A fish for the experienced aquarist. The young are dark with vertical stripes and these acclimatise well to captivity. They are intolerant of poor water conditions. Feed on invertebrates, either live or frozen, include green food and if possible have algae in the aquarium for the fish to graze on. They grow large and require careful handling so do not buy them unless you can cope with this.

Breeding
Not known.

24–26°C
75–79°F

38 cm (15 in)

(247)

Family: POMACANTHIDAE	
Common name: ROCK BEAUTY	
Distribution: Western Atlantic	
Size: 30 cm (12 in)	
Food: Meaty and green food	
Temperature range: 24–26°C / 75–79°F	
pH: 8.4 Salinity: 1.023–1.027	

A common fish, the young are yellow with a black spot edged in blue in the rear upper part of the body. When adult, the head, belly region and caudal fin are yellow and the rest of the body, the dorsal and anal fins are black. Adults are territorial and quarrelsome so it is advisable to keep only a single specimen in the community aquarium. Juveniles can be a challenge to acclimatise to aquarium life if only because in nature they feed on sponges, so the first hurdle is to get them to eat. But, once they are settled, they feed on frozen food and algae.

HOLACANTHUS TRICOLOR
(BLOCH, 1795)

Breeding
Not known.

24–26°C
75–79°F   30 cm (12 in)

POMACANTHUS ANNULARIS
(BLOCH, 1787)

Family: POMACANTHIDAE	
Common name: BLUE-RINGED ANGELFISH	
Distribution: Indo-Pacific	
Size: 25 cm (10 in)	
Food: OMNIVOROUS	
Temperature range: 24–26°C / 75–79°F	
pH: 8.4 Salinity: 1.023–1.027	

The Blue-ringed Angel is a delicate creature, requiring copious amounts of algae in its diet. It should also be

24–26°C
75–79°F   25 cm (10 in)

offered meaty food, especially live food. The colour transformation between juvenile and adult is drastic: juveniles are dark blue with vertical fine blue and white lines, adults are a coppery colour with broader blue lines that go along the body turning upwards so that they all converge towards the rear of the dorsal fin. Keep one fish in the community aquarium as they are territorial.

Breeding
Not known.

Family: POMACANTHIDAE	
Common name: EAR-SPOT ANGELFISH	
Distribution: Indian Ocean	
Size: 25 cm (10 in)	
Food: Algae, meaty food	
Temperature range: 24–26°C / 75–79°F	
pH: 8.4 Salinity: 1.023–1.027	

Little is known about this fish. It is seldom imported so aquarium-care details are sketchy. Juveniles have the standard dark coloration with vertical light stripes. It is believed that this fish has crossed with *Pomacanthus maculosus* in the wild to produce a hybrid which is very dark with orange markings on the body and a bright orange caudal fin. This fish was seen off Malindi in Kenya.

Breeding
Not known.

24–26°C
75–79°F   25 cm (10 in)

POMACANTHUS CHRYSURUS
(CUVIER, 1831)

PYGOPLITES DIACANTHUS
(BODDAERT, 1772)

Family: POMACANTHIDAE
Common name: REGAL ANGELFISH, ROYAL EMPRESS ANGELFISH
Distribution: Red Sea, Indo-Pacific
Size: 25 cm (10 in)
Food: OMNIVOROUS
Temperature range: 24–26°C/75–79°F
pH: 8.4 Salinity: 1.023–1.027

The Regal Angelfish can be difficult to feed. Given optimum water conditions and patience they do, usually, acclimatise. Although their natural diet is sponges and algae, they take frozen food and eventually even flake.

Breeding
Not known.

24–26°C
75–79°F
 25 cm (10 in)

POMACANTHUS IMPERATOR
(BLOCH, 1787)

Family: POMACANTHIDAE
Common name: EMPEROR ANGELFISH
Distribution: Indo-Pacific
Size: 40 cm (16 in)
Food: OMNIVOROUS
Temperature range: 24–26°C/75–79°F
pH: 8.4 Salinity: 1.023–1.027

A really majestic fish, it has been grown by aquarists from the dark juvenile stage to the full glory of the adult. They are peaceful in the aquarium and feed readily on frozen meaty food, algae and even flake. To keep them for any length of time in good condition the water has to be as good as possible.

Breeding
Not known.

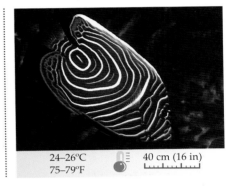

24–26°C
75–79°F
40 cm (16 in)

Family: POMACANTHIDAE
Common name: FRENCH ANGELFISH
Distribution: Western Atlantic
Size: 30 cm (12 in)
Food: OMNIVOROUS
Temperature range: 24–26°C/75–79°F
pH: 8.4 Salinity: 1.023–1.027

A beautiful fish at every stage of its life, the young are black with yellow vertical bars. As they mature they lose the bars and most scales then have a yellow rear edge. When fully adult this yellow becomes a finer white edge, the head is dusky and the body colour deepening until it is black at the rear of the fish. Young fish act as cleaners. Feed on meaty food and make sure that there is plenty of algae to graze on.

POMACENTRUS PARU
(BLOCH, 1787)

Breeding
Not known.

24–26°C
75–79°F
30 cm (12 in)

ABUDEFDUF CYANEUS
(QUOY & GAIMARD, 1825)

Family: POMACENTRIDAE
Common name: BLUE DAMSEL
Distribution: Indo-Pacific
Size: 6 cm (2½ in)
Food: Small meaty food, flake
Temperature range: 24–26°C/75–79°F
pH: 8.4 Salinity: 1.023–1.027

Can be a little quarrelsome so either keep a single fish or keep in a shoal of about eight or more fish. They are hardy and are often one of the first fish kept in the new aquarium. They are very active and are invariably seen – until you want to catch them, when they disappear in among the rocks. They have been bred and females can be differentiated from males by the shape of the ovipositor.

Breeding
They breed in a similar manner to the freshwater Cichlids. The eggs are laid on a flat surface and guarded.

24–26°C
75–79°F
6 cm (2½ in)

MARINE GROUP

AMPHIPRION AKALLOPISOS
(BLEEKER, 1853)

Family: POMACENTRIDAE
Common name: SKUNK CLOWN
Distribution: Indo-Pacific
Size: 7 cm (3 in)
Food: OMNIVOROUS
Temperature range: 24–26°C/75–79°F
pH: 8.4 Salinity: 1.023–1.027

Very peaceful but must be kept with
anemones, to be precise *Heteractis
magnifica*. An adult pair will usually
inhabit a single anemone. In the wild
they are found at depths of 3–25 m /
10–82 ft. Feeding them poses no
problems: offer live, frozen, green and
flake food.

Breeding
Bred commercially.

24–26°C 7 cm (3 in)
75–79°F

AMPHIPRION CLARKI
(BENNETT, 1830)

Family: POMACENTRIDAE
Common name: CLARKE'S ANEMONEFISH,
TWO-BANDED ANEMONEFISH, BANDED
CLOWNFISH
Distribution: Indo-Pacific
Size: 12 cm (4½ in)
Food: OMNIVOROUS
Temperature range: 24–26°C/75–79°F
pH: 8.4 Salinity: 1.023–1.027

An attractive fish, its coloration can
vary according to the catching locality.
It is a peaceful fish that may be kept
with others and preferably with an
anemone so that a pair and any young
can inhabit it. In the aquarium it will
eat most small food including green
and flake food.

Breeding
Eggs are laid close to an anemone and
these and the fry are tended by the
parents. *A. clarkii* is bred commercially
for the trade.

24–26°C 12 cm (4½ in)
75–79°F

Family: POMACENTRIDAE
Common name: TOMATO CLOWN, FIRE CLOWN,
BRIDLED CLOWN
Distribution: Pacific
Size: 7 cm (3 in)
Food: OMNIVOROUS
Temperature range: 24–26°C/75–79°F
pH: 8.4 Salinity: 1.023–1.027

Readily available in the trade, the
Tomato Clown needs an anemone to
inhabit. A pair may be kept but ensure
the aquarium is of a reasonable size as
they sometimes squabble. Feeding is
simple: live, frozen, vegetable and flake
food are eagerly consumed.

Breeding
Raised in good numbers for the
aquarium trade.

24–26°C 7 cm (3 in)
75–79°F

AMPHIPRION FRENATUS
BREVOORT, 1856

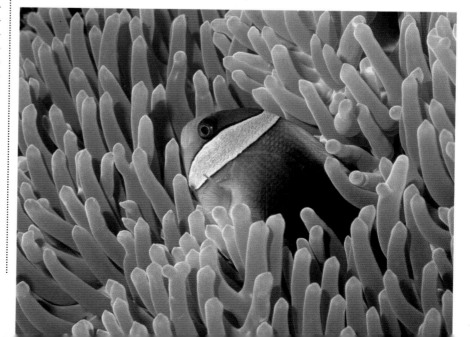

AMPHIPRION OCELLARIS
CUVIER, 1830

Family: POMACENTRIDAE	
Common name: PERCULA CLOWN, COMMON CLOWN	
Distribution: Indo-Pacific	
Size: 8 cm (3 in)	
Food: OMNIVOROUS	
Temperature range: 24–26°C / 75–79°F	
pH: 8.4 Salinity: 1.023–1.027	

Provide several anemones if you wish to keep more than a pair of these fish otherwise the fish will squabble over the anemone. Very easy to keep, they will eat most small food. The colour can vary and this has led to many heated debates as to whether a particular fish is *A. ocellaris* or *A. percula*. It could well be that they are one and the same fish, as the colour varies across its very wide range including even black.

Breeding
As for *A. clarkii*.

24–26°C
75–79°F   8 cm (3 in)

CHROMIS CAERULEA
CUVIER, 1830

Family: POMACENTRIDAE	
Common name: GREEN CHROMIS	
Distribution: Red Sea, Indo-Pacific	
Size: 10 cm (4 in)	
Food: OMNIVOROUS	
Temperature range: 24–26°C / 75–79°F	
pH: 8.4 Salinity: 1.023–1.027	

These very active fish like the company of their own kind, so should be kept as a shoal. They can be finicky about feeding, but once established they grow on slowly, although rarely attaining their full wild size. 6–7 cm (2½–3 in) is nearer the norm for aquarium specimens.

Breeding
Reported to breed among filamentous algae. The male guards the eggs until hatching three or four days later.

24–26°C
75–79°F   10 cm (4 in)

PSEUDOCHROMIS PACCAGNELLAE
AXELROD, 1973

Family: PSEUDOCHROMIDAE	
Common name: FALSE GRAMMA, DOTTYBACK, ROYAL DOTTYBACK, PACCAGNELLA'S DOTTYBACK	
Distribution: Pacific	
Size: 5 cm (2 in)	
Food: Very small meaty food	
Temperature range: 24–26°C / 75–79°F	
pH: 8.4 Salinity: 1.023–1.027	

This fish is very often confused with the Royal Gramma, *Gramma loreto*. The difference, sometimes very hard to see, is a fine white line that separates the two colours. It requires almost identical conditions to the Royal Gramma. Ensure that there are plenty of hiding places in the aquarium.

Breeding
Not known.

24–26°C
75–79°F   5 cm (2 in)

PTEROIS VOLITANS
LINNAEUS, 1758

Family: SCORPAENIDAE
Common name: LIONFISH, SCORPIONFISH
Distribution: Indo-Pacific
Size: 35 cm (14 in)
Food: CARNIVOROUS
Temperature range: 24–26°C / 75–79°F
pH: 8.4 Salinity: 1.023–1.027

A really impressive fish, it has an aura of mystique around it because it is poisonous. Handle it with extreme care. If you are stung by one of these creatures, bathe the affected area with hot water as this will help to ease the pain and coagulate the poison. They hunt by drifting through the water and gulping in unsuspecting prey. In captivity they can normally be persuaded to accept dead food, but be prepared to have to feed live fish in the first instance. May be kept with other fish provided their companions are too big to be swallowed!

Breeding
The eggs are produced in a gelatinous ball that floats in the upper levels of the water. When the fry are about 10 mm / ⅜ in long they sink to the bottom of the aquarium.

 24–26°C 75–79°F   35 cm (14 in)

CHROMILEPTIS ALTIVELIS
(VALENCIENNES IN CUVIER & VALENCIENNES, 1878)

Family: SERRANIDAE
Common name: PANTHER GROUPER, POLKA-DOT GROUPER
Distribution: Indo-Pacific
Size: 50 cm (20 in)
Food: CARNIVOROUS
Temperature range: 24–26°C / 75–79°F
pH: 8.4 Salinity: 1.023–1.027

A hunter, this fish loves live food but may be persuaded to accept dead fish.

In the aquarium it is always on the move, drifting through the water until it spots possible prey, when it lunges at it. They may be kept with others of their kind and make a splendid sight. Ensure that its companions are not small enough to be eaten. Young fish have few, large black blotches on white, adults have more, smaller dark blotches on white.

Breeding
Not known.

 24–26°C 75–79°F   50 cm (20 in)

SYMPHORICHTHYS SPILURUS
(GUNTHER, 1874)

Family: SERRANIDAE
Common name: MAJESTIC SNAPPER
Distribution: Pacific
Size: 30 cm (12 in)
Food: CARNIVOROUS
Temperature range: 24–26°C / 75–79°F
pH: 8.4 Salinity: 1.023–1.027

This creature may be kept in the community aquarium provided two criteria are met: the first is that there are no fish small enough for it to eat; the second is that there are no fish likely to bite or nip the long trailing fin filaments of the Majestic Snapper. Provide a large, spacious aquarium as this fish loves to swim. It will accept a range of meaty food.

Breeding
Not known.

 24–26°C 75–79°F   30 cm (12 in)

SIGANUS VULPINUS
(EVERMANN & SEALE, 1907)

Family: SIGANIDAE

Common name: FOXFACE, FOXFISH, BADGERFISH

Distribution: Pacific

Size: 25 cm (10 in)

Food: OMNIVOROUS

Temperature range: 24–26°C / 75–79°F

pH: 8.4 Salinity: 1.023–1.027

An accommodating fish, it adapts readily to aquarium life. It will take most food but there must be a high vegetable content in the diet. An aquarium with plenty of algae will suit it and it can graze over the algae. For the most part it is peaceful but it may be a little picky with others of the same species. Quite active, it likes a lot of swimming space.

Breeding
No report of this particular species spawning but others of the family are reported to have been possibly triggered by water changes.

24–26°C 75–79°F		25 cm (10 in)

DUNKEROCAMPUS DACTYLIOPHORUS
(BLEEKER, 1853)

Family: SYNGNATHIDAE

Common name: BANDED PIPEFISH

Distribution: Pacific

Size: 16 cm (6 in)

Food: Small live food

Temperature range: 24–26°C / 75–79°F

pH: 8.4 Salinity: 1.023–1.027

A strange looking fish, it should be kept either in a species aquarium or with very calm fish. They like a tank with plenty of rocks and crevices to poke about in to find food. If keeping with other fish, ensure that the Pipefish gets sufficient food. They require large amounts of small live food such as brine shrimp.

Breeding
May breed in the aquarium. The male carries the eggs around on the underside of his body. Copious amounts of tiny live food are needed to feed the fry.

24–26°C 75–79°F		16 cm (6 in)

HIPPOCAMPUS KUDA
(BLEEKER, 1852)

Family: SYNGNATHIDAE

Common name: YELLOW SEAHORSE, GOLDEN SEAHORSE, PACIFIC SEAHORSE

Distribution: Indo-Pacific

Size: 25 cm (10 in)

Food: Small live food

Temperature range: 24–26°C / 75–79°F

pH: 8.4 Salinity: 1.023–1.027

Best kept in a species aquarium with coral branches for them to hold on to. Feeding can be difficult as they require small, live food such as brine shrimp, *Daphnia*, etc, in quite large amounts. They will even take the fry of livebearers such as Mollies.

Breeding
They will breed in the aquarium. The male broods the eggs and fry in a special brood pouch. It takes about four weeks before the eggs hatch. Copious amounts of very small live food is required to raise the fry.

24–26°C 75–79°F		25 cm (10 in)

INDEX OF SCIENTIFIC NAMES

INDEX OF COMMON NAMES